Maui

Contents

GREEN MAUI, P66

WINDSURFING, P49

MATT MUNRO/LONELY PLANET ©

/GETTY IMAGES ©

Contents

Welcome to Maui

Maui lures travelers with an invigorating mix of natural beauty and outdoor fun, all shared with warm alohas.

Outdoor Adventure

When it comes to outdoor recreation, Maui wins best in show. Just look at that zipliner launching into a canopy of green. Or the mountain biker hurtling past eucalyptus and pine. Hiking trails wind through lava flows and bamboo forests. Along the coast, surfers barrel through waves and snorkelers glide among fish-filled reefs and coral.

And we haven't even mentioned the Valley Isle's most iconic adventures, like driving the Road to Hana. Watching the sunrise from the summit of Haleakalā. Paddling a kayak in Makena Bay. In sum? Amazing.

Natural Beauty

The golden sands of Keawakapu Beach. The rumpled green flanks of Haleakalā. The graceful beauty of Wailua Falls. These gorgeous sights have drawn admirers for generations. But it's funny, just when you think you have a handle on Maui's sublime scenery, an unexpected view catches you by surprise. It's these unplanned glimpses of beauty that linger. Maybe it's the *'ahinahina* (silversword) staking out a claim on a stark crater slope. Or the jagged lava along the Ke'anae Peninsula, looking protective for a moment, not menacing. And the Waiakoa Loop Trail at Polipoli? Spookily pretty – until that baby boar snuffles into view.

Food & Drink

A top-notch dining scene enhances Maui's natural charms. And the best part? No matter the view or adventure, you're always a short drive from a delicious meal. Unless it's 8pm in Hana and you're looking for dinner... From scrappy food trucks to white-linen dining rooms, eateries are embracing locally sourced food, from Upcountry vegetables to grass-fed beef from the ranch down the road. And the local food? The names may be unfamiliar – *loco moco,* shave ice, *kalua* pork – but the flavors are rich and delicious, and the portions typically hearty.

History

As you hike over the uncomfortable lava rocks on the King's Hwy near La Perouse Bay, gazing out to sea and broiling under the sun, it's easy to connect with ancient travelers who surely felt the same mix of awe and discomfort. Maui is dotted with such spots, where natural formations and historic structures are direct portals to the past. Downtown Lahaina, with its old wooden storefronts and rowdy pubs, channels the whaling era. You'd hardly blink if Edward Bailey, an 1800s missionary, stepped from the stairwell at the Bailey House. And the 100-year-old Komoda Bakery? The past still makes tasty cream puffs.

Why I Love Maui

By Amy C Balfour, Writer

On my first visit to Maui I hiked the Waiheʻe Ridge Trail and ziplined through the West Maui mountains. Thanks to those adventures, I'm hooked on the island's outdoor charms. Since then I've kayaked Makena Bay, hiked into a moonscape crater and snorkeled Molokini Crater. It's the mix of beautiful scenery and easy-to-access adventures that pulls me back. That and the genuine alohas from the residents, who have invited me to book-club meetings and a backyard party. I even had an inn manager, running late, send me to Monkeypod Kitchen with a fistful of cash and instructions to have fun. Aloha and *mahalo*!

For more about our writers, see p320

Above: Haleakalā National Park (p194)

Maui

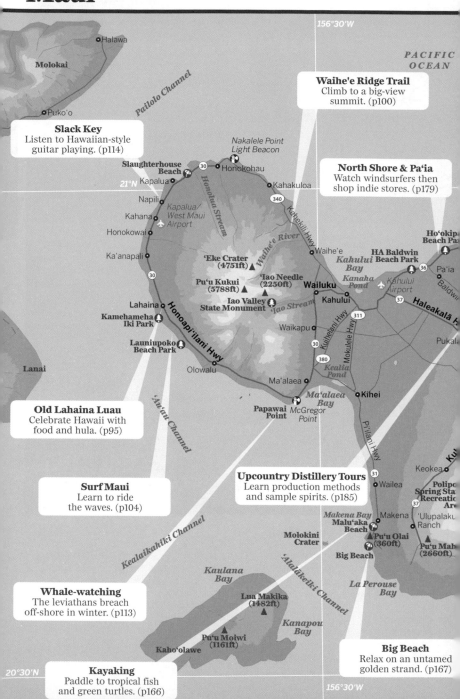

Waihe'e Ridge Trail
Climb to a big-view summit. (p100)

Slack Key
Listen to Hawaiian-style guitar playing. (p114)

North Shore & Pa'ia
Watch windsurfers then shop indie stores. (p179)

Old Lahaina Luau
Celebrate Hawaii with food and hula. (p95)

Surf Maui
Learn to ride the waves. (p104)

Upcountry Distillery Tours
Learn production methods and sample spirits. (p185)

Whale-watching
The leviathans breach off-shore in winter. (p113)

Big Beach
Relax on an untamed golden strand. (p167)

Kayaking
Paddle to tropical fish and green turtles. (p166)

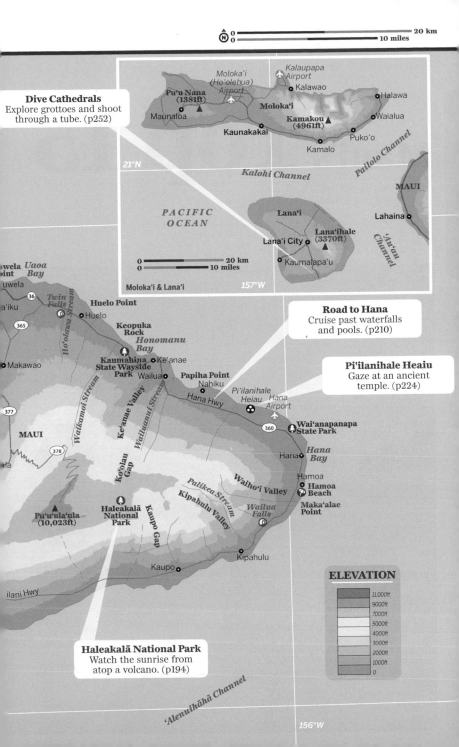

N 0 — 20 km
0 — 10 miles

Dive Cathedrals
Explore grottoes and shoot through a tube. (p252)

Kalaupapa Airport

Moloka'i (Ho'olehua) Airport

Pu'u Nana (1381ft)

Kalawao

Halawa

Maunaloa

Moloka'i

Kamakou (4961ft)

Waialua

Kaunakakai

Puko'o

Kamalo

Pailolo Channel

21°N

Kalohi Channel

MAUI

PACIFIC OCEAN

Lana'i

Lahaina

Lana'i City

Lana'ihale (3370ft)

0 — 20 km
0 — 10 miles

Kaumalapa'u

'Au'au Channel

Moloka'i & Lana'i

157°W

wela oint

Uaoa Bay

uwela

36

Twin Falls

Huelo Point

a'iku

365

Huelo

Keopuka Rock

Ho'olawa Stream

Makawao

Honomanu Bay

Kaumahina State Wayside Park

Ke'anae

Wailua

Papiha Point

Nahiku

Road to Hana
Cruise past waterfalls and pools. (p210)

377

Waikamoi Stream

Pi'ilanihale Heiau

Hana Hwy

Hana Airport

MAUI

378

Ke'anae Valley

Ko'olau Gap

Wailuanui Stream

360

Wai'anapanapa State Park

Pi'ilanihale Heiau
Gaze at an ancient temple. (p224)

la

Pu'u'ula'ula (10,023ft)

Haleakalā National Park

Kaupo Gap

Palikea Stream

Kipahulu Valley

Hana

Hana Bay

Waiho'i Valley

Hamoa

Hamoa Beach

Wailua Falls

Maka'alae Point

ilani Hwy

Kaupo

Kipahulu

ELEVATION

11,000ft
9000ft
7000ft
5000ft
4000ft
3000ft
2000ft
1000ft
0

Haleakalā National Park
Watch the sunrise from atop a volcano. (p194)

'Alenuihāhā Channel

156°W

Maui's **Top 15**

Sunrise at Haleakalā National Park

1 As you shiver in the inky darkness, bumping elbows with strangers and wishing for your warmer coat, it's easy to grumble, 'What was I thinking?' But then a soft, orange glow pierces the darkness. The crowd leans forward, holding its breath. Cottony clouds appear, stretching to horizon's end, encircling your lofty summit perch (p207). Rich tones of amber and ocher blaze on the crater floor below. Elemental. Communal. Spiritual. To quote Mark Twain: 'The sublimest spectacle I ever witnessed.' And to quote the park service: 'Reserve before you go!' Yep, reservations now required.

Driving the Road to Hana

2 Buckle up. Of all the heart-stoppingly dramatic drives in Hawaii, this is the Big Kahuna. A roller-coaster of a ride, the twisting Hana Hwy (p210) winds down jungly valleys and back up towering cliffs, curling around 600 twists and turns along the way. Some 54 one-lane bridges cross nearly as many waterfalls – some of them eye-popping torrents and others so gentle they beg a dip. But the ride's only half the thrill. Swim in a Zen-like pool, stroll a ginger-scented trail and stop once, maybe twice, for banana bread.

PIERRE LECLERC/SHUTTERSTOCK ©

AMIT BASU PHOTOGRAPHY/GETTY IMAGES ©

Snorkeling at 'Turtle Beach'

3 Packed with coves, reefs and lava rocks, the Maui coast is made for do-it-yourself snorkeling. Grab a map at the dive shop, rent gear, hit the beach and off you go. From stunning Malu'aka Beach (p166) in Makena, simply swim in the direction of the tour boats. Before you get halfway you'll likely spot a magnificent green sea turtle nibbling algae on the ocean floor, and another swimming gracefully through the surf. The underwater sights at 'Turtle Beach' are mesmerizing – and a great introduction to snorkeling in Maui.

Whale-Watching

4 Breaching. Lunging. Ever-mysterious spy hopping. Humpback whales keep things lively off Maui's western coast in winter, when thousands arrive to court, mate and calve. If you're there at the same time – typically December through April – treat yourself to a whale-watching cruise. Whales are also readily spotted from cliffside lookouts such as Papawai Point (p113), west-facing beaches and oceanfront condos. Snorkelers and divers who stick their heads underwater at the right time can even hear them singing: love songs, we presume!

PHOTO BY MEREDITH NARROWE/GETTY IMAGES ©

GREG ELMS/GETTY IMAGES ©

Waiheʻe Ridge Trail

5 Hiking doesn't get much better than the Waiheʻe Ridge Trail (p100), an inviting footpath that climbs the rugged green slopes of the West Maui Mountains. The trail is alternately covered and exposed, winding through a dense grove of guava trees before darting up a grassy ridgeline with bird's-eye views of cloud-topped peaks and overgrown valleys. After 2.5 miles of gentle climbing, the lonely summit is a sweet reward.

Big Beach (Oneloa), Makena State Park

6 If one beach captures the spirit of Maui, this is it: wild, vast and in a completely natural state. But unvisited, no. Big Beach (p167) is where Mauians come to celebrate Maui the way it used to be. An endless expanse of gleaming sands, no development in sight and unbelievably blue water. For a sweeping view of the place – and an iconic photograph – climb the rocky outcrop just north. Take a few steps. Turn. And whoa. Paradise.

Old Lahaina Luau

7 They had us at aloha, but who are we to refuse the cool mai tai and sweet-smelling lei that followed? At Maui's most authentic luau (p95), Hawaiian history, culture and culinary prowess are the focus. Highlights? The unearthing of the *imu*-cooked pig, the dancing of the *hula kahiko* and, of course, the savoring of the feast – a spread of hearty salads, fresh fish, and grilled and roasted meats. But it's the sense of shared community that will linger longest in your memory.

ULLSTEIN BILD/GETTY IMAGES ©

Diving the Cathedrals

8 Want to hear divers gush about a diving spot? Then listen to them describe the grottoes, hideaways and arch at the Cathedrals dive site just off the southern coast of Lana'i (p252). It's an adventurous place with unusual geologic sights around every bend. When the water surges, divers can make a wild exit from the Cathedrals through a narrow tube, better known as the Shotgun. And the marine life? Eels, turtles, sharks and loads of tropical fish.

Upcountry Distillery Tours

9 Deep ocean water, pineapples and *panio-los* (Hawaiian cowboys) on the label. When it comes to producing spirits, distilleries in Kula and Hali'imaile embrace all things Hawaiian. Even better? They share their secrets on engaging tours that always end with a tasting. At the new Hali'imaile Distilling Company (p185), guides spotlight the handcrafted stills and the fun-loving products – just look at the mustachioed barrels aging the Paniolo Whiskey. It all feels a bit rock and roll. They do produce Sammy Hagar's own Beach Bar Rum, after all.

Surfing West Maui

10 This is Hawaii – of course you're going to catch some waves. The best part is, you don't have to be Laird Hamilton to enjoy the Maui surf. Just stick to Lahaina and West Maui, where the waves are more accessible, and you' be hanging ten in no time. Up-and-at-em surf schools cluster near Kamehameha Iki Park in Lahaina (p86), ready to launch newbies on easy waves beside the breakwall. Got your surf legs? Check out one of the beginner-friendly surf spots between Lahaina and Ma'alaea.

Pi'ilanihale Heiau

11 Standing in front of Hawaii's largest temple (p224) – five stories high – it's impossible not to feel dwarfed by the scale. The remote setting on a windswept coast adds to the sense of being in a sacred place. Be still. You can almost hear the footsteps of the ancients and see the high priest walking up the terraced stone steps to offer sacrifices to the gods. The surrounding Polynesian gardens – swaying coconut palms, sturdy breadfruit trees – add depth to the vision of how it must have looked centuries ago.

The North Shore & Pa'ia

12 Ready for small-town adventuring? On the North Shore the surf is wild, the shops and eateries unique, and the vibe laid-back – dare we say crunchy? If you're a player on the pro-windsurfing circuit, meet your buddies at Ho'okipa Beach Park (p179). The rest of us will watch the death-defying action from the adjacent hills. Follow Ho'okipa's windsurfing theatrics by immersing yourself in the funky vibe of nearby Pa'ia, Maui's hippest burg, home to artsy shops, cool surfer haunts, a roadside stupa and one awesome deli buffet. Pa'ia

'Iao Valley State Monument

13 Nowhere is Maui's verdant, moody beauty better captured than at 'Iao Valley (p141), where the 'Iao Needle – a phallic-shaped, emerald-green pinnacle – shoots up from the valley floor. Snuggled into deep folds of lush rainforested mountains, 'Iao is such a sumptuous sight it's hard to imagine that it was the scene of a violent interisland battle in the late 18th century. This unusual melding of breathtaking scenery and tragic history makes the valley a uniquely compelling place for reflection. The Monument is due to complete flood-damage repairs and reopen imminently.

Masters of Hawaiian Slack Key Guitar Concert Series

14 You'll feel like you're part of a family jam session at this intimate slack key guitar concert (p114) series in Napili. Slack key tuning, with its simultaneous playing of bass and melody, virtually defines Hawaiian music. The host, Grammy Award–winning musician George Kahumoku Jr, interweaves the music with an upbeat banter on growing up Hawaiian-style. The weekly guest list features some of the finest slack key guitar players on the planet.

George Kahumoku Jr

13

Kayaking

15 Hawaii's first settlers were skilled ocean navigators who crossed thousands of miles of open ocean in canoes loaded with passengers, livestock and supplies. Today, members of outrigger-canoe clubs ply the waves regularly, their graceful vessels skimming across the surf just offshore. Want to test your paddle skills? Many resorts offer guided outrigger trips that push off from adjacent beaches. For do-it-yourself views of green sea turtles, and maybe a breaching whale, join a trip with Aloha Kayaks, who will get you out to sea.

Need to Know

For more information, see Survival Guide (p297)

Currency
US dollar ($)

Language
English, Hawaiian

Visas
Generally not required for stays of up to 90 days for citizens of Visa Waiver Program countries.

Money
ATMs common. Credit cards widely accepted; often required for car and hotel reservations.

Cell Phones
International travelers need GSM multiband phones. Buy prepaid SIM cards locally. Coverage can be spotty outside developed areas.

Time
Hawaii does not observe daylight saving time. It has about 11 hours of daylight in midwinter and almost 13½ hours in midsummer. In midwinter the sun rises at about 7am and sets at about 6pm. In midsummer it rises before 6am and sets after 7pm.

When to Go

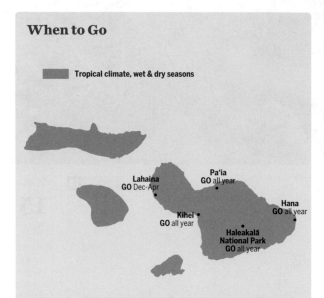

Tropical climate, wet & dry seasons

Lahaina
GO Dec-Apr

Pa'ia
GO all year

Hana
GO all year

Kihei
GO all year

Haleakalā
National Park
GO all year

High Season
(mid-Dec–mid-Apr)
➡ Highest accommodation prices
➡ Coincides with Christmas holidays
➡ Prices high through whale season

Shoulder
(Jun–Aug)
➡ Coincides with school vacations
➡ Book rental car early; fleets may be reduced
➡ Lots of festivals in June and July

Low Season
(Apr & May, Sep–mid-Dec)
➡ Between whale season and summer
➡ Slow between Thanksgiving and Christmas
➡ Look for online specials and cheap airfares

Useful Websites

Hawaii Visitors and Convention Bureau (www.gohawaii.com/maui) Official tourism site; comprehensive events calendar and multilingual planning guides.

The Maui News (www.mauinews.com) Find out the latest headlines about the Valley Isle.

Maui Time (http://mauitime.com) Weekly newspaper with in-depth locals news features and entertainment listings.

Lonely Planet (www.lonelyplanet.com/usa/hawaii/maui) Destination information, hotel bookings, traveler forum and more.

Important Numbers

Emergency	911
Country code	1
Area code	808
International access code	011

Exchange Rates

Australia	A$1	$0.74
Canada	C$1	$0.72
Europe	€1	$1.09
Japan	Y100	$0.88
New Zealand	NZ$1	$0.69
UK	£1	$1.29

For current exchange rates see www.xe.com

Daily Costs

Budget: Less than $150

➡ Hostel dorm: $29–34

➡ Semi-private hostel room, guesthouse or budget B&B: $69–112

➡ Groceries, fast food: $6–12

➡ Walks, beach days: free

➡ Maui Bus one-way fare: $2

Midrange: $150–350

➡ Most B&Bs, hotel room or condo: $100–275

➡ Local rental car: per day/week from $35/175

➡ Dinner at midrange restaurant: $20–35

➡ Museums, snorkeling, hiking: free–$30

Top End: over $350

➡ Beach resort room: from $275

➡ New rental car: per day/week from $45/233

➡ Three-course meal at top restaurant: $75–100

➡ Diving, zip-lining, spa treatment, sunset cruise: from $69

Opening Hours

Opening hours may vary slightly throughout the year. We've provided high-season opening hours; hours generally decrease in shoulder and low seasons.

Banks 8:30am–4pm Monday to Friday; some to 6pm Friday and 9am–noon or 1pm Saturday

Bars & clubs noon–midnight daily; some to 2am Thursday to Saturday

Businesses 8:30am–4:30pm Monday to Friday

Post offices 8:30am–4:30pm Monday to Friday; some also 9am–noon Saturday

Shops 9am–5pm Monday to Saturday, some also noon–5pm Sunday; major shopping areas and malls keep extended hours

Arriving in Maui

Kahului International Airport (808-872-3830; http://hawaii.gov/ogg; 1 Kahului Airport Rd)

Private shuttle To Kihei $29–33, Lahaina $48–50

Taxi To Kihei/Lahaina from $30/70

Rental car $35–110 per day; major rental companies have airport rental booths.

Maui Bus The Upcountry Islander and Haiku Islander routes stop at the airport. Transfers are required for West and South Maui. $2 per ride.

Top Tips

➡ Never turn your back on the ocean when swimming or wading. Powerful waves can take you by surprise.

➡ Tackle the sunrise at Haleakalā and other early-morning adventures at the start of your trip before you've adjusted to the time change.

➡ When snorkeling, don't step on the coral. It's fragile.

➡ Don't touch the green turtles or get too close.

➡ Don't feed fish or animals.

➡ Stay aware of your surroundings while exploring the outdoors and slow down on slippery trails.

➡ Watch for clouds and surging water while wading in pools and streams, which are susceptible to flash floods.

➡ Fill up with gas before driving the Road to Hana. The only gas station on the route is in Hana.

➡ Keep valuables in your hotel room, not in your car.

➡ Slow down, enjoy the conversations and embrace living on island time.

For much more on **getting around**, see p32

What's New

Haleakalā National Park

Advance reservations are now required for entry between 3am and 7am: be alert if you want to watch the sunrise from the volcano summit. The reservation fee (separate from general admission) is $1.50 per vehicle. (p194)

Microbreweries

Two craft breweries have opened. In Kihei, tours run daily at the Maui Brewing Co (p113) production facility. Sample the Talk Story, an American pale ale, at Koholā Brewery (p94) in Lahaina.

Craft Distilleries

Locally owned distilleries share their production secrets on tours in the Upcountry. Check out the homemade still at Hali'imaile Distilling Co (p185) or follow your guide past the Upcountry sugarcane fields at Hawaii Sea Spirits Organic Farm & Distillery (p185).

Sheldon Simeon

Former Top Chef contender Sheldon Simeon has opened Tin Roof in Kahului in a low-key strip mall. In 2016 Simeon's lease expired on Migrant at the Marriott, but plans are afoot to reopen it in Wailuku. (p136)

Wai'anapanapa State Park

The popular housekeeping cabins have reopened to guests. Look for new furniture, flooring and fixtures. In a separate project, construction crews have been reconfiguring walkways, steps and overlooks along the coastline. (p224)

Hotel Openings and Rebrands

With the opening of an all-suites Residence Inn Marriott in Wailea, your midrange options just improved. Kihei's long-running Maui Sunseeker has both new owners and name (Kohea Kai Resort) but the vibe remains progressive. Four Seasons Resort Lana'i has reopened with glossy style. (p30)

Hali'imaile General Store

For the first time, chef Bev Gannon's beloved destination Hawaiian fusion restaurant is offering happy-hour food and drink specials (mid-April to mid-December; p185)

Hana Burger Food Truck

Road to Hana drivers are pulling over for grass-fed beef burgers from Hana Ranch, served from a roadside truck. Look for the truck and picnic tables just beyond Hana Town, toward Kipahulu. (p238)

'Iao Valley State Monument

This lush state park was closed after suffering extensive damage following severe storms and flooding in September of 2016, but at the time of writing was due to reopen imminently. Check the park website for details. (p141)

Resort Closure

Longtime favorite Makena Beach & Golf Resort in Makena shut in 2016, after a 30-year run as a resort.

For more recommendations and reviews, see **lonelyplanet.com/maui**

If You Like...

Beaches

From black sands to golden crescents, the coves and coasts will keep your camera busy.

Big Beach Free of commercial and residential development, this wild beach welcomes sunbathers ready to escape the crowds. (p167)

Keawakapu Beach For swimming, oceanfront cocktails and one magnificent sunset, hit this Kihei show-off. (p154)

Wailea Beach Sunbathe like a star on this busy golden strand, favored by celebrities and water sports fans. (p162)

Napili Beach We're not fond of the cliche 'hidden gem,' but this time the term fits. (p114)

Pa'iloa Beach A photogenic black-sand beach fronts wild surf along the ancient King's Highway. (p225)

Hamoa Beach For a visual taste of the South Pacific, visit this lush beach south of Hana. (p235)

Hulopo'e Beach Ferries drop off day-trippers at this sun-kissed playground fronting gleaming Manele Bay on Lana'i. (p251)

Epic Views

Volcanic moonscapes. Lush tropical trails. A splashy blowhole. The landscapes here aren't what you see at home.

Sunrise on Haleakalā Thick clouds and dazzling light welcome the day in breath-taking style from atop a volcano. (p202)

Waihe'e Ridge Trail Catch a look at the wild north coast before the clouds roll in on this lush hike to a 2563ft-tall peak. (p100)

Ho'okipa Beach Park & Overlook Expert windsurfers skim across the waves while surfers ride the consistent breaks. (p179)

Ali'i Kula Lavender Take in the sweeping panorama of the Maui isthmus and the southern coast while surrounded by lavender. (p190)

Pu'u o Kahaula Hill Flanked by a large cross and tiki torches, the view from this landmark hill sweeps to Hana Bay. (p235)

'Ahihi-Kina'u Natural Area Reserve One word for the drive through the centuries-old lava flow? Otherworldly. (p168)

Nakalele Blowhole The anticipation is half the fun while waiting – from afar – for the ocean to blast skyward. (p121)

Kalaupapa Overlook On Moloka'i, this clifftop viewpoint overlooks a broad peninsula. (p262)

Scenic Drives

Road to Hana The serpentine Hana Highway twists along the rumpled east Maui coast beside waterfalls and pools. (p210)

Haleakala Highway This country byway switchbacks through pastures and forest to the top of Maui's highest volcano. (p64)

Kahekili Highway Hold tight for a wild spin along the rugged and rural north coast, home to the mighty Kahakuloa Head. (p119)

Waipoli Road Hairpinning upwards from Ali'i Kula Lavender, this stunner shares views of paragliders, the isthmus and the coast. (p64)

Kula Highway A drive along this Upcountry thoroughfare that unfurls along the fertile slopes of Haleakalā. (p64)

Food & Drink

There are serious *'ono grinds* (good eats) in Maui. When deciding where to eat, you'll rarely go wrong with fresh, local, island-style dishes.

Poke Tasty varieties of this raw-fish salad abound, but a *poke* bowl from Foodland is always a good choice.

Loco Moco Try this hearty Hawaiian breakfast of rice, fried egg, and a burger – all covered in gravy – at **Kihei Caffe**. (p158)

Da Kitchen Express Hearty servings of local dishes, with a variety of plate lunches including kalua pork and teriyaki chicken. (p159)

Mama's Fish House This special-occasion restaurant is famed for its fresh local fish. (p183)

Monkeypod Kitchen Fantastic pub grub with a Hawaiian twist from chef Peter Merriman. (p164)

Komoda Store & Bakery This 100-year-old bakery in Makawao draws morning crowds for its cream puffs and stick doughnuts. (p188)

Ululani's Hawaiian Shave Ice Grab napkins for Hawaii's favorite chilly treat: exuberant and colorful snow cones bursting with tropical flavors. (p90)

Maui Brewing Co Tour the new production facility then take your pick of two-dozen beers. (p160)

Waterfalls

Wailua Falls Tour buses stop for this 100ft-high beauty in the deep green folds of Kipahulu. (p240)

Three Bears Falls If one is never enough, pull off the Hana Hwy for three cascades tumbling behind one bridge. (p221)

'Ohe'o Gulch These powerful falls drop into terraced pools in the Kipahulu District of **Haleakalā National Park** like beauty untamed – and dangerous. (p240)

Pipiwai Trail This streamside hike climbs to bridal-veil Makahiku Falls and the 400ft-high Waimoku Falls. (p199)

Moa'ula & Hipuapua Falls Head to the Halawa Valley on Malaka'i for these twin 250ft falls. (p245)

Top: Three Bears Falls
Bottom: Haleakalā National Park

Month by Month

January

The Friday Town Parties rotate weekly between Wailuku, Lahaina, Makawao and Kihei and feature live music, food trucks and arts and crafts. There's a fantastic slack key guitar show every Wednesday night at the Napili Kai (p114).

🏃 PGA Tournament of Champions

The season opener for the PGA tour tees off in Kapalua in early January, when the previous year's golf champions compete for a multimillion-dollar purse (p117).

✨ Chinese New Year Festival

Fireworks and lion dancers welcome the New Year in January or February at the Maui Mall.

February

Between December and April, about 12,000 humpback whales return to Hawaii to breed and give birth in the shallow waters. View them up and down the West Maui coast. February is the best month for spotting them.

✨ Whale Day Celebration

A whale of a bash, this beachside celebration in Kihei in mid-February honors Maui's favorite winter visitor – the splashy North Pacific humpback whale. (p158)

March

✨ Celebration of the Arts

In late March, the Ritz-Carlton, Kapalua hosts traditional artisans from across the Hawaiian islands, with craft-making demonstrations, live entertainment and a focus on Native customs and beliefs (p118).

April

Got the post-winter blues? April is shoulder season in Maui, a nice time to rejuvenate between winter's whale-watching crowds and the arrival of summer's families. Quirky festivals keep the scene entertaining.

✨ Banyan Tree Birthday Party

Celebrate Maui's most-renowned tree with a birthday party under its sprawling branches, which cover an entire square in Lahaina. The beloved banyan is more than 140 years old. The event occurs the weekend closest to April 24.

✨ East Maui Taro Festival

Hana, Maui's most Hawaiian town, throws the island's most Hawaiian party in late April, with everything from hula dances and a Hawaiian music festival to a taro-pancake breakfast. (p236)

May

✨ East Maui Brewers Festival

Head to the Maui Arts & Cultural Center in mid-May to sip microbrews from 40 local and national craft breweries. There's also live music and local food.

June

June and July have a busy festival schedule. You'll find at least one big summer celebration in almost every region.

★ King Kamehameha Day Parade & Celebration

In early June, head to Front St in Lahaina to honor the birthday of King Kamehameha I with food, live music and a bright floral parade. Also known as Kamehameha the Great, this warrior chieftain eventually united the islands of Hawaii.

★ Kapalua Wine & Food Festival

Hawaii's hottest chefs vie for attention in this culinary extravaganza of cooking demonstrations and wine tasting for four days in mid-June. (p118)

★ Maui Film Festival

In mid-June, movie lovers gather in Wailea, where the golf course is transformed into the 'Celestial Theater' and Hollywood stars show up for added bling. (p164)

★ Ki Ho'alu Slack Key Guitar Festival

Slack key guitar music doesn't get any better than this. In late June, this one-day event brings in all the big-name players from throughout the state. Plan to spend the afternoon and early evening at the Maui Arts & Cultural Center in Kahului (p135).

July

Lahaina throws the biggest Fourth of July party on Maui. Head to Banyan Tree Sq and Front St for live music, entertainment, arts and fireworks.

☆ Makawao Paniolo Parade

A colorful parade through downtown showcases the Upcountry's *paniolo* (Hawaiian cowboy) past, held on the weekend closest to Independence Day.

★ Lana'i Pineapple Festival

Pineapples, the symbol of hospitality, are feted on the island of Lana'i on the weekend of July 4 with live music, food and fireworks.

September

☆ Maui County Fair

Maui is a garden, so it's no surprise that its old-fashioned agricultural fair is a bountiful event with orchids, luscious produce and lots of good food. Plus plenty of carnival rides. Late September or early October in Kahului (p132).

October

★ Halloween in Lahaina

Lahaina hosts Maui's biggest street festival on Halloween night, attracting more than 15,000 revelers with music, dancing and costume contests. Fun for families early in the night; later things get a bit more wild.

November

☆ Hula O Nā Keiki

Talented *keiki* (children) are the headliners of this annual hula competition at the Ka'anapali Beach Hotel in early to mid-November, with arts, crafts and workshops (p112).

☆ First Light: Academy Screenings

The folks behind the Maui Film Festival show Hawaii movie premiers and special screenings at the Maui Arts & Cultural Center from mid-November though December (www.mauifilmfestival.com/fl_index.php).

☆ Nā Mele O Maui

Children's choral groups sing native Hawaiian music at this culture-rich event, held in late November at the Maui Arts & Cultural Center in Kahului (p137).

December

☆ Holiday Lighting of the Banyan Tree

On the first weekend of December, Lahaina illuminates America's oldest banyan tree with thousands of bright, colorful holiday lights. Even Santa stops by for this one.

Itineraries

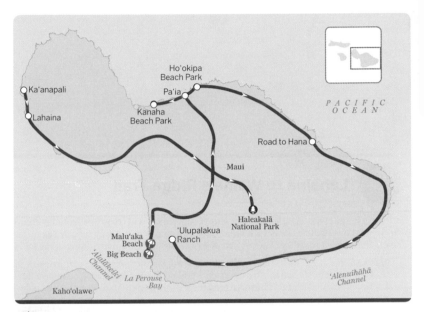

 Island Tour

To embrace the magic that is Maui, remember: quality over quantity. Yes, the ziplines are fun, the restaurants excellent and the resorts posh, but spending time in small towns and remote parks will connect you with the land and its people. This trip covers many places, but allow yourself to readjust if the mana (elemental magic) is strong.

Splash into the scene with an ocean dip in coastal **Ka'anapali**, followed by a sunset cruise. Next, stroll the historic whaling town of **Lahaina** then treat yourself to the **Old Lahaina Luau**. Still got jet lag? Drive to **Haleakalā National Park** to catch a breathtaking sunrise and hike into the crater.

The next few days are all about those gorgeous beaches. Begin by snorkeling with turtles at **Malu'aka Beach**, followed by a picnic at magnificent **Big Beach**. For adventure, check out **Kanaha Beach** for the sailboarding scene.

Head to **Pa'ia** for Maui's hippest cafe scene and check out the surf action at **Ho'okipa Beach Park**. Wrap up with waterfalls galore on the most legendary drive in Hawaii, the wildly beautiful **Road to Hana**. On your last day look out for leviathans on a whale-watching cruise or savor a fine dinner on the western coast.

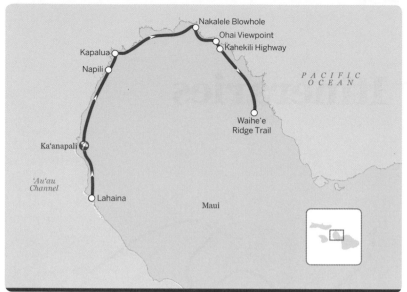

4 DAYS Lahaina to Waihe'e Ridge Trail

History buffs, hikers and those with a sense of adventure will enjoy this multiday excursion in West Maui. The trip starts with urban exploring and ends with a wild drive along a remote and rugged coastline. There's a bit of snorkeling and Hawaiian dining in the middle.

The exhibits at the **Lahaina Heritage Museum** set the tone for adventure, with tales of warring ancient Hawaiians, hardy whalers and determined missionaries. From here, relax under the USA's largest **banyan tree** then stroll around Maui's captivating old whaling town, which is packed tight with historic buildings, art galleries, great restaurants and indie shops. In the evening, feast your stomach and your eyes at the **Old Lahaina Luau**, where the Hawaiian buffet and the storytelling – through hula – are highlights.

The next morning, plunge into Maui with a dip in the sea at **Ka'anapali Beach**. Snorkel out to **Pu'u Keka'a** (Black Rock) to check out Maui's dazzling underwater scenery, then pop into the **Whalers Village Museum** to learn more about the island's whaling history. Enjoy the sunset on a sailboat cruise or from shore at the **Hula Grill**.

Start day three early – and we mean early – at the Gazebo restaurant in **Napili** for chocolate macnut pancakes. Swimmers should then head to **Kapalua Bay**, bodysurfers to **DT Fleming Beach** and snorkelers to **Honolua Bay**. Kapalua's menu of adventures also includes hiking and ziplining. And golfers? You probably already know about Kapalua's courses from the tournament coverage. Catch the sunset at **Merriman's Kapalua**. In the morning, stroll beside a string of beaches on the lovely **Coastal Trail**.

Hit the road on your last day with an adventurous early-morning drive around the northern tip of Maui. Follow the Kahekili Hwy to **Nakalele Blowhole**, and don't miss **Ohai Viewpoint**. Other than fruit stands, dining options are few but **Julia's Best Banana Bread** should see you through.

In the early afternoon lace up your hiking boots. Lofty mountain views and waterfalls are just starters on the fun **Waihe'e Ridge Trail**, which heads deep into the West Maui Mountains. Return to Lahaina or spend the night in Pa'ia.

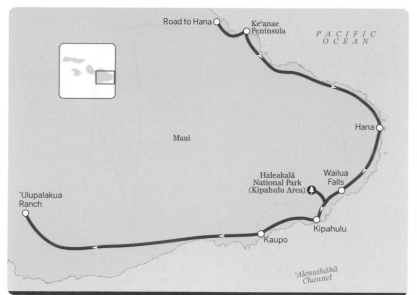

3 DAYS The Road to Hana to 'Ulupalakua Ranch

This magical drive along the remote east Maui coast is lined with waterfalls and lush scenery. If you want to get away from the resort scene while digging into local culture and exploring untamed nature, this your trip. And there's no need to rush – you're spending two nights midway in Hana.

This trip begins on the Hana Hwy, dubbed **The Road to Hana**. The roadway begins as Hwy 36 then flips to Hwy 360 at mile marker 16. Waterfalls, pools and thick forests line the route. About halfway to Hana, swing down to **Ke'anae Peninsula** for wind-swept views of the rough lava coast, pounded by surf. You'll be humbled by Hawaii's largest temple at **Kahanu Garden**. Views of the striking black-lava coast and the unusual black-sand beach at **Wai'anapanapa State Park** will linger in your memory.

The old Hawaiian community of **Hana** is well worth a poke around and a two-night stay. Enjoy Thai food for lunch, visit Hana's museum and the **Hasegawa General Store**, and the marvelous beaches. Be sure to hike to the top of **Pu'u o Kahaula Hill** for a broad view of the town and Hana Beach.

It's time for more local exploring in the morning. First stop? **Wailua Falls**. This roadside cascade is a top contender for Maui's most-gorgeous waterfall. The road rolls through the Kipahulu Area of **Haleakalā National Park**, home to 'Ohe'o Gulch and its 24 pools, each backed by its own little waterfall. Make time to hike to the 200ft plunge of Makahiku Falls on the **Pipiwai Trail**.

In jungle-tangled **Kipahulu**, seek out the grave of aviator **Charles Lindbergh** before returning to Hana for drinks and live music at posh but hospitable Travaasa Hana. In the morning you'll follow the lonely Pi'ilani Hwy for an occasionally hair-raising drive with memorable hairpin turns, which eventually straighten out in the cowboy region of **Kaupo**.

End your trip with a taste of Maui Splash, a refreshing pineapple wine, at the tasting room at Maui Wine on the **'Ulupalakua Ranch**. Spend the night in the **Upcountry**, home to several inviting B&Bs and inns.

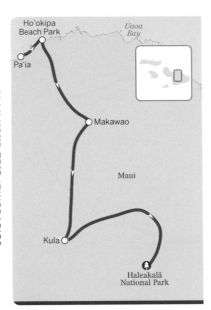

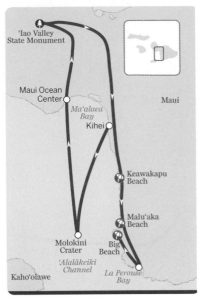

3 DAYS Pa'ia to Haleakalā National Park

The Upcountry may not have the flash of West and South Maui, but that's why many people like it. This itinerary includes several small towns on the flanks of Haleakalā, from the surf-and-granola vibe of Pa'ia to the artsy charms of Makawao. It ends with a scenic bang in Haleakalā National Park.

On your first day, explore downtown **Pa'ia** to find the right breakfast joint then wander the boutiques or hit the beach. At **Ho'okipa Beach Park** watch the windsurfers from the overlook. Splurge for dinner at the renowned **Mama's Fish House**.

It's *paniolo*-meets-Picasso in **Makawao**, a gallery-filled cowboy town. After shopping, enjoy a melt-in-your-mouth cream puff from **Komoda Store & Bakery** or hit the trails at the **Makawao Forest Reserve**.

For Upcountry's sweetest green scene, visit **Ali'i Kula Lavender** in **Kula** and munch on lavender scones while soaking up rainbow-lit coastal views from the farm.

The next morning, leave early to catch the sunrise atop **Haleakalā** volcano in its namesake national park. Follow with a hike into the crater and walk around the otherworldly cinder cones.

2 DAYS Kihei to Big Beach

If you like your adventures sprinkled with history and science, then consider this short trip. It heads out to sea then dives into the wild and rugged heart of central Maui.

Kihei Caffe is a good place to fuel up before a morning of snorkeling. And for offshore fish-gazing, it's hard to beat **Molokini Crater**, a sunken volcanic crater rim harboring brilliant fish and coral.

Right where the Molokini boat docks you'll find the **Maui Ocean Center**, an inviting tropical aquarium. In the afternoon, drive to **'Iao Valley State Monument**, known for its cool streams, misty mountains and Maui's emerald jewel, the 'Iao Needle.

The star of Kihei's beaches, **Keawakapu Beach** is tops for sunset. The next morning, relax on the sand or slip on a snorkel and swim to the coral gardens at **Malu'aka Beach**, dubbed Turtle Beach: sea turtles nibble algae as you swim past.

Continue south to **La Perouse Bay**, a stunning volcanic landscape at road's end, to ponder the twisted black lava flows.

On your way back to Kihei, stop at **Big Beach** for another fine sunset.

Top: 'Ohe'o Gulch,
Haleakalā National
Park (p240)

Bottom: Maui Ocean
Center (p144)

Maui: Off the Beaten Track

HALE PA'I PRINTING MUSEUM

Students ran the press that produced Hawaii's first newspaper, printed in a cottage that stands today on the grounds of Lahainaluna High School, 2 miles northeast of downtown Lahaina. Check out a reproduction of the original press. (p83)

KAHAKULOA

A striking rock formation watches over this drowsy village that's tucked beside a bay near the western edge of the wild Kahekili Hwy. The town hot spot? The front porch of the banana-bread hut. (p122)

Honokohau
Kapalua
KAHAKULOA
Napili
Kahana
Honokowai
Ka'anapali
Waihe'e
Ho'okipa Beach Park
'Eke Crater (4751ft)
Kahului Bay
Pa'ia
'Iao Needle (2250ft)
Pu'u Kukui (5788ft)
Wailuku
HA Baldwin Beach Park
HALE PA'I PRINTING MUSEUM
Lahaina
Kahului
Kamehameha Iki Park
'Iao Valley State Monument
Launiupoko Beach Park
Waikapu
Pukalani
KING KAMEHAMEHA GOLF CLUB
Olowalu
Ma'alaea
Maalaea Bay
Kihei
Keokea
Wailea
POLIPOLI SPRING STATE RECREATION AREA
Makena
Pu'u Mahoe (2660ft)

KING KAMEHAMEHA GOLF CLUB

Frank Lloyd Wright designed a golf clubhouse? Say what? That's right, this striking enclave on a Waikapu hillside was created and adapted by the renowned architect. Visitors are welcome to look around. (p142)

POLIPOLI SPRING STATE RECREATION AREA

Polipoli is the broody poet of Maui's state parks. Dark woods, flitting clouds, and a damp chill in the air, all befitting a melancholy tale. But this is Maui, so swap a snuffling boar for a chain-clanking ghost. (p193)

LA PEROUSE BAY

A jagged field of lava rock meets a pristine bay at the end of the road in South Maui. Check out historic ruins, scan for spinner dolphins or start a trek to a royal highway. (p169)

0 / 0 20 km / 10 miles

'ULA'INO ROAD

Waterfalls on the Hana Hwy may blur in your memory. But the mysterious temple and the dark lava tube on 'Ula'ino Rd? They'll likely stay sharp in your thoughts for years to come. Make time for these unique destinations. (p224)

KIPAHULU AREA

Unbeknownst to many, Haleakalā National Park holds two separate and distinct units. The lesser known is Kipahulu, a lush oceanfront wonderland of waterfalls, pools and one awesome bamboo grove. (p209)

PACIFIC OCEAN

Pa'uwela Point
Uaoa Bay
O Pa'uwela
O Ha'iku
Huelo Point
Huelo O
Honomanu Bay
Kaumahina State Wayside Park
O Ke'anae
O Makawao
Wailua O   Papiha Point
O Nahiku
Ke'anae Valley
'ULA'INO ROAD   Wai'anapanapa State Park
O Hana
O Kula
Ko'olau Gap
Waiho'i Valley   O Hamoa
Kipahulu Valley
Maka'alae Point
Pu'u'ula'ula (10,023ft)   Haleakalā National Park
Kaupo Gap
PI'ILANI HIGHWAY   Kaupo O   Kipahulu O   KIPAHULU AREA

PI'ILANI HIGHWAY

Rewards are earned on the challenging back road to Hana, where landscapes are lonely but dramatic: tropical flora, volcanic slopes, crumbly cliffs and vast ranchlands. (p228)

Accommodations

Accommodation Types

Maui has a wide range of accommodations, and it's generally advisable to book in advance as prices fluctuate depending on availability. Also, watch out for added tax, resort fees and parking charges.

➡ **B&Bs** Homes or small lodgings. Owner usually lives on-site. Fruit, pastries and bread are typically served for breakfast.

➡ **Condominiums** Individually owned units grouped in one complex. Typically include a full kitchen.

➡ **Hotels** Price is usually based on room size and view, with bigger rooms and full ocean views attracting top rates.

➡ **Camping** Maui's national, state and county parks offer campgrounds: book permits in advance.

Booking Accommodations

Condominiums and vacation rentals (which may include rooms, cottages and entire houses) can be found across most of the island. You'll find listings by searching online sites such as HomeAway (www.homeaway.com), Vacation Rentals by Owner (VRBO; www.vrbo.com), Flipkey (www.flipkey.com) and AirBnB (www.airbnb.com).

Condominiums

➡ Condos are incredibly popular on Maui. Indeed, some top destinations such as Kihei and Napili have far more condominiums than hotels.

➡ Condos are more spacious than hotel rooms, and are often furnished with everything a visitor needs, from a kitchen to a washer and dryer. They typically work out cheaper than hotels.

➡ In most places condo units are individually owned and then placed in a rental pool, so furnishings and decor can vary by unit.

➡ Most condos, especially those handled through rental agencies, have a three- to seven-day minimum stay.

➡ Maui condos usually have built-in discounts for longer stays: as a general rule the weekly rate is six times the daily rate and the monthly rate three times the weekly.

➡ Ask about cleaning fees, which might be tacked onto your bill.

➡ Some condo complexes are booked only through rental agencies. Others operate more like a hotel with a front desk, though even in these places some units are usually still handled by rental agencies. Some properties may charge a reservation fee.

Vacation Rentals

➡ Typically, a vacation rental means renting an entire house (with no on-site manager and no breakfast provided).

➡ Ask about mandatory cleaning fees.

B&Bs

➡ If you're considering a B&B stay on Maui, plan ahead. Most B&Bs (also known as inns) are small operations with just a few rooms, so they can book out weeks in advance.

➡ Some accept reservations only through agencies, and others require a minimum stay of a few days. Same-day reservations are hard to get, though there are sometimes last-minute openings and, if you're lucky, you may snag a one-night rental. But do always call ahead – B&B owners don't want unannounced visitors disturbing their guests.

➡ B&B booking services include Affordable Paradise (www.affordable-paradise.com) and Hawaii's Best B&B (www.bestbnb.com).

Paliku campground (p197)

PLAN YOUR TRIP ACCOMMODATIONS

CAMPGROUNDS & CABINS INSIDE A VOLCANO

Who needs a resort when you can camp near the summit of a dormant volcano? Amenities include dark skies, storied sunrises from the summit and sweet isolation. Yep, if you like a touch of adventure with your vacationing, consider an overnight stay at Haleakalā National Park, which offers free backcountry camping on the crater floor with a permit, as well as $75 cabin rentals. Visit www.nps.gov/hale for more details.

Top Choices
Best Maui Stays

➡ **Pa'ia Inn, Pa'ia** (www.paiainn.com; r $239-699, ste $569-599) Classy boutique hotel

➡ **Ho'oilo House, Lahaina** (www.hooilohouse.com; r $329) A calming retreat.

➡ **Banana Bungalow, Wailuku** (www.mauihostel.com; s/d $95/105) Fun hostel.

➡ **Montage Kapalua Bay, Kapalua** (www.montagehotels.com; ste from $915) Swanky yet inviting 24-acre resort.

➡ **Hamoa Bay House & Bungalow, Hana** (www.vrbo.com/28451; bungalow 1 bedroom $285, house 2 bedroom $325-395) Romantic retreat.

Warmest Alohas

➡ **Hale Napili, Napili** (www.halenapili.com; studio $199-299, 1 br $349) Island hospitality

➡ **Ocean Breeze Hideaway, Kihei** (www.hawaiibednbreakfast.com; r $125-139) Low-key and welcoming.

➡ **Punahoa, Kihei** (www.punahoabeach.com; studio $224, 1/2 bedroom $299/$315) Classy boutique condo with clear ocean views.

➡ **Old Wailuku Inn, Wailuku** (www.mauiinn.com; r $165-265) Elegant period home.

Best for Families

➡ **Hyatt Regency Maui Resort & Spa, Ka'anapali** (www.maui.hyatt.com; r/ste from $344/663) Kids will love the water slides.

➡ **Grand Wailea Resort Hotel & Spa, Wailea** (www.grandwailea.com; r/ste from $479/1259) Exuberant, join-the-crowd fun.

➡ **Honua Kai Resort & Spa, Ka'anapali** (www.honuakai.com; studio/ste $301-1495) Breezy, stylish oasis.

➡ **Ka'anapali Beach Hotel, Ka'anapali** (www.kbhmaui.com; r $165-275) Welcoming, comfy resort.

Best on a Budget

➡ **Paliku Cabin & Campground, Haleakalā National Park** (www.nps.gove/hale; campground free; per cabin with 1-12 people $75) Sleep in the Haleakalā Crater.

➡ **Camp Olowalu, Olowalu** (www.campolowalu.com; campsites per adult/child 6-12yr $20/5) The setting here is pure *Survivor*.

➡ **Wailuku Guesthouse, Wailuku** (www.wailukuhouse.com; 1br $110-150, 2br $180) Affordable, friendly, family-run guesthouse.

➡ **YMCA Camp Ke'anae, Ke'anae** (www.ymcacampkeanae.org; campsite single/family $25/40, cabin per person $25) Bluff-top location.

Getting Around

For more information, see Transportation (p305)

Traveling by Car

Car Hire

To explore Maui thoroughly and reach off-the-beaten path sights, you'll need your own wheels.

All the major car rental firms have offices at Kahului Airport. Most of these firms also have branches in Ka'anapali and will pick you up at the nearby Kapalua Airport. For a green option, consider Bio-Beetle in Kahului. Also check out Kihei Rent A Car (p161).

Be sure to check for any road restrictions on your vehicle rental contract. Some car rental agencies, for instance, may prohibit driving on the Kahekili Hwy between Honokohau and Waihe'e and in the Kaupo district of the Pi'ilani Hwy.

Driving Conditions

Most main roads on Maui are called highways whether they're busy four-lane thoroughfares or just quiet country roads. Indeed there are roads in remote corners of the island that are barely one lane but nonetheless are designated highways.

➡ Islanders refer to highways by name, and rarely by number. If you stop to ask someone how to find Hwy 36, chances are you'll get a blank stare – ask for the Hana Hwy instead.

➡ Most Maui roads are paved. Some, like the Hana Hwy, are extremely curvaceous. The notorious **Pi'ilani Hwy** (p228) in southeast Maui is only part-paved but is usually passable for cars. Check the conditions of these roads after rains.

➡ Cell-phone use without a hands-free device is prohibited. Seat-belt use is mandatory.

RESOURCES

American Automobile Association (www.hawaii.aaa.com; ☎800-736-2886) Members are entitled to discounts on select car rentals, hotels, sightseeing and attractions, as well as free road maps and travel-agency services. For emergency roadside assistance and towing call ☎800-222-4357. AAA has reciprocal agreements with automobile associations in other countries (eg CAA). Bring your membership card from home.

Hawaii Department of Transportation (http://hidot.hawaii.gov/highways/roadwork/maui) Road closures.

Maui Now (mauinow.com/tag/maui-traffic) Online newspaper articles highlighting current road conditions and closures.

No Car?

Bus

Maui Bus (📞808-871-4838; www.mauicounty.gov/bus; single ride $2, day pass $4) offers an extensive public bus system between the main towns, but not to out-of-the-way places, such as Haleakalā National Park or Hana. Buses come with front-load bike racks.

The main routes run every hour daily, roughly 7am to 8pm. Kahului is a hub.

Routes The handiest routes for visitors:

➡ Haiku Islander (Kahului–Ha'iku)

➡ Ka'anapali Islander (Lahaina–Ka'anapali)

➡ Kihei Islander (Kahului–Wailea)

➡ Kihei Villager (Ma'alaea–Kihei)

➡ Lahaina Islander (Kahului–Lahaina)

➡ Napili Islander (Ka'anapali–Napili)

➡ Wailuku Loop (Kahului–Wailuku)

The Upcountry Islander and Haiku Islander routes stop at Kahului Airport.

Costs Fares are $2 per ride, regardless of distance. There are no transfers; you have to pay the fare each time you board a bus. A day pass costs only $4.

Carry-on You can carry on only what fits under your seat or on your lap, so forget the surfboard.

Resort Shuttle Many of the Ka'anapali resorts operate shuttles for guests that serve the resort areas and Lahaina.

Bicycle

Cyclists on Maui face a number of challenges: narrow roads, an abundance of hills and mountains, and the same persistent winds that so delight windsurfers. Maui's stunning scenery certainly will entice hard-core cyclists, but casual riders hoping to use a bike as a primary source of transportation around the island may well find such conditions daunting.

Getting around by bicycle within a small area can be a reasonable option for the average rider. For example, the tourist enclave of Kihei is largely level and now has cycle lanes on its two main drags, S Kihei Rd and the Pi'ilani Hwy. Elsewhere, bike lanes are still sparse.

It's easy to rent a bike in most tourist areas of Maui. Rates range from $15 to $60 per day, depending on the style and quality of the bike.

Bringing your own bike to Hawaii costs upwards of $100 on flights from the mainland. The bicycle can usually be checked at the airline counter, the same as any baggage, but you'll need to prepare the bike by doing some disassembly. Check with the airlines for details.

In general, bicycles are required to follow the same state laws and rules of the road as cars. State law requires all cyclists under the age of 16 to wear helmets.

PLAN YOUR TRIP GETTING AROUND

DRIVING FAST FACTS

➡ **Right or left:** Right

➡ **Top speed limit:** 55mph

➡ **Signature car:** Jeep Wrangler

➡ **Gas stations on the Road to Hana:** 0

➡ **Gas stations in Hana:** 1

ROAD DISTANCES (MILES)

	Lahaina	Kihei	Kapalua	Kahului
Kihei	22			
Kapalua	10	32		
Kahului	24	10	33	
Hana	72	58	82	51

Mama's Fish Ho

Plan Your Trip

Eat & Drink Like a Local

We love cuisine in Maui because of its tasty exuberance and no-worries embrace of foreign flavors. The plate lunch. Loco moco (rice, fried egg and hamburger patty with gravy). Even Spam musubi (rice ball) has a sassy – if salty – international charm. So join the fun, sample the unknown and savor the next bite.

The Year in Food

It's always a good time to dig into produce grown in Maui's Upcountry. Due to the island's consistently warm tropical climate, most fruits and vegetables are harvested year-round.

Spring (April)

Head to Hana to celebrate taro, a unique and revered Hawaiian plant with a starchy potato-like quality. It's used in burgers, chips and mashed into a pastelike pudding called poi.

Fall (October)

To check out the range of produce grown on the island, wander the aisles at the Maui County Fair in early October in Kahului. As Halloween approaches, take the family to the pumpkin patch at Kula Country Farms, where there's also a corn maze.

Food Experiences

Meals of a Lifetime

➜ **Lahaina Grill** (p93) Savor seafood and steaks in artsy digs in downtown Lahaina.

➜ **Mama's Fish House** (p183) Celebrate a special occasion with exquisite fish, impeccable service and a prime beach view.

➜ **Monkeypod Kitchen** (p164) It's your favorite neighborhood restaurant, done Hawaiian-style.

➜ **Geste Shrimp Truck** (p136) These hot bundles of spicy goodness demand a stack of napkins.

➜ **Mana Foods** (p182) What? An organic grocery? Well, have you tried the deli buffet? Feel the mana at this locals' joint.

➜ **Hana Farms Clay Oven Pizza** (p238) The wood-fired pizzas are loaded with locally grown veggies.

➜ **Mana'e Goods & Grindz** (p260) Local food that's legendary on Moloka'i's rural eastern side.

Best Breakfasts

➜ **Gazebo** (p114) Dig into macadamia-nut pancakes beside the Napili coast.

➜ **Plantation House** (p119) Did somebody says crab-cakes Benedict? Oh yes, they did.

➜ **Kihei Caffe** (p158) Quick and hearty is the name of the game at this Kihei hotspot.

➜ **Colleen's** (p185) Join the surfer crowd for breakfast burritos and egg-stuffed croissants.

➜ **808 Bistro** (p159) The decadent 'whale pie' encourages gluttony, but the dapper surroundings will keep you polite.

Dare to Try

Spam musubi A rice ball topped with sautéed Spam and wrapped with dried seaweed. Locals of all stripes enjoy this 'only in Hawaii' creation.

Local Specialties

Hawaiian food can be divided into three general categories: local food, Native Hawaiian and Hawaii Regional Cuisine.

Local Food

Day-to-day eats reflect the state's multi-cultural heritage, with Asian, Portuguese and native Hawaiian influences the most immediately evident. Cheap, fattening and tasty, local food is also the stuff of cravings and comfort. Can be found across the island.

➜ **Plate lunch** The classic example of local food is the ubiquitous plate lunch. Picture this: chunky layers of tender kalua pork, a dollop of smooth, creamy macaroni and two hearty scoops of white rice. Yum, right? The pork can be swapped for other proteins like fried mahimahi (fish) or teriyaki chicken. Served almost like street food, the plate lunch is often presented on disposable plates and eaten using chopsticks. A favorite breakfast combo includes fried egg and spicy Portuguese sausage (or bacon, ham, Spam etc) and, always, two scoops of rice.

➤ **Pupu** The local term used for all kinds of munchies or 'grazing' foods is *pupu*. Much more than just cheese and crackers, *pupu* represent the ethnic diversity of the islands and might include boiled peanuts in the shell, edamame (boiled fresh soybeans in the pod) and universal items such as fried shrimp.

➤ **Poke** Raw fish marinated in *shōyu* (soy sauce), oil, chili peppers, green onions and seaweed, *poke* comes in many varieties. Sesame ahi (yellowfin tuna) is particularly delicious and goes well with beer.

➤ **Spam musubi** (p35)

➤ **Shave ice** Ignore joyless cynics who'll tell you that shave ice is nothing more than a snow cone. Shave ice is not just a snow cone. It's a tropical 21-gun salute – the most spectacular snow cone on earth. The specifics? The ice is shaved as fine as powdery snow, packed into a paper cone and drenched with sweet fruit-flavored syrups in dazzling hues. For added decadence, add Kaua'i cream, azuki beans and ice cream.

Native Hawaiian

Across Maui you'll find preparation methods and dishes that trace back to the island's first settlers.

➤ **Kalua pig and poi** These are the 'meat and potatoes' of native Hawaiian food. Kalua pork is traditionally baked in an underground oven. Poi is served as the main side dish with every Hawaiian-style meal. The purple paste is pounded from cooked taro roots, with water added to make it puddinglike. It's nutritious and easily digested, but for many nonlocals it is also

Shave ice

an acquired taste, largely because of its pasty consistency.

➤ **Laulau** This common main dish is a bundle of pork or chicken and salted butterfish wrapped in a taro leaf that's steamed until it has a soft spinachlike texture.

➤ **Baked 'ulu** Breadfruit which has a texture similar to a potato.

➤ **Haupia** This delicious pudding is made of coconut cream thickened with cornstarch or arrowroot. *Haupia* ice cream made on Maui offers a nice cross between traditional and modern cuisine.

Hawaii Regional Cuisine

Twenty years ago Hawaii was a culinary backwater. Sure, you could slum it on local grinds (food) and get by on the slew of midrange Asian eateries, but fine dining was typically a European-style meal that ignored locally grown fare and the islands' unique flavors.

Then, in the 1990s, a handful of island chefs smashed this tired mold and created a new cuisine, borrowing liberally from Hawaii's various ethnic influences. They partnered with local farmers, ranchers

---

SPAM A LOT

Spam arrived in Hawaii during WWII, when fresh meat imports were replaced by this standard GI ration. By the war's end, Hawaiians had developed a taste for the fatty canned stuff. Today, Hawaiians consume about 7 million cans of Spam annually!

Spam looks and tastes different in Hawaii. It's eaten cooked (typically sautéed to a light crispiness in sweetened *shōyu*), not straight from the can, and served as a tasty meat dish.

Beachfront dining, Lahaina

and fishers to highlight fresh local fare and transform their childhood favorites into grown-up, gourmet masterpieces. The movement was dubbed 'Hawaii Regional Cuisine' and the pioneering chefs became celebrities. A trio with Maui connections are Roy Yamaguchi of Roy's Ka'anapali (p110), Beverly Gannon of Hali'imaile General Store (p185) and Mark Ellman of Frida's Mexican Beach House (p93), Mala Ocean Tavern (p93) and Honu (p92) in Lahaina.

The real catchwords for Hawaii Regional Cuisine are fresh, organic and locally grown. Think Upcountry greens, Maui chèvre (goat cheese), Kula onions, free-range Hana beef and locally caught fish. The spread of the movement has been a boon to small-scale farmers who are contributing to a greening of Maui's gardens and menus.

How to Eat & Drink

When to Eat

Maui locals eat meals early and on the dot. Restaurants are packed around the habitual mealtimes, but they clear out an hour or two later, as locals are not lingerers. If you dine at 8:30pm you might not have to wait at all. But bear in mind that restaurants also close early and night owls must hunt for places to eat.

➡ **Breakfast** Typically 6am.

➡ **Lunch** Noon.

➡ **Dinner** Locals eat at 6pm.

Where to Eat

For top-end restaurants in Maui, book a week in advance, and earlier during the winter holiday season.

➡ **Plate-lunch eateries** Great choices for quick takeout. They pack things tidily so you can carry your meal to a nearby beach for an impromptu picnic lunch. One tip: at lunchtime, decide what you want before reaching the register. Lines typically move quickly and the indecisive can muck up the system.

➡ **Food trucks** Known as *kaukau* (food) wagons, food trucks have become common on Maui. They typically park near the beach or shopping centers. Bring cash.

FOOD GLOSSARY

Hawaii's cuisine is multi-ethnic and so is the lingo.

adobo – Filipino chicken or pork cooked in vinegar, *shōyu*, garlic and spices

'awa – kava, a Polynesian plant used to make a mildly intoxicating drink

bentō – Japanese-style box lunch

broke da mout – delicious; literally 'broke the mouth'

char siu – Cantonese barbecued pork

chirashizushi – assorted sashimi served over rice

crack seed – Chinese-style preserved fruit; a salty, sweet and/or sour snack

donburi – Japanese-style large bowl of rice topped with a protein (eg pork *katsu*)

furikake – catch-all Japanese seasoning or condiment, usually dry and sprinkled atop rice; in Hawaii, sometimes mixed into *poke*

grind – to eat

grinds – food (usually local)

guava – fruit with green or yellow rind, moist pink flesh and lots of edible seeds

haupia – coconut-cream custard, often thickened with arrowroot or cornstarch

hulihuli chicken – rotisserie-cooked chicken with island-style barbecue sauce

imu – underground earthen oven used to cook *kalua* pig and other luau food

'inamona – roasted, ground *kukui* (candlenut), used as a condiment (eg mixed into *poke*)

izakaya – Japanese pub serving tapas-style dishes

kalbi – Korean-style grilled meats, typically marinated short ribs

kalo – Hawaiian word for taro, often pounded into *poi*

kalua – Hawaiian method of cooking pork or other luau food, traditionally in an *imu*

kare-kare – Filipino oxtail stew

katsu – Japanese deep-fried cutlets, usually pork or chicken

kaukau – food

laulau – bundle of pork or chicken and salted butterfish, wrapped in taro and *ti* leaves and steamed

li hing mui – sweet-salty preserved plum, a type of crack seed; also refers to the flavor powder

liliko'i – passion fruit

loco moco – hearty dish of rice, fried egg and hamburger patty topped with gravy or other condiments

➡ **Cafes** These are the best places to relax over a good lunch in an engaging setting at a fair price. If the setting isn't important, there are plenty of diner-style Asian restaurants with Formica tables and vinyl chairs, no view and no decor. They generally offer quick service and often have surprisingly good food at decent prices.

➡ **Top-end restaurants** These are outright impressive and include some of the most highly rated chef-driven places in Hawaii. These establishments are typically found on prime oceanfront perches as well as in resorts and golf-course clubhouses. Most forgo the pompous fastidiousness common to upscale urban restaurants on the US mainland. Meals start at $30 per person. To sample top cuisine at a good price, visit during happy hour when prices of appetizers are often reduced.

➡ **Groceries** Chains and locally owned markets can be found across the island. You'll find local specialties like *poke* bowls and Spam *musubi* at most of them.

lomilomi salmon – minced, salted salmon with diced tomato and green onion

luau – Hawaiian feast

mai tai – tiki-bar drink typically containing rum and tropical fruit juices

malasada – sugar-coated, fried Portuguese doughnut (no hole), often filled with flavored custard

manapua – Chinese *bao* (baked or steamed buns) with *char siu* or other fillings

manjū – Japanese steamed or baked cake, often filled with sweet bean paste

mochi – Japanese pounded-rice cake, sticky and sweet

musubi – Japanese *onigiri* (rice ball or triangle) wrapped in *nori*

noni – type of mulberry with strong-smelling yellow fruit, used medicinally by Hawaiians

nori – Japanese seaweed, usually dried

ogo – crunchy seaweed, sometimes added to *poke; limu* in Hawaiian

okazu-ya – Japanese take-out delicatessen, often specializing in home-style Hawaiian and local dishes

'ono – delicious

'ono kine grinds – good food

pau hana – happy hour (literally 'stop work')

pipikaula – Hawaiian beef jerky

poha – cape gooseberry

poi – staple Hawaiian starch made of steamed, mashed taro (*kalo*)

poke – cubed, marinated raw fish

ponzu – Japanese citrus sauce

pupu – snacks or appetizers

saimin – local-style noodle soup

shave ice – cup of finely shaved ice doused with sweet syrups

shōyu – soy sauce

star fruit – translucent green-yellow fruit with five ribs like the points of a star, and sweet, juicy pulp

taro – plant with edible corm used to make *poi* and with edible leaves to wrap around *laulau; kalo* in Hawaiian

uni – sea urchin

➡ **Farmers markets & produce stands** Local farms and food purveyors share their fare at kiosk-lined farmers markets in West Maui, Central Maui, South Maui and the Upcountry. Most farmers markets occur once per week. Fruit and farm stands are common along the Road to Hana, in Hana and in Kula. As of 2013, about 90% of groceries were imported to Hawaii from the mainland, including milk, fruit, vegetables and beef. If absolute freshness means something to you, choose locally raised beef, island-caught fish and Maui-grown produce.

Habits & Customs

➡ **Food portions** Locals tend to consider quantity as important as quality – and the portion sizes are telling, especially at plate-lunch places. If you're a light eater, feel free to split a meal or take home the leftovers.

Papaya

➡ **Potluck meals** Home entertainment for local folks always revolves around food, which is usually served 'potluck style' with all the guests adding to the anything-goes smorgasbord. Locals rarely serve dinner in one-at-a-time courses. Rather, meals are served 'family style,' where diners help themselves. Throwaway paper plates and wooden chopsticks make for an easy clean-up, and the rule is 'all you can eat' (and they definitely mean it!).

➡ **Dinner guest** If you're invited to someone's home, show up on time and bring a dish – preferably homemade, but a bakery cake or *manju* (Japanese cakes filled with sweet bean paste) from Sam Sato's (p140) in Wailuku are always a certain hit. Remove your shoes at the door. And don't be surprised if you're forced to take home a plate of leftovers.

Menu Decoder

You'll find a few staples in just about every Hawaiian meal. One word of caution:

Maui's attempts at nonlocal classics such as pizza, bagels, croissants and southern BBQ can be disappointing. Stick with local-local food.

➡ **Sticky white rice** More than just a side dish in Hawaii, sticky white rice is a culinary building block, an integral partner in everyday meals. Without rice, Spam *musubi* would be a slice of canned meat. *Loco moco* would be nothing more than an egg-covered hamburger. And without two-scoop rice, the plate lunch would be a ho-hum conversation between meat and macaroni rather than a multicultural party. And by the way, sticky white rice means sticky white rice. While you might find couscous or mashed potatoes at fancy restaurants, day-to-day meals are served with sticky white rice. Not flaky rice. Not wild rice. Not flavored rice. And definitely not Uncle Ben's. Locals can devour mounds of the stuff and it typically comes as two scoops. The top condiment is soy sauce, known by its Japanese name *shōyu,* which combines well with sharp Asian flavors such as ginger, green onion and garlic.

➡ **Protein** Meat, chicken or fish are often key components of a meal, too. For quick, cheap eating, locals devour anything tasty, from Portuguese sausage to hamburger steak to corned beef. But the dinner-table highlight is always seafood, especially freshly caught fish.

Price Ranges

The following price ranges refer to a standard main on Maui. Prices don't include tax.

$ less than $15

$$ $15–25

$$$ more than $25

Top: Picnicking,
Hawaii-style

Bottom: *Loco moco*

MIKACO LTD/GETTY IMAGES ©

Plan Your Trip
Diving & Snorkeling Maui

The underwater scenery around Maui is just as impressive as what you'll see on land. Dive companies run frequent trips to hot spots like Molokini. Many of the best snorkeling areas are only a few kicks from shore.

Diving & Snorkeling Outfitters

Lahaina Divers (p86) Boat dives and snorkeling; departs from Lahaina.

Maui Dive Shop (p113) Boat dives and snorkeling; departs from Lahaina.

Maui Dreams Dive Co (p156) Shore dives and boat dives; departs from Kihei and Ma'alaea.

Pacific Whale Foundation (p144) Snorkeling; departs from Ma'alaea.

Aloha Kayaks (p168) Kayak-snorkeling; departs from Makena Landing.

South Pacific Kayaks & Outfitters (p157) Kayak-snorkeling; departs from Makena Landing.

Maui Kayaks (p86) Kayak-snorkeling; departs the West Maui and South Maui coasts.

Best Snorkeling Spots

➡ **Honolua Bay** Fish-filled reefs and loads of coral in West Maui.

➡ **'Ahihi-Kina'u Natural Area Reserve** (p168) Enter the water beside the new 'fish' sign in this marine conservation area.

➡ **Molokini Crater** Oh yes, you will see colorful tropical fish inside this volcanic rim.

➡ **Malu'aka Beach** (p166) Come to Turtle Beach to ogle graceful green sea turtles.

➡ **Ulua Beach** (p162) For easy-access snorkeling in Wailea, grab a parking spot at this beach near the Andaz Maui.

Diving

Excellent visibility. Warm water temperatures. Hundreds of rare fish species... Maui is a diving mecca for a reason. Here you can often see spinner dolphins, green sea turtles, manta rays and moray eels. With luck, you might even hear humpback whales singing underwater – you'll never forget it if you do.

Most dive operations on Maui offer a full range of dives as well as refresher and advanced certification courses. Introductory dives for beginners get you beneath the surface in just a couple of hours. Experienced divers needn't bring anything other

MOLOKINI CRATER

This fascinating volcanic crater lies midway between the islands of Maui and Kahoʻolawe. Extremely popular with travelers, this underwater site can see more than 1000 visitors in a day. Half of the crater rim has eroded away, leaving a crescent-moon shape that rises 160ft above the ocean surface, with a mere 18 acres of rocky land high and dry. But it's what's beneath the surface that draws the crowds. Snorkelers and divers will be thrilled by steep walls, ledges, white-tipped reef sharks, manta rays, turtles and abundant fish.

The legends about Molokini are myriad. One says Molokini was a beautiful woman who was turned to stone by jealous Pele, goddess of fire and volcanoes. Another claims one of Pele's lovers angered her by secretly marrying a *moʻo* (shape-shifting water lizard). Pele chopped the sacred lizard in half, leaving Molokini as its tail and Puʻu Olaʻi in Makena as its head. Yet another tale alleges that Molokini, which means 'many ties' in Hawaiian, is the umbilical cord left over from the birth of Kahoʻolawe.

The coral reef that extends outward from Molokini is awesome, though it's lost some of its variety over the years. Most of the black coral, once prolific in Molokini's deeper waters, made its way into Lahaina jewelry stores before the island was declared a marine conservation district in 1977. During WWII the US Navy shelled Molokini for target practice, and live bombs are still occasionally spotted on the crater floor. In 2006 a tour boat with an inexperienced captain sank at Molokini. No one was injured, but after an inept salvage job, 1200 coral colonies had been destroyed. The company incurred a $396,000 state-imposed fine.

There are a few things to consider when planning a Molokini excursion. The water is calmest and clearest in the morning, so don't fall for discounted afternoon tours – go out early for the smoothest sailing and best conditions. For snorkelers, there's simply not much to see when the water's choppy. The main departure points for Molokini trips are Maʻalaea and Lahaina Harbors. You'll get out there quicker if you hop a boat from Maʻalaea, which is closer to Molokini. Going from Lahaina adds on more sail time, but if it's winter it'll also increase the possibilities for spotting whales along the way, so it's sometimes worth an extra hour out of your day.

than a swimsuit and certification card. Don't monkey around with activity desks – book directly with the dive operators.

On Maui, the granddaddy of dives is crescent-shaped Molokini. The other prime destination is the untouched Cathedrals on the south side of Lanaʻi, which takes its name from the amazing underwater caverns, arches and connecting passages.

For a basic but helpful map of dive and snorkel spots around Maui, pick up Maui Dive Shop's free pull-out map at one of its stores (www.mauidiveshop.com), which are scattered across West and South Maui.

Responsible Diving

The popularity of diving is placing immense pressure on many sites. Consider the following tips to help preserve the ecology and beauty of reefs while on Maui:

➡ Avoid touching living marine organisms with your body or dragging equipment across the reef. Polyps can be damaged by even the gentlest contact. Never stand on coral. If you must hold on to the reef, touch only exposed rock or dead coral.

➡ Be conscious of your fins. Even without contact, the surge from heavy fin strokes near the reef can damage delicate organisms. When treading water in shallow reef areas, take care not to kick up clouds of sand. Settling sand can easily smother the delicate organisms of the reef.

➡ Don't use reef anchors and take care not to ground boats on coral.

➡ Minimize your disturbance of marine animals. It is illegal to approach endangered marine species too closely; these include whales, dolphins, sea turtles and the Hawaiian monk seal. In particular, don't ride on the backs of turtles!

➡ Practice and maintain proper buoyancy control. Major damage can be done by divers descending too fast and colliding with the reef.

Maui: Diving & Snorkeling

HONOLUA BAY

A short walk through tropical flora ends at this pristine bay, a conservation district loaded with tropical fish. Reefs and coral hug the edge of the bay. (p118)

PU'U KEKA'A (BLACK ROCK)

A legendary lava promontory is an easy snorkel spot if you're staying in Ka'anapali. Look for tropical fish, coral and the occasional green sea turtle. Strong swimmers may find more fish in the cove at the tip of the rock. (p107)

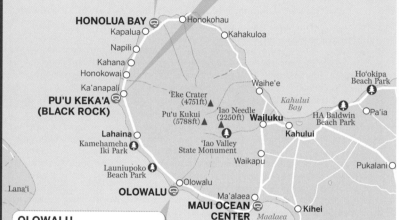

OLOWALU

Check out the shallow coral reef here if you're driving toward Lahaina from the airport and just can't wait to look for fish. (p104)

MAUI OCEAN CENTER

Drop into the 750,000-gallon ocean tank at this oceanside aquarium for an inside dive with reef sharks and hammerheads. (p144)

MOLOKINI CRATER

Hop aboard a boat for a snorkel or dive trip to this crescent-shaped volcanic rim, a marine conservation district. Boats fill the inner rim in the morning, when visibility is best. Experienced divers also like to explore the back wall. (p144)

MAKENA BAY

Paddle out into the bay in a kayak then hop overboard to snorkel past colorful fish and green sea turtles. There's even an underwater arch to ogle. Scan for whales in winter. Also a popular spot for shore dives. (p166)

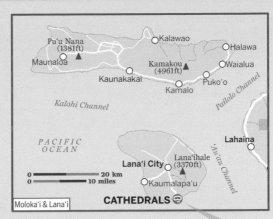

Moloka'i & Lana'i

CATHEDRALS

Ride a boat to the south shores of Lana'i for fantastic diving. Kick through grottoes and swoosh through a short tube. Look for sharks, turtles and tropical fish. (p252)

MALU'AKA BEACH

Dubbed Turtle Town, this is the place to come if you'd like to glide beside honu, Maui's beloved green sea turtles. Remember, look but don't touch. Fantastic coral is about 100 yards out – head south. (p166)

'AHIHI KINA'U NATURAL RESERVE

Fishing is prohibited in this natural reserve near the edge of an old lava flow, so there are fish aplenty. The secret is out, however, and this remote spot can now see 500 snorkelers per day. Arrive early and enter the water at the fish sign. It's a good spot to look for rainbow parrot fish. (p168)

Make sure you are correctly weighted and that your weight belt is positioned so that you stay horizontal.

➡ Resist the temptation to feed marine animals. You might disturb their normal eating habits, encourage aggressive behavior or feed them food that is detrimental to their health.

➡ Spend as little time in underwater caves as possible, as your air bubbles may be caught within the roof and leave previously submerged organisms high and dry.

➡ Don't leave any rubbish, and remove any litter you find. Plastics in particular are a serious threat to marine life. Turtles can mistake plastic for jellyfish and eat it.

➡ Don't collect (or buy) coral or shells. Aside from the ecological damage, taking home marine souvenirs depletes the beauty of a site and spoils the enjoyment of others.

➡ **Divers Alert Network** (DAN; ☎800-446-2671, emergency 919-684-9111; www.diversalertnetwork.org) gives advice on diving emergencies, insurance, decompression services, illness and injury.

➡ Protect fragile reefs by wearing a coral-safe sunscreen (p164).

Snorkeling

The waters around Maui are a kaleidoscope of coral, colorful fish and super-big sea turtles. Best of all, you don't need special skills to view them. If you can float, you can snorkel – it's a cinch to learn. If you're a newbie, fess up at the dive shop or beach hut where you rent your snorkel gear – mask, snorkel and fins – and they'll show you everything you need to know. And it's cheap: most snorkel sets rent for $10 or less per day.

Snorkelers should get an early start. Not only does the first half of the morning offer the calmest water, but at some of the popular places crowds begin to show by 10am.

The hottest spots for snorkeling cruises are the largely submerged volcanic crater of Molokini, off Maui's southwest coast, and Lana'i's Hulopo'e Beach. Both brim with untouched coral and an amazing variety of sealife.

Remember to wear reef-safe sunscreen lotion before kicking off. Many modern lotions are reef killers. Safe ingredients are titanium dioxide and zinc oxide. Avoid sunscreens with oxybenzone and other chemical UV-radiation filters.

Plan Your Trip
On the Water

The Pacific Ocean is Maui's ultimate playground. And take note, when renting ocean gear, you'll pay premium prices at resort beach shacks. Stop by a surf or snorkel shop in town for the best rates.

Best Beaches for Water Sports

Honolua Bay
Surfing in winter, snorkeling in summer. (p118)

DT Fleming Beach Park
A beauty that will make you wonder if you've reached the South Pacific. (p115)

Ka'anapali Beach
A happening resort beach with all the expected facilities. (p107)

Keawakapu Beach
The perfect beach for a sunset swim. (p154)

Malu'aka Beach
The best place to snorkel with turtles. (p166)

Big Beach
For long beach strolls, bodyboarding and bodysurfing. (p167)

Bodysurfing & Bodyboarding

If you want to catch your waves lying down, bodysurfing and bodyboarding are suitable water activities for anybody.

There are good beginner to intermediate shorebreaks at the Kama'ole Beach Parks and Charley Young Beach in Kihei, and at Ulua Beach and Wailea Beach in Wailea. Experienced bodysurfers should head to DT Fleming Beach Park and Slaughterhouse Beach in Kapalua, Big Beach in Makena, and HA Baldwin Beach Park near Pa'ia.

Special bodysurfing flippers, which are smaller than snorkel fins, will help you paddle out. Bodyboard rentals range from $7 to $20 per day.

Kayaking

There's a lot to see underwater just off Maui's coast, so most outfitters offer snorkel-kayak combos. The top spot is Makena, an area rich with marine life, including sea turtles, dolphins and wintering humpback whales. In the calmer summer months, another excellent option is Honolua–Mokule'ia Bay Marine Life Conservation District at Slaughterhouse Beach and Honolua Bay north of Kapalua, where there are turtles aplenty and dolphin sightings. Water conditions around Maui are usually clearest and calmest early in the morning.

For tours try Aloha Kayaks (p168), or South Pacific Kayaks (p157), which also rents kayaks.

Kitesurfing

Kitesurfing is a bit like strapping on a snowboard, grabbing a huge kite and riding with the wind across the water. It looks damn hard and certainly takes stamina, but if you already know how to ride a board, there's a good chance you'll master it quickly. According to surf legend Robby Naish, who pioneered kitesurfing, it's the most accessible of all extreme sports.

There's no better place to learn than on Maui's Kite Beach, at the western end of Kanaha Beach Park. Visiting kitesurfers need to check with locals to clarify the no-fly zones. Get the lowdown from the Maui Kiteboarding Association (www.mauikiteboardingassociation.com) and Maui Kitesurfing Community (www.mauikitesurf.org).

Outrigger Canoeing

Polynesians were Hawaii's first settlers, paddling outrigger canoes across 2000 miles of open ocean – so you could say canoeing was Hawaii's earliest sport. The first Europeans to arrive were awestruck at the skill Hawaiians displayed, timing launches and landings perfectly and paddling among the waves like dolphins.

Today canoe clubs keep the outrigger tradition alive. Hawaiian Sailing Canoe Adventures (p164) in Wailea offers guided outrigger canoe tours, sharing cultural insights as you paddle along the coast. Some resorts, including the Four Seasons (p162) and **Andaz Maui** (3550 Wailea Alanui Dr), also offer tours.

Stand Up Paddle Boarding

The stand up paddle surf invasion has begun. For proof, drive from Papawai Point northwest to Lahaina and look seaward. Platoons of paddle-wielding surfers, standing on 9ft to 11ft boards, are plying the waves just off the coast at seemingly every beachside park.

Abbreviated to SUP, and known in Hawaii as *ku hoe he'e nalu*, the sport is great for less limber adventurers since you don't need to pop up into a stance. It takes coordination to learn but isn't harder than regular surfing – although you should be a strong swimmer. Consider a class with paddle surf champ Maria Souza (p156) in Kihei, or with the instructors at Maui Wave Riders (p86) in Lahaina. Beachside rentals run $25 to $50 per hour.

Whale-Watching

With their tail-slaps, head lunges and spy hops, humpback whales sure know how to impress a crowd. Each winter, about 12,000 of these graceful leviathans – two-thirds of the entire North Pacific humpback whale population – come to the shallow coastal waters off the Hawaiian Islands to breed and give birth. And like other discerning visitors to Hawaii, these intelligent creatures favor Maui. The western coastline of the island is their chief birthing and nursing ground. Luckily for whale-watchers, humpbacks are coast-huggers, preferring shallow waters to protect their newborn calves.

Much of Hawaii's ocean waters are protected as the Hawaiian Islands Humpback Whale National Marine Sanctuary (p155), whose Kihei headquarters is abuzz with cool whale happenings. Along the coast there's great whale-watching at many places, including Papawai Point, and along beach walks in Kihei and Wailea.

If you want to get within splashing distance of 40-ton leviathans acrobatically

---

PARKS & BEACHES
....
Details about county parks and beaches in Maui, including contact information and lifeguard availability, can be found on the Maui County government (www.mauicounty.gov) website.

---

jumping out of the water, take a whale-watching cruise. No one does them better than the Pacific Whale Foundation (p88), a conservation group that takes pride in its green, naturalist-led whale-watching trips. Maui's peak whale-watching season is from January through March, although whales are usually around for a month or so on either side of those dates.

Windsurfing

This sport reaches its peak on Maui. Ho'okipa Beach, near Pa'ia, hosts top international windsurfing competitions. The wind and waves combine at Ho'okipa in a way that makes gravity seem arbitrary, but this beach is for experts only, as hazards include razor-sharp coral and dangerous shorebreaks. For kick-ass wind without risking life and limb, the place to launch is Kanaha Beach in Kahului, but avoid the busy weekends when the water becomes a sea of sails.

Overall, Maui is known for its consistent winds. Windsurfers can find action in any month, but as a general rule the best wind is from June to September and the flattest spells are from December to February.

At Ma'alaea, where the winds are usually strong and blow offshore toward Kaho'olawe, conditions are ripe for advanced speed sailing. In winter, on those rare occasions when *kona* (leeward) winds blow, the Ma'alaea–Kihei area can be the only place windy enough to sail.

Most windsurfing shops are based in Kahului and handle rentals, lessons and gear sales.

Plan Your Trip
Surfing Maui

Maui lies smack in the path of all the major swells that race across the Pacific, creating legendary peaks for surfing. The island's north shore sees the biggest waves, which roll in from November to March, though some places, like famed Hoʻokipa Beach, have good wave action year-round. Get a surf and weather report online at OMaui (www.omaui.com).

Helpful Resources

Knowing the when and size of the next swell is essential. This is where streaming webcams, surf reports and forecasts come in. For Maui, the following sources are very useful; and don't forget common sense – if conditions look intimidating, stay on shore.

Surf News Network (www. surfnewsnetwork.com) Provides comprehensive island weather-and-wave reports.

Live Surf Cam Hawaii (http://livesurf camhawaii.com) An index to scores of live surf cams on Maui and across the state.

Omaui (www.omaui.com) Get surf and weather reports here.

Surfline (www.surfline.com) Great omnibus site with massive amounts of information.

Wavewatch (www.wavewatch.com) Has surf reports and forecasts.

Maui Surf Beaches & Breaks

For action sports, head to Maui's beaches. On the north shore, near the town of Ha'iku, is the infamous big-wave spot known as Pe'ahi, or Jaws (p182). Determined pro surfers, such as Laird Hamilton, Dave Kalama and Darrick Doerner, helped put the planet's largest, most perfect wave on the international map. Jaws' waves are so high that surfers must be towed into them by wave runners. At Ho'okipa Beach (p180) near Pa'ia, surfers have their pick of four different breaks, which can churn out large waves in winter.

Not into risking your life? No worries, there are plenty of other waves to ride. Maui's west side, especially around Lahaina, offers a wider variety of surf. The fun reef breaks at Lahaina Breakwall (p88) and Harbor cater to both beginner and intermediate surfers. Try The Cove (p156) for good beginner waves in Kihei. To the south is Ma'alaea Pipeline (p144), a fickle right-hand reef break that is often considered one of the fastest waves in the world. On the island's northwest corner is majestic Honolua Bay. Its right point break works best on winter swells and is considered one of the premier points not just in Hawaii, but around the world.

Gentler shorebreaks good for bodysurfing can be found around Pa'ia, Kapalua and the beaches between Kihei and Makena.

Beginners

Newbies should head directly to Lahaina, which has beginner-friendly waves and instructors who can get you up on a board in just one lesson. You won't be tearing across mammoth curls, but riding a board is easier than it looks and there's no better place to get started. Two primo owner-operated surf schools that have the perfect blend of patience and persistence are Goofy Foot Surf School (p86) and Maui Surf Clinics (p86).

Surfing Etiquette

Just as Hawaiian royalty had certain breaks reserved just for them, so goes it on Maui's surf breaks today. Respect locals and local customs or you might end up with a black eye (and a bad reputation). Tourists are welcome but deference to local riders is always recommended.

In the water, basic surf etiquette is vital. The person closest to the peak of the wave has the right of way. When somebody is already up and riding, don't take off on the wave in front of them. Don't paddle straight through the lineup. Rather, head out through the channel where the waves aren't breaking and then find your way into the lineup. When you wipe out – and you'll do this plenty – try to keep track of your board.

Maui: Surfing

HONOLUA BAY

Facing northwest, the right point break provides some of the best surfing in the world when the winter swells arrive. (p118)

HO'OKIPA BEACH

Experienced surfers can take their pick of four breaks. In winter the really big waves roll in. Windsurfers take over at The Point, the break furthest west in the bay, in the afternoon. (p180)

HONOLUA BAY
Kapalua
Napili
Kahana
Honokowai
Ka'anapali

Honokohau
Kahakuloa

Pailolo Channel

'Eke Crater (4751ft)
Pu'u Kukui (5788ft)
'Iao Needle (2250ft)

Waihe'e

Kahului Bay

HO'OKIPA BEACH
Pa'ia
HA Baldwin Beach Park

LAHAINA
Lahaina
Kamehameha Iki Park
Launiupoko Beach Park
Olowalu

Wailuku
Kahului

'Iao Valley State Monument
Waikapu

Pukalani

Lana'i

Ma'alaea
MA'ALAEA
Kihei

Papawai Point
Maalaea Bay

KIHEI

Keokea
Polipoli Spring State Recreation Area

Wailea

Makena

'Ulupalakua Ranch
Pu'u Mahoe (2660ft)

'Alalakeiki Channel

La Perouse Bay

LAHAINA

If you want to learn to surf, and you're staying in West Maui, head to the Lahaina Breakwall just south of Banyan Tree Sq. These gentle reef breaks are newbie-friendly. Surfing outfitters line Front St. (p88)

MA'ALAEA

The fast Ma'alaea Pipeline is a right-hand reef break. (p144)

KIHEI

Beginners in South Maui can test their skills on the small waves at The Cove just south of Kalama Park. Surf instructors await along South Kihei Rd. (p156)

N 0 ▬▬▬▬▬ 20 km
0 ▬▬▬▬▬ 10 miles

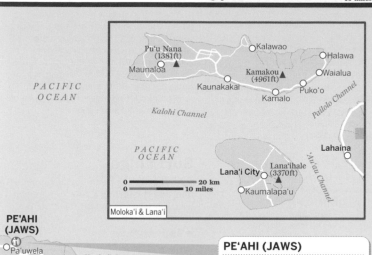

PACIFIC
OCEAN

Pu'u Nana
(1381ft)
Maunaloa ▲

Kalawao

Halawa

Kamakou
(4961ft) ▲

Waialua

Kaunakakai

Puko'o

Kamalo

Kalohi Channel

Pailolo Channel

PACIFIC
OCEAN

0 ▬▬▬▬▬ 20 km
0 ▬▬▬▬▬ 10 miles

Lahaina

Lana'i City

Lana'ihale
(3370ft) ▲

'Au'au Channel

Kaumalapa'u

Moloka'i & Lana'i

PE'AHI
(JAWS)

Pa'uwela

Ha'iku

Huelo Point

Huelo

Honomanu Bay

Kaumahina State
Wayside Park

Ke'anae

PE'AHI (JAWS)

Pros only for monster waves so huge
they require a tow-in. Big-wave riders
Laird Hamilton, Dave Kalama and
Darrick Doerner brought the spotlight
to this North Shore spot. (p182)

Makawao

Wailua

Papiha Point

Nahiku

Ke'anae Valley

Wai'anapanapa
State Park

Hana

Kula

Ko'olau Gap

Waiho'i Valley

Hamoa

Kipahulu Valley

Maka'alae
Point

Pu'u'ula'ula
(10,023ft) ▲

Haleakalā
National
Park

Kaupo Gap

Kaupo

Kipahulu

'Alenuihāhā Channel

THE ORIGINAL BOARDRIDERS

Hawaii is the birthplace of surfing. Researchers have traced chants mentioning *he'e nalu* (surfing) and petroglyphs depicting surfers back to at least 1500 AD.

When the first missionaries arrived in Hawaii in the 1820s they promptly started stamping out the 'hedonistic' act of surfing and, save a few holdouts, by 1890 surfing was all but extinct.

Then in the early 1900s modern surfing's first icon, Duke Kahanamoku, stepped off the beach and into history. Kahanamoku grew up on the sands of Waikiki, where he rode the reefs on traditional *olo*-style boards. After winning Olympic gold in swimming at Stockholm in 1912, Duke began to travel the world demonstrating the Hawaiian 'Sport of Kings.'

Also, remember you're a visitor out in the lineup, so don't expect to get every wave that comes your way. There's a definite pecking order and, frankly, as a tourist you're at the bottom. That said, usually if you give a wave, you'll get a wave in return.

As a tourist in Hawaii, there are some places you go and there are some places you don't go. For many local families the beach parks are meeting places where generations gather to celebrate life under the sun. They're tied to these places by a sense of community and culture, and they aren't eager for outsiders to push them out of time-honored surf spots.

Surf Lingo

Hawaii has a wonderful linguistic tradition, and the surfing lexicon here is fabulous. A few words you definitely want to know.

➡ **Aggro** Aggressive.

➡ **Barney** Defined in the classic 1987 surf movie *North Shore* as a 'kook in and out of the water,' it means somebody who doesn't know what they are doing.

➡ **Betty** Hot surfer chic.

➡ **Brah** Brother or friend.

➡ **Green room** The inside of a wave's tube.

➡ **Grom or Grommet** Younger surfers (who are probably better than you).

➡ **Howlie** White person or non-Hawaiian.

Ziplining

Plan Your Trip
On the Land

Adventures here aren't limited to the sea; there is a plethora of things to do on land. Maui's hiking and horse trails traverse some of the most unique ecosystems on earth. And if knocking around a little white ball is your thing, would-be pros can stalk the very greens where the professionals play.

Ancient Hawaii's Extreme Sports

Never let it be said that ancient Hawaiians didn't know how to play. Every male ruler had to prove his prowess in sports – to demonstrate *mana* (spiritual essence) – and the greater the danger, the better. No contest topped the *hōlua* – an ancient sled just a little wider than a book, on which Hawaiians raced down mountains at speeds of up to 50mph. Not every sport was potentially deadly, though many involved gambling – like foot and canoe racing, wrestling and *'ulu maika* (stone bowling). Annual makahiki harvest celebrations featured four months of feasting, hula dancing, religious ceremonies and sports competitions.

West Maui tour (30 minutes) Takes in tropical rainforest, remote waterfalls and 'Iao Valley – this is Maui's prettiest face.

East Maui tour (45 minutes) Spotlights Hana, Haleakalā Crater and 'Ohe'o Gulch. Keep in mind that this is the rainiest side of Maui. The good news: waterfalls galore stream down the mountainsides if you hit clear weather after a rainstorm. The bad news: it can be socked in with clouds.

Circle Island tour (one hour) Combines the West and East Maui tours.

West Maui & Moloka'i tour (one hour) Includes the drama of West Maui as well as a zip along the spectacular coastal cliffs of Moloka'i. Definitely the Big Kahuna of knockout photo ops!

All operate out of the Kahului Heliport, at the southeast side of Kahului Airport. Discounts off the list prices are common; ask when you book or look for coupons online or in the free tourist magazines.

Golf

Surrounded by scenic ocean vistas and emerald mountain slopes, golfing just doesn't get much better. The most prestigious of Maui's courses is the Plantation course (p117) in Kapalua, which kicks off the year for the PGA tour. Only slightly less elite are the championship greens at Wailea (p162) and Ka'anapali (p109).

At the other end of the spectrum, you can enjoy a fun round at the friendly Waiehu Municipal Golf Course (p123) and at lesser-known country clubs elsewhere around the island.

A good resource, with course reviews, is Maui Golf (www.golf-maui.com).

Helicopter Tours

Helicopters go into amazing places that you otherwise might not experience. When you book, ask about seat guarantees, and let it be known you want a seat by a window, not a middle seat. On Maui, winds pick up by midday and carry clouds up the mountains with them. For the clearest skies and calmest ride, book a morning flight. There are four main tours:

Horseback Riding

With its abundant ranchland and vibrant cowboy culture, Maui offers some of Hawaii's best riding experiences. Choose a ride based on the landscape you'd like to see, since all are friendly, reputable outfitters. Most rides last a few hours and often include lunch or a snack. Many outfitters also offer sunset rides.

Makena Stables (p169) takes riders along the volcanic slopes that overlook pristine La Perouse Bay, while **Mendes Ranch** (p123) offers rides along the cliffs of the Kahekili Hwy. Families will like the easy trips at **Thompson Ranch** (✆808-878-1910; www.thompson-ranchmaui.com; cnr Middle & Polipoli Rds; morning/sunset/picnic rides $150/175/200; ⊙tour 10am; ⏺) in Keokea. Families with older kids and riders with a sense of adventure can explore lava fields in the volcanic Ka'naio region, with longer rides leading to a remote beach. You won't see many other people! The folks at long-running **Pi'iholo Ranch Stables** (p186) are now offering a Cowboy for a Day experience, allowing guests to help round up cattle. Traditional horseback rides across its Upcountry ranch, with mountain and valley views, are also on offer here.

Spas

Hawaiian spa treatments may sound a bit whimsical, but they're based on herbal traditions. Popular body wraps and 'cocoons' use seaweed to nourish; ginger, papaya and healing plants are applied as moisturizers. Other tropical treatments sound good enough to eat: coconut-milk baths and coffee-chocolate scrubs...mmm.

Most spas are in the large resort hotels, such as the Travaasa Hana (p236), Grand Wailea Resort Hotel & Spa (p163) and the spa at Montage Kapalua Bay (p117). You can enjoy a massage in an oceanside *hale* – a thatched hut – at the spa at the Four Seasons Maui at Wailea (p162). But if you prefer a more traditional setting away from the resorts, consider the Luana Spa (p236), which offers treatments under a thatched hut in Hana.

Tennis

Singles? Doubles? Or perhaps a lesson? Take your pick at the world-class facilities at Wailea Tennis Club (p163), Royal Lahaina Tennis Ranch (p109) in Ka'anapali and Kapalua Tennis Garden (p117). At Kapalua, they'll match you with another player if you need an opponent. If you just want to knock a ball around, many hotels have tennis courts for their guests and the county maintains free tennis courts at many public parks.

Ziplining

Click in. Grab tight. Thumbs up. And whooooosh...you're off. Quick as a flash, Maui's ziplines let you soar freestyle on a series of cables over gulches, woods and waterfalls while strapped into a harness. The hardest part is stepping off the platform for the first zip – the rest is pure exhilaration!

RON DAHLQUIST/GETTY IMAGES ©

The 3600ft-long line at the Flyin Hawaiian Zipline (p142) is impressing riders while the Pi'iholo Ranch Stables (p186) zipline in Makawao is winning rave reviews with its 2800ft final line. It also offers side-by-side ziplines, allowing you to swoop the course alongside up to three of your friends. First on the Maui scene was Skyline Eco-Adventures' (p191) Haleakalā tour, which often books out months in advance. The company has opened a second zipline in the hills above the Ka'anapali Resort; this one is pricier but easier to book. In Kapalua, the Kapalua Ziplines (p117) course offers side-by-side zipping on dual lines as well as moonlight rides. If you have younger kids or are wary about ziplining, try the low-key Maui Zipline (p143) in Waikapu.

Haleakalā National

Plan Your Trip

Hiking & Biking Maui

The diversity is what makes hiking and cycling on Maui so cool. Trails here hug lofty ridges, twist through bamboo forests and green jungles, and meander across rough lava fields.

Maui's National, State & County Parks

The commanding Haleakalā National Park (p194), with its steep slopes and cloud-capped volcanic peaks, gives rise to east Maui. The park has two distinct faces. The main section encompasses Haleakalā's summit with its breathtaking crater-rim lookouts and lunarlike hiking trails. In the park's rainforested Kipahulu section you're in the midst of dramatic waterfalls, swimming holes and ancient Hawaiian archaeological sites.

Top among Maui's state parks is 'Iao Valley State Monument (p141), whose towering emerald pinnacle rises picture-perfect from the valley floor. For the ultimate stretch of unspoiled beach, head to Makena State Park (p166). On the east side of Maui, Wai'anapanapa State Park (p225) sits on a distinctive black-sand beach.

Maui's county parks center on beaches and include the windsurfing meccas of Kanaha Beach Park (p132) and Ho'okipa Beach Park (p180). Details about county parks and beaches, including contact information and lifeguard availability, can be found on the Maui County government website: www.mauicounty.gov.

Hiking

The most extraordinary trails are in Haleakalā National Park (p196), where hikes range from half-day walks to quad-busting multiday treks meandering across the moonscape of Haleakalā Crater. In the Kipahulu ('Ohe'o Gulch) section of the park, linked trails climb past terraced pools and on to the towering waterfalls that feed them.

In Maui's Upcountry, Polipoli Spring State Recreation Area (p193) has an extensive trail system in cloud forest, including the breathtaking Skyline Trail

that connects with Haleakalā summit. For a walk through a fantasy-novel forest, spend an hour or two among the tall trees on the Kahakapao Trail Loop in the Makawao Forest Reserve (p186).

North of Wailuku is the lofty Waihe'e Ridge Trail (p100). This wonderful footpath penetrates deep into the misty West Maui Mountains, offering sweeping views of green valleys and the rugged northern coast. Near Ma'alaea Bay, the Lahaina Pali Trail (p126) follows an old footpath on the drier western slope of the same mountain mass.

At the Kapalua Resort the Coastal Trail (p101) links Kapalua Beach and DT Fleming Beach.

Several pull-offs along the road to Hana offer short nature walks that lead to hidden waterfalls and unspoiled coastal views, including the **Waikamoi Nature Trail** (Map p218; https://hawaiitrails.org; Hana Hwy). A longer coastal trail between Wai'anapanapa State Park and Hana Bay follows an ancient Hawaiian footpath past several historic sights, as does the Hoapili Trail (p150) (the King's Hwy) from La Perouse Bay on the other side of the island.

Short nature walks that combine bird- and whale-watching include the Kealia Coastal Boardwalk (p146) in Ma'alaea and the **Kihei Coastal Trail** (p151).

One of Maui's top environmental shakers, the **Sierra Club** (www.mauisierraclub.org/hikes-service-programs), sponsors guided hikes, often educational, to various places around the island. Everyone is welcome; nonmembers are asked to pay a $5 donation. Not only will you be sharing the trails with other eco-minded hikers, but the Sierra Club sometimes hikes into fascinating places that are otherwise closed to the public.

Hiking Considerations

➡ Maui has no snakes, no poison ivy and few wild animals that will fuss with hikers. There's only the slimmest chance of encountering a large boar in the backwoods, but they're unlikely to be a problem unless cornered.

➡ Be careful on the edge of steep cliffs since cliffside rock in Maui tends to be crumbly.

➡ Flash floods are a potential threat in many of the steep, narrow valleys on Maui that require stream crossings. Warning signs include a distant rumbling, the smell of fresh earth and

Maui: Hiking

KAPALUA TRAILS

Walk along the coast or ascend into a wet rainforest on trails that crisscross the grounds of the Kapalua Resort. (p101)

WAIHE'E RIDGE TRAIL

This lush trail has it all: tropical foliage, a heart-pumping climb and sweeping views of the coast, waterfalls and rumpled green valleys. And there's a picnic table at the summit. (p100)

Pailolo Channel

Honokohau
Kapalua KAPALUA Kahakuloa
Napili TRAILS
Kahana
Honokowai
Ka'anapali WAIHE'E RIDGE
TRAIL
Ho'okipa
Beach Park
'Eke Crater Waihe'e
(4751ft) Kahului
Pu'u Kukui 'Iao Needle Bay Pa'ia
(5788ft) (2250ft) Wailuku HA Baldwin
Lahaina 'Iao Valley Kahului Beach Park
Kamehameha State Monument
Iki Park Waikapu
Lana'i Launiupoko
Beach Park Olowalu LAHAINA Pukalani
PALI TRAIL Ma'alaea

LAHAINA PALI TRAIL

This exposed hike follows the route of the old King's Hwy. During whale season, from the West Maui trailhead climb a short distance for great views of the frolicking humpback whales. (p126)

Papawai Maalaea
Point Bay Kihei

Keokea

KAHAKAPAO LOOP TRAIL

A loop trail on the slopes of the volcano swoops through thick groves of non-native trees. The multi-use trail is popular with dog-walkers and mountain bikers. (p172)

Wailea
POLIPOLI SPRING
STATE RECREATION
Makena AREA

Pu'u Mahoe
(2660ft)
HOAPILI
TRAIL
'Alalakeiki Channel La Perouse
Bay

POLIPOLI SPRING STATE RECREATION AREA

Thick forests, darting mists and a remote location – yep, there's a distinct touch of spookiness while hiking the network of trails on the southwest slopes of Haleakalā. (p193)

HOAPILI TRAIL

From La Perouse Bay, the trail unfurls past lava rock ruins then follows the coast. The path turns inland to join the the ancient King's Hwy through a vast plain of lava. The scenery is amazing, but the sun is hot! Start early. (p150)

0 ——— 20 km
0 ——— 10 miles

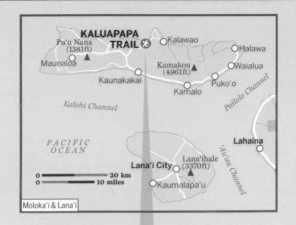

KALUAPAPA TRAIL

Pu'u Nana (1381ft)

Maunaloa

Kalawao

Halawa

Kaunakakai

Kamakou (4961ft)

Waialua

Puko'o

Kamalo

PACIFIC OCEAN

Kalohi Channel

Pailolo Channel

PACIFIC OCEAN

0 ——— 20 km
0 ——— 10 miles

Lana'i City

Lana'ihale (3370ft)

'Au'au Channel

Lahaina

Kaumalapa'u

Moloka'i & Lana'i

KALAUPAPA TRAIL

You'll tackle 26 switchbacks on this steep cliffside path that ends at a beach near a former Hansen's disease (leprosy) settlement. Mules carrying visitors also use this 3-mile trail. (p263)

Pa'uwela Point

Uaoa Bay

Pa'uwela

Ha'iku

Huelo Point

Huelo

Honomanu Bay

Makawao

Kaumahina State Wayside Park

Ke'anae

KAHAKAPAO LOOP TRAIL

Wailua

Papiha Point

Nahiku

Ke'anae Valley

Wai'anapanapa State Park

Kula

HALEAKALĀ NATIONAL PARK (SUMMIT)

Hana

Waiho'i Valley

Hamoa

Pu'u'ula'ula (10,023ft)

Kaupo Gap

Kipahulu Valley

Maka'alae Point

HALEAKALĀ NATIONAL PARK (KIPAHULU)

Kaupo

Kipahulu

HALEAKALĀ NATIONAL PARK (SUMMIT)

Hike into the lunarlike crater of the volcano to see cinder cones and silverswords. On the slopes, explore a non-native forest. (p196)

HALEAKALĀ NATIONAL PARK (KIPAHULU)

Trails climb past waterfalls and terraced pools, with a swing through a towering bamboo forest. (p199)

PRESERVING HIKING TRAILS

Of special interest to hikers and naturalists is the work of **Nā Ala Hele** (www.hawaii trails.org), a group affiliated with Hawaii's Division of Forestry and Wildlife (DOFAW). Nā Ala Hele was established in 1988 with the task of coordinating public access to hiking trails and also maintaining and preserving historic trails. On Maui, the group has negotiated with private landowners and the military to gain access to previously restricted areas and re-establish abandoned trails. Visit its website for trail descriptions.

The Nā Ala Hele logo signpost – a brown sign featuring a yellow hiking petroglyph figure – marks an increasing number of trailheads.

a sudden increase in the stream's current. If the water begins to rise, get to higher ground immediately.

➡ A walking stick is good for bracing yourself on slippery approaches, gaining leverage and testing the depth of streams.

➡ Darkness falls fast once the sun sets, and ridgetop trails are no place to be caught unprepared in the dark. Always carry a flashlight. Wear long pants for protection from overgrown parts of the trail, and sturdy footwear with good traction. Pack 2 quarts (2L) of water per person for a day hike, carry a whistle to alert rescue workers if necessary, wear sunscreen and start early.

Biking

Mountain Biking

To explore the wilderness on a mountain bike, head to the Upcountry. Experienced downhill riders will find adrenaline-stoked thrills on the Skyline Trail (p206), which follows the mountain's spine from Haleakalā National Park into Polipoli Spring State Recreation Area. Closer in, you'll find single track trails at the Makawao Forest Reserve (p186). There, several short trails intersect with the 5.75-mile Kahakapao Trail Loop, giving riders a variety of options. The reserve also has pump tracks and skills courses. See **West Maui Cycles** (www.westmauicycles.com) for a basic map of the reserve's trails.

You can rent mountain bikes at West Maui Cycles, which is in Lahaina, or at South Maui Bicycles (www.southmauibicycles.com) in Kihei.

Road Cycling

Road cyclists on Maui face a number of challenges: narrow roads, heavy traffic, an abundance of hills and mountains, and the same persistent winds that so delight windsurfers. Many roads, however, including the Pi'ilani Hwy in South Maui, do have bike lanes. Reliable shops include West Maui Cycles (p86) in Lahaina, South Maui Bicycles (p157) in Kihei and Island Biker (p133) in Kahului.

The full-color *Maui County Bicycle Map* is no longer being published, but you can peruse it online on the websites for West Maui Cycles and South Maui Bicycles. The map is outdated, but it shows all the roads on Maui that have been suitable for cycling and gives other nitty-gritty details. It's worth a look if you intend to explore by pedal power. The West Maui Cycles' website also provides basic maps for several mountain-biking trails on the island.

Garden of the Gods, p254

Plan Your Trip

Scenic Drives in Maui

You'll find a world-class scenic drive in just about every region of Maui. Most offer views of the ocean and various mountains, but a few step up their game with waterfalls, tropical flora and roadside fruit stands.

Guided Driving Tours

A number of tour-bus companies operate half-day and full-day sightseeing tours on Maui, covering the most visited island destinations. Popular routes include day-long jaunts to Hana, and Haleakalā trips that take in the major Upcountry sights.

Polynesian Adventure Tours (p304) Part of Gray Line Hawaii, it's a big player among Hawaiian tour companies; offers tours to Haleakalā National Park, Central Maui and 'Iao Valley State Monument, and the Road to Hana. Also runs short trips from Maui to Pearl Harbor in Oahu (from adult/child $378/357).

Roberts Hawaii (p304) In operation for more than 70 years, Roberts Hawaii runs three tours: Hana, 'Iao Valley and Lahaina, and Haleakalā National Park.

Valley Isle Excursions (p304) Costs a bit more but it's hands-down the best Road to Hana tour. Vans take just 12 passengers and guides offer more local flavor and less canned commentary. Includes continental breakfast and, in Hana, a BBQ chicken lunch.

Across the island, there are also specialized adventure tours such as whale-watching cruises, snorkeling trips to Lana'i and hiking excursions through tropical forests. Details are in the Activities sections for each town.

Scenic Drives

The best scenic drives in Maui twist, squeeze and bounce between their start points and their end points. In other words, the iconic driving routes here are pretty, but you have to respect the roads and your fellow drivers by paying attention to your surroundings. And though Maui sounds relatively small – 48 miles long and 26 miles across at her widest – lengthy driving times make the island feel much bigger. Always give yourself extra time.

The Road to Hana (p76) We'll go ahead and brag: the Road to Hana is one of the world's most epic drives. From the Twin Falls Farm Stand to the community of Hana, the Hana Hwy is 33 miles of waterfalls, crystal pools, tropical foliage, bamboo forests and rough lava coastlines. The rental car of choice for this visual feast? It's all Jeeps and convertible Mustangs. And remember, when it comes to the Road to Hana, the old adage is true – the journey is the destination.

Pi'ilani Highway (p228) The remote 'back road' to Hana is becoming less lonely as word gets out about its scenic appeal. Yep, the best part of this drive is the diversity of the landscapes, which switch up every few miles. Hwy 31 rolls from lush tropical flora to steep coastal cliffs to rolling ranchlands to a centuries-old plain of black lava. The final flourish? Eight graceful windmills beside the coast. The drive begins where the Hana Hwy ends – on the edge of lush Kipahulu in East Maui.

Kahekili Highway (p119) The distance between Kapalua and Waihe'e on Route 360 is only 25 miles, but this chipper road packs in more adventure per mile than any other road on the island. A powerful blowhole. Otherworldly lava cliffs. Ocean baths. Coastal trails. And a towering volcanic seaside dome. Plus some breathtaking hairpin turns. And have we mentioned the banana bread? If you're staying in West Maui or don't have time for the Road to Hana, kick it on the Kahekili Hwy.

Haleakalā Highway From Pukalani this highway, also known as Crater Rd, twists through green pastures and thick forests as it climbs the western slope of Haleakalā, the mighty volcano anchoring Maui's Upcountry. The sense of anticipation builds as views of the coast expand and clouds start to appear *below* you as the road switchbacks ever higher – with no guardrails. And if you're driving up before sunrise? Well, maybe it's better you can't see the steep drop-offs beside the road. Once in the park, overlooks offer bird's-eye views of the volcanic crater. The end-of-drive reward: the highest point on the island, which tops off at 10,023ft.

Kula Highway The level of skill needed for driving this flat road, which ribbons through the Upcountry, is minimal. But c'mon, it's nice to have one island drive that's not a wheel-clutching, one-lane horror show. Also known as Hwy 31, the road links to small farms, botanical gardens, inviting green parks and one awesome coffee shop (p192) in Keokea. Continue on to ranch country to stroll the grounds and sample a wine or two at Maui Wine (p193).

Waipoli Road Holy cow! What's happening?! Yep, this devilish road sneaks up on you. One minute you're gazing tranquilly over a pretty lavender

farm (p190), the next minute you're navigating a tight series of rising blind curves that surely can't fit two cars at once. And wait, was that the bottom of my rental car scraping the edge of the road? OK, try to relax. Just watch the paragliders floating overhead. They sure are pretty. Twist. Turn. Twist. Will this road ever end? Yep, for most rental cars it ends at the entrance to the Kula Forest Reserve, where signage makes it clear that 4WD vehicles are the only way forward on the unpaved nightmare just ahead.

Thompson Road We tucked this drive at the end of the list, hoping no one would actually see it. This short but luscious road in Keokea rolls past emerald green pastures and lava-rock walls, with the crystal blue sea as a backdrop. Heavenly. Let's keep it low key, shall we?

Ali'i Kula Lave

Plan Your Trip
Green Maui

Maui has a long history of protecting its environment. Islanders of all backgrounds are activists, from Native Hawaiians volunteering to restore an ancient fishpond to scientists fighting invasive plants. The island has no polluting heavy industry and not a single roadside billboard to blight the wonderful natural vistas.

RON DAHLQUIST/GETTY IMAGES ©

Sites for Agritourism

Ali'i Kula Lavender On the slopes of Haleakalā with views of the isthmus and central coasts, this vast lavender farm is a pleasant place to wander and to shop for lavender-based products. Walking tours also offered. (p190)

Surfing Goat Dairy Famous for its fresh chevre, which comes in numerous flavors, Surfing Goat is open for dairy tours. Children and adults can join the 'Evening Chores & Milking Tours' or simply check out the playful young goats. Free samples. (p190)

O'o Farm lunch tour This organic farm offers tours of its produce fields as well as its coffee trees. Enjoy a meal as part of your tour, with coffee samples also served on the coffee tour. (p191)

Maui Wine In the far reaches of the Upcountry, Maui's only winery offers tastings as well as tours at its historic property, a longtime ranch and a favorite spot of King David Kalakaua, the Merrie Monarch. (p193)

Ono Organic Farms Tropical fruit is a highlight at this farm tucked in the lush foliage of East Maui. Tours offered on Tuesday afternoons. You can also stop by their fruit stand in Hana. (p240)

Maui Goes Green

Today, Maui and its residents are leaders in eco-activism. Maui was the first island in Hawaii to approve a ban on single-use plastic bags. Businesses and restaurants that violate the ordinance, which went into effect on January 11, 2011, will incur a $500 daily fine. A powerful incentive!

Parks, forest reserves and watersheds cover nearly half of the island. The crowning glory is Haleakalā National Park, which, thanks to the collaborative work of environmental groups, now extends from its original perch in the center of Maui clear down to the south coast. On the first and third Sunday of every month, volunteers can visit the park to work and help rid Hosmer Grove of invasive pine trees.

More than 35% of Maui Electric's electricity came from renewable sources, including wind power and the burning of bagasse, the byproduct of sugar production, in 2015. Will the 2016 closure of Hawaiian Commercial & Sugar Company, the island's last sugarcane plant, affect this percentage? Stay tuned. The eight turbines at the new Auwahi Wind farm on 'Ulupalakua Ranch produce enough electricity to power about 14,500 typical Maui homes. You'll find 34 wind turbines, operated by Kaheawa Wind Power, on the slopes above wind-whipped Ma'alaea, which can power 18,000 homes.

Sustainable Maui

As you plan your trip, consider your impact on the island. There are numerous ways to lighten your tourist footprint.

Sustainable Icon ✐

It seems like everyone's going 'green' these days, but how can you know which Maui businesses are genuinely ecofriendly and which are simply jumping on the sustainability bandwagon? Throughout the guide, this Sustainable icon indicates listings that we are highlighting because they demonstrate an active sustainable-tourism policy. Some are involved in conservation or environmental education, while others maintain and preserve Hawaiian identity and culture. Many are owned and operated by local and indigenous operators.

Transportation

On a short trip to Maui, consider ditching the car. The Maui Bus (http://www.maui-county.gov/609/Maui-Bus-Public-Transit-System) loops past convenient stops in Lahaina, Ka'anapali, Kihei, Kahului and Wailuku. It also runs several 'islander' routes between major towns and resorts. In Ka'anapali and Kapalua, free resort shuttles swing past major hotels and beaches.

For longer stays, rent a smaller, less gas-guzzling vehicle. Not only will that be gentler on Maui's environment, but the island's narrow roads will be easier to negotiate. Consider renting a Bio-Beetle (p138), which runs on recycled cooking oil.

Treading Lightly

Before arriving on Maui, clean your shoes and wipe off your luggage so you don't inadvertently bring seeds or insects from elsewhere, introducing yet another invasive species. This advice especially applies if you're arriving on Maui from the Big Island, where Rapid 'Ohi'a Death (p68) fungal disease has recently killed hundreds of thousands of *'ohi'a lehua,* a native tree.

When hiking, stay on trails; when snorkeling, stay off the coral.

Don't disturb cultural sites, and respect the 'Kapu – No Trespassing' signs that you'll see around the island.

Eating Locally

Every food product not grown or raised on Maui is shipped to the island by boat or plane. Considering the great distances and the amount of fuel used, that makes the 'locavore' or 'eat local' movement particularly relevant.

Recycling

Many beach parks on Maui have a bin for recycling aluminum cans, and you can often find ecofriendly businesses with bins

Organic gardening

for plastic and glass as well. Ask at your hotel how they recycle: should you keep your cans and bottles separate? If they're not committed recyclers, asking helps raise their awareness, also.

Tap water on Maui is perfectly fine for drinking, so resist those California spring-water imports. At the very least, refill your plastic bottle once it's emptied.

GREEN BEER

OK, so the beer at Maui Brewing Company (p160) isn't *green*, but the folks who brew it are committed to eco-minded business practices. For example, used vegetable oil from the brewpub is converted to diesel fuel, which powers the cars of owners Garrett and Melanie Marrero as well as the delivery truck. Spent grain is given to local ranchers for composting, and the brewery's retail beers are sold in recyclable cans. Cans over glass? Yep, cans aren't breakable, so they're less of a threat on the beach. Cans are also lighter than glass, meaning you can move more product in one trip, saving fuel and ultimately leaving a smaller environmental footprint. For a sudsy and sustainable toast, visit its Kahana brewpub (p113) for one of the ecofriendly pint nights, when 50% of the nightly beer-sale profits benefit a local environmental group. Cheers for green beers!

On the Ground and in the Sea

There are environmentally friendly organizations across Maui that offer ways to be active and adventurous with lower environmental impact.

Instead of a boat dive, try a shore dive (no diesel fuel, no dropped anchors) with a company that specializes in them, such as Maui Dreams Dive Co (p156) in Kihei. Opt for a sailboat cruise over a motorboat cruise. Riding with the wind is more ecofriendly, plus sailboats get closer to whales and dolphins, which are repelled by motorboat noise. Consider companies

Outrigger canoes, North Kihei

such as Trilogy Excursions (p88) that fly a green flag, indicating that the boat adheres to strict environmental practices and doesn't discharge waste into the ocean.

To really go local, take an outrigger-canoe trip with Hawaiian Sailing Canoe Adventures (p164).

Local farms sell fruits and vegetables at farmers markets in the Upcountry, Kihei and Honokowai, and at the Maui Swap Meet in Kahului. More and more eateries and restaurants are showcasing locally caught seafood as well as Maui-raised beef and Maui-grown produce. The range of restaurants is wide, from the deli at Mana Foods (p182) in Pa'ia to the burgers

at Hana Burger Food Truck (p238) to the gourmet pub grub at Monkeypod Kitchen (p164) in Wailea. One buy-local restaurant, Flatbread Company (p182) in Pa'ia, gives a cut of the night's profits to local environmental groups who show up to rap with customers every Tuesday night.

Buying Maui-made products supports the local economy and often helps sustain the environment as well. Ali'i Kula Lavender (p190) in Kula produces organic lavender blossoms that are used by two dozen home-based businesses to make lavender jams, vinegars and salad dressings sold at the farm. For picnics, buy cheese from Surfing Goat Dairy (p190) and wine from Maui Wine (p193).

Maui Ocean Center (

Travel with Children

Children are welcome everywhere on Maui. Hawaiians love kids – large families are common and *na keiki* (children) are an integral part of the scenery. Maui has everything for a child on vacation: sandy beaches, fun hotel pools, tasty food and outdoor activities galore. Maui also offers cool cross-cultural opportunities, from hula lessons to outrigger-canoe rides.

Best Regions for Kids

Lahaina

First stop? Banyan Tree Sq to play among those wonderful banyan-tree branches. Kids will find lots of water attractions at the adjacent harbor, from a submarine ride to surfing lessons.

West Maui

Water sports galore, especially for older kids – think swimming, snorkeling, bodyboarding, catamaran sails, whale-watching, kayaking and stand up paddle boarding. On land, kids can hike and zipline. The Whalers Museum is well-suited to kids curious about history.

South Maui

Another great place to hit the water, with surf lessons in Lahaina and kayaking in Makena Bay. Many beaches have lifeguard stands as well as grassy areas for picnics. Try an outrigger-canoe trip, available at many resorts.

Haleakalā National Park

Every kid loves playing astronaut on a crunchy walk into the wildly lunarlike crater, plus you can join a ranger talk or complete the requirements to become a Junior Ranger.

Maui for Kids

Eating

Maui's family-oriented, casual atmosphere means children will feel at home almost everywhere. Sit-down restaurants are quick to accommodate kids, with high chairs and booster seats.

You might assume that all fancy restaurants frown on parties that include children, but many cater to them with special kids' menus. The trend toward exhibition-kitchen restaurants – one large open area with a loud dining room – means that child chatter will blend into the overall din. At hotel luau, kids receive a discount and most will enjoy the show (they might even get invited to go on stage and enjoy the fun!). As for the food, the local palate tends toward the sweet and straightforward, which typically agrees with kids' tastes, without too much garlic or pungent flavor.

Children love a picnic, and impromptu picnicking on Maui is a cinch – you can scarcely go a mile without finding a park with picnic tables. Many restaurants pack food for takeout, and grocery stores invariably have extensive deli sections with grab-and-go meals. Finding treats is also easy. Premium ice cream, shave ice, home-style cookies and chocolate-covered macadamias are omnipresent temptations.

When you're traveling around the island, stop at roadside fruit stands to let everyone pick their own healthful snack. It's fun watching a coconut being cracked open with a machete, then slurping up the coconut water through a straw.

Children's Programs

➡ Many of Maui's beach resorts have *keiki* (child) day programs where kids can do fun things while you head for the spa.

➡ Visitors to Haleakalā National Park should take advantage of the free junior ranger program, geared to ages seven to 12.

➡ The Pacific Whale Foundation (p88) provides a free Junior Marine Naturalist handbook that introduces kids to Hawaii marine life through quizzes, anagrams and the like. Pick up one on board a whale-watching cruise.

Festivals

Keep watch for festivals, even small local events, while on Maui. They're invariably family oriented with plenty of *keiki*-geared activities included in the fun. The weekly Friday Town Parties (www.maui fridays.com) are entertaining and filled with distractions.

Children's Highlights

Restaurants, hotels and attractions that especially welcome children and have good facilities for families are marked with the family-friendly icon (⊞) throughout this guide.

Water Adventures

➡ **Surf lessons in Lahaina** Gentle waves! Surf schools line the streets.

➡ **Snorkeling at Honolua Bay** Fantastic underwater sights are a few kicks from shore. Careful on the slippery entry!

➡ **Whale-watching** From mid-December to April, hop on a boat in Lahaina or Ma'alaea to glimpse these mighty beasts.

➡ **Outrigger-canoe tour** Join a family-friendly trip to look for green sea turtles in a traditional Hawaiian canoe.

Plants & Animals

➡ **Maui Ocean Center** (p144) A 54ft clear tunnel funnels families through a fish-filled 750,000-gallon tank.

➡ **Surfing Goat Dairy** (p190) Kids can hang with the kids – of the goat variety.

➡ **Ono Organic Farm** (p240) Sample exotic fruit as you explore a 300-acre farm.

➡ **Maui Tropical Plantation** (p142) Enjoy two ziplines, a touch of history and exotic fruit at the Coconut Station.

Easy Exploring

➡ **Banyan Tree Square** (p82) With its sprawling canopy and thick trucks, this tree would make the Swiss Family Robinson feel at home.

➡ **Kealia Coastal Boardwalk** (p146) Burn off energy at this elevated boardwalk through coastal wetlands.

➡ **Kalakupua Playground** (p184) In Ha'iku, this jungle gym at the Fourth Marine Division Memorial Park looks like a sprawling castle.

➡ **Kula Country Farms** (p192) In October, bring the little ones to the pumpkin patch.

Older Kids & Teens

➡ **Skyview Soaring** (p235) From Hana, glide above the slopes of Haleakalā in a sailplane.

➡ **Haleakalā National Park** (p196) Hike into the crater to see cinder cones and silverswords.

➡ **Makena Bay** (p166) Paddle from shore to find green sea turtles, tropical fish and maybe a breaching whale.

➡ **Hana Lava Tube** (p224) (Ka'eleku Caverns) Wander through a long underground tunnel formed by lava.

➡ **Molokini Crater** (p43) Snorkel among tropical fish inside the rim of an underwater volcano.

➡ **Makena Stables** (p169) Ride through coastal lava fields on horseback.

➡ **Ho'okipa Beach Park & Overlook** (p179) Watch windsurfers skim the waves.

Museums & Cultural Sites

➡ **Whalers Village Museum** (p107) In West Maui, kids can imagine life aboard a 19th-century whaling ship, complete with harpoons and scrimshaw carvings.

➡ **Old Lahaina Luau** (p95) Hawaii's most authentic, aloha-filled luau comes with music, hula and children's games.

➡ **Pi'ilanihale Heiau** (p224) Near Hana, gaze up at an enormous ancient temple.

➡ **La Perouse Bay** (p169) Walk past the lava-rock ruins of an early Hawaiian coastal settlement.

Kid-Friendly Resorts

➡ **Grand Wailea Resort Hotel & Spa** (p163) Slides, caves and waterfalls across nine pools! You won't see the kids until dinner.

➡ **Four Seasons Maui at Wailea** (p162) The Kids for All Seasons program offers fun and educational Maui-inspired programs for the youngsters, plus there's a resort game room.

➡ **Hyatt Regency Maui Resort & Spa** (p106) Swim-through grottoes and water slides in the pool are fun, plus there are exotic animals in the lobby.

➡ **Ka'anapali Beach Hotel** (p112) Kids can pick up an Aloha Passport spotlighting 12 activities, plus there are daily Hawaiian activities for children.

Planning
Am I Old Enough?

Some popular activities on Maui require that children be of a certain age, height or weight to participate. Always ask about restrictions when making reservations, to avoid disappointment.

To learn how to surf Kids who can swim comfortably in the ocean are candidates for lessons. Teens can usually join group lessons, although younger kids may be required to take private lessons.

To take a snorkel cruise Depending on the outfitter and type of boat (catamaran, raft), tours sometimes set minimum ages, usually from five to eight years. Larger boats may allow tots as young as two to ride along.

To go ziplining Minimum age requirements range from eight to 10 years, depending on the company. Participants must also meet weight minimums (usually 60lb to 80lb).

To ride a horse For trail rides the minimum age ranges from eight to 13 years, depending on the company. It helps if the child already has some riding experience.

Practicalities

➡ Children are welcome at hotels throughout Maui. Those under 17 typically stay free when sharing a room with their parents and using existing bedding.

➡ Many sights and activities offer discounted children's rates, sometimes as cheap as half price.

➡ Car-rental companies on Maui lease child-safety seats, but they don't always have enough on hand so don't book your car at the last minute.

➡ If you're traveling with infants and forget to pack some of your gear, go online to www.mauibabyequipment.com to rent cribs, playpens, pushchairs and other baby items.

➡ For an evening out alone, the easiest and most reliable way to find a babysitter is through the hotel concierge.

➡ Maui is an open-minded place, and although public breast-feeding is not commonplace, it's unlikely to elicit unwanted attention.

Need to Know

Car-safety seats Reserve in advance with your car rental.

Changing facilities Found in shopping malls and resorts.

Cots/Cribs Request in advance when booking a room.

High chairs Available at most restaurants.

Kids' menus Family-oriented restaurants have them.

Nappies/Diapers Grocery and convenience stores sell them.

Pushchairs/Strollers Bring your own or rent in Maui.

Helpful Books & Resources

Travel with Children (Lonely Planet) Loaded with valuable tips and amusing tales, especially for first-time parents.

lonelyplanet.com Ask questions and get advice from other travelers on the Thorn Tree's online 'Kids to Go' and 'USA' Forums.

Go Hawaii (www.gohawaii.com) The state's official tourism website lists family-friendly activities, special events and more – easily search the site using terms such as 'kid' or 'family'.

Maui Family Magazine (www.mauifamilymaga zine.com) Geared to locals, but the website does have a weekend guide for families.

Regions at a Glance

Ready for an adventure? Whether you're seeking outdoor fun, great food, engaging history, cultural distractions or natural beauty, Maui offers a top-notch experience. The weather's darn nice, too. Each region has a few specialties. Lahaina lures 'em in with history and great restaurants. West Maui entertains honeymooners and families with bustling resorts and a lively beach scene. Ancient history and modern hustle collide in central Maui. Kihei is the quintessential beach town, while Wailea with its posh resorts and golf courses feels like a tropical country club. The Road to Hana offers waterfalls while Hana shares history and Old Hawaiian charm. The landscapes and the sunrise bring the masses to Haleakalā National Park, but you can get away from the crowds on the islands of Lana'i and Moloka'i.

Lahaina

Food
History
Shopping

Sheer Diversity

From food trucks and shave-ice stands to oceanfront lunch spots to white-linen romantic hideaways, Lahaina's range of dining establishments is broad. Food choices abound too, with seafood restaurants, burger joints and ethnic cuisines.

Whalers & Missionaries

Two forces collided in Lahaina the mid-1800s. Missionaries spread God's word while rowdy whalers sought a good time. Museums and homes spotlight their lifestyles.

Galleries & Outlet Stores

Art galleries and shopping discounters don't usually frequent the same neighborhoods, except here in Lahaina. Along Front St you'll find both local art and brand-name outlet stores.

p78

West Maui

Beaches
Water Sports
Accommodations

Sunbathing Heaven

From Ka'anapali to Kapalua, the beaches are wide, golden crescents with gorgeous views of the coast and nearby islands. Come here to catch a tan, enjoy a beach read and show off your bikinis and board shorts.

Snorkeling & Paddleboarding

West Maui's beach coves are ready-made for low-key water sports. Kick off from shore to snorkel the many reefs, or hop aboard a stand up paddle board for an hour of easy paddling.

Resorts & Condos

Two types of lodging flank the west coast's gorgeous beaches: resorts catering to your every need and do-it-yourself condominium complexes. Both are typically upscale.

p98

'Iao Valley & Central Maui

History
Offshore Adventures
Nature

Chieftains & Church Life

Steeped in ancient Hawaiian legend, the 'Iao Valley was also the site of a terrible battle between Kamehameha the Great and Maui warriors. The nearby Bailey House was home to missionaries.

Kanaha Beach Park

Winds blast through the flat Maui isthmus, providing sustained power for the windsurfer and kiteboarder skimming across the ocean off this mile-long beach.

Kealia Pond National Wildlife Refuge

Look for endangered Hawaiian seabirds in the pond and the marshy waters buffering it from the sea. The coastal boardwalk is a nice place for a late-afternoon stroll.

p124

Kihei & South Maui

Beaches
Food
Happy Hours

Family Fun

The three Kama'ole Beach parks feature picnic tables, showers, restrooms and lifeguards, making them great spots for birthday parties and long days at the beach with the kids.

Local Food

Loco moco, shave ice and lunch plates are easy to find in Kihei – just drive down Kihei Rd, which is lined with eateries. From breakfast through dinner, all meals are local-style in Da Kitchen Express.

5 Palms

Overlooking Keawakapu Beach, this buzzy place does happy hour right, with great food and drink deals, welcoming bartenders and a darn fine sunset.

p148

North Shore & Upcountry

Food & Drink
Outdoors
Shopping

Nature's Bounty

Loaded with farms and fertile volcanic soils, the Upcountry is the island's fruit basket. The Maui produce, cheese and beef found on menus across the island are all grown and produced here.

Land & Sea

Surfers and windsurfers enjoy some of the best waves and winds in the world on the north shore. Hikers and mountain bikers head to Makawao Forest Reserve's trails. Pa'ia and Haiku are prime adventure base camps.

Shopping

Cool boutiques and beloved mom-and-pop businesses line the main roads in Pa'ia and Makawao, while roadside fruit stands and bountiful farmers markets draw chefs and cooks in search of the freshest fare.

p170

Haleakalā National Park

Landscape
Hiking
Flora & Fauna

Craters & Cascades

In the Summit District, cinder cones dot the lunarlike floor of the crater atop the park's namesake volcano. In Kipahulu, waterfalls drop from lofty heights and splash into terraced pools.

Summit Trails

The crater is the park's marquee attraction, with a handful of trails crisscrossing the vast depression. These trails pass cinder cones, big views and peaks shrouded in fog.

Endangered Species

Silver-spiked leaves adorn the *'ahinahina* (silversword) flowers, which dot the summit. The rare nene, a native goose, can sometimes be seen near the Park Headquarters Visitor Center.

p194

The Road to Hana

Natural Beauty
Flora & Fauna
History

Waterfalls

They say every time you cross a bridge on the Road to Hana you also pass a waterfall – and that sounds about right. Waterfalls are the star attraction on this lush drive along the windward coast.

Tropical Gardens

Stretch your legs on a walk through the well-manicured plants at the Garden of Eden then gaze at an ancient temple bordered by Kahanu Garden, a lovely 294-acre ethnobotanical garden beside the sea.

King's Highway

Follow the ancient King's Hwy in Wai'anapanapa State Park. You can still see ancient stepping stones along this striking coastal path.

p210

Hana & East Maui

Beaches
Culture
Landscape

Hamoa Beach

Lined with thick tropical greenery and flanked by black lava reefs, this golden crescent is your Maui postcard. Dr Beach dubbed it one of the country's best in 2015.

Old Hawaii

Daily rhythms are slow on the backside of Haleakalā, where conversation is key, homegrown-food trucks dominate the dining scene and the Hasegawa General Store stocks everything from hardware to liquor.

From Lush to Lava

The Pi'ilani Hwy twists along the lonely eastern coastline, linking the green tropical flora of Kipahulu and its environs with the black-lava fields covering Haleakalā's southern slopes.

p226

Lana'i & Moloka'i

Remoteness
History
Water Sports

Ferries & Planes

Getting to Lana'i or Moloka'i takes a bit of planning. To access either island, hop aboard a ferry in Lahaina or catch an interisland flight.

Kalaupapa National Historic Park

Hike, or ride a mule, down a steep cliffside trail to the Kalaupapa Peninsula, the site of a long-running settlement for people with Hansen's disease (leprosy). Obligatory tours include stories about life here in the past.

Diving

Shhh...divers may not want to share the existence of the Cathedrals, a fantastic dive site off near Manele Bay in Lana'i with lava-made caverns, ledges, walls and the exciting 'Shotgun' lava tube.

p242

On the Road

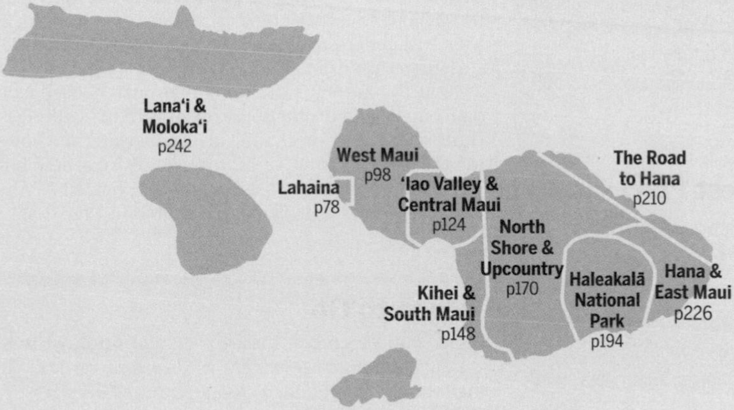

Lana'i &
Moloka'i
p242

West Maui
p98

Lahaina
p78

'Iao Valley &
Central Maui
p124

The Road
to Hana
p210

North
Shore &
Upcountry
p170

Kihei &
South Maui
p148

Haleakalā
National
Park
p194

Hana &
East Maui
p226

Lahaina

☎ 808 / POP 11,900

Best Places to Eat

➡ Lahaina Grill (p93)

➡ Pacific'O (p93)

➡ Star Noodle (p92)

➡ Ululani's Hawaiian Shave Ice (p90)

➡ Choice Health Bar (p90)

Best Places to Watch the Sunset

➡ Front St, just south of Lahainaluna Rd

➡ Fleetwood's (p94) rooftop bar

➡ Old Lahaina Luau (p95)

➡ Kimo's (p92)

➡ Mala Ocean Tavern (p93)

Why Go?

With its weathered storefronts, narrow streets and bustling harbor, plus a few chattering mynahs, Hawaii's most historic town looks like a port-of-call for Captain Ahab. Is this the 21st century, or an 1850s whaling village? In truth, it offers a mix of of both.

Tucked between the West Maui Mountains and a tranquil sea, Lahaina has long been a popular convergence point. Ancient Hawaiian royals were the first to gather here, followed by missionaries, whalers and sugar plantation workers. Today it's a base for creative chefs, passionate artists and dedicated surf instructors.

Near the harbor, storefronts that once housed saloons, dance halls and brothels now teem with art galleries, souvenir shops and, well, still plenty of watering holes. As for the whalers, they've been replaced by a new kind of leviathan hunter: whale-watchers as dedicated as Ahab in their hunt. Between January and March, they don't have to look hard.

When to Go

From mid-December through to mid-April, visitor can watch the humpback whales as they feed on krill during their annual migration.

The King Kamehameha Day Parade takes place in June, with floats, historical figures on horseback and a festival.

Winter begins with famous Halloween revelry and ends with the lighting of the Banyan Tree.

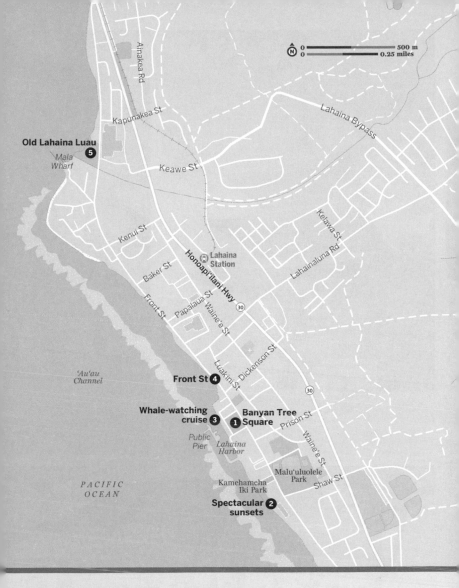

Lahaina Highlights

1 Banyan Tree Square
(p82) Reveling in the
improbable beauty of
Lahaina's central landmark,
including the Old Lahaina
Courthouse.

2 Spectacular Sunsets
(p93) Thrilling to the
polychromatic spectacle over
the Pacific from the terrace of

a waterfront restaurant such
as Pacific'O.

3 Whale-watching Cruise
(p88) Going whale-watching
in winter when odds are
good that you'll see a whale,
especially when you're in the
hands of an operator such as
Pacific Whale Foundation.

4 Front St (p95) Strolling

while viewing dawdling
sailboats and a languid Lana'i,
and browsing alluring galleries.

5 Old Lahaina Luau (p95)
Celebrating Hawaiian culture
with traditional hula, tropical
cocktails and food a few
cuts above the average luau
experience.

. Lahaina Jodo Mission (p83)

his mission's 12ft-high bronze Buddha, cast in
yoto, is the largest of its kind outside Japan.

. Banyan Tree Square (p82)

ahaina's favorite tree has 16 major trunks,
eaching across the better part of an acre.

. *Carthaginian* (p88)

his sunken sailing brig, which is one of the sights
sible during the *Atlantis* submarine tour, played a
ading role in the 1965 movie *Hawaii*.

. Aloha Mixed Plate (p91)

iendly, open-air and beside the beach, this is the
awaii you came to find.

History

In ancient times Lahaina – then known as Lele – housed a royal court for high chiefs and was the breadbasket (or, more accurately, the breadfruit basket) of West Maui. After Kamehameha the Great unified the islands, he chose the area as his base. The capital remained here until 1845, centered on Moku'ula Island & Mokuhinia Pond Site (p89). The first Christian missionaries arrived in the 1820s and within a decade Hawaii's first stone church, missionary school and printing press were in place.

Lahaina became the dominant port for whalers, not only in Hawaii but in the entire Pacific. The whaling years reached their peak in the 1840s, with hundreds of ships pulling into port each year. When the whaling industry fizzled in the 1860s, Lahaina became all but a ghost town. In the 1870s sugarcane came to Lahaina and it remained the backbone of the economy until tourism took over in the 1960s.

◉ Sights

Lahaina's top sights cluster around the harbor, with other sights either on Front St or within a few blocks of it. This makes Lahaina an ideal town to explore on foot. The top free sight? The sunset view from Front St, at its intersection with Lahainaluna Rd.

★ Old Lahaina Courthouse   MUSEUM
(Map p84; ☏ visitor center 808-667-9193; http://lahainarestoration.org/old-lahaina-court house/; 648 Wharf St, Banyan Tree Park; ⊙9am-5pm) FREE Tucked in the shadows of the iconic banyan tree, Lahaina's 1859 courthouse is a repository of history and art. Its location beside the harbor is no coincidence. Smuggling was so rampant during the whaling era that officials deemed this the ideal spot for customs operations, the courthouse and the jail – all neatly wrapped into a single building. It also held the governor's office. On August 12, 1898, the US annexation of Hawaii was formally concluded here.

The excellent Lahaina Visitor Center (p96) is on the building's 1st floor.

There are also two art galleries operated by the Lahaina Arts Society (p95), one is in the old jail in the basement (entrance outside). It was given the Greek Revival style you see today in 1925 and was used until the 1970s.

Lahaina Heritage Museum   MUSEUM
(Map p84; www.lahainarestoration.org; 648 Wharf St, Banyan Tree Park; ⊙9am-5pm) FREE On the 2nd floor of the Old Lahaina Courthouse, this museum celebrates Lahaina's prominent role in Maui's history. Exhibits spotlight ancient Hawaiian culture, 19th-century whaling, and local plantations and mills. Check out the lemon-shaped sling stones. Made from volcanic rock, they were deadly projectiles used in early Hawaiian warfare.

★ Banyan Tree Square   PARK
(Map p84; cnr Front & Hotel Sts) A leafy landmark (the largest tree in Hawaii), stands in the center of Lahaina. Remarkably, it sprawls across the entire square. Planted as a seedling on April 24, 1873, to commemorate the 50th anniversary of missionaries in Lahaina, the tree has become a virtual forest unto itself, with 16 major trunks and scores of horizontal branches reaching across the better part of an acre. The square was recently given a major restoration, that fixed the paving tiles and fixed the teak benches.

The songs of thousands of mynah birds keep things lively at night. Most weekends artists and craftsmen set up booths beneath the tree's shady canopy.

Fort Ruins   RUINS
(Map p84; cnr Wharf & Canal Sts) Just south of the Old Lahaina Courthouse, an imposing cluster of coral stone blocks stands at attention. This is a reconstruction of a section of an 1832 fort, originally built to keep rowdy whalers in line. Each day at dusk a Hawaiian sentinel would beat a drum to alert sailors to return to their ships. Stragglers who didn't make it in time were imprisoned here.

Baldwin House   MUSEUM
(Map p84; ☏ 808-661-3262; www.lahainaresto ration.org/baldwin-home-museum; 120 Dickenson St; adult/child incl admission to Wo Hing Museum $7/free; ⊙10am-4pm, candlelit tours 6-8:30pm Fri) Reverend Dwight Baldwin, a missionary doctor, built this house in 1834–35, making it the oldest surviving Western-style building in Lahaina. It served as both his home and the community's first medical clinic. The coral-and-rock walls are a hefty 24in thick, which keeps the house cool year-round. The exterior walls have been plastered over, but you can get a sense of how they originally appeared next door at the Masters' Reading Room (p96), which now houses an art gallery.

HALE PA'I PRINTING MUSEUM

This small white cottage ([☎]808-662-0560; http://lahainarestoration.org/hale-pai-museum/; 980 Lahainaluna Rd) on the grounds of Lahainaluna High School housed Hawaii's first printing press. Although its primary mission was making the Bible available to Hawaiians, the press also produced, in 1834, Hawaii's first newspaper. Named *Ka Lama (The Torch)*, it held the distinction of being the first newspaper west of the Rockies.

The adjacent school was founded in 1831, and students operated the press. Typography tools and a replica of the original Rampage Press are displayed. The original press was so heavily used that it wore out in the 1850s. Displays discuss various items and publications printed on the press. There's also an exhibit explaining the history of Hawaii's 12-letter alphabet and a reprint of an amusing 'Temperance Map', drawn by an early missionary to illustrate the perils of drunkenness. Don't be alarmed if an ear-splitting siren breaks your 1850s reverie; it's the high school's 'bell'. Boarding students, about 10% of the student body, have traditionally worked in neighboring fields – so the bell has to be loud.

Call in advance: Hale Pa'i is staffed by volunteers so hours can vary. To get there, follow Lahainaluna Rd uphill for 2 miles northeast from downtown Lahaina.

It took the Baldwins 161 days to get here from their native Connecticut, sailing around Cape Horn at the southern tip of South America. Dr Baldwin's passport and representative period furniture are on display. A doctor's 'scale of fees' states that $50 was the price for treating a 'very great sickness', while a 'very small sickness' cost $10. It's only a cold, Doc, I swear.

★**Wo Hing Museum**   MUSEUM
(Map p84; www.lahainarestoration.org/wo-hing-museum; 858 Front St; adult/child incl admission to Baldwin House $7/free; ⊙10am-4pm) This three-story temple, built in 1912 as a meeting hall for the benevolent society Chee Kung Tong, provided Chinese immigrants with a place to preserve their cultural identity, celebrate festivities and socialize in their native tongue. After WWII, Lahaina's ethnic Chinese population spread far and wide and the temple fell into decline. Now restored and turned into a cultural museum, it houses ceremonial instruments, a teak medicine cabinet c 1900, jade pieces dating back thousands of years and a Taoist shrine.

The tin-roof **cookhouse** out back holds a tiny theater showing films of Hawaii shot by Thomas Edison in 1898 and 1906, soon after he invented the motion-picture camera. These grainy black-and-white shots capture poignant images of old Hawaii, including *paniolo* (cowboys) herding cattle, cane workers in the fields and everyday street scenes.

Hale Pa'ahao Prison   MUSEUM
(Stuck-in-Irons House; Map p84; www.lahaina restoration.org/hale-paahao-prison; 187 Prison St; ⊙10am-4pm) [FREE] A remnant of the whaling era, this shady coral stone jail was built in 1852 and looks much as it did 150 years ago thanks to a 1988 restoration. One of the tiny reconstructed cells displays a list of arrests in 1855. The top three offenses were drunkenness (330 arrests), 'furious riding' (89) and lascivious conduct (20). Other transgressions of the day included profanity, aiding deserting sailors and drinking *'awa* (kava; native plant used to make an intoxicating drink).

Pioneer Mill Smokestack   MUSEUM
(Map p84; www.lahainarestoration.org; 275 Lahainaluna Rd; ⊙sunrise-sunset) [FREE] The hard-to-miss Pioneer Mill smokestack is a local icon. Outdoor exhibits spotlight equipment and vehicles used on the company's sugar plantation, in operation from 1860 until 1999. There are two restored late 1800s steam locomotives, formerly used by Pioneer Mill. Excellent informational signs explain the history of sugarcane plantations in Lahaina.

Lahaina Jodo Mission   BUDDHIST TEMPLE
(Map p87; [☎]808-661-4304; 12 Ala Moana St; ⊙sunrise-sunset) A 12ft-high bronze Buddha sits serenely in the courtyard at this Buddhist mission, looking across the Pacific toward its Japanese homeland. Cast in Kyoto, the Buddha is the largest of its kind outside Japan and was installed here in 1968 to celebrate the centennial of Japanese immigration to Hawaii. The grounds also hold a 90ft pagoda and a whopping 3.5-ton temple bell, which is rung 11 times each evening at 8pm. Inside the temple are priceless Buddhist paintings by Haijin Iwasaki.

Lahaina Downtown

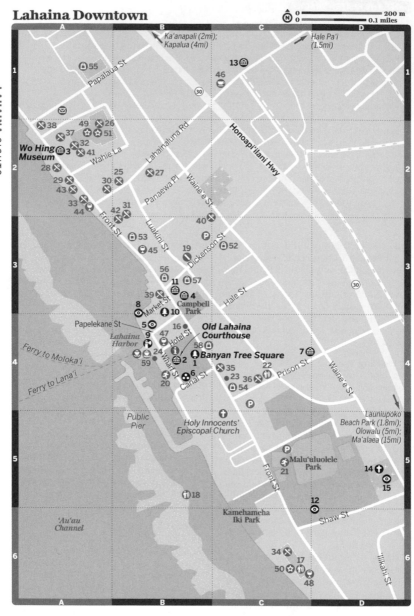

Hauola Stone   HISTORIC SITE

(Map p84; off Market St) At the northern shoreline of the small plaza behind the Lahaina Public Library, look beneath the water's surface for the middle of three lava stones. In the 14th and 15th centuries royal women gave birth to the next generation of chiefs and royalty here.

Lahaina Public Library Grounds   PARK

(Map p84; 680 Wharf St) This was once a royal taro field where Kamehameha II toiled in

Lahaina Downtown

the mud to instill in his subjects the dignity of labor. Today the gardens offer a bit of a green respite near the historic waterfront.

Brick Palace   HISTORIC SITE
(Map p84; off Market St) The first Western-style building in Hawaii, the Brick Palace was erected by Kamehameha I around 1800 so he could keep watch on arriving ships. Despite the name, this 'palace' was a simple two-story structure built by a pair of ex-convicts from Botany Bay. All that remains is a vague representation of the excavated foundation. It's behind the Lahaina Public Library.

Lahaina Lighthouse   LIGHTHOUSE
(Map p84; Wharf St) Directly in front of the Pioneer Inn (p94) is the site of the first lighthouse in the Pacific. It was commissioned in 1840 to aid whaling ships pulling into the harbor. The current concrete structure dates from 1916.

🏖 Beaches

Launiupoko Beach Park   PARK
(☑808-661-4685; Honoapiilani Hwy/Hwy 30) This small park about 3 miles south of central Lahaina is good for families and can be reached via a nice walk or bike ride; otherwise it's a

short drive. There's a rock-protected beach with negligible surf that's good for small children, as well as a regular beach with larger waves, which is enjoyed by surfers, kayakers and those perched on SUPs (stand up paddle surfing). Trees offer shade, palms offer atmosphere and small dunes offer a diversion. It gets busy on weekends.

Wahikuli Wayside Park　　　　　PARK
(☑808-661-4685; Honoapiilani Hwy) Just 2 miles north of the heart of Lahaina and right on the road to Ka'anapali, this long county park follows the shore and is great for walking and cycling. There are dozens of shady picnic tables, reef-protected beaches and fine views of Lana'i. It's a short bike ride or nice stroll from central Lahaina.

🏃 Activities

Lahaina is not known for its beaches, which are generally shallow and rocky, though you can find good ones at parks just north and south of the center. It is a good place to take a surfing lesson.

For a sunset cruise, a whale-watching tour or other maritime adventures, head to Lahaina Harbor. Dive boats leave from Lahaina Harbor, offering dives suitable for all levels.

★**Lahaina Divers**　　　　　DIVING
(Map p84; ☑808-667-7496; www.lahainadivers. com; 143 Dickenson St; 2-tank dives from $160; ☺8am-8pm) Offers a full range of dives, from night dives to 'discover scuba' dives for newbies. The latter go to a reef thick with green sea turtles – a great intro to diving. There are also lessons and a huge range of packages.

★**Snorkel Bob's**　　　　　SNORKELING
(Map p87; ☑808-661-4421; www.snorkelbob. com; 1217 Front St; snorkel gear package per week from $35; ☺8am-5pm) With 11 shops on four islands, Snorkel Bob's is famous for cheap snorkel-set rentals. A huge range of equipment and deals are offered by the day or week. You can even pick up your gear in Lahaina and return it on another island. The store is on Front St north of downtown.

West Maui Cycles　　　　　CYCLING
(Map p87; ☑808-661-9005; www.westmaui cycles.com; 1087 Limahana Pl; per day $15-130; ☺9am-5pm Mon-Sat, 10am-4pm Sun) Quality hybrid and mountain bikes for rent, as well as cheaper cruisers fine for kicking around town. Check the website for route maps and trail locations. Car racks cost $5 per day. The office is a mecca for cyclists.

Maui Kayaks　　　　　KAYAKING
(Map p84; ☑808-214-3491; www.mauikayaks.com; 505 Front St; guided tour adult/child from $60/50; ☺store 8am-4pm, reservations 8am-6pm) This locally owned operation offers guided kayaking and kayaking-snorkel tours along the western coast of Maui. The Lahaina Paddle trip doubles as a whale-watching excursion in season. Kayak rentals are also available (per two hours/day $25/35).

Malu'uluolele Park Tennis Courts　　　TENNIS
(Map p84; Front St, Malu'uluolele Park) The popular public tennis courts at Malu'uluolele Park have lights to enable night playing.

Surfing

If you've never surfed before, Lahaina is a great place to learn, with first-class instructors, gentle waves and ideal conditions for beginners. The section of shoreline known as Lahaina Breakwall, north of Kamehameha Iki Park, is a favorite spot for novices. Surfers also take to the waters just offshore from Launiupoko Beach Park.

Several companies in Lahaina offer surfing lessons.

Maui Surf Clinics　　　　　SURFING
(Map p84; ☑808-244-7873; www.mauisurf clinics.com; 505 Front St, Suite 201; 2hr lesson from $85; ☺lessons daily; 🚸) This welcoming school implements the techniques of its founder Nancy Emerson, who was winning international surfing contests by the time she was 14. It offers a huge range of group and private lessons, including ones geared to children (from $100). It also offers SUP lessons.

Goofy Foot Surf School　　　　　SURFING
(Map p84; ☑808-244-9283; www.goofyfootsurf school.com; 505 Front St, Suite 123; 2hr lesson from $65; ☺6:30am-8pm Mon-Sat, 8am-8pm Sun; 🚸) This top surf school combines fundamentals with fun. In addition to lessons, it runs daylong surf camps. Pick up a free beginner surf map with safety guidelines at the shop. SUP lessons also offered. Also rents surfboards and SUP boards to experienced surfers and paddlers – if you've taken a lesson or been on a board, you're good.

Maui Wave Riders　　　　　SURFING
(Map p84; ☑808-661-0003; www.mauiwave riders.com; 133 Prison St; 90min class adult/child from $65/55; ☺7am-4pm Mon-Sat) Offers surfing classes for all ages as well as SUP lessons. Also has gear rentals, with a huge range of boards.

North Lahaina

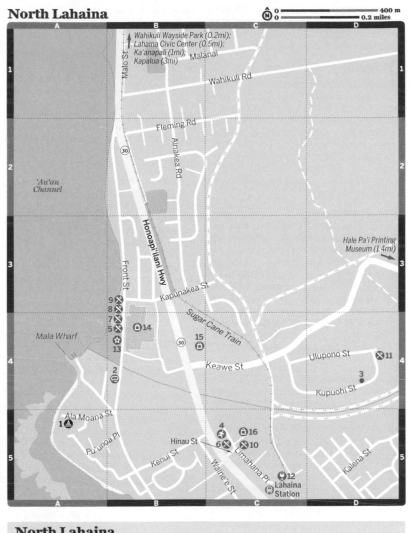

North Lahaina

◎ Sights
1 Lahaina Jodo Mission A5

⊕ Activities, Courses & Tours
2 Snorkel Bob's B4
3 Trilogy Excursions D4
4 West Maui Cycles C5

⊗ Eating
5 Aloha Mixed Plate B4
6 Choice Health Bar C5
7 Frida's Mexican Beach House............. B4
8 Honu Seafood & Pizza........................ B3
9 Mala Ocean Tavern............................. B3

10 Nobu's Lunch Wagon........................... C5
11 Star Noodle D4

⊖ Drinking & Nightlife
Aloha Mixed Plate......................... (see 5)
12 Kohola Brewery C5

⊛ Entertainment
13 Old Lahaina Luau................................ B4

⊕ Shopping
14 Lahaina Cannery Mall B4
15 Lahaina Gateway B4
16 Ole Surfboards.................................... C5

Lahaina Breakwall
SURFING

(Map p84) The section of shoreline known as Lahaina Breakwall, north of Kamehameha Iki Park, is a favorite spot for novices.

Tours

Catamarans and other vessels in Lahaina Harbor cater to tourists, and outfitters staff booths along the harbor's edge. Most companies offer discounts or combo deals on their websites. Check with the company for the specifics about where to meet pre-trip.

During whale season from mid-December to mid-April, snorkeling trips and cocktail cruises often double up as whale-watching excursions.

★ Trilogy Excursions
BOATING

(Map p87; ☑ 888-225-6284, 808-874-5649; www.sailtrilogy.com; 207 Kupuohi St; 4hr snorkel trip adult/child from $120/60; ⊙ 8:30am-4pm Mon- Fri, noon-3pm Sun) Offering snorkeling tours in Maui for more than 40 years, this family-run operation specializes in catamaran tours. There's a variety of trips, including ones to the reef at Olowalu and the much-loved islet of Molokini. In season there are whale-watching trips as wells as dinner and sunset cruises. Day trips to Lana'i are popular.

★ Pacific
Whale Foundation
WHALE WATCHING

(Pac Whale Eco Adventures; Map p84; ☑ 808-667-7447; www.pacwhale.com; 612 Front St; whale-watching adult/child from $33/20; ⊙ store 6am-8pm; ⊕) ✐ The whale-watching cruises, which depart several times a day in winter, are immensely popular. In the unlikely event you don't spot whales, your next trip is free. Well-versed naturalists add context to the trips. Snorkel and dolphin-watching cruises (adult/child $94/52) are popular year-round. There are other snorkeling trips as well as various sunset and dinner cruises. Most trips leave from Lahaina Harbor. Other trips depart from Ma'alaea Harbor to the south.

The company also offers several highly recommended volunteer opportunities in Maui through its **Volunteers on Vacation** (☑ ext 1 808-249-8811; www.volunteersonvacation.org) program.

Makai Adventures
WHALE WATCHING

(Map p84; ☑ 808-495-1001; www.makaiadventures.com; 675 Wharf St, Slip 16, Lahaina Harbor; 2hr trips $40-50; ⊙ sales booth 7am-7pm, trips mid-Dec–mid-Apr) Runs well-regarded whale-watching trips several times a day during the humpback-whale season. The small boat carries a maximum of 20 people.

Scotch Mist II
CRUISE

(Map p84; ☑ 808-661-0386; www.scotchmistsailingcharters.com; 675 Wharf St, Slip 2, Lahaina Harbor; adult/child from $60/40) The *Scotch Mist II*, a beautiful 50ft sailing yacht, serves champagne, wine, beer and chocolate-covered macadamia nuts on its sunset cruise. Book in advance as the boat (which is available for group charters) carries just 18 passengers per sail. Snorkel cruises and whale-watching trips (December to April) are also available.

Hawaii Ocean Project
CRUISE

(Map p84; ☑ 808-667-6165; www.hawaiioceanproject.com; 675 Wharf St, Lahaina Harbor; dinner cruise adult/child $90/58; ⊙ 8am-8pm) Operated by the Lahaina Cruise Company, this flotilla of boats includes the 70ft-long *Kaulana*, the largest catamaran in the harbor. It's used for snorkeling tours along with the 65ft-long *Lahaina Princess* (from adult/child $90/58). The sunset dinner cruise on the 120ft-long *Maui Princess* includes open-air table service and live music.

Atlantis Submarine
BOATING

(Map p84; ☑ 808-667-2494; www.atlantisadventures.com; 658 Wharf St, Best Western Pioneer Inn; adult/child $105/38; ⊙ tours hourly 9am-2pm, office 7:30am-6pm; ⊕) To see Maui's undersea wonders without getting wet, consider a trip on the *Atlantis*. The price is steep, but this 65-footer is a real sub, and it dives to a depth of more than 100ft. Sights include coral, tropical fish and the sunken *Carthaginian:* a sailing brig that played a leading role in the 1965 movie *Hawaii.*

Check in at the office, which is inside the Pioneer Inn building. The office opens onto Front St. One child under 13 years admitted free with an adult.

✯ Festivals & Events

Lahaina's top festivals draw huge crowds, with Front St closed to traffic during many of these events. Check http://visitlahaina.com/events/ for the latest schedule.

★ King Kamehameha Day Parade
PARADE

(⊙ mid-Jun) Traditionally dressed Hawaiian riders on horseback, marching bands and floral floats take to Front St to honor Kamehameha the Great on this public holiday in

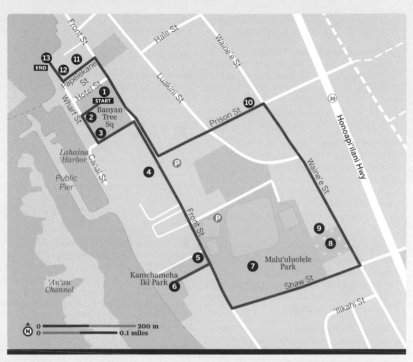

🏃 Walking Tour
Ancient & Historic Lahaina

START BANYAN TREE SQ
END HAUOLA STONE
LENGTH 1.25 MILES; TWO HOURS

Lahaina has old sights that date to times before the arrival of Europeans and Americans. Visit the **❶ Lahaina Visitor Center** (p96) for a brochure ($2) describing the historic sites. Interpretive markers are placed in front of historic sites throughout downtown.

Begin at **❷ Banyan Tree Square** (p82). Its landmark banyan is a testament to extraordinary natural architecture. The **❸ Old Lahaina Courthouse** (p82) symbolizes the start of the modern era. Just south, the **❹ Fort Ruins** (p82) recalls efforts to assert control over whalers in the 1830s.

Turn right onto Front St to reach **❺ Holy Innocents' Episcopal Church**, at No 561. The site was once a summer home of Hawaii's last monarch, Queen Lili'uokalani.

Just south is the foundation of **❻ Hale Piula**, Lahaina's attempt at a royal palace. It was abandoned mid-construction because

Kamehameha III preferred sleeping nearby on Moku'ula Island. Fronted by **❼ Kamehameha Iki Park**, the site now has a thatched-roof pavilion used for events and carvers building outrigger canoes.

Across the street in Malu'uluolele Park, pause to ponder the **❽ Moku'ula Island & Mokuhinia Pond Site**. Where today there's bland grass, 100 years ago was a freshwater pond and a sacred island used as a home by generations of Hawaiian royalty.

Pivotal figures in 19th-century Maui are buried in **❾ Waiola Cemetery**. Evocative inscriptions and cameos adorn many tombstones. Just north is the troubled **❿ Waine'e Church**. At the corner of Prison and Waine'e Sts, **⓫ Hale Pa'ahao Prison** (p83) held drunken whalers and was built with coral stone blocks from the Fort Ruins.

Near the harbor behind the Lahaina Public Library Grounds (p84), look for the barely there legacy of the **⓬ Brick Palace** (p85) and finish at the ancient **⓭ Hauola Stone** (p84) while gazing out to the ocean, which has been so pivotal in Lahaina's history.

mid-June. An awards ceremony and arts festival follow at Kamehameha Iki Park.

★ **Whale & Ocean Arts Festival** CULTURAL
(◎ early Mar) Celebrate the annual humpback-whale migration at Banyan Tree Sq during this weekend-long celebration with Hawaiian music, hula and games. Naturalists are on hand to share their knowledge about whales. Also features marine-themed art.

**Holiday Lighting
of the Banyan Tree** CHRISTMAS
(◎ Dec) Lahaina illuminates Hawaii's biggest tree on the first weekend in December with thousands of colorful lights, accompanied by hula performances, carolers, cookie decorating and a craft show. And, of course, Santa shows up for the *na keiki* (children).

Friday Town Party CARNIVAL
(www.mauifridays.com; ◎ 6-9pm) This outdoor festival features music and food vendors. It's held the second Friday of the month at Campbell Park, which is across from the Pioneer Inn on Front St.

Halloween in Lahaina CARNIVAL
(◎ Oct 31) Front St morphs into a costumed street festival on Halloween night. The party is fun for families in the late afternoon, with a *na keiki* costume parade, but things gets a bit wilder as the night goes on – although a strong police presence keeps rowdiness in check. Forget parking; take a shuttle or taxi.

Banyan Tree Birthday STREET CARNIVAL
(◎ Apr) Lahaina's favorite tree gets a two-day birthday party, complete with a birthday cake, music and art, plus piñatas for the *na keiki* (children). It's held on the weekend closest to April 24. The tree celebrates its 145th birthday in 2018.

Fourth of July FIREWORKS
(◎ 4 Jul) Enjoy a concert on the lawn of the public library from 5pm then watch fireworks light up the sky over the harbor at 8pm.

✖ Eating

Lahaina has the finest dining scene on Maui and a huge range of choices. But remember, fine food draws hungry hordes. Many folks staying in Ka'anapali pour into Lahaina at dinnertime and traffic jams up. Allow extra time and book popular places in advance.

★ **Ululani's Hawaiian Shave Ice** SWEETS $
(Map p84; www.ululanisshaveice.com; 819 Front St; small ice $5; ◎ 12:30-9pm) For over-the-top (literally) shave ice, amble up to the counter at Ululani's Hawaiian Shave Ice and take your pick of tropical flavors. A second **location** (Map p84; www.ululanishawaiianshaveice.com; 790 Front St; ◎ 10:30am-9pm) is one block south.

★ **Choice Health Bar** HEALTH FOOD $
(Map p87; ✆ 808-661-7711; www.choicehealth bar.com; 1087 Limahana Pl; mains $8-18; ◎ 8am-6pm Mon-Sat; ✐) This breezy box of healthy deliciousness whips up addictive organic fare. The fruit-stuffed acai bowls – loaded with berries, greens and granola – are invigorating. The Buddha Bowl is a triple-layered nirvana of grains topped by soup then a salad. Smoothies, juices and health shots are

---

RIGHTEOUS & ROWDY

Two diametrically opposed groups of New Englanders clashed in Lahaina in the 1820s – missionaries and whalers.

In 1823 William Richards, Lahaina's first missionary, converted Maui's native governor, Hoapili, to Christianity and persuaded him to pass laws against 'drunkenness and debauchery.' However, after months at sea, sailors weren't looking for a prayer service when they pulled into port – to them there was 'no God west of the Horn.' Missionaries and whalers almost came to battle in 1827 when Governor Hoapili arrested a whaler captain for allowing women to board his ship. The crew retaliated by shooting cannonballs at Richards' house. The captain was released, but laws forbidding liaisons between seamen and Hawaiian women remained in force. This actually proved popular with many ship captains as their crews were less likely to become incapacitated while docked in Lahaina as opposed to Honolulu, which was something of a den of iniquity.

It wasn't until Governor Hoapili's death in 1840 that laws prohibiting liquor and prostitution were no longer enforced and whalers began to frolic in Lahaina. Among the sailors who roamed Lahaina's streets was Herman Melville in 1843; he later penned *Moby Dick*.

perfect for travelers on the go. Menu items and ingredients reflect what's in season.

Nobu's Lunch Wagon
HAWAIIAN $

(Map p87; 1058 Limahana Pl; mains $9; ⊙10:30am-2:30pm Mon-Fri) One of Maui's best food trucks is in a dubious location in an industrial park, across from a Taco Bell. The namesake owner prepares a variety of plate lunches including meatballs, garlic mushroom chicken and daily specials. Sides like noodles and mac salad are excellent. Enjoy your lunch as a picnic just north at Wahikuli Wayside Park (p86).

Lahaina Luna Cafe
HAWAIIAN $

(Map p84; ☑808-757-8286; http://lahainaluna cafe.com; 790 Front St; mains $10-14; ⊙10:30am-9pm; ☑) Comfort food with a farm-to-table ethos. Locally sourced foods are used for tasty salads, burgers, sandwiches, tacos and much more at this open-air cafe on a small courtyard off the street. Grab a table under an umbrella and order from the counter. Soon your well-presented meal will emerge from the busy and skilled kitchen. There's a good kid's menu.

Maui Sugar Shop
BAKERY $

(Map p84; ☑808-662-0033; www.mauisugar shop.com; 878 Front St, Suite A10; treats from $3; ⊙7am-8:30pm Mon-Fri, from 8am Sat, 10am-4pm Sun) The organic treats are all gluten-free at this tiny storefront bakery on the backside of a tired strip mall. Cakes, cupcakes, muffins and a lot more sell fast through the day. The wizards at the mixing bowls use over 40 kinds of flour among other exotic ingredients.

TaquerEATa
MEXICAN $

(Map p84; ☑808-866-7078; 741 Waine'e St; mains from $4; ⊙8am-3pm Sun-Fri) Breakfast and lunch tacos can be customized in myriad ways at this silver-hued food truck, part of a pod of trucks. The lines form early for the super fresh and tasty fare. Choose from an array of housemade salsas that sparkle with fresh flavors.

Cafe Cafe
CAFE $

(Map p84; ☑808-661-0006; http://cafecafe maui.com; 129 Lahainaluna Rd, Old Lahaina Center; mains $8-12; ⊙7am-7pm) A great place for cof-fee coffee. This laid-back island casual joint serves extraordinary coffee drinks and teas. Out front is a collection of ragtag tables. Enjoy a bevy of fruit and veggie smoothies as well as bagel sandwiches and breakfast treats.

Sunrise Cafe
BREAKFAST $

(Map p84; ☑808-661-8558; 693 Front St; mains $6; ⊙7am-3pm) Right next to the verdant gardens of the Lahaina Public Library is a great reason to get out of bed: Sun-rise Cafe serves up fantastic cheap break-fasts. Choices include cinnamon rolls, lox Benedicts, breakfast burritos and good old bacon and eggs. The small dining area un-der a tin roof gets crowded and waits can be long. It's cash-only.

Pho Saigon 808
VIETNAMESE $

(Map p84; ☑808-661-6628; http://phosaigon 808.com; 658 Front St, Wharf Cinema Center; mains $11-22; ⊙11am-9pm) Excellent Asian fare is cooked up fast and fresh at this small res-taurant buried back in the recesses of the Wharf Cinema Center mall. Choose from a huge number of noodle dishes, pho and cur-ries. There's a smattering of Thai dishes as well. They deliver.

Prison Street Pizza
PIZZA $

(Map p84; ☑808-662-3332; http://prison streetpizza.com; 133 Prison St; mains $8-15; ⊙10am-10pm Mon-Sun) This low-key pizza joint is just a few steps from Banyan Tree Sq and serves Jersey-style pizza (soft crust, load-ed with ingredients and plenty of tomatoes in the base). Other menu items include calzones and a few sandwiches. Eat in the simple din-ing room, grab takeout or get delivery. Large pizzas ($28) serve several people.

Aloha Mixed Plate
HAWAIIAN $

(Map p87; ☑808-661-3322; www.alohamixedplate. com; 1285 Front St; mains $8-20; ⊙8am-10pm; ☑) Aloha Mixed Plate is the Hawaii you came to find: friendly, open-air and beside the beach (although the view is somewhat obscured). The food's first-rate, the prices reasonable. For a thoroughly Hawaiian ex-perience, order the Ali'i Plate, packed with *laulau, kalua* pig, *lomilomi* salmon, poi (steamed, mashed taro) and *haupia* (coco-nut pudding) – and, of course, macaroni sal-ad and white rice.

The restaurant serves breakfast, includ-ing dishes such as *loco moco* and *kalua* pig omelets.

Ono Gelato Co
GELATO $

(Map p84; ☑808-495-0203; www.onogelato company.com; 815 Front St; small gelato $5; ⊙8am-10pm) At Ono Gelato Co there's al-ways a crowd gazing at the stunning array of smooth gelati. There is also a fine coffee bar.

Scoops ICE CREAM $

(Map p84; ☑ 808-661-5632; 888 Front St, Old La-haina Center; ice cream from $4; ☺9am-10pm) Scoops serves locally made ice cream, but we'll make the choice easy: Kauai Pie, a luscious mix of Kona coffee ice cream, coco-nut, macadamia nuts and fudge. Cash only. Known for its fresh waffle cones.

★Star Noodle ASIAN $$

(Map p87; ☑ 808-667-5400; www.starnoodle.com; 286 Kupuohi St; shared plates $3-20, mains $7-15; ☺10:30am-10pm) This hillside hotspot is constantly busy – and rightly so. Inside this sleek noodle shop, grazers can nibble on an eclectic array of Asian-fusion share plates. Those seeking heartier fare can dive into garlic noodles, kimchi ramen and a local saimin (local-style noodle soup; Spam in-cluded). A central communal table and the chatty bar keep the vibe lively.

It's about 1½ miles from the center of Lahaina, in an otherwise humdrum indus-trial park.

Paia Fishmarket SEAFOOD $$

(Map p84; ☑808-662-3456; http://paiafish market.com; 632 Front St; mains $10-20; ☺11am-9:30pm) This branch of the Maui original is located in an appealing vintage building near the banyan tree. There are picnic tables on a shady terrace, while inside it's all bright and airy. Of course the reason to come here is the superb seafood. The menu changes daily depending on what's fresh.

You can always count on fish and chips, fish tacos, excellent *ono* (white-fleshed wa-hoo), burgers and more.

Sale Pepe ITALIAN $$

(Map p84; ☑ 808-667-7667; www.salepepe maui.com; 878 Front St, Old Lahaina Center; mains $14-24; ☺11am-2pm, 5-10pm Mon-Sat) Who needs the ocean? The only view at this at-tractive Italian restaurant trapped inside a strip mall is of fabulous pastas and pizza. The rigatoni, spaghetti, lasagna and more are made fresh daily, as are the many sauc-es, including the rich tomatoey one used on the superb pizzas. Most ingredients are sourced locally except for certain essential items imported from Italy.

Koa's Seaside Grill SEAFOOD $$

(Map p84; ☑808-667-7737; www.koasgrill.com; 839 Front St; mains $20-38; ☺9am-9pm) Push back through a trinket-filled gift shop to find a wide-open dining room built over tidal water and rocks. Thrill to incredible views over the water to Lana'i. But for an even better view, climb the stairs to the rooftop deck. Enjoy sunset cocktails from the long list and then browse the steak and seafood menu.

Honu Seafood & Pizza SEAFOOD, PIZZA $$

(Map p87; ☑ 808-667-9390; www.honumaui.com; 1295 Front St; mains $14-48; ☺11am-9:30pm) Named for Maui's famous green sea turtles, this stylish venture from restaurateur Mark Ellman is wowing crowds with expansive ocean views and a savory array of popular wood-fired pizzas, fresh salads and comfort foods like burgers. The fresh seafood is sea-soned with global flavors. The beer list fea-tures over 50 brews (10 on tap).

As you dine, scan the water beside the rocky coast – you might just glimpse a green sea turtle.

Thai Chef THAI $$

(Map p84; ☑ 808-667-2814; www.thaichef restaurantmaui.com; 878 Front St, Old Lahaina Center; mains $12-22; ☺11am-2pm Mon-Fri, 5-9pm Mon-Sat; ☑) Hidden in the back of an aging strip mall, this place looks like a dive from the outside, but the food's incredible. Start with the fragrant ginger coconut soup and the fresh summer rolls and then move on to savory curries that explode with flavor. It's BYOB so pick up refreshments from the nearby Foodland.

Vegetarians and vegans are well catered for.

Cool Cat Cafe DINER $$

(Map p84; ☑ 808-667-0908; www.coolcatcafe.com; 658 Front St, Wharf Cinema Center; mains $10-27; ☺10:30am-10:30pm; ☑) It's a hunka-hunka burger love at Cool Cat Cafe, a lively 2nd-floor doo-wop diner where most of the burg-ers, sandwiches and salads are named for 1950s icons, honoring the likes of Marilyn Monroe, Chubby Checker and, of course, Elvis Presley. The burgers get rave reviews. The view from the large open terrace over-looking Banyan Tree Sq isn't bad either.

Kimo's HAWAIIAN $$

(Map p84; ☑ 808-661-4811; www.kimosmaui.com; 845 Front St; lunch mains $14-34; ☺11am-10:30pm; ☑) One of the best oceanfront patios on Front St. A locally beloved standby, Hawai-ian-style Kimo's keeps everyone happy with reliably good food, a superb water view and a family-friendly setting. Try one of the fresh fish dishes and the towering hula pie. At lunch, order the delicious Caesar salad. Mai tais are served in glass totems; there's a tasty happy-hour menu.

There is live music some nights.

★ Frida's Mexican Beach House
MEXICAN $$$

(Map p87; ☑808-661-1287; http://fridasmaui.com; 1287 Front St; mains $20-40; ☺11am-9:30pm) Not your cheap taco joint, Frida's (with plenty of imagery from the namesake Frida Kahlo) has a superb waterfront location, with a large open dining area on a terrace that will have your blood pressure falling minutes after arriving. Steaks and seafood with a Latin flair feature on the upscale menu. Cocktails are creative; yes there are margaritas!

★ Lahaina Grill
HAWAIIAN $$$

(Map p84; ☑808-667-5117; www.lahainagrill. com; 127 Lahainaluna Rd; mains $33-89; ☺from 5:30pm) The windows at the Lahaina Grill frame a simple but captivating tableau: beautiful food being enjoyed in beautiful surrounds. Once inside, expectations are confirmed by the service and the food. The menu uses fresh local ingredients sourced from top local purveyors. The steak and seafood dishes are given innovative twists and presented with artistic style.

A seafood standout is the Maui onion-seared ahi (yellowfin tuna) with vanilla-bean jasmine rice. The Lahaina Grill tops local restaurant polls every year.

★ Pacific'O
ASIAN $$$

(Map p84; ☑808-667-4341; www.pacifico maui.com; 505 Front St; lunch mains $15-18, mains $30-45; ☺11:30am-9:30pm) 🥬 Enjoy Pacific Rim cuisine prepared with contemporary flourishes at Chef James McDonald's chic oceanside restaurant. Bold and innovative seafood and beef dishes are accompanied by the best of Maui's garden bounty. Lunch is a less fancy affair, with island-inspired salads, sandwiches and tacos, but the same up-close ocean view across a small beach.

Ask about tours of the restaurant's own organic **O'o Farm** (www.oofarm.com) in upcountry Maui, which gives true meaning to their boast of farm-to-table.

Gerard's
FRENCH $$$

(Map p84; ☑808-661-8939; www.gerardsmaui. com; 174 Lahainaluna Rd; mains from $39, 8-course prix fixe per person $105; ☺seatings 6-8pm) Where has all the romance gone? To the front porch of Gerard's, where white linens and flickering shadows are an invitation for murmurings of love. Or exclamations of culinary bliss. Chef Gerard Reversade, who infuses fresh Lahaina-caught seafood with

flavors from the French countryside, has earned many plaudits. The extensive wine lists are noteworthy; order an extra bottle and retire upstairs to the **Plantation Inn** (☑808-667-9225, reservations 800-433-6815; www.theplantationinn.com; r/ste from $180/300; P❄🐾🛜🏊).

Mala Ocean Tavern
FUSION $$$

(Map p87; ☑808-667-9394; www.malaocean tavern.com; 1307 Front St; mains brunch $8-15, lunch $15-26, dinner $20-46; ☺11am-9pm Mon-Fri, 9am-9pm Sat & Sun) This waterfront bistro from local restaurateur Mark Ellman fuses Mediterranean and Pacific influences with sophisticated flair. Tapas dishes include comfort foods like burgers. For main meals, the choices are much more sophisticated: anything with fish is a sure pleaser. At sunset, tiki torches on the waterfront lanai (porch, balcony or veranda) add a romantic touch.

Foodland
SUPERMARKET

(Map p84; ☑808-661-0975; www.foodland.com; 878 Front St, Old Lahaina Center; ☺6am-midnight) Has everything you need for self-catering, as well as a good deli. The ahi *poke* (raw tuna) is served fresh, cheap and in numerous varieties at the seafood counter. For discounts, you can use your phone number in place of a customer card.

🍷 Drinking & Nightlife

Front St is the center of the action. Check the entertainment listings in the free *MauiTime Weekly* (www.mauitime.com), published on Thursdays, or the *Lahaina Times* (www.lahainanews.com). Many of Lahaina's waterfront restaurants have live music at dinnertime. Happy hours with live music before 5pm and after 8pm are common.

DON'T MISS

If it's Friday night, suit up for a party in the street. The **Maui Friday Town Parties** (www.mauifridays.com) celebrate local art, food and musicians. On the first Friday of the month the party is held in downtown Wailuku. It moves to Lahaina the second Friday, followed by Makawao and Kihei on the third and fourth Fridays respectively. For exact locations, check the website. Festivities typically start at 6pm.

Local food trucks are a town party highlight, graze your way through myriad treats.

★**Koholā Brewery** BREWERY

(Map p87; ☑ 808-868-3198; www.koholabrewery.com; 910 Honoapiilani Hwy, no 55; ⊗11am-9pm, tours 2-4pm Fri) Bags of barley and corrugated metals give this microbrewery an industrial vibe. But you'll hardly notice the spartan surrounds as you sample the brews that include American pale ale, lager, pilsner, American wheat, porter and many seasonal specials. The beers are some of the best in the islands and bartenders are great at offering samples of the latest creations.

You can also find Koholā beers at Lahaina restaurants including Frida's, Honu Seafood & Pizza, Down the Hatch, Fleetwood's and Kimo's.

★**Down the Hatch** BAR

(Map p84; ☑ 808-661-4900; www.dthmaui.com; 658 Front St, Wharf Cinema Center; ⊗11am-2am) Lahaina's best late-night bar is on the lower level of the mall. All open-air, its fountains are drowned out by the raucous revelry of the mixed crowd of locals and visitors. There's a long happy hour (3pm to 7pm) when you can enjoy the long list of drinks at big discounts. The piña coladas and other tropical treats are excellent.

The bar food features seafood and is served late.

★**Fleetwood's on Front St** BAR

(Map p84; ☑ 808-669-6425; www.fleetwoodsonfrontst.com; 744 Front St; ⊗2-10pm) With its comfy pillows, cushy lounges and ornate accents, this rooftop oasis – owned by Fleetwood Mac drummer Mick Fleetwood – evokes Morocco. But views of the Pacific and the West Maui Mountains keep you firmly rooted in Hawaii. At sunset, a conch-shell blast announces a tiki-lighting ceremony that's followed by a bagpipe serenade – from a kilt-wearing Scot.

Drinks are 50% off during happy hour (2pm to 5pm). Hungry? The top-end dinner menu features complex Med-flavored dishes. If you see the red flag flying, it means Mick is on the island. On many nights there is live music, sometimes featuring Mick: check the website for schedules.

Spanky's Riptide SPORTS BAR

(Map p84; ☑ 808-667-2337; www.spankysmaui.com; 505 Front St; ⊗11am-10pm) Want to catch the big game? Try the lovably rowdy Spanky's Riptide. Follow the whoops and cheers, stroll right in, step around the dog, pick your brew, then look up at the wall of action-packed TV screens. Happy hours are 2pm to 4pm and 7pm to 8pm.

Cheeseburger In Paradise BAR

(Map p84; ☑ 808-661-4855; www.cheeseburgerland.com; 811 Front St; ⊗8am-10pm) Perched above the sea at the corner of Front St and Lahainaluna Rd, this open-air spot is a lively – and iconic – place to watch the sunset. The music (no surprise) is Jimmy Buffett–style, and the setting is pure tropics, from the rattan decor to the frosty piña coladas. Live soft rock from 4:30pm to 10:30pm nightly.

Opened in 1989, this original location spawned an empire. It was recently completely reconstructed.

Pioneer Inn Bar PUB

(Map p84; ☑ 808-661-3636; www.pioneerinn-maui.com; 658 Wharf St; ⊗7am-10pm) Ahoy matey! If Captain Ahab himself strolled through the swinging doors, no one would look up from their grog. With its whaling-era atmosphere and scenic harborfront lanai, the captain would blend right in at this century-old landmark. Although the food is nothing special, the drinks are well-priced (happy hour 3pm to 6pm). Local musicians perform familiar standards outside at night.

Aloha Mixed Plate BAR

(Map p87; ☑ 808-661-3322; www.alohamixedplate.com; 1285 Front St; ⊗8am-10pm; 🖥) Let the sea breeze whip through your hair while you linger over a heady mai tai – come between 2pm and 6pm and they're cheap. After sunset, you can listen to Old Lahaina Luau's music beating next door. The restaurant menu is cheap and good.

MauiGrown Coffee COFFEE
(Map p84; ☑ 808-661-2728; www.mauigrown coffee.com; 277 Lahainaluna Rd; ⏱ 6:30am-5pm Mon-Sat) Your view from the lanai at Maui-Grown's historic bungalow? The famous Pioneer Mill Smokestack (p83) and the cloud-capped West Maui Mountains. There's a fine range of locally grown and roasted coffees on offer.

☆ Entertainment

When it comes to hula and luau (Hawaiian feast), Lahaina offers several options. And if you just want music, check out the bars and lounges during happy hour and later.

★ Old Lahaina Luau LUAU
(Map p87; ☑ 808-667-1998; www.oldlahaina luau.com; 1251 Front St; adult/child $120/79; ⏱ 5:15-8:15pm Oct-Feb, 5:45-8:45pm Mar-May & Sep, 6:15-9:15pm Jun-Aug; 👪) From the warm aloha greeting to the feast and hula dances, everything here is premium (including the drinks). No other luau on Maui comes close to matching this one for its authenticity, presentation and all-around aloha. The feast is good, with typical Hawaiian fare that includes *kalua* pork, ahi *poke, pulehu* (broiled) steak and an array of salads and sides.

It's held on the beach at the north side of town. One caveat: it often sells out a month in advance, so book ahead.

Feast at Lele LUAU
(Map p84; ☑ 808-667-5353; www.feastatlele. com; 505 Front St; adult/child $131/99; ⏱ from 5:30pm Oct-Jan, 6pm Feb-Apr & Sep, 6:30pm May-Aug) 🍴 Food takes center stage at this intimate four-hour Polynesian luau held on the beach. Dance performances in Hawaiian, Maori, Tahitian and Samoan styles are each matched to a food course. With the Hawaiian music, you're served *kalua* pork and *pohole* ferns; with the Maori, duck tenderloin salad and so on for a total of five courses. Premium drinks are included.

'Ulalena DANCE
(Map p84; ☑ 808-856-7900; www.mauitheatre. com; 878 Front St, Old Lahaina Center; adult/child from $70/30; ⏱ 5pm Mon, Tue, Thu & Fri) This Cirque du Soleil–style extravaganza has its home at the 680-seat Maui Theatre. The theme is Hawaiian history and storytelling; the medium is modern dance, with colorful stage sets, acrobatics, no shortage of energy and elaborate costumes.

Burn'n Love LIVE MUSIC
(Map p84; ☑ 808-856-7900; www.burnnlove. com; 878 Front St, Old Lahaina Center; adult/child from $70/free; ⏱ 7pm Mon, Tue, Thu, Fri & Sun) This ode to Elvis celebrates the King's time in the Hawaiian Islands. How much you enjoy it will really depend on your own demographic.

🛍 Shopping

Classy boutiques, tacky souvenir shops and flashy art galleries run thick along Front St, with notable outlets on surrounding streets.

★ Village Galleries ARTS & CRAFTS
(Map p84; ☑ 808-661-4402; www.villagegalleries maui.com; 120 Dickenson St; ⏱ 9am-9pm) Stop here for fine art – Hawaiian-style.

★ Lahaina Arts Society ARTS & CRAFTS
(Map p84; ☑ 808-661-0111; www.lahainaarts.com; 648 Wharf St, Old Lahaina Courthouse; ⏱ 9am-5pm) A nonprofit collective representing more than 90 island artists, it runs two galleries in the Old Lahaina Courthouse (p82). The Banyan Tree Gallery is on the 1st floor, in the former post office. The Old Jail Gallery is in the basement, the entrance to the jail is outside, on the north side of the building.

Many of Maui's best-known artists got their start here, and there are some gems among the collection.

★ Maui Hands ARTS & CRAFTS
(Map p84; ☑ 808-667-9898; www.mauihands. com; 612 Front St; ⏱ 10am-7:30pm Mon-Sat, to 7pm Sun) Excellent selection of island-made crafts from more than 300 local artists, jewelers and craftspeople. One of four locations on the island.

Ole Surfboards SPORTS & OUTDOORS
(Map p87; ☑ 808-661-3459; 277 Wili Ko Pl; ⏱ hours vary) Bob 'Ole' Olson has come far from South Dakota where he was born in 1929. One of the world's foremost surfboard shapers still plies his trade in an obscure warehouse close to the center of Lahaina. Using only hand tools, he designs and shapes boards for some of the world's best surfers. For the right price, he'll outfit you as well.

Peter Lik Gallery PHOTOGRAPHY
(Map p84; ☑ 808-661-6623; www.lik.com/galleries/lahaina.html; 712 Front St; ⏱ 9am-10pm) Vibrant colors, stunning landscapes – nature is king in the stylish lair of Australian

photographer Peter Lik (who has galleries worldwide). The pillars in front of this store are remnants of a bank that was here until the tragic Lahaina 1919 fire.

Lahaina Town Surf Clothing Co CLOTHING
(Map p84; ☑808-283-4100; www.ltownsurf.com; 675 Front St, Wharf Cinema Center; ☺11am-7pm) Lahaina- and Hawaii-themed T-shirts and other clothing are sold from this open-air kiosk in the mall across from the banyan tree. All proceeds go to funding programs that give free surfing lessons to local kids.

Hale Zen Home Decor & More HOMEWARES
(Map p84; ☑808-661-4802; www.halezen.com; 180 Dickenson St; ☺10am-6pm Mon-Sat, to 4pm Sun) This inviting shop embraces stylish island living with candles, lotions and gifts as well as crafted furniture and cute children's clothes.

Lahaina Printsellers ART, MAPS
(Map p84; ☑808-667-5815; www.printsellers.com; 764 Front St; ☺10am-10pm) Hawaii's largest purveyor of antique maps, including fascinating originals dating back to the voyages of Captain Cook. Lahaina Printsellers also sells affordable reproductions. This location shares space with Lahaina Giclee, a gallery selling a wide range of fine quality Hawaiian giclée (zhee-clay) digital prints.

Village Gifts & Fine Arts ARTS & CRAFTS
(Map p84; ☑808-661-5199; www.villagegalleries maui.com; cnr Front & Dickenson Sts; ☺10am-6pm, to 9pm Fri) This one-room shop in the historic **Masters' Reading Room** (Map p84; cnr Front & Dickenson Sts) sells prints, wooden bowls and other crafts. For fine art, visit the shop's sister property, the Village Galleries (p95), which is located in a separate building behind the store, across the parking lot.

Wharf Cinema Center MALL
(Map p84; ☑808-661-8748; www.thewharfcinema center.com; 658 Front St) Lots of shops and restaurants in an open-air mall just across from Banyan Tree Sq.

Lahaina Gateway MALL
(Map p87; www.lahainagateway.com; 305 Keawe St; ☺9:30am-10pm) Just off Hwy 30 is the Lahaina Gateway strip mall. Here you'll find Barnes & Noble bookstore and other chain stores.

Outlets of Maui MALL
(Map p84; ☑808-661-8277; www.theoutletsof maui.com; ☺9:30am-10pm) Factory-store retailers at this open-air outlet mall include all the same chains you'll find at outlet malls everywhere.

Lahaina Cannery Mall MALL
(Map p87; ☑808-661-5304; www.lahainacannery.com; 1221 Honoapi'ilani Hwy; ☺9:30am-9pm Mon-Sat, to 7pm Sun) Lots of shops in one gloomy location.

❶ Information

For urgent but not critical care, try the **Minit-Medical** (☑808-667-6161; www.minit-medical.com; 305 Keawe St, Lahaina Gateway; ☺8am-6pm Mon-Sat, 8am-4pm Sun). Otherwise call ☑911 for transport to the ER in Wailuku.

Post Office (Map p84; 132 Papalaua St, Old Lahaina Center; ☺10am-4pm Mon-Fri) Lahaina's place for mail.

Lahaina Visitor Center (☑808-667-9175; www.visitlahaina.com; 648 Wharf St, Old Lahaina Courthouse; ☺9am-5pm) Located inside the Old Lahaina Courthouse (p82), this is an excellent tourist office. You can get gifts, books, information and a walking tour map ($2).

❶ Getting There & Away

It takes about one hour to drive between Lahaina and the airport in Kahului.

Hawaii Executive Transportation provides van service between the airport and Lahaina, and serves most addresses in town.

A taxi between Lahaina and the airport costs about $80.

The **Maui Bus** (☑808-871-4838; www.maui county.gov/bus; single ride $2, day pass $4) runs the Lahaina Islander route 20 between Kahului bus hub and Lahaina (one hour), stopping at Ma'alaea Harbor, where a connection can be made to Kihei (various stops) via the Kihei Villager. Another route, the Ka'anapali Islander, connects Lahaina and Ka'anapali (30 minutes). Both Islander routes depart from the Wharf Cinema Center hourly from 6:30am to 8:30pm.

The **Expeditions Ferry** to Lana'i uses the **Ferry Dock** (Map p84; off Wharf St) in Lahaina Harbor. The Moloka'i ferry no longer runs.

❶ Getting Around

BUS

In Lahaina, the **Maui Bus** Lahaina Villager route runs hourly along Front St downtown and connects to Lahaina Cannery Mall and Lahaina Gateway. Many of the Ka'anapali resorts operate shuttles for guests, which serve the resort areas and Lahaina.

FERRY

Expeditions Ferry (Map p84; ☑ 808-661-3756; www.go-lanai.com; Lahaina Harbor; adult/child one way $30/20) Worth it just for the ride, this ferry links Lahaina Harbor with Manele Bay Harbor on Lana'i (one hour) several times daily. In winter there's a fair chance of seeing humpback whales; spinner dolphins are a common sight all year, especially on morning sails.

SHUTTLE

Hawaii Executive Transportation (☑ 808-669-2300; www.hawaiiexecutivetransportation. com; 1/2/3/4 passengers $51/59/64/66; ⊙ reservations 7am-11pm) Has van service from Kahului airport; does custom pick-ups and drop-offs.

TAXI

For a taxi in Lahaina, call **Maui Pleasant Taxi** (☑ 808-344-4661; www.mauipleasanttaxi. com) or **West Maui Taxi** (☑ 808-661-1122, 888-661-4545; www.westmauitaxi.com). Expect to pay $14 to $20 one way between Lahaina and Ka'anapali. Uber and Lyft are usually cheaper.

West Maui

Best Places to Dine with a View

➡ Hula Grill & Barefoot Bar (p110)

➡ Gazebo (p114)

➡ Plantation House (p119)

➡ Burger Shack (p119)

➡ Merriman's Kapalua (p119)

Best Beaches

➡ Ka'anapali Beach (p107)

➡ Kapalua Beach (p115)

➡ Oneloa Beach (p115)

➡ DT Fleming Beach Park (p115)

➡ Napili Beach (p114)

Why Go?

For sun-kissed fun, West Maui is the place to be. Whether you want to snorkel beside lava rocks, zipline down the mountains, thwack a golf ball, hike through the jungle or sail beneath the setting sun, the adventures are as varied as the landscape. Ka'anapali is West Maui's splashy center, a look-at-me town luring travelers with world-class golf courses, stylish resorts, oceanfront dining and a dazzling, mile-long crescent of beach.

Further north, Hawaiian history and swanky exclusivity have formed an intriguing, sometimes uneasy, alliance in Kapalua, where luxurious lodgings and a PGA golf course preen near a lush mountain watershed, an ancient burial ground and several gorgeous beaches. To escape this glittery scene, hunker down in Kahana or Napili, lovely seaside communities known for their condos and budget-friendly prices. For off-the-grid excitement, only one adventure will do – a breezy, sometimes hair-raising, drive around the untamed northern coast.

When to Go

The best time to visit is generally whale-watching season – between mid-December and mid-April.

West Maui has great weather all year round. Average temperatures range from the mid-70s to the low-80s Fahrenheit (23–30°C). Rain showers are more likely the further west you go, but they often blow over quickly.

Good deals can be found between mid-April and mid-June and between September and mid-December.

Visit in June for the Kapalua Wine & Food Festival (p118) held over four days at the Ritz-Carlton. It features renowned winemakers and Hawaii's hottest chefs, offering cooking demonstrations and wine tastings.

West Maui Highlights

❶ **Ka'anapali Beach** (p107) Snorkeling beside Pu'u Keka'a (Black Rock) then strutting your stuff resort-style at 'Dig-Me Beach.'

❷ **Papawai Point** (p113) Crying 'Thar she blows!' at this cliffside perch, a primo whale-watching spot come winter.

❸ **Waihe'e Ridge Trail** (p100) Climbing into the clouds on this scenic five-miler with sweeping north coast views.

❹ **Balancing on a board** (p104) Surfing, bodyboarding and stand up paddling: everyone's catching waves.

❺ **Masters of Hawaiian Slack Key Guitar Concert Series** (p114) Enjoying these old-style jams in Napili, cultural celebrations that make everyone feel like 'ohana (extended family).

HIKING IN WEST MAUI

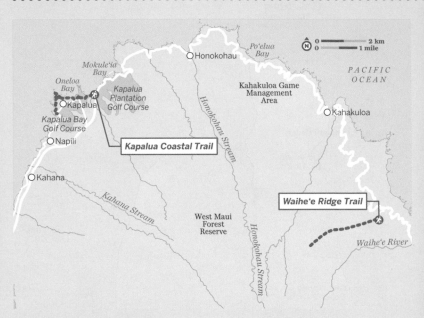

WAIHE'E RIDGE TRAIL

START CAR PARK TO THE WAIHE'E RIDGE TRAIL
END THE PEAK OF LANILILI
LENGTH 5 MILES ROUND-TRIP; ROUGHLY 3 HOURS
DIFFICULTY MODERATE

For jaw-dropping views over the long, lush carpets of Waihe'e Gorge, cascading waterfalls, tropical forests and a bird's eye view of Wailuku and Maui's wild northern coast, it doesn't get much better than the Waihe'e Ridge Trail.

To get to the trailhead, take the one-lane paved road that starts on the inland side of the Kahekili Hwy just south of the 7-mile marker. You'll find parking before the trailhead (currently open 7am to 7pm). Begin your walk by climbing a sheer concrete ramp, and pass blue water tanks on the right.

Suitable for solo walkers, fit seniors and active kids, the initial path is a bit steep and can get boggy – Waihe'e means 'slippery

water' in Hawaiian, but don't let this dishearten you. It's a fairly steady climb to the 2563ft summit of Lanilili Peak, but it's not a strenuous one. Be prepared to walk back down the mountain afterwards. There are intervals of flat terrain throughout the trail. It's best to bring good walking shoes to tackle mud, stones and exposed tree roots. Set off before 8am to beat the heat and the clouds, which can obscure the view later in the morning. Perhaps grab one of the walking sticks/tree branches, often left behind by hikers, at the gate leading onto the trail, if you are in need of some extra support.

Starting at an elevation of 1000ft, it's already possible to spy the vast blue ocean. The trail, which crosses reserve land, climbs a ridge, passing from mainly shaded humid woodland areas of ancient undergrowth to open pastures nearer the summit. Guava trees and groves of eucalyptus are prominent, and the aroma of fallen fruit may accompany you after a rainstorm. From the 0.75-mile post, panoramic views open up, with a scene

Whether you're after an easy coastal stroll or a trek through tropical flora, West Maui has a trail for you.

that sweeps clear down to the ocean along the Waihe'e Gorge and deep into pleated valleys.

Continuing on, you'll enter ohia forest; look out for butterflies and native birds like the bright crimson *'apapane*. A clearing offers a bench in prime view of the cascading Makamaka'ole Falls in the distance. On the ridge, views are similar to those you'd see from a helicopter, and you'll probably see a handful of them dart into the adjacent valley like gnats on a mission.

There are several natural pausing spots along the trail to stop and soak up the scenery and remarkable stillness. Birdsong, chirping insects, a rushing stream, muffled bits of hiker conversation below – these are the only interruptions. The trail ends with a series of sharp bends and a steep climb to a picnic table on the 2563ft **peak of Lanilili**. You'll be rewarded with a staggering 360-degree view, and with clear skies it's possible to see Haleakalā volcano in the distance. If it's foggy, wait about 10 minutes or so; it may blow off.

The Division of Forestry and Wildlife claims 50 to 100 people hike the trail daily, so expect company. See www.hawaiitrails.org for more details.

KAPALUA COASTAL TRAIL
START DT FLEMING BEACH PARK
END KAPALUA BEACH CAR PARK
LENGTH 1.76 MILES; 40 MINUTES TO ONE HOUR
DIFFICULTY EASY

This spectacular, easy **hike** (www.kapalua.com/activities/hiking-trails; ☉ sunrise-sunset) is one you can do solo. Wear a good pair of walking shoes, as some coastal sections cross sharp rocks. The path crosses pristine resorts, beautiful beaches and an ancient burial ground and runs adjacent to the jagged **Makaluapuna Point** (p115). The western end of the trail, next to **DT Fleming Beach Park** (p115), has far more parking spaces.

From here, a green-and-white wooden church and the entrance to the **Mahana Ridge Trail** marks the walk's beginning. Don't take the Mahana dirt path up; instead, follow the road east past the **Ritz Carlton's Burger Shack** (p119) towards the resort's immaculate, shell-lined lawns, cultivated garden beds and tennis courts. Coastal winds pick up here, cooling walkers as they stroll. At the top of the hill there's an arresting view of the ocean and, in the winter, a chance to spot whales. A hotel pool to the left jars with the **Honokahua burial site** (p116) to the right. This graveyard – dating back to AD 610, and marked with a single plaque – is off-limits to the general public. An estimated 2000 Hawaiians have been laid to rest here and it's believed that their ancestral spirits watch over these lands.

A slight detour onto the road leads to **Oneloa Beach** (p115); take the alley towards the bluest of sea views, where the trail turns into a raised boardwalk adjacent the beach. It is flanked with tropical, pink-petaled *pohuehue* and *'akia* plants, with orange fruits and tiny yellow flowers. Surfers and kiteboarders ride waves out to sea and holiday-makers occupy luxury condos to the left. Stairs down to the beach offer the chance to dip your toes in the sea. At the end of the beach, the boardwalk turns into a rocky path onto the cliffside. Follow the bridge over the channel at the eastern side of **Hawea Point** or explore the impressive razor-sharp lava formations of the point, which jut out to sea and upwards to three feet. Be careful not get too close to the edge or disturb the signposted nesting areas of seabirds.

Rejoining the main path, follow arrows sprayed onto the paved pathway, through plush condos and the **Montage Kapalua Bay** (p117) resort on **Kapalua Beach** (p115). This calm crescent-shaped bay is excellent for snorkeling; at the west side of the beach it's possible to spot the former Hawaii State Fish *humuhumunukunukuapua'a* (Hawaiian triggerfish), as well as goat fish, porcupine fish, parrotfish and more (hire equipment at the water-sports shack on Kapalua Beach). The path continues under lime trees, and ends with a foot tunnel to restrooms and a car park with limited spaces.

CARL SHANEFF/GETTY IMAGES ©

1. Waiehu Municipal Golf Course (p123)
This county-run golf course offers an affordable and easily walkable 18 holes, plus a 24-tee driving range.

2. Ka'anapali Beach (p107)
Surfers, bodyboarders, parasailers, snorkelers and sailing enthusiasts all enjoy this vibrant spot.

3. Honolua Bay (p118)
Honolua Bay has thriving reefs and abundant coral along its rocky edges.

4. Olowalu Petroglyphs (p104)
These carved figures are 200 to 300 years old.

WEST MAUI

Lahaina to Ma'alaea

The drive between Lahaina and Ma'alaea is bursting with staggering views of the wild West Maui mountains on one side and the shimmering ocean on the other. In winter this section of Honoapi'ilani Hwy is like a ready-made whale-watching safari. Stay alert, though! Too many distracted drivers have their heads facing the shore, trying to spot humpback whales cruising just off land. Stand up paddleboarders and surfers are also a common sight.

Puamana Beach Park & Launiupoko Beach Park

Beaches

Launiupoko Beach Park   BEACH
(🖼) The park is an ideal spot for families; *na keiki* (children) have a blast wading in the large rock-enclosed shoreline pool and good picnic facilities invite you to linger. Launiupoko is at the traffic lights at the 18-mile marker on Honoapi'ilani Hwy. Beginner and intermediate surfers head to this beach park, a popular wave 3 miles south of Lahaina.

The southern side of the beach has small waves ideal for beginner surfers, while the northern side ratchets it up a notch for those who have honed their skills. You're also likely to see stand up paddle surfers (SUP) weaving through Launiupoko's surf.

Puamana Beach Park   BEACH
This shady beach park, 1.5 miles south of Lahaina, is rocky but sometimes has good conditions for beginner surfers – otherwise it's mostly a quick stop for a seaside view, particularly at sunset. Not a great spot for lying out.

🏃 Activities

Middles   SURFING
Situated at Launiupoko Beach Park, this beautiful slow wave breaks left and right and is ideal for beginners and long-boarders. As with most Maui breaks, it's better in the morning before the wind picks up. It's a mellow reef break, but beginners should wear booties as rocks can be sharp underfoot. It gets very busy, especially at weekends.

Guardrails   SURFING
Peeling straight off Honoapi'ilani Hwy, between the 18- and 19-mile markers, the welcoming beginner/intermediate reef break has long right and left rides and is uncrowded. Be aware, currents here can be stronger than other spots and it's tricky getting in and out of the water, as you have to negotiate the rocks as the waves crash in.

Olowalu

The West Maui Mountains form a scenic backdrop, giving Olowalu its name, which means 'many hills'.

Beaches

Olowalu Beach   BEACH
(Honoapi'ilani Hwy, at 14-mile marker) The coral reef of Olowalu Beach, which is popular with snorkelers, is shallow and silty, and the 'sharks may be present' signs lining the beach mean what they say. There was a reported minor shark attach near Olowalu in March 2016.

⊙ Sights & Activities

Olowalu Petroglyphs   ARCHAEOLOGICAL SITE
A short walk behind the general store leads to 200–300-year-old petroglyphs (ancient Hawaiian stone carvings). Park just beyond the water tower at the back of Olowalu's general store and it's a 440yd walk up a dirt road; keep the cinder cone straight ahead of you as you follow the road. Bear left at the Olowalu Cultural Reserve sign.

As with most of Maui's petroglyphs, these figures are carved into the vertical sides of cliffs (rather than on horizontal lava as they are on Hawai'i, the Big Island). Most of the Olowalu figures have been damaged, but you can still make out some of them. Don't climb the rocks for a better look, however, and do watch for falling rocks. There's a picnic table and interpretive signage at the site.

If you have mobility issues it's OK to drive to the site, instead of walking, but be careful on the bumpy dirt road and be respectful of neighboring landowners.

✕ Eating

⭐**Leoda's Kitchen & Pie Shop**   BAKERY $
(☎808-662-3600; www.leodas.com; 820 Olowalu Village Rd, on Honoapi'ilani Hwy; breakfast $6-19, lunch & dinner $6-16, dessert pies $4-9; ⊙7am-8pm; 🛜) Wear your stretchy pants to Leoda's.

West Maui

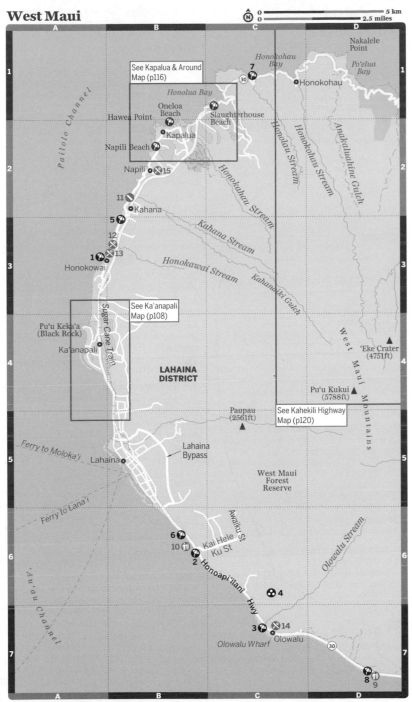

0 ____ 5 km
0 ____ 2.5 miles

Nakalele Point

Po'elua Bay

Honokohau Bay

See Kapalua & Around Map (p116)

7

30

Honokohau

Honolua Bay

Oneloa Beach

Slaughterhouse Beach

Hawea Point

Kapalua

Honolua Stream

Honokohau Stream

Anakaluahine Gulch

Napili Beach

Napili

15

11

Kahana

5

12

13

1

Honokowai

Kahana Stream

Honokawai Stream

Kahanaiki Gulch

West Maui Mountains

See Ka'anapali Map (p108)

Sugar Cane Train

Pu'u Keka'a (Black Rock)

Ka'anapali

LAHAINA DISTRICT

'Eke Crater (4751ft)

Pu'u Kukui (5788ft)

See Kahekili Highway Map (p120)

Paupau (2561ft)

Ferry to Moloka'i

Lahaina

Lahaina Bypass

West Maui Forest Reserve

Ferry to Lana'i

'Au'au Channel

Patiolo Channel

Olowalu Stream

6

10

2

Awaiku St

Kai Hele Ku St

Honoapi'ilani Hwy

4

3

14

Olowalu

Olowalu Wharf

30

8

9

West Maui

Diet-busters at this simple-but-stylish restaurant include savory pot pies, topping-laden burgers and rich sandwiches such as the 'pork, pork...mmm pork.' Save room for one of the mini dessert pies – gorgeous creations vying for attention at the front counter. It's also a great breakfast spot on your way into or out of Lahaina.

Located at the 15-mile marker on the Honoapi'ilani Hwy.

Ukumehame Beach Park & Around

Heading south from Lahaina, look for Ukumehame Beach Park at the 12-mile marker on Honoapiilani Hwy.

The pull-off for the western end of the Lahaina Pali Trail (p126) is just south of the 11-mile marker, on the inland side of the road.

 Beaches

Ukumehame Beach Park   BEACH
(Honoapi'ilani Hwy, at 12-mile marker) Home to the **Thousand Peaks** surf spot, toward Ukumehame's western end, this uncrowded break is a good option for long-boarders and beginner

surfers wanting to get away from the crowds of nearby beaches like Launiupoko (p104). The thin stretch of sand is popular for picnicking and fishing, but there are prettier beach spots. Dive and snorkel boats hover on the horizon, here to explore the Coral Gardens underwater. (Otherwise the gardens are quite a swim from the shore, and the currents can be strong.)

 Activities

Grandma's   SURFING
One of the few surf breaks you can camp right next to is at Pāpalaua Wayside Park between mile markers 11 and 12 on Honoapi'ilani Hwy. Waves on this reef break are not as well formed as Thousand Peaks next door, but are gentle, often long rides, good for beginners, and uncrowded.

Lahaina to Ka'anapali

The drive between Lahaina and Ka'anapali offers great ocean views out to the island of Lana'i, plus a couple of roadside beach parks including Hanaka'o'o Beach Park and Wahikuli Wayside Park, both good spots to get away from the crowds of Ka'anapali and Lahaina.

 Beaches

Wahikuli Wayside Park   BEACH
(Honoapi'ilani Hwy) Two miles north of Lahaina, Wahikuli Wayside Park occupies a narrow strip of beach, with three separate parking areas, flanked by the busy highway. Although the beach is mostly backed by a black-rock retaining wall, there's a small sandy area north of the central parking area. Swimming conditions are usually fine and, when the water's calm, you can snorkel near the lava outcrops at the park's southern end. The park has showers and restrooms.

Hanaka'o'o Beach Park   BEACH
The long, sandy Hanaka'o'o Beach Park, extending south from **Hyatt Regency Maui Resort & Spa** (200 Nohea Kai Dr), has a sandy bottom and water conditions that are usually safe for swimming. However, southerly swells, which sometimes develop in summer, can create powerful waves and shorebreaks, while the occasional *kona* (leeward) storm can kick up rough water conditions in winter. Snorkelers head to the second clump of rocks on the southern side of the park, but it really doesn't compare with sites further north.

Hanaka'o'o Beach is also called 'Canoe Beach,' as West Maui outrigger-canoe clubs practice here in the late afternoon.

The park has full facilities and is one of only two beaches on the entire West Maui coast that has a lifeguard. A small immigrant cemetery dating from the 1850s marks the entrance.

Ka'anapali

Honeymoons, anniversaries, girlfriend getaways – Ka'anapali is a place to celebrate. Maui's flashiest resort destination welcomes guests with 3 miles of sandy beach, a dozen oceanfront hotels, two 18-hole golf courses and an ocean full of water activities. You can sit at a beachfront bar with a tropical drink, soak up the gorgeous views of Lana'i and Moloka'i across the channel and listen to guitarists strum their wiki-wacky-woo.

🏖 Beaches

★ Ka'anapali Beach   BEACH
Home to West Maui's liveliest beach scene, this gorgeous stretch of sand unfurls alongside Ka'anapali's resort hotels, linking the Hyatt Regency Maui with the Sheraton Maui (p112) 1 mile north. Dubbed 'Dig-Me Beach' for all the preening, it's a vibrant spot. Surfers, bodyboarders and parasailers rip across the water, snorkelers admire the sea life, and sailboats pull up on shore. There are no lifeguards, so check with the hotel beach huts before jumping in: water conditions vary with the season and currents are sometimes strong.

For the best snorkeling, try the underwater sights off Pu'u Keka'a. This lava promontory protects the beach in front of the Sheraton Maui. Novices stick to the sheltered southern side of the landmark rock – where there's still a lot to see – but the shallow coral here has been stomped to death. If you're a confident swimmer, the less-frequented horseshoe cove cut into the tip of the rock is the real prize, teeming with tropical fish, colorful coral and sea turtles. There's often a current to contend with off the point, which can make getting to the cove a bit tricky, but when it's calm you can swim right in. Pu'u Keka'a is also a popular shore-dive spot.

Kahekili Beach Park   BEACH
This idyllic golden-sand beach at Ka'anapali's less-frequented northern end is a good place to lose the look-at-me crowds strutting their

stuff further south. The swimming's better, the snorkeling's good and the park has everything you'll need for a day at the beach – showers, restrooms, a covered picnic pavilion and barbecue grills. Access is easy and there's ample free parking.

👁 Sights

Whalers Village Museum   MUSEUM
(Whale Center Hawaii; ☑ 808-661-5992; www.whalersvillage.com/museum.htm; 2435 Ka'anapali Pkwy, Whalers Village; adult/child 6-18yr $3/1; ⊙10am-4pm; 🚶) Lahaina was a popular restocking stop for whaling ships traveling between Japan, the Arctic and New England during the Golden Age of whaling (1825–60). This fascinating museum was going through a refurbishment at the time of writing, but a free exhibition is currently running at Whalers Village (p112) until it reopens. Until then, fascinating display cabinets sit around the shopping complex detailing whaling history and facts about the anatomy of these large mammals.

At the entrance of Whalers Village, look up: there's a life-size sperm-whale skeleton suspended from the ceiling.

Pu'u Keka'a   DIVE SITE
(Black Rock) You'll find the best underwater sights off Pu'u Keka'a, also known as Black Rock, the lava promontory that protects the beach in front of the Sheraton. First-time snorkelers will be happy with the coral and fish at the protected southern side of Pu'u Keka'a, but the highlight is the horseshoe cove cut into the tip of the rock, where

---

SPIRIT'S LEAP
••••••••••••••••••••••••••••••••••••••

According to traditional Hawaiian beliefs, **Pu'u Keka'a** (Black Rock), the westernmost point of Maui, is a place where the spirits of the dead leap into the unknown to be carried to their ancestral homeland. The rock is said to have been created during a scuffle between the demigod Maui and a commoner who questioned Maui's superiority. Maui chased the man to this point, froze his body into stone then cast his soul out to sea. Today, daring teens wait their turn to leap off the rock, to a resounding splash into the cove below.

Ka'anapali

N
0 ———— 500 m
0 ———— 0.25 miles

there's more pristine coral, abundant tropical fish and the occasional turtle.

There's often a current to contend with off the point, which can make getting to the cove a little risky, but when it's calm you can swim right around into the horseshoe. Pu'u Keka'a is also a popular shore-dive spot. If you want to see what the horseshoe cove looks like, take the short footpath to the top of the rock, where you can peer right down into it.

🏃 Activities

Tour of the Stars STARGAZING
(☑ 808-667-4727; www.maui.hyatt.com; 200 Nohea Kai Dr, Hyatt Regency Maui Resort & Spa; guest adult/child 6-12yr $25/15, nonguest $30/20; ⊙ viewing 8pm & 9pm) Enjoy stellar stargazing in a secret observatory atop the Hyatt resort. These 50-minute viewings are limited to 14 people, use a 14in-diameter telescope and are held on clear nights. Romantic types should opt for the couples-only viewing at 10pm Friday and Saturday, which rolls out champagne and chocolate-covered strawberries (guest/nonguest $40/45)

Skyline Eco-Adventures ZIPLINING
(☑ 808-878-8400; www.zipline.com; 2580 Keka'a Dr, Fairway Shops; 3.5hr outing $156; ⊙ hourly departures 7am-2pm) 🍃 Zoom through the lush West Maui mountains among tree canopies, at speeds of around 20mph on an adrenaline-fueled zipline adventure. The Ka'anapali course takes you 2 miles up the wooded cliffsides to platforms and drops of up to

Ka'anapali

150ft. You can free-glide along eight separate lines (3½ hours) or 11 lines (four hours) above waterfalls, stream beds and valleys.

If it's drizzly and windy? Hold on tight and no cannonballs! You can also drop from a line into a mountain pool on the new Zip & Dip tours (book in advance). Skyline is 100% carbon neutral and donates 1% of sales to eco-friendly causes as a member of 1% for the Planet.

Teralani Sailing BOATING
(☑ 808-661-7245; www.teralani.net; outings adult/child 3-12yr from $71/50; ☺ check-in 3:30pm winter, 4pm summer; ⚐) This friendly outfit offers a variety of sails on two custom-built catamarans that depart from the beach beside Whalers Village (p112). The easygoing sunset sail offers an inspiring introduction to the gorgeous West Maui coast. Snorkel sails and whale-watching outings are additional options but, no matter which you choose, you'll find an amiable crew, refreshing cocktails and decent food.

Note the 24-hour cancellation policy.

Ka'anapali Dive Company DIVING
(☑ 808-661-2179; www.goscubamaui.com; Westin Maui Resort & Spa; 1-tank dive $79; ☺ reservations 7am-5pm) Want to learn to scuba dive? These are the people you want to see. The introductory two-tank dive ($110) for novices, with equipment, starts with instruction in a pool and moves on to a guided dive from the beach. It also offers one-tank beach dives for certified divers. No separate rentals. Walk up or call to make a reservation.

Trilogy Ocean Sports WATER SPORTS
(☑ 808-661-7789; www.sailtrilogy.com; Ka'anapali Beach; 5hr tour adult/child $119/$59.50; ☺ 6.30am-5pm) Trilogy runs snorkel trips from Ka'anapali Beach to nearby sites, including Honolua, located just north of Kapalua. Here marine life, including tropical fish and turtles, can be seen underwater and dolphins can occasionally be spied from the boat. All equipment is provided, plus cinnamon rolls and teriyaki BBQ chicken for lunch. And, the bar opens on the return sail to shore.

Ka'anapali Golf Courses GOLF
(☑ 808-661-3691; www.kaanapaligolfcourses.com; 2290 Ka'anapali Pkwy; greens fee nonguests $205-255; ☺ hours vary seasonally, from 6:30am) Get away from the buzzing beach for a golf session at Ka'anapali's two courses. Advanced golfers prefer the Royal Ka'anapali Golf Course – the place to practice your precise putting. Meanwhile, Ka'anapali Kai Golf Course is shorter and has wonderful views of islands Lana'i and Moloka'i. Staying at Ka'anapali Resort? The guest rate will save you about $80.

👉 **Tours**

Ka'anapali Surf Club WATER SPORTS
(☑ 808-662-8794; www.kaanapalisurfclub.com; next to Marriott on Ka'anapali Beach Walk; surfboard hire from $25, group surfing classes from $75, kayak tours per person from $99; ☺ 7am-5pm) Pop by the desk next to Marriott to rent a surfboard or SUP, or join the early-morning kayak tour (7:30am check in), taking groups out to Black Rock at the north of the beach, where you can jump out of the boat to snorkel (equipment provided). It's teeming with marine life here – including parrotfish, turtles and snapper.

Hula Girl SAILING, SNORKELING
(☑ 808-665-0344; www.sailingmaui.com; snorkeling tour adult/child 2-12yr $100/85; ☺ reservations 7am-9pm) You'll sail in style from Ka'anapali to Honolua Bay, one of Maui's top snorkeling spots, on the 65ft *Hula Girl* catamaran. Divers are welcome, too. Food and cocktails are not included in trip rates, but the prices are reasonable and choices may be more impressive than those you'll find on all-inclusive trips. Honolua Bay trips are five hours (departures 9:30am and 2.30pm).

See website for additional tours, all departing from the beach in front of Leilani's (p110) at Whalers Village.

🍴 **Courses**

Royal Lahaina Tennis Ranch TENNIS
(☑ 808-667-5200; www.royallahaina.com/activities.cfm; 2780 Keka'a Dr; per half-day per person $10; ☺ pro shop 8am-noon daily, 2-6pm Mon-Fri, 2-5pm Sat-Sun) Previously named the Facility of the Year by the United States Tennis Association, this is the largest tennis complex in West Maui, with four courts lit for night play. Racket hire is $2.50 per visit. Private lessons and group clinics are available. Courts with floodlights are open until 9pm; book ahead if you'd like to use these.

🎊 **Festivals & Events**

Hula O Nā Keiki DANCE
(www.kbhmaui.com; 2525 Ka'anapali Pkwy; ☺ Nov) Children take center stage at this hula-dance competition in early to mid-November,

which features some of the best *keiki* dancers in Hawaii. It's held at the Ka'anapali Beach Hotel (p112).

Eating

Joey's Kitchen
HAWAIIAN **$**

(📞 808-868-4474; Whalers Village, 2435 Ka'anapali Pkwy; mains from $12; ⏱ 7.30am-9pm; 🍴) Chef Joey Macadangdang has lived on Maui for more than 20 years and fuses Hawaiian-island flavors with Filipino dishes at this no-frills canteen-style eatery: expect breakfast, lunch and dinner on paper plates. What it lacks in ambience Joey's makes up for in flavor – the seafood is freshly caught and prepared as ahi *poke* bowls with rice, mahimahi tacos, or coconut shrimp with fries.

Huli-huli (rotisserie-grilled) chicken and beef short ribs are also on the menu. Ingredients are locally sourced and the marinades are homemade.

⭐ Hula Grill & Barefoot Bar
HAWAIIAN **$$$**

(📞 808-667-6636; www.hulagrillkaanapali.com; 2435 Ka'anapali Pkwy, Whalers Village; bar lunch $14-20, dining-room mains $29-44; ⏱ bar 10:45am-10pm, dining room 4:45-9:30pm) Coconut-frond umbrellas, sand beneath your sandals, guy strumming guitar. The Barefoot Bar is the best spot on the beach walk to sip mai tais and nibble *pupu* (ceviche, sashimi and coconut calamari snacks). There are two menus, for bar and dining room. The bar menu is cheaper but it's not a romantic experience; instead you watch the chefs at work.

Japengo
SUSHI, STEAKS **$$$**

(📞 808-667-4909; www.maui.hyatt.com; 200 Nohea Kai Dr, Hyatt Regency Maui Resort & Spa; sushi $8-24, mains $24-54; ⏱ 5-10pm) Got the sun-kissed tan and the windswept hair? Japengo's bar-restaurant is the place to show off your Ka'anapali glow. At the tiki-lit patio bar, enjoy an artist's array of tropical cocktails before tucking into sushi as the sun goes down. Roasted meat and seafood dishes, like the grilled ahi (yellowfin tuna) with Hamakua mushrooms and wasabi butter, have Pacific Rim flair.

Roy's Ka'anapali
HAWAIIAN **$$$**

(📞 808-669-6999; www.royshawaii.com; 2290 Ka'anapali Pkwy, Ka'anapali Resort; dinner mains $32-49; ⏱ lunch 11am-2pm, bar pupus 2-5pm, dinner from 5pm) The Maui outpost of Chef Roy Yamaguchi's upscale dining empire sits inside the golf-course clubhouse at the Ka'anapali resort (p109). At this spot, big-windowed views of the greens are a pleasant backdrop for the exquisitely prepared island and regional fare. Main meals include the sashimi-like blackened ahi with Chinese mustard, and Roy's meatloaf with Maui cattle beef-onion rings and mushroom gravy.

Drinking & Nightlife

Bars in Whalers Village (p112) and at many Ka'anapali resorts offer live music in the evening. It's typically Jimmy Buffett–style guitar tunes, occasionally spiced up with some ukulele strumming. Luau and hula shows are also popular. Check www.mauitime.com for performers and schedules.

Hula Grill & Barefoot Bar
BAR

(📞 808-667-6636; www.hulagrillkaanapali.com; Whalers Village, 2435 Ka'anapali Pkwy; ⏱ bar 10:45am-10pm, grill 4:45pm-9pm) This is your Maui postcard: coconut-frond umbrellas, sunset mai tais, sand beneath your sandals and the lullaby sounds of Hawaiian slack key guitar.

Leilani's
LIVE MUSIC

(📞 808-661-4495; www.leilanis.com; 2435 Ka'anapali Pkwy, Whalers Village; ⏱ 11am-10.30pm) This open-air bar and restaurant beside the beach is a pleasant place to linger over a cool drink while catching a few rays. It also has a good grill and *pupu* menu. Live music Wednesday through Sunday from 3pm to 5pm.

Sangrita Grill & Cantina
BAR

(📞 808-662-6000; www.sangritagrill.com; 2580 Keka'a Dr, Fairways Shops; mains $14-27, cocktails $9-12; ⏱ 11am-9.30pm) The chicken enchiladas, like the parking lot view, are somewhat uninspiring at this Mexican restaurant in the Fairways Shops. But the cocktails? Now we're having some fun. The Ruby Red martini includes Maui's Organic Ocean Vodka and the Lilikoi margarita blends tequila with passion fruit. The lengthy tequila menu and the sultry interior is also worth a look.

☆ Entertainment

Drums of the Pacific
LUAU

(📞 808-667-4727; www.maui.hyatt.com; 200 Nohea Kai Dr, Hyatt Regency Maui Resort & Spa; adult/child 6-12yr from $99/70; ⏱ from 5pm Oct-Mar, from 5:30pm Apr-Sep; 🍴) Ka'anapali's best luau includes an *imu* ceremony (unearthing of a roasted pig from an underground oven),

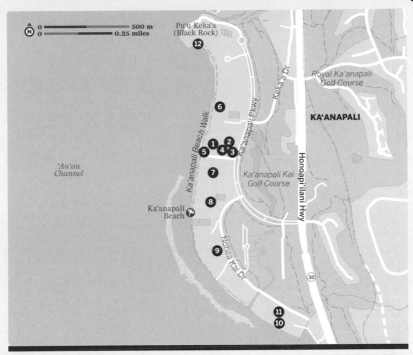

🏃 Walking Tour
Ka'anapali Beach Walk

START HULA GRILL & BAREFOOT BAR
END PU'U KEKA'A (BLACK ROCK)
LENGTH 1 MILE; 40+ MINUTES

For people-watching or a romantic stroll, walk between Maui's biggest, fanciest strip of resorts. The paved pathway, sandwiched between the flash hotels, tiki bars and white sand, is always busy with holiday-makers promenading under the fronds, snapping pictures of the pristine 3-mile beach, and catching snippets of early evening ukulele or guitar entertainment from outdoor restaurants like **①Hula Grill & Barefoot Bar** (p110).

Take a stroll into the adjacent **②Whalers Village** (p112) for exhibitions on the area's whaling past and the mammals in these waters. Pick up some art or apparel at boutiques **③Martin & MacArthur** (p112) or **④Sand People**. Back on the promenade, sailboats and the outline of Lana'i and Moloka'i can be seen on the horizon. Tour operators **⑤Teralani Sailing** (p109) and **⑥Trilogy Ocean Sports** (p109) operate off the beach. Adjacent resorts,

⑦Westin Maui Resort & Spa, **⑧Kaanapali Alii** and **⑨Marriott's Maui Ocean Club**, are buzzing with activity, with people making use of cabanas and hammocks, dazzling garden statuary and fairy-tale landscaping.

Vendors are dotted along the route, selling beachwear and tickets to the nightly **⑩Drums of the Pacific** (p110) luau, situated at the end of the walk. Detour into the **⑪Hyatt Regency Maui Resort & Spa** (p106) for its swan and flamingo ponds and black African penguins. South of the Hyatt, a 17ft-high bronze sculpture, named *The Acrobats*, makes a dramatic silhouette at sunset.

Make **⑫Pu'u Keka'a (Black Rock)** (p107) your final stop. Sheraton Maui hosts a torch-lit cliff-diving ritual every day at sunset for King Kahekili, the last chief of Maui, who once demonstrated his strength by cliff diving here. The cliffside water is a popular place to snorkel. Beach-access parking can be found at Whalers Village (p112; $3 per half-hour, free when validated at certain shops).

an open bar, a Hawaiian-style buffet and a South Pacific dance-and-music show.

Ka'anapali Beach Hotel   HULA
(☑ 808-661-0011; www.kbhmaui.com; 2525 Ka'anapali Pkwy; ☺ 6-9pm Tue-Sun; 👪) Maui's most Hawaiian hotel cheerfully entertains with a free hula show and Hawaiian music. Enjoy mai tais and brews at the adjacent Tiki Bar (10am to 10pm), with music and dancing nightly in the Tiki Courtyard.

Sheraton Maui   LIVE PERFORMANCE
(☑ 808-661-0031;www.sheraton-maui.com; 2605 Ka'anapali Pkwy; ☺ sunset) Everybody swings by to watch the Sheraton-organized torch-lighting and cliff-diving ceremony from Pu'u Keka'a (p107) that takes place at sunset. Afterwards, there's live music at the Sheraton's Cliff Dive Grill.

Whalers Village   HULA, DANCE
(☑ 808-661-4567; www.whalersvillage.com; 2435 Ka'anapali Pkwy; ☺ hula shows 7-8pm Sat, hula lessons 3-4pm Thu; 👶) Ka'anapali's shopping center hosts Polynesian and Tahitian dance and hula performances. Check out the website for a monthly calendar of events and classes.

🛍 Shopping

You'll find more than 60 shops and restaurants at **Whalers Village** (☑ 808-661-4567; www.whalersvillage.com; 2435 Ka'anapali Pkwy; ☺ 9:30am-10pm) shopping center, from surf brands and local Hawaii-inspired fashion and decor, to rare local arts and crafts at **Martin & MacArthur** (☑ 808-667-7422; www.martinandmacarthur.com; Whalers Village, 2435 Ka'anapali Pkwy; ☺ 9:30am-10pm). Check out **Malibu Shirts** (☑ 808-667-2280; www.malibushirts.com; Whalers Village, 2435 Ka'anapali Pkwy; ☺ 9am-10pm) for its retro styles and its displays spotlighting surfing history.

ℹ Getting There & Away

Popular Ka'anapali is one of the easiest areas to get to on Maui. It takes roughly 50 minutes by road (Hwy 380 and Hwy 30) from Kahului Airport. It's also easy to get from Ka'anapali to the nearby towns of Lahaina (10 minutes away heading south on Hwy 30) and Kapalua (15 minutes' drive heading north on Hwy 30).

ℹ Getting Around

BUS

Maui Bus (☑ 808-871-4838; www.mauicounty.gov; bus stop at entrance to Whalers Village; per trip $2; ☺ most routes 6:30am-8pm) currently connects Whalers Village shopping center in Ka'anapali with the Wharf Cinema Center (p96) in Lahaina, hourly on the Ka'anapali Islander from 6am to 9pm and half-hourly between 2pm and 6pm. The Napili Islander runs north up the coast to Kahana (12 minutes) and Napili (29 minutes) from 6am to 8pm. Single journeys cost $2.

The free **Ka'anapali Trolley** loops between the Ka'anapali hotels, Whalers Village and the golf courses every 20 to 30 minutes between 10am and 8pm (with lunch and dinner breaks for the driver). The trolley schedule is posted at the Whalers Village stop.

CAR & MOTORCYCLE

For Harley-Davidson motorcycle rentals, try **Eagle Rider** (☑ 808-667-7000; www.eaglerider.com; 30 Halawai Dr A-3; motorcyle per day incl helmet from $139; ☺ 9am-5pm), located just north of Ka'anapali off the Honoapi'ilani Hwy. The company shares space with **Aloha Motorsports** (☑ 808-667-7000; http://alohamotorsports.com; 30 Halawai Dr; ☺ 9am-5pm), which rents scooters.

TAXI

Cabs are often found outside Ka'anapali's resorts and Whalers Village on Ka'anapali Pkwy. Alternatively you can book one with **Ka'anapali Taxi** (☑ 808-665-1777; www.kaanapalitaxi-maui.com).

Honokowai

This is the best place in West Maui to spot passing whales right from your room lanai (balcony) over the winter months. The main road, which bypasses the condos, is Honoapi'ilani Hwy (Hwy 30). The parallel shoreline road is Lower Honoapi'ilani Rd, which leads into Honokowai and continues north into Kahana and Napili.

◉ Sights & Activities

Honokowai Beach Park   BEACH
(👪) The real thrills here are on land, not in the water. This family-friendly park in the center of Honokowai has playground facilities and makes a nice spot for a picnic. But forget swimming. The water is shallow and the beach is lined with a submerged rock shelf. Water conditions improve at the southern side of town, and you could continue walking along the shore down to lovely Kahekili Beach Park (p107) at the northern end of Ka'anapali.

WHALE-WATCHING

During the winter humpback whales occasionally breach as close as 100yd from the coast of West Maui: 40 tons of leviathan suddenly exploding straight up through the water can be a real showstopper!

Beach parks and pull-offs along the Honoapiilani Hwy offer great vantage points for watching the action. The very best spot is Papawai Point, a cliffside perch jutting into the western edge of Ma'alaea Bay, and a favored humpback nursing ground (not to mention a great place to catch a sunset). The **Pacific Whale Foundation** (☑ 800-942-5311; www.pacificwhale.org; 300 Ma'alaea Rd, Ma'alaea Harbor; ⏰ 6am-9pm) posts volunteers at the parking lot to share their knowledge and point out the whales (8am to 2pm mid-December to mid-April).

Papawai Point is midway between the 8- and 9-mile markers on the highway, about 3 miles north of Ma'alaea. Note that the road sign simply reads 'scenic point,' not the full name, but there's a turning lane to the point, so slow down and you won't miss it.

Boss Frog   SNORKELING
(☑ 808-665-1200; www.bossfrog.com; 3636 Lower Honoapi'ilani Rd; snorkel set per day from $1.50; ⏰ 8am-6pm) Offers great prices for rental mask, snorkel and fins.

✗ Eating

Farmers Market Deli   DELI $
(☑ 808-669-7004; 3636 Lower Honoapi'ilani Rd; sandwiches $6; ⏰ 7am-7pm; ☑) ✿ For healthy and tasty take-out fare, stop at this welcoming market. The salad bar (with free samples; $9 per pound) includes organic goodies and hot veggie dishes and the smoothies are first-rate. The place becomes even greener on Monday, Wednesday and Friday mornings (7am to 11am), when vendors sell locally grown produce in the parking lot.

★ Honokowai Okazuya   INTERNATIONAL $$
(☑ 808-665-0512; 3600 Lower Honoapi'ilani Rd; mains $10-19; ⏰ 11am-2:30pm & 4:30-8:30pm Mon-Sat) Okayuza's appeal is not immediately apparent: the place is tiny, prices seem a little high and the choices weird (*kung pao* chicken *and* spaghetti with meatballs?). Then you nibble the Mongolian beef. Hmm, it's OK. Chomp, chomp. That's pretty interesting. Gulp, gulp. What is that spice? Savor, savor – until the whole meal is devoured. Here, plate lunches take a delicious gourmet turn. Primarily take-out. Cash only.

Kahana

Trendy Kahana, a village just north of Honokowai, boasts million-dollar homes, upscale beachfront condominiums and a Maui microbrewery. This sleepy enclave is for those who like privacy and marine life – you can often see turtles swimming in the water from your hotel lanai.

⊙ Sights & Activities

The sandy **beach** fronting Kahana village offers reasonable swimming. Park at seaside **Pohaku Park** and walk north to get there. Pohaku Park itself has an offshore break, called **S-Turns** (Pohaku Beach Park) that attracts intermediate surfers.

Maui Dive Shop   DIVING, SNORKELING
(☑ 808-669-3800; www.mauidiveshop.com; 4405 Honoapi'ilani Hwy, Kahana Gateway; 2-tank beach dives from $90, snorkel sets per day $9; ⏰ 7am-7pm Mon-Sat, 7am-6pm Sun) Come here for information about a full range of dives and to rent snorkel gear.

✗ Eating & Drinking

Maui Brewing Co   BREWERY
(☑ 808-669-3474; www.mauibrewingco.com; 4405 Honoapi'ilani Hwy, Kahana Gateway; mains $12-19; ⏰ 11am-10pm) ✿ From burgers made from local beef to the wild-pork flatbread, bar food takes a Hawaiian spin at this cavernous brewpub. The company, which has been honored as one of Hawaii's top green businesses, implements sustainable practices where possible. Happy hour runs from 3pm to 6pm daily, with $1 off a selection of craft beers.

The Bikini Blonde lager, Mana Wheat, Big Swell IPA and Coconut Porter are always on tap, supplemented by seasonal and specialty brews.

In 2015, ever-growing Maui Brewing added a new production facility and taproom to its line-up, housed together in Kihei (p160).

BEST BUDGET EATS

➡ Leoda's Kitchen & Pie Shop (p104)

➡ Honolua Store (p118)

➡ Joey's Kitchen (p110)

➡ Farmers Market Deli (p113)

➡ Gazebo (p114)

Hawaiian Village Coffee CAFE $
(☑ 808-665-1114; 4405 Honoapi'ilani Hwy, Kahana Gateway; pastries $6, sandwiches $8-10; ⊙ 5:30am-6pm Mon-Sat, 5:30am-5pm Sun; 🛜) Off-duty surfers shoot the breeze at this low-key coffee shop, which sells sweet pastries, cupcakes and the probiotic drink kombucha (on tap from $2).

Napili

👁 Sights

Napili is a bayside oasis flanked by the posh grounds of Kapalua to the north and the hustle and bustle of Kahana and Ka'anapali to the south. For an oceanfront retreat that's a bit more affordable – and not far from the action – we highly recommend this sun-blessed center of calm.

Napili Beach BEACH
The deep golden sands and gentle curves of Napili Beach offer good beachcombing at any time and excellent swimming and snorkeling when it's calm. Look for green sea turtles hanging out by the rocky southern shore. Big waves occasionally make it into the bay in winter, and when they do it's time to break out the skimboards – the steep drop at the beach provides a perfect run into the surf.

🍴 Eating & Drinking

⭐ **Gazebo** CAFE $
(☑ 808-669-5621; 5315 Lower Honoapi'ilani Rd, Outrigger Napili Shores; mains $8-14; ⊙ 7:30am-2pm) Locals aren't kidding when they advise you to get to the Gazebo early to beat the crowds. But a 7:10am arrival is worth it for this beloved open-air restaurant – a gazebo on the beach – with a gorgeous waterfront setting. The tiny cafe is known for its breakfasts, and those with a sweet tooth love the white-chocolate–macnut pancakes.

Meal-size salads, hearty sandwiches and the *kalua* pig plate steal the scene at lunch.

Maui Tacos MEXICAN $
(☑ 808-665-0222; www.mauitacos.com; 5095 Napilihau St, Napili Plaza; mains $6-12; ⊙ 9am-9pm) The burritos are huge at Maui Tacos, where the Mexican fare is island-style healthy. The salsas and beans are prepared fresh daily, trans-fat-free oil replaces lard, and fresh veggies and local fish feature on the menu. It's fast-food style and good for a quick meal.

Sea House Restaurant HAWAIIAN $$$
(☑ 808-669-1500; www.seahousemaui.com; 5900 Lower Honoapi'ilani Rd, Napili Kai Beach Resort; breakfast $9-15, lunch $10-18, dinner $28-40; ⊙ 7am-9pm) Pssst, want a $9 meal framed by a million-dollar view? Sidle up to the bar at this tiki-lit favorite, order a bowl of the smoky seafood chowder then watch as the perfectly framed sun drops below the horizon in front of you. Bravo! If you stick around, and you should, seafood and steak dishes are menu highlights.

Happy hour (2pm to 4.30pm) draws crowds for a $2 to $5 discount on *pupus* and cocktails.

Napili Coffee Store CAFE
(☑ 808-669-4170; www.napilicoffeestore.com; 5095 Napilihau St, Napili Plaza; pastries from $5, sandwiches & salads from $7; ⊙ 6am-6pm; 🛜) The ice-blended mocha at Napili's favorite coffee shop is nothing less than aloha in a cup. Utterly delicious. Locals also line up for the pleasant service and the pastries, from banana bread to pumpkin-cranberry muffins and chocolate peanut-butter bars. For heartier fare, try a slice of quiche or a turkey sandwich with basil pesto.

⭐ Entertainment

⭐ **Masters of Hawaiian Slack Key Guitar Concert Series** LIVE MUSIC
(☑ 808-669-3858; www.slackkeyshow.com; 5900 Lower Honoapi'ilani Rd, Napili Kai Beach Resort; $38-95; ⊙ 7:30pm Wed & Thu) Ledward Kaapana and other top slack key guitarists appear regularly at this exceptional concert series. George Kahumoku Jr, a slack key legend in his own right, is the weekly host. As much a jam session as a concert, this is a true Hawaiian cultural gem that's worth going out of your way to experience. Reservations recommended.

Kapalua & Northern Beaches

Kapalua has long been a sacred place for Native Hawaiians, but now it's more known for world-class golf courses, an adventure zipline company and glitzy five-star resorts. The rugged northern coast is not far from Kapalua's manicured greens, where untamed views are guaranteed to replenish your soul. The nightlife doesn't exactly sizzle here, but the beaches – all with public access – sure do.

In the 1900s this area was the site of a productive pineapple plantation, and hikes around the area will take adventurers though forests planted by DT Fleming, the tree surgeon who developed Maui's pineapple industry.

If uninterrupted sunshine is your goal in West Maui, note that Kapalua can be a bit rainier and windier than points south.

 Beaches

★ **Kapalua Beach**   BEACH
For a long day on the beach, it's hard to beat this crescent-shaped strip at the southwestern tip of Kapalua. Snorkel in the morning, grab lunch at the Sea House, try stand up paddle surfing, then sip cocktails at Merriman's (p119) next door. Or simply sit on the sand and gaze across the channel at Moloka'i. Long rocky outcrops at both ends of the bay make Kapalua Beach the safest year-round swimming spot on this coast.

You'll find colorful snorkeling on the right side of the beach, with abundant tropical fish and orange slate-pencil sea urchins. There's a rental hut here for beach gear.

Take the drive immediately north of **Napili Kai Beach Resort** (5900 Lower Honoapi'ilani Rd) to get to the beach parking area, where there are restrooms and showers. A tunnel leads from the parking lot north to the beach. This is also a starting point for the Coastal Trail (p101).

Oneloa Beach   BEACH
Fringed by low sand dunes covered in beach morning glory, this white-sand jewel is a picturesque place to soak up the rays. On calm days swimming is good close to shore, as is snorkeling in the protected area along the rocky point at the northern side of the beach. When there's any sizable surf, strong rip currents can be present.

The half-mile strand – Oneloa means 'long sand' – sits beside the Coastal Trail (p101) and is backed by gated resort condos and restricted golf greens. Beach access requires a sharp eye. Turn onto Ironwood Lane and then left into the small parking lot opposite the Ironwoods gate. Arrive early or at lunchtime to get a parking space, freshly emptied by the people leaving.

DT Fleming Beach Park   BEACH
(Honoapi'ilani Hwy) Surrounded by ironwood trees and backed by an old one-room schoolhouse, this sandy crescent looks like an outpost from another era. In keeping with its Hawaiian nature, the beach is the domain of wave riders. Experienced surfers and bodysurfers find good action here, especially in winter. The shorebreaks can be brutal, however, and the beach is a hot spot for injuries. The reef on the right is good for snorkeling in summer when the water is very calm.

DT Fleming Beach Park has restrooms, showers, grills, picnic tables and a lifeguard. The access road is off Honoapi'ilani Hwy (Hwy 30), immediately north of the 31-mile marker.

◉ Sights

Makaluapuna Point   NATURAL FEATURE
(Dragon's Teeth) Razor-sharp spikes crown rocky Makaluapuna Point, known informally by the nickname Dragon's Teeth. The formation does look uncannily like the mouth of an imaginary dragon. The 3ft-high spikes are the work of pounding winter waves that have ripped into the lava rock point, leaving the pointy 'teeth' behind. The point is also potentially hazardous. It is subject to powerful waves, particularly the northern winter swells, and covered by uneven, sometimes sharp, rocks.

Signage states that the outcropping is sacred to Native Hawaiians. Although the public is allowed access to the ocean by law, visitors are strongly discouraged from walking onto the formation out of respect for native customs. The adjacent Honokahua burial site is off-limits to the general public. Both sites are of cultural significance to Native Hawaiians and should not be inspected up close. Respect the signage.

For a view of Makaluapuna Point, you can skirt along the outside of the 13-acre burial site below the parking area, but don't enter areas marked 'Please Kokua,' which

Kapalua & Around

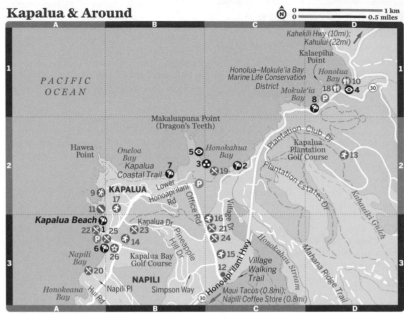

Kapalua & Around

are easily visible islets of stones bordering the Ritz's manicured golf greens. Do not walk across the greens.

Get here by driving north to the very end of Lower Honoapi'ilani Rd, where you'll find parking and a plaque detailing the burial site. The path to the point leads down from the plaque along the northern edge of the Kapalua Bay Golf Course.

Honokahua Burial Site   RUINS
This site is of cultural significance to Native Hawaiians and is off-limits to the general public. There are an estimated 2000 Hawaiians laid to rest here, dating back

to AD 610. The burial site is covered with well-maintained grass and flanked by a native *hau* hedge. Hawaiians believe that their ancestors' spirits continue to protect these lands; please respect the signage.

Activities

Stop by the **Kapalua Village Center** (☎808-665-4386; www.kapalua.com/activities; 2000 Village Rd; ☉8am-5pm) to book activities around the resort.

Kapalua Golf
GOLF

(☎877-527-2582, 808-669-8044; www.golfat kapalua.com) ⌘ Kapalua boasts two of the island's top championship-golf courses, both certified by Audubon International as sanctuaries for native plants and animals. How's that for green greens? The **Bay course** (☎808-662-7720; www.kapalua. com/golf; 300 Kapalua Dr; twilight/midday/standard round $159/189/219; ☉pro shop 6am-7pm, 1st tee 6:40am) is the tropical ocean course, meandering across a lava peninsula. The challenging **Plantation course** (2000 Plantation Club Dr; twilight/midday/standard round $199/239/299) ⌘ sweeps over a rugged landscape of hills and deep gorges.

Book tees by phone or at either of the course's pro shops, open 6am to 7pm.

Coconuts
SURFING

Considered by many as one of best surf spots in the world, Coconuts is an expert point-break on the far outside of Honolua Bay, producing big, fast right-hand rides. Winds and currents are strong. Parking is very limited off Honoapi'ilani Hwy, and car break-ins are common.

The Cave
SURFING

Named after a small Honolua Bay cave, which has occasionally trapped surfers. Strong northwesterly offshore winds help produce first-rate barrels here in the bay. It's a superlocal spot for advanced surfers only. Be courteous and don't go dropping in on anyone. Parking is very limited off Honoapi'ilani Hwy, and car break-ins are common.

Kapalua Tennis Garden
TENNIS

(☎808-662-7730; www.kapalua.com/activities/ tennis; 100 Kapalua Dr; per person per day $15, racket rental $6; ☉8am-5pm Mon-Fri, 8am-4pm Sat-Sun) Maui's premier full-service tennis club has 10 Plexipave courts, with four lit for evening games, plus an array of clinics. If you're on your own, give the club a ring

and they'll match you with other players for singles or doubles games.

Kapalua Bay Beach Crew
DIVING

(☎808-649-8222; Kapalua Bay; ☉8am-5pm) Rent a basic snorkel set for $20 per day and a SUP board for $40 per hour. An SUP lesson is $139 for an hour (you can keep the board for the rest of the day). Look for its hut at the northern end of Kapalua Beach.

Kapalua Ziplines
ZIPLINING

(☎808-756-9147; www.kapaluaziplines.com; 500 Office Rd; 4-/7-line zip $177/208; ☉6:45am-5pm) Ready to soar across the West Maui Mountains for nearly 2 miles? On the signature tour (4¼ hours) you'll glide down seven ziplines, two of them extending a breathtaking 2000ft in length. The tour has a dual track, allowing you to zip beside a friend. The seven-line tour includes refreshments and water.

Moonlight tours take place in the summer months and are a chance to experience three lines with headlamps and glow sticks.

Spa Montage Kapalua Bay
SPA

(☎808-665-8282; www.spamontage.com; 1 Bay Dr; body therapies from $35, massages from $210, spa day pass per person $55; ☉9:00am-7:00pm) This soothing place has a top spa including a eucalyptus steam room, cedar-wood sauna, whirlpool, bamboo rainfall showers and aesthetically pleasing treatment areas. It embraces native Hawaiian ingredients and traditions from both *mauka* (mountain) and *makai* (sea). This is the place for a couple's massage or a Lomi Lomi massage ($210 for 60 minutes), which follows the rhythmic motions of the ocean.

Post-treatment, continue invigorating with a fresh fruit juice or smoothie from the on-site cafe and juice bar (7am to 1pm; juices and smoothies for around $12).

Courses

Kapalua Golf Academy
GOLF

(☎808-662-7740; www.golfatkapalua.com; 1000 Office Rd; 1hr private lesson $185, half-day school $275; ☉7am-5pm) Hawaii's top golf academy is staffed by PGA pros.

Festivals & Events

PGA Tournament of Champions
SPORTS

(www.pgatour.com; ☉early Jan) Watch Tiger and friends tee off at the PGA Tour's season opener at the Kapalua Plantation Golf

Course, vying for a multimillion-dollar purse.

Celebration of the Arts ART & CRAFT
(www.celebrationofthearts.org; Ritz-Carlton Kapalua; ⊙ early May) This festival celebrates traditional Hawaiian culture with art, hula, music, films and cultural panels.

Kapalua Wine & Food Festival FOOD & DRINK
(www.kapaluawineandfoodfestival.com; Ritz-Carlton Kapalua; ⊙ mid-Jun) A culinary extravaganza held over four days in mid-June. It features renowned winemakers and Hawaii's hottest chefs, offering cooking demonstrations and wine tastings.

Xterra World Championship SPORTS
(www.xterraplanet.com/maui; Ritz-Carlton Kapalua; ⊙ Oct) A major off-road triathlon race boasting a $105,000 purse. It starts with a 1-mile rough water swim, followed by a 20-mile dirt-trail bike ride through a ravine and tropical landscape, and then a 6.5-mile trail run through forest and across beach.

Eating

The dining scene in Kapalua is among the island's best. It's hard to get a bad meal in this area, whether you go for low-end or high-end options.

Honolua Store DELI $
(☎ 808-665-9105; 502 Office Rd; breakfast $6-9, lunch $5-13; ⊙ store 6am-8:30pm, deli 6am-7pm) This porch-wrapped bungalow, which was revamped and expanded in 2013, opened in 1929 as the general store for the Honolua Pineapple Plantation. Today, Honolua Store is a nod to normalcy in the midst of lavish exclusiveness. The deli is known for its reasonable prices and fantastic plate lunches. Grab-and-go sandwiches and bento items are available in the deli case.

Sansei Seafood
Restaurant & Sushi Bar JAPANESE $$
(☎ 808-669-6286; www.sanseihawaii.com; 600 Office Rd; sushi from $3, mains from $16; ⊙ dinner 5:15-10pm Sat-Wed, to 1am Thu & Fri) The

---

HONOLUA–MOKULE'IA BAY MARINE LIFE CONSERVATION DISTRICT

The narrow Kalaepiha Point separates **Slaughterhouse Beach** and **Honolua Bay**. Together they form the Honolua–Mokule'ia Bay Marine Life Conservation District, which is famed for its snorkeling and surfing.

Honolua Bay is a surfer's dream. It faces northwest and when it catches the winter swells it has some of the gnarliest surfing in the world. In summer snorkeling is excellent in both bays, thanks in part to prohibitions on fishing in the preserve. Honolua Bay is the favorite, with thriving reefs and abundant coral along its rocky edges.

Spinner dolphins sometimes hang near the mouth of the bays, swimming just beyond snorkelers. When it's calm, you can snorkel around Kalaepiha Point from one bay to the other, but forget it after heavy rains: Honolua Stream empties into its namesake Bay and the runoff clouds the water.

The land fronting Honolua Bay has long been owned by Maui Land & Pineapple. The company has allowed recreational access to the bay for no fee. A few families have the right to live on this land, but they cannot charge an access fee or restrict visiting hours. In 2014, with community support, the state of Hawaii purchased more than 240 acres beside the bay to protect them from development.

Once you reach the bay, read the signage about protecting the coral (sunscreen, for example, should be avoided) then enter via the rocky coastline. Do not enter the water via the concrete boat ramp, which is very slippery and potentially hazardous.

When the waters are calm the bays offer superb kayaking. Slaughterhouse Beach is also a top-rated bodysurfing spot during the summer. Its attractive white-sand crescent is good for sunbathing and beachcombing – look for glittering green olivine crystals in the rocks at the southern end of the beach.

Just north of the 32-mile marker, there's public parking and a concrete stairway leading down the cliffs to Slaughterhouse Beach. After passing Slaughterhouse Beach, look ahead for a large parking area on the left. Here you'll find a nice view of Honolua Bay below. A half-mile past the 32-mile marker there's room for about six cars to park adjacent to the path down to Honolua Bay, or continue around a couple of bends and park beside the port-o-johns. From here, follow the gravel path through the junglelike flora to the bay.

innovative sushi menu is the draw, but the non-sushi house specials, which often blend Japanese and Pacific Rim flavors, shouldn't be overlooked. The spicy Dungeness crab ramen with truffle broth is noteworthy. Order before 6pm for an early-bird dinner special. No reservation? Queue up early for one of the seats at the sushi bar.

The wine and cocktail menus are worth a look, too: try the refreshing Kai Lemongrass Vodka with lemon and lime juice and coconut water.

Burger Shack BURGERS $$
(☑808-669-6200; DT Fleming Beach Park; mains from $15; ⊙11:30am-5pm; ⚡) This casual oceanfront joint sells burgers, shakes and inventive cocktails under the coconut trees. Creative patties include a *katsu* burger with ramen chicken breast, a smoked slow-roasted pork burger, and a black bean, beet and tofu burger.

Plantation House HAWAIIAN $$$
(☑808-669-6299; www.theplantationhouse.com; 2000 Plantation Club Dr, Plantation Golf Course Clubhouse; breakfast $9-19, lunch $10-20, dinner $29-50; ⊙8am-9:30pm) The crab-cake Benedict at this open-air restaurant is a fluffy, hollandaise-splashed affair that will have you kissing your plate and plotting your return. Adding to the allure are stellar views of the coast and Moloka'i, as well as the world-famous golf course below. For dinner, fresh fish and beef dishes are prepared with global flair.

Pineapple Grill HAWAIIAN $$$
(☑808-669-9600; www.cohnrestaurants.com; 200 Kapalua Dr, Kapalua Bay Golf Course Clubhouse; breakfast $8-16, lunch & dinner $12-29; ⊙8am-late) This beauty's got it all, from a sweeping hilltop view to a sleek exhibition kitchen that whips up creative Pacific Asian seafood and meat dishes accompanied by locally sourced vegetables. Plus, happy hour *pupu* (snacks) cost under $10 between 3pm and 6pm.

Merriman's Kapalua HAWAIIAN $$$
(☑808-669-6400; www.merrimanshawaii.com/kapalua; 1 Bay Club Pl; restaurant mains $27-75, happy-hour menu $9-26; ⊙restaurant 5:30-9pm, bar 3pm-close) We especially like Merriman's at happy hour (3pm to 5pm). Perched on a scenic point between Kapalua Bay and Napili Bay, the tiki- and palm-dotted Point Bar is a gorgeous place to unwind after braving the Kahekili Hwy. At the acclaimed restaurant,

Maui-caught fish and locally sourced meats and produce are the highlights. There's live music daily in the dining room from 5.30pm to 8.30pm.

Kahekili Highway

Bring your hat, water, suncreen, your scrambling shoes and your sense of adventure on this challenging 20- to 35-mile road trip, which hugs the rugged northern tip of Maui. Optimistically called a highway (Route 340), the route is generally driven from east of Punalau Beach, where Honoapi'ilani Hwy/Route 30 turns into the Kahekili Hwy. It charges around hairpin turns, careens over one-lane bridges and teeters beside treacherous cliffs. The road finishes in Wailuku. It's one of Maui's most adventurous drives. The area is so ravishingly rural that it's hard to imagine trendy West Maui could hold such untouched countryside.

Not for the faint of heart, some sections slow to just 5mph as the road wraps around blind curves; a lengthy stretch around the village of Kahakuloa (p122) is just one lane with cliffs on one side and a sheer drop on the other – if you meet oncoming traffic here you may be doing your traveling in reverse! But if you can handle that, this largely overlooked route offers all sorts of adventures, with horse and hiking trails, a mighty blowhole and delicious banana bread.

Don't be fooled by car-rental maps that show the road as a dotted line – it's paved and open to the public the entire way. There are no services, so gas up beforehand. Give yourself a good two hours' driving time, not counting stops. If you get stuck behind a slow-moving vehicle, it could take much longer.

Property between the highway and the coast is both privately and publicly owned. Trails to the shore are often uneven, rocky and slippery, and the coast is subject to dangerous waves. If you decide to explore, take appropriate precautions, and get access permission when possible.

◉ Sights

Punalau Beach BEACH
Manicured golf courses and ritzy enclaves drop away and the scenery gets wilder as you drive toward Maui's northernmost point. Ironwood-lined Punalau Beach, 0.7 miles

Kahekili Highway

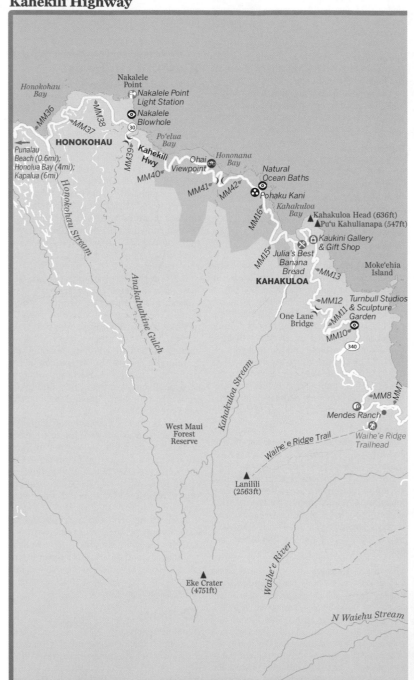

Honokohau
Bay

Nakalele
Point

Nakalele Point
Light Station

Nakalele
Blowhole

MM36

MM37

MM38

30

HONOKOHAU

MM39

Punalau
Beach (0.6mi);
Honolua Bay (4mi);
Kapalua (6mi)

Po'elua
Bay

Kahekili
Hwy

Ohai
Viewpoint

Hononana
Bay

Natural
Ocean Baths

MM40

MM41

MM42

Pohaku Kani

Honokohau Stream

Kahakuloa
Bay

Kahakuloa Head (636ft)
Pu'u Kahulianapa (547ft)

MM16

Kaukini Gallery
& Gift Shop

Julia's Best
Banana
Bread

MM15

Moke'ehia
Island

KAHAKULOA

MM13

Anakaluahine Gulch

MM12

Turnbull Studios
& Sculpture
Garden

One Lane
Bridge

MM11

MM10

340

Kahakuloa Stream

MM8

MM7

Mendes Ranch

West Maui
Forest
Reserve

Waihe'e Ridge Trail

Waihe'e Ridge
Trailhead

Lanilili
(2563ft)

Eke Crater
(4751ft)

Waihe'e River

N Waiehu Stream

after the 34-mile marker on Honoapi'ilani Hwy, makes a worthy stop if you're up for a solitary stroll. Swimming is a no-go though, as a rocky shelf creates unfavorable conditions for water activities.

Nakalele Point

The terrain turns hilly after Punalau Beach, with rocky cattle pastures punctuated by tall sisal plants. At a number of pull-offs you can stop and explore. Lush pastures are quite enticing, willing you to traipse down the cliffs and out along the rugged coastline.

At the Kahekili Hwy's 38-mile marker, a mile-long trail leads to a **light station** at the end of windswept Nakalele Point. Here you'll find a coastline of arches and other formations carved out of the rocks by the pounding surf. There are several worn paths leading toward the light station, but you can't really get lost – just walk toward the point. Bring water and wear a hat, as there's little shade.

The **Nakalele Blowhole** (Kahekili Hwy, 38-mile marker) roars when the surf is up but is a sleeper when the seas are calm. To check on its mood, park at the boulder-lined pull-off 0.6 miles beyond the 38-mile marker. You can glimpse the action, if there is any, a few hundred yards beyond the parking lot. It's a 15-minute scramble down a jagged moonscape of lava rocks to the blowhole, which can shoot up to 100ft. Keep a safe distance and watch your footing carefully. A tourist fell into the hole and vanished in 2011. Another died after falling from a cliff in the area in 2013. And it probably goes without saying, but don't sit on, or peer into, the blowhole!

Eight-tenths of a mile after the 40-mile marker look for the **Ohai Viewpoint**, on the *makai* (seaward) side of the road. The viewpoint isn't marked but there's a sign announcing the start of the Ohai Trail, a 1.2-mile loop with interpretative signage and views off the coast. For the best views, bear left from the trailhead and walk to the top of the point for a jaw-dropping coastal panorama that includes a glimpse of the Nakalele Blowhole. If you have kids, be careful – the crumbly cliff edge has a sudden drop of nearly 800ft!

OCEAN BATHS & BELLSTONE

After the 42-mile post on the Kahekili Hwy (coming from Lahaina), the mile-markers

KAHAKULOA

An imposing 636ft-tall volcanic dome guards the entrance to Kahakuloa Bay like a lurking, watchful dragon. They say this photogenic landmark, known as **Kahakuloa Head**, believed to be a favorite cliff-diving spot of Chief Kahekili in the 18th century. Before the road drops into the valley, there's a pull-off above town providing a bird's-eye view.

The bayside village of Kahakuloa, tucked at the bottom of a lush valley and embraced by towering sea cliffs, retains a solidly Hawaiian character. Kahakuloa's isolation has protected it from the rampant development found elsewhere on Maui. Farmers tend taro patches, dogs wander across the road, and a missionary-era Protestant church marks the village center. One of Hawaii's most accomplished ukulele players, Richard Ho'opi'i, grew up here.

You won't find any stores, but villagers set up hard-to-miss roadside stands selling fruit and snacks to day-trippers. For shave ice, hit Ululani's hot-pink stand. For chilled homemade lemonade and free samples of macadamia nuts, coconut candy and 'ono (delicious) banana bread, stop at **Julia's lime-green shack** (www.juliasbananabread. com; Kahekili Hwy, mile-marker 13; ☺9am-5:30pm or until sold out).

change; the next marker is 16 and the numbers drop as you continue.

One-tenth of a mile before the 16-mile marker, look seaward for a large dirt pull-off and a well-beaten path that leads 15 minutes down lava cliffs to **natural ocean baths** (Kahekili Hwy, at 16-mile mark) on the water's edge. Cut out of slippery lava rock and encrusted with olivine minerals, these incredibly clear pools sit in the midst of roaring surf.

Some have natural steps, but if you're tempted to go in, size it up carefully – people unfamiliar with the water conditions here have been swept into the sea and drowned. If the rocks are covered in silt from recent storm runoffs, or the waves look high, forget about it – it's dangerous. Although the baths are on public land, state officials do not recommend accessing them due to the hazardous conditions, including slippery rocks, large and powerful surf, waves crashing over ledges and strong currents.

The huge boulder with concave marks on the inland side of the road just before the pull-off is a bellstone, **Pohaku Kani** (Kahekili Hwy, at 16-mile mark). If you hit it with a rock on the Kahakuloa side, where the deepest indentations are, you might be able to get a hollow sound. It's a bit resonant if you hit it

just right, though it takes some imagination to hear it ring like a bell.

Kahakuloa to Waihe'e

On the outskirts of Kahakuloa, after a heart-stopping, narrow climb (coming from Lahaina), you'll reach the hilltop **Kaukini Gallery & Gift Shop** (☎808-244-3371; www.kaukinigallery.com; Kahekili Hwy, at mile-marker 13; ☺10am-5pm), on Kahekili Highway. Filled with trinkets, local jewelry, art, and tableware, the shop makes a nice place to browse and grab a soda before hitting the road again.

Look for the towering giraffe statue east of the 10-mile marker. It marks the entrance for **Turnbull Studios & Sculpture Garden** (☎808-244-0101; www.turnbullstudios.org; 5030 Kahekili Hwy; ☺10am-5pm Mon-Sat). Here you can view Bruce Turnbull's ambitious bronze and wood creations, peer into a working studio and wander through a small gallery selling an attractive collection of work by local artists.

Continuing around beep-as-you-go blind turns, the highway gradually levels out atop sea cliffs. For an Edenic scene, stop at the pull-off 175yd north of the 8-mile marker and look down into the ravine below, where you'll see a cascading **waterfall** framed by double pools.

For a real *paniolo* (Hawaiian cowboy) experience, saddle up at **Mendes Ranch** (☑ 808-871-5222; www.mendesranch.com; 3530 Kahekili Hwy; 1½hr rides $110; ⊘ rides 8:45am & 12:15pm), a working cattle ranch near the 7-mile marker and the road to Waiheʻe Ridge Trail (p100). The picture-perfect scenery on these rides includes everything from jungle valleys to lofty sea cliffs.

Waiheʻe to Wailuku

Aside from the world-class Waiheʻe Ridge Trail, the other activity in this sleepy part of West Maui is a round of golf. The county-run **Waiehu Municipal Golf Course** (☑ 808-243-7400; www.mauicounty.gov; 200 Halewaiu Rd; greens fee from $50, twilight rate $40, optional cart $20; ⊘ 7am-5pm Mon-Fri, 6am-5pm Sat & Sun) offers an affordable and easily walkable 18 holes on the coast, plus a 24-tee driving range at which to let off some steam.

'Iao Valley & Central Maui

Best Places to Eat

➡ Geste Shrimp Truck (p136)

➡ Farmacy Health Bar (p140)

➡ Ichiban Okazuya (p140)

➡ Sam Sato's (p140)

Best Nature Spots

➡ 'Iao Valley State Monument (p141)

➡ Kealia Coastal Boardwalk (p146)

➡ Maui Ocean Center (p144)

➡ Maui Nui Botanical Gardens (p132)

Why Go?

Welcome to the flat bit. Central Maui is the isthmus connecting the West Maui Mountains to mighty Haleakalā, giving the island its distinctive three-part shape. This odd wedge of topography, Maui's most arable piece of land, was once known only for its fields of waving sugarcane, but it now boasts a potpourri of attractions. To the north, the island's commercial center, Kahului, contains windswept Kanaha Beach, a hub for water sports. Sister-city Wailuku is a funky up-and-comer with the best lunch scene, and the gateway to the lush 'Iao Valley. On the southern coast, Ma'alaea is home to a top-notch aquarium and its harbor is the launchpad for a Molokini cruise.

When to Go

Central Maui is a beacon for kiteboarders and windsurfers who take advantage of the windy north shores. The strongest winds happen during the summer months, while surfers prefer the big swells of the winter months.

Kahului is predominantly warm and dry year-round, as it sits in between Maui's two giant mountainous regions. Meanwhile, the lush 'Iao Valley and Wailuku Town get daily precipitation.

The best flight and accommodation deals for Central Maui can be found in the fall, or between mid-April and mid-June. The most expensive flights into Kahului and coastal hotel rooms are during the whale-watching winter months.

In late November and early December a celebration of Hawaiian culture named Na Mele O Maui takes place in Kahului.

'Iao Valley & Central Maui Highlights

1 Kanaha Beach Park
(p132) Kite- and windsurfing this beautifully blustery stretch.

2 Blue Hawaiian Helicopters (p135) Taking an unforgettable aerial trip through the West Maui Mountains to Moloka'i.

3 King Kamehameha Golf Club (p142) Teeing off at the island's only 18-hole course where the club house is a stunning Frank Lloyd Wright design.

4 'Iao Valley State Monument (p141) Exploring Maui's lush interior and soaring emerald peaks.

5 Maui Swap Meet (p137) Browsing tent after tent of local arts, crafts and food.

HIKING IN CENTRAL MAUI

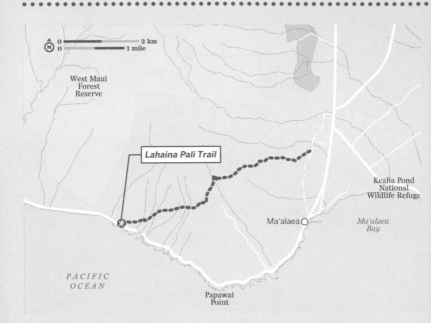

Lahaina Pali Trail

West Maui
Forest
Reserve

Kealia Pond
National
Wildlife Refuge

Ma'alaea ○

Ma'alaea
Bay

PACIFIC
OCEAN

Papawai
Point

LAHAINA PALI TRAIL
START LAHAINA TRAILHEAD
END MA'ALAEA TRAILHEAD
LENGTH 5 MILES ONE-WAY; THREE OR
MORE HOURS
DIFFICULTY DIFFICULT

This spectacular and challenging **route** (https://hawaiitrails.ehawaii.gov) was used more than a century ago by missionaries traveling by horse and foot from Lahaina to Wailuku. The old road is now used by able hikers on a pulse-pounding climb up and down rocky pathways, ascending 1600ft above sea level to a 36-turbine wind farm. Mesmerizing views stretch to the north and south coastlines, the central valley, Haleakala volcano and Kealia Pond National Wildlife Refuge.

The climb is arguably easier than the higgledy-piggledy descent over boulders all shapes and sizes, yet you'll likely see skilled hill runners hopping down it at speed – sprinting down is only for experts: loose rocks can be treacherous.

Find the **Lahaina trailhead** on Honoapi'ilani Hwy after Olowalu Tunnel (if heading towards Lahaina). The first part of the trail from here is shaded, although some of the trees have suffered from brushfires. The pathway quickly becomes arid and exposed – bring sunscreen, a hat and plenty of water and start early before the sun is overhead. Beautiful sweeping views appear almost immediately. Examine the blue ocean hues for whales in winter, and look for petroglyphs and stone walls along the trail, marking the resting spots of ancient travelers. The path winds up the mountain, passing cavernous, moody valleys. Lone trees provide moments of shade. Distractions from the silence include fluttering butterflies, the hum of crickets and an occasional plane on its way to Kahului airport. The blades of the **windmills** mark the breezy midpoint of the route. On a clear day from this area, known as the **Kaheawa Pastures**, you can see Molokini islet and Kaho'olawe to the south, the West Maui mountains to the west and Haleakala to the east. It's all downhill from here. Phew!

Follow in the footsteps of missionaries on a high and scrubby trail that's a prime lookout for whale-watching in winter.

Choose to continue, or return the way you've come.

You can reach the trailheads on either side of the route by car; there's parking on the Ukumehame side (just after the tunnel on the right, before Ukumehame Beach Park at the 12-mile marker) and Ma'alaea side near Maui Demolition on Honoapi'ilani Hwy. If you plan to complete the entire trail you'll need two cars, one parked at either end. Alternatively, walk the route again or book a Uber/taxi to your parked car (check car availability before you set off).

ANN CECIL/GETTY IMAGES ©

MARK GIBSON/GETTY IMAGES ©

JOE WEST/SHUTTERSTOCK ©

1. Kiteboarding
Central Maui is a beacon for kiteboarders and windsurfers.

2. 'Iao Needle (p142)
Maui's iconic landmark and centerpiece of the 'Iao Valley State Monument.

3. Ae'o (Hawaiian black-necked stilt)
Kanaha Pond Bird Sanctuary (p132) is a haven for rare Hawaiian birds.

4. Ma'alaea (p143)
The cute little harbor village of Ma'alaea is a jumping-off point for whale-watching and snorkeling trips.

ʻIao Valley & Central Maui

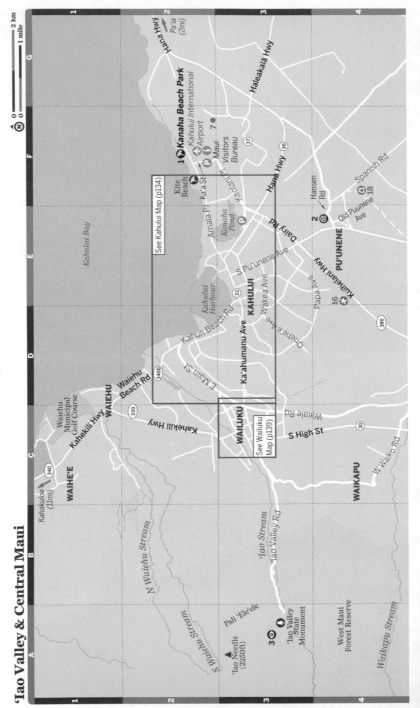

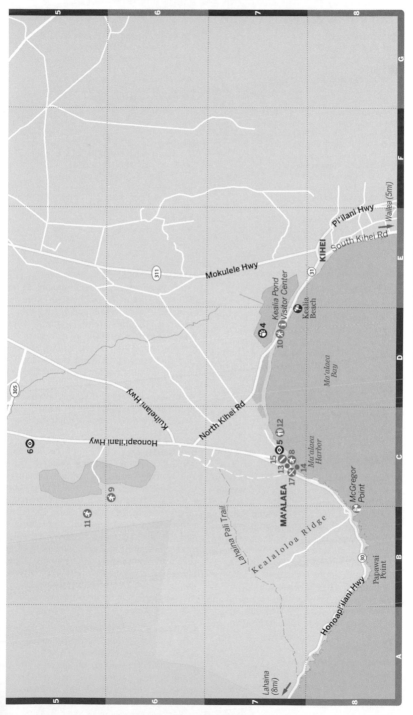

'Iao Valley & Central Maui

Kahului

Most Hawaiian Islands have a working town like Kahului, full of warehouses, strip malls, shopping centers, and that island-wide magnet, the big-box store. Like its counterparts, Kahului also contains Maui's main harbor and airport, turning it, in the eyes of many, into a transit stop. But at the same time, you'll find a great swath of local life here if you linger a little longer. You can talk to the locals at the Saturday swap meet, watch a concert on the lawn of the cultural center and join the wave-riders at Kanaha Beach.

🏝 Beaches

★ Kanaha Beach Park   BEACH
(Map p130) Well, you can't judge a beach by its cover. Wedged between downtown Kahului and the airport, and hidden behind a strip of ironwood trees, this mile-long stretch of sand is surf city, with scores of brilliant sails zipping across the waves. Kitesurfers converge at the southwest end, known as **Kite Beach**, while windsurfers head northeast. A roped-off swimming area lies in-between. Facilities include restrooms, showers and shaded picnic tables. There's no better place to learn how to ride the wind – or just to watch the action.

◉ Sights

Story of Hawaii Museum   MUSEUM
(Map p134; ☑808-871-4547, 808-871-4547; www. storyofhawaiimuseum.com; 2nd flr, Queen Ka'ahumanu Center, 275 W Kaahumanu Ave; suggested donation adult/child $7/5; ⊘11am-5pm) This quirky place offers a fascinating look at the history of Hawaii as told through centuries of maps. The collection encompasses early explorers, the monarchy, territorial days, WWII, statehood and the golden era of the Matson cruise line. Of particular note is a map that suggests Captain Cook may not have been the first European to discover Hawaii.

To unlock the cartographic tale, the 30-minute, docent-led tour is a must. You can also buy giclée prints of what you see.

Kanaha Pond
Bird Sanctuary   BIRD SANCTUARY
(Map p134; Hwy 37; ⊘sunrise-sunset) 🏆 **FREE**
You wouldn't expect a wildlife sanctuary to be so close to a main road, but a short walk leaves it behind. This shallow marsh is a haven for rare Hawaiian birds, including native coots, black-crowned night herons, and the ae'o (Hawaiian black-necked stilt), a graceful wading bird with long orange legs that feeds along the pond's marshy edges. According to various Fish & Wildlife surveys the ae'o population probably hovers around 1500 statewide, but you can count on spotting some here.

Maui Nui Botanical Gardens   GARDENS
(Map p134; ☑808-249-2798; www.mnbg.org; 150 Kanaloa Ave; adult/child under 13yr $5/free, Sat free; ⊘8am-4pm Mon-Sat) 🍃 For all of those botanophiles interested in native Hawaiian plants, this garden on the grounds of a

former zoo has a wealth of knowledge. An excellent new audio tour ($5 or free with admission) brings it to life. Don't expect the exotic tropicals that dominate most Hawaiian gardens; do expect dedicated staff. Staff also lead personal guided tours from 10am to 11:30am Tuesday to Friday by appointment (suggested donation $10).

Schaefer International Gallery   MUSEUM
(Map p134; ☑808-242-2787; www.mauiarts.org; 1 Cameron Way; ☉10am-5pm Tue-Sun) FREE This art gallery at the Maui Arts & Cultural Center (p137) has six exhibitions per year, ranging from native Hawaiian arts to contemporary local artists working in all mediums.

Kahului Harbor   HARBOR
(Map p134) Kahului's large protected harbor is the island's only deep-water port, so all boat traffic, from cruise ships to cargo vessels, docks here. But it's not all business. Late afternoon you might see outrigger canoe clubs like Na Kai 'Ewalu (www.nakaiewalucanoe-club.org) practicing near **Ho'aloha Park** – a timeless scene.

🏃 Activities

Kanaha Beach Park is the best place to windsurf on Maui, unless you're an aspiring pro ready for Ho'okipa. Board-and-rig rentals start at $59/387 per day/week, while beginner group introductory classes cost around $100. For more info see www.maui windsurfcompany.com.

Kitesurfing (or kiteboarding) is enormously popular in Kahului. The action centers on **Kite Beach**, the southwest end of Kanaha Beach Park. Here you can learn the ropes from some real pros, and you're likely to see vans from various water-sports companies parked in the lot. Expect to pay about $100 for discovery intro lesson. Check out the scene live at www.kitebeach cam.com.

Be sure to shop around and ask about discounts on lessons and rentals.

Kanaha Kai   WATER SPORTS
(Map p134; ☑808-877-7778; www.kanahakai.com; 96 Amala Pl; rental per day SUP $35, windsurfing rigs from $57; ☉9.30am-6pm Mar-Oct, to 5pm Nov-Feb) Windsurfing, SUP (stand up paddle surfing), kitesurfing and surfing rentals and lessons. Very competitive pricing. Look out for prebooked offers on the website.

Naish Maui Pro Center   ADVENTURE SPORTS
(Map p134; ☑808-871-1500; www.naishmaui.com; 111 Hana Hwy, Suite 108; daily SUP rental from $45; ☉9am-5pm) For SUP, windsurfing and kitesurfing equipment hire.

Hi-Tech Surf Sports   WATER SPORTS
(Map p134; ☑808-877-2111; www.surfmaui.com; 425 Koloa St; rental per day surfboard from $25, SUP from $35, windsurf equipment $60; ☉9am-6pm) Surfboard, SUP and windsurfing rentals.

Aqua Sports Maui   KITESURFING
(Map p134; ☑808-242-8015; www.mauikiteboard-inglessons.com; 3hr intro from $225) Specializes in kitesurfing lessons.

Maui Windsurf Company   WINDSURFING
(Map p134; ☑808-877-4816; www.mauiwindsurf-company.com; 22 Hana Hwy; 2½hr lesson per person from $100; ☉8.30am-5.30pm) Want to get up and riding on a windsurf board? Maui Windsurf Company is friendly and all equipment is included in your lesson.

Crater Cycles   MOUNTAIN BIKING
(Map p134; ☑808-893-2020; www.cratercy-cleshawaii.com; 400 Hana Hwy; downhill bikes per day $65; ☉9am-6pm Mon-Sat) Rents quality full-suspension downhill and road bikes, complete with helmet, pads and a roof rack. Provides good trail maps on its website.

Island Biker   CYCLING
(Map p134; ☑808-877-7744; www.islandbiker maui.com; 415 Dairy Rd; per day/week $60/250; ☉9am-5pm Mon-Fri, to 3pm Sat) Rents quality mountain bikes and road bikes.

The Dunes at Maui Lani   GOLF
(Map p130; ☑808-873-0422; www.dunesat mauilani.com; 1333 Maui Lani Pkwy; greens fee incl cart before 1pm $95, after 1pm $78, club hire $35; ☉6:30am-6pm) With Maui's second-highest USGA course rating, this 18-hole course will give scratch golfers playing from the tips a lot of fun. It's easy to underestimate, but it has the highest slope rating of any course on Maui. Follow Dairy Rd south and it appears on the right.

👉 Tours

In Hawaii the best helicopter tours operate out of Maui and Kaua'i. So if you aren't visiting the latter, this is your shot at the top. Various tour routes are available, but the finest combines the West Maui Mountains with the eastern end of Moloka'i, a jaw-dropping,

Kahului

0 — 1 km
0 — 0.5 miles

Kanaha Beach Park (0.4m)

Kahului (0.5m)

Pa'ia (5m)

Haleakala Hwy

Hana Hwy

Kahului Bay

Kanaha Pond

Hana Hwy

Kahului Harbor

Ho'aloha Park

S Pu'unene Ave

Ka'ahumanu Ave

Department of Parks & Recreation – Central District

Downtown Wailuku (0.5m)

Ma'alaea (7m); Lahaina (20m)

Kahului

uninhabited region of unspoiled emerald-green valleys and waterfalls.

Several tour companies operate out of Kahului Heliport, alongside the airport. Check online and in free tourist magazines for significant discounts and ask about fuel surcharges.

★ **Blue Hawaiian Helicopters**   TOURS
(Map p130; ☑808-871-8844; www.bluehawaiian.com; 1 Kahului Airport Rd, Hangar 105; tours $152-510) Industry-leader Blue Hawaiian flies the hi-tech Eco-Star, which has an enclosed tail rotor. Excellent visibility means you see everything, noise-cancelling headsets let you hear everything, and digital in-flight video brings the entire experience home. Tour prices depend on the itinerary and chopper; it also flies A-Stars, the industry workhorse. Professional staff operate like clockwork.

The signature West Maui Mountains tour by Eco-Star starts from $185 if booked online.

Air Maui Helicopter Tours   TOURS
(Map p130; ☑808-877-7005; www.airmaui.com; 1 Kahului Airport Rd, Hangar 110; tours $100-350) A full range of tour options in A-Stars. Professionally run and good value. Solo travelers should check for single-seater deals from $100 before booking.

Sunshine Helicopters   TOURS
(Map p130; ☑808-270-3999; www.sunshinehelicopters.com; 1 Kahului Airport Rd, Hangar 107; tours $225-515) Well-established firm operating on four islands.

★☆ Festivals & Events

★ **Ki Ho'alu Slack Key Guitar Festival**   MUSIC
(www.mauiarts.org; ⊙Jun) Top slack key guitarists take the stage at this fun event, held on the lawn of the Maui Arts & Cultural Center each June.

Maui Marathon   SPORTS
(www.mauimarathonhawaii.com; ⊙mid-Sep) This road race begins in Kahului and ends 26.2 miles later at Whalers Village in Ka'anapali.

Maui Ukulele Festival   MUSIC
(www.ukulelefestivalhawaii.org; ⊙mid-Oct) Held outdoors at the Maui Arts & Cultural Center on a Sunday in mid-October, this aloha event showcases uke masters from Maui and beyond.

Nā Mele O Maui   MUSIC
(www.mauiarts.org; ⊙Nov/Dec) This celebration of Hawaiian culture features children's choral groups singing native Hawaiian music. The aloha-rich event is held in late November/early December at the Maui Arts & Cultural Center (p137).

ISLAND INSIGHTS

While most historians credit Captain Cook with the European discovery of Hawaii, there is evidence that the Spanish may have preceded him. From South America to the Philippines, the vast Pacific was once part of Spain's overseas empire. For over two centuries galleons made the trip from Mexico to Manila and back at the mercy of the winds. Is it possible that they discovered Hawaii? Conversely, is it possible that in hundreds of round-trips they did *not*? Spanish tradition contains references to the Islas del Rey, Islas de los Jardines, Islas de las Tables and Islas de las Mesas, any one of which could be Hawaii. Top candidates for Discoverer include Juan Gaytan, based on his rudimentary account of a trip outbound from New Spain in 1555, and Francisco Gauli, whose 1582 expedition strayed from the normal galleon route.

To review some of the evidence yourself, check out the fascinating **Story of Hawaii Museum** (p132) in Kahului. Not only does it have a Spanish map showing the Islas de las Mesas, but the map was captured from the Spanish by a British warship. In other words, Captain Cook's navy had evidence of a mid-Pacific archipelago well before Cook himself. Perhaps the good captain had a better compass than we think.

✗ Eating

★ Geste Shrimp Truck
SEAFOOD $

(Map p134; ☎808-298-7109; www.gesteshrimp.com; Kahului Beach Rd; mains $13; ⊘11am-5:30pm Tue-Sat) Beside Kahului Harbor, this small white food truck – emblazoned with a giant shrimp – serves the tastiest shrimp on Maui – maybe even the world! A dozen costs $13 and you'll get a scoop of crab mac salad and rice to go with them. It's a messy meal so bring something to wipe your hands on, don't wear white and don't eat in your car! Nearby Maui Nui Botanical Gardens has picnic tables.

Tin Roof
JAPANESE, HAWAIIAN $

(Map p134; ☎808-868-0753; www.tinroofmaui.com; 360 Papa Pl; mains from $5-10; ⊘10am-2pm Mon-Sat) The latest venture from celebrity chef Sheldon Simeon proves that a restaurant can be successful no matter the venue – in this case a tin-roofed outlet next to Payday Loans. Be prepared to queue for his tasty *kau kau* tins of flavorsome pork belly, rice and salsa, or mochiko chicken marinated in ginger sake shoyu, topped with su-miso sauce, gochujang aioli, and mochi crunch.

Wow-Wee Maui's
Kava Bar & Grill
BURGERS, SANDWICHES $

(Map p134; ☎808-871-1414; www.mauikavabar.com; 333 Dairy Rd; mains $7-17; ⊘10.30am-9pm) The grill dominates the kava at this buzzing local joint, but it's still your best chance to try *piper methysticum,* a ceremonial drink made from the kava plant that has an earthy taste and numbs your

mouth. The rest of the restaurant offers good burgers, wraps, and mains including Hawaiian BBQ pork, grilled salmon and baby back ribs.

Tasaka Guri-Guri
ICE CREAM $

(Map p134; ☎808-871-4513; 70 E Ka'ahumanu Ave, Maui Mall; 2 scoops/quart $1.30/6; ⊘9am-6pm Mon-Sat, to 4pm Sun) For the coolest treat in town, queue up at this hole-in-the-wall shop dishing up homemade pineapple sherbet. The *guri-guri,* as it's called, is so popular that locals take it to friends on neighboring islands. Cash only.

Pa'ina Food Court
FOOD HALL $

(Map p134; www.mauiculinary-campusdining.com; 310 W Ka'ahumanu Ave, Maui College; mains $6-9; ⊘7:30am-2pm Mon-Thu, to 1pm Fri) With tenants like Paniolo Grill and World Plate, this multi-stall food court isn't your average campus fare. Run by students from Maui College's acclaimed culinary arts program, it's worth a detour for choice alone. The food court is inside the Pa'ina Building, which borders the parking lot beside the easy-to-find Maui Swap Meet grounds off Wahinepio Ave.

Thailand Cuisine II
THAI $$

(Map p134; ☎808-873-0225; www.thailandcuisinemaui.net; 70 E Ka'ahumanu Ave, Maui Mall; mains $12-21; ⊘11am-2:30pm Mon-Sat, 5-10pm Mon-Sun; ✪) This family-run eatery is one of Maui's best ethnic restaurants. Start with the shrimp summer rolls, then move on to aromatic green curries or perhaps the ginger-grilled mahimahi.

Da Kitchen
HAWAIIAN **$$**

(Map p134; ☑ 808-871-7782; www.dakitchen.com; 425 Koloa St, Triangle Sq; mains $10-27; ⊘ 11am-9pm Mon-Sat) Tasty *grinds* (local foods) attract all kinds to this strip mall eatery. The *kalua* pork is, as they say, 'so tender it falls off da bone', while the more expensive plate lunches are big enough to feed two. Expect a crowd at lunch but the service is quick.

★ Bistro Casanova
MEDITERRANEAN **$$$**

(Map p134; ☑ 808-873-3650; www.casanovamaui.com; 33 Lono Ave; lunch $9-20, dinner $14-36; ⊘ 11am-9:30pm Mon-Sat) An offshoot of the popular Casanova in Makawao, this is Kahului's classiest dining option, with happy hour offers on wine, cocktails and beer (from $5) between 4pm and 6pm. On the dinner menu the seafood and steaks are good and come with plenty of Kula veggies. The setting is upscale and urban. Reservations are recommended at dinner, when the bistro can fill with a pre-theater crowd en route to a show at the Maui Arts & Cultural Center.

Leis Family Class Act
INTERNATIONAL **$$$**

(Map p134; ☑ 808-984-3280; www.mauiculinary-campusdining.com; 310 W Ka'ahumanu Ave, Maui College; prix fixe per person $30-42; ⊘ 11am-12:30pm Wed & Fri) Maui Culinary Academy's fine-dining restaurant connects an ocean view with the opportunity to watch up-and-coming chefs create a four-course locavore meal. The menu rotates between countries. Reserve online.

Whole Foods
SUPERMARKET

(Map p134; ☑ 808-872-3310; www.wholefoodsmarket.com; 70 E Ka'ahumanu Ave, Maui Mall; ⊘ 7am-9pm) Whole Foods carries island-grown produce, fish and beef, and is a good place to pick up lei.

Safeway Kahului
SUPERMARKET

(Map p134; ☑ 808-877-3377; www.safeway.com; 170 E Kamehameha Ave; ⊘ 24hr) For groceries, the Safeway in the town center never closes.

🍸 Drinking & Nightlife

Maui Coffee Roasters
CAFE

(Map p134; ☑ 800-645-2877; www.mauicoffeeroasters.com/cafe; 444 Hana Hwy; pastries $4-9, sandwiches & wraps $7-10; ⊘ 7am-6pm Mon-Sat, 8am-4pm Sun; 🛜) Enjoy good vibes and good java at this bright and upbeat cafe where locals sip lattes and nibble wraps while surfing free wi-fi. Kitchen hours 7am to 5pm Monday to Saturday and 8am to 2:30pm Sunday.

Kahului Ale House
SPORTS BAR

(Map p134; ☑ 808-877-0001; www.alehouse.net; 355 E Kamehameha Ave; ⊘ 11am-10.30pm) With 35 flat-screen TVs, Maui's top sports bar won't let you miss a single play. Pub grub includes burgers, sandwiches and pizzas. Live music from about 5pm to 8pm or so daily. The kitchen is open late.

☆ Entertainment

Maui Arts & Cultural Center
CONCERT VENUE

(MACC; Map p134; ☑ 808-242-7469; www.mauiarts.org; 1 Cameron Way) This snazzy performance complex opened in 1994 and boasts two indoor theaters and an outdoor amphitheater. As Maui's main venue for music, theater and dance, the MACC hosts everything from ukulele jams to touring rock bands. Look out for the Ki Ho'alu Slack Key Guitar Festival (p135), usually in June, and the Maui Ukulele Festival held every year in October.

Be sure to stop by the Schaefer International Gallery beforehand, to see the latest art exhibition.

🛍 Shopping

Kahului hosts Maui's big-box discount chains of the Wal-Mart and Costco variety, as well as its reigning shopping mall, **Queen Ka'ahumanu Center** (Map p134; ☑ 808-877-3369; www.queenkaahumanucenter.com; 275 W Ka'ahumanu Ave; ⊘ 9:30am-9pm Mon-Sat, 10am-5pm Sun).

★ Maui Swap Meet
MARKET

(Map p134; ☑ 808-244-3100; www.mauiexposition.com; 310 Ka'ahumanu Ave, Maui College; adult/child 12yr & under 50¢/free; ⊘ 7am-1pm Sat) Don't be misled by 'swap meet'. This outdoor market is not a garage sale, nor a farmers market, but an arts and crafts show of the highest order. Scores of white tents, set up behind Maui College, are chock-full of fascinating, high-quality merchandise, most of it locally made, including jewelry, sculptures, clothing and Hawaii memorabilia. Come here for a meaningful souvenir.

Bounty Music
MUSIC

(Map p134; ☑ 808-214-1591; www.bountymusic-maui.com; 111 Hana Hwy; ⊘ 9am-6pm Mon-Sat, 10am-4pm Sun) Hawaiian music lovers should step inside for all sorts of ukuleles, from inexpensive imported models to handcrafted masterpieces. Rentals, too. And if you're lucky you might catch some impromptu live music.

ⓘ Information

Bank of Hawaii (☑ 808-871-8250; www.boh. com; 11 E Kamehameha Ave; ⊗ 8:30am-4pm Mon-Thu, to 6pm Fri, 9am-1pm Sat) ATM available here.

Department of Parks & Recreation – Central District (Map p134; ☑ 808-270-7389; www. mauicounty.gov; 700 Halia Nakoa St, War Memorial Gymnasium; ⊗ 8am-4pm Mon-Fri) Useful for updates on national parks and to apply for camping permits.

Longs Drugs (☑ 808-877-0068; 70 E Ka'ahumanu Ave, Maui Mall; ⊗ 24hr; pharmacy 8am-10pm Mon-Fri, to 7pm Sat & Sun) More than just a pharmacy – a local institution offering everything from flip-flops to souvenirs.

Maui Memorial Medical Center (☑ 808-244-9056; www.mauimemorialmedical.org; 221 Mahalani St; ⊗ 24hr) The island's main hospital. For extreme emergencies, flying to Queen's Medical Center in Honolulu may be preferable.

Mahalani St is off W Kaahumanu Ave, right between Kahului and Wailuku.

Maui Visitors Bureau (Map p130; ☑ 808-872-3893; www.gohawaii.com/maui; Kahului Airport; ⊗ 5am-10pm) This staffed booth in the airport's arrivals area has tons of tourist brochures.

ⓘ Getting There & Away

Most people fly into **Kahului International Airport** (OGG; Map p130; ☑ 808-872-3830; http://hawaii.gov/ogg; 1 Kahului Airport Rd), Maui's main airport, which is located at the eastern side of town, just a short taxi ride from the restaurants and shops of the city. Direct flights arrive here from the US mainland and Canada.

The majority of the car-hire companies on the island operate from the airport. Local **Bio-Beetle** (☑ 808-873-6121; https://mauicarrentals.us; 55 Amala Pl; per day $50-90, per week $150-400) rents a spread of ecofriendly vehicles, including biodiesel VW bugs, gas and electric Chevy Volts, and the purely electric Nissan Leaf. Free airport pick-up and drop-off is offered.

ⓘ Getting Around

Maui Bus (www.co.maui.hi.us) connects Kahului airport with downtown Kahului via the Haiku Islander (route 35) and the Upcountry Islander (route 40), both of which run hourly throughout the day. Maui Bus routes also connect with Wailuku, Paia and Haiku. Each route costs $2. Infants under two years old travel for free.

Shuttle services from the airport, including **Roberts Hawaii** (☑ 1800-831-5541; www. robertshawaii.com), run to various destinations in Maui. Fares start from $10 one way, while a taxi from the airport to central Kahului costs from $13.

Wailuku

Four streams feed the lush landscape surrounding Wailuku, which made the area an important food source and landholding for Maui chieftains. Missionaries took up residence here in the 1800s. Today, while offering more sights on the National Register of Historic Places than any other town on Maui, Wailuku sees few tourists. And that is its appeal. An earthy mishmash of curio shops, galleries and mom-and-pop stores surround the modern center of the county capital, all begging to be browsed. If you're here at lunchtime you're in luck. Thanks to a combination of low rent and hungry government employees, Wailuku dishes up tasty eats at prices that shame more touristy towns.

◉ Sights

A cluster of historic buildings anchor the small downtown. Hawaii's best-known architect, Maui-born CW Dickey, left his mark here before moving on to fame in Honolulu. The c 1928 Wailuku Public Library is a classic example of his distinctive regional design, and its double-pitched hip roof is his signature element. Another Dickey creation, the Territorial Building, sits across the street. To learn more, pick up a copy of the free Wailuku Historic District walking map at the Hale Hō'ike'ike at the Bailey House or download it at www. mauimuseum.org. Five buildings along the walk are on the National Register of Historic Places.

★ Hale Hō'ike'ike
at the Bailey House   MUSEUM
(☑ 808-244-3326; www.mauimuseum.org; 2375a Main St; adult/child 7-12yr $7/2; ⊗ 10am-4pm Mon-Sat) This small but historically evocative museum occupies the 1833 home of Wailuku's first Christian missionary, Edward Bailey. He was the second missionary to occupy the house and lived here nearly 50 years. The home gives you a sense of what it was like to live in missionary times while also containing

Wailuku

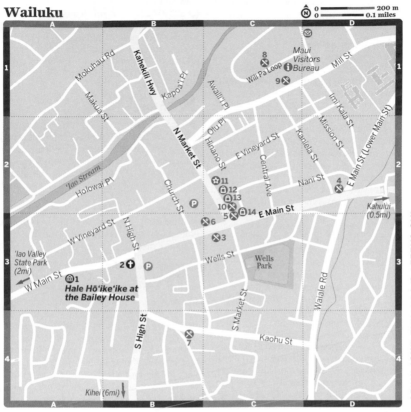

Wailuku

⊚ Top Sights

1 Hale Hōʻikeʻike at the Bailey House...... A3

⊚ Sights

2 Kaʻahumanu Church............................. B3

⊗ Eating

3 808 on Main... C3
4 A Saigon Café....................................... D2
5 Farmacy Health Bar............................ C3
6 Giannotto's Pizza................................ C3
7 Ichiban Okazuya.................................. B4

8 Sam Sato's... C1
9 Tasty Crust.. C1
10 Wailuku Coffee Co............................. C2

⊕ Entertainment

11 'Iao Theater.. C2

⊕ Shopping

12 Bird-of-Paradise Unique
    Antiques.. C2
13 Brown-Kobayashi................................ C2
14 Native Intelligence............................. C2

a collection of interesting artifacts, including a shark-tooth dagger and a notable collection of native wood bowls, stone adzes, feather lei and tapa cloth.

Outside there's a historic koa canoe (c 1900) and a 10ft redwood board used by surfing legend Duke Kahanamoku.

Kaʻahumanu Church   CHURCH
(103 S High St) This handsome missionary church is named for Queen Kaʻahumanu, who cast aside the old Hawaiian gods and allowed Christianity to flourish. The clock in the steeple, brought around the Horn in the 19th century, still keeps accurate time.

The church is usually locked, but hymns still ring out in Hawaiian at services on Sundays.

Haleki'i-Pihana Heiau State Monument
RUINS

(Map p134; Hea Pl; ⊙7am-7pm) Haleki'i-Pihana Heiau is the hilltop ruins of two of Maui's most important heiau (ancient stone temples). The site was the royal court of Kahekili, Maui's last ruling chief, and the birthplace of Keopuolani, wife of Kamehameha the Great. After his victory at the battle of 'Iao in 1790, Kamehameha marched to this site to worship his war god Ku, offering the last human sacrifice on Maui.

With this history, it is surprising to find the site overgrown and nearly forgotten. Even the parking lot is closed. Yet, surprisingly, the ravages of time add something to the visit. Instead of merging with another bus tour group, you'll likely be by yourself, reflecting on the contrast between these ancient temples and the modern suburb lapping at their doorstep. Concentrate on the wild ocean and mountain vistas, and you might notice a certain mana (spiritual essence) still permeating the air.

The site is about 2 miles northeast of central Wailuku. From Waiehu Beach Rd (Hwy 340), turn inland onto Kuhio Pl, then take the first left (Hea Pl, missing sign) and park near the end on the residential street. Follow the closed road up to the site. Haleki'i, the first heiau, has stepped stone walls that tower above 'Iao Stream, the source for the stone used in its construction. The pyramid-like mound of Pihana Heiau is a five-minute walk beyond. Some faded placards provide historical background. A round-trip is a quarter mile.

✨ Festivals & Events

★ Wailuku First Friday
CARNIVAL

(www.mauifridays.com; ⊙1st Fri of the month 6pm-9pm) On the first Friday of every month, Market St turns into a pedestrian zone and laid-back street party, with several bands, lots of tasty food options, and even a beer garden. This is Wailuku at its finest, so don't miss it if you're nearby.

Maui County Fair
FAIR

(www.mauifair.com; ⊙Sep or Oct) Get a feel for Maui's agricultural roots at this venerable fair held in late September or early October, with farm exhibits, tasty island *grinds* and a dazzling orchid display.

E Ho'oulu Aloha
CULTURAL

(☑808-244-3326; www.mauimuseum.org; ⊙Nov & Dec) This old-Hawaii-style festival held towards the end of the year at the Bailey House Museum features hula, music, crafts and food. You won't find a friendlier community scene. Phone the museum to check dates.

Eating

★ Sam Sato's
JAPANESE $

(☑808-244-7124; 1750 Wili Pa Loop; mains under $10; ⊙7am-2pm Mon-Sat) On busy days, Sam Sato's may use 350lb of noodles to keep the crowds sated. A Hawaii classic, this place packs them in with steaming bowls of noodles and delicious *manju* (Japanese cakes filled with sweet bean paste). You'll find yourself waiting for a table at lunchtime, but there's often room at the counter. The dry mein is the signature dish.

Farmacy Health Bar
HEALTH FOOD $

(☑808-866-4312; www.facebook.com/farmacy healthbar; 12 N Market St; smoothies $9, mains $10-14; ⊙8am-5.30pm Mon-Sun) The acai creations are so cold they chill your teeth at this spare but inviting health-food eatery where you'll feel invigorated just reading the menu. Smoothies are packed with fruit, and a handful of good-for-you salads come with locally grown veggies. Sandwiches can be made with sourdough, wheat, pita or gluten-free bread. Best for takeout. And check out those bright green walls!

Ichiban Okazuya
JAPANESE $

(☑808-244-7276; 2133 Kaohu St; mains $9-12; ⊙10am-8pm Mon-Fri) Little more than a tin-roofed shed, this place tucked behind the government buildings has been dishing out tasty Japanese-style plate lunches to office workers for half a century, so you'd better believe it has the recipes down pat.

Wailuku Coffee Co
CAFE $

(☑808-495-0259; www.wailukucoffeeco.com; 26 N Market St; ⊙7am-5pm Mon-Sat, 8am-3pm Sun; ☜🖉) Located in the bays of a 1920s gas station, this is (as a sign proclaims) 'where the hip come to sip.' But if you're a few years behind the times, don't worry: in Wailuku this means surfing the web in your T-shirt while downing a toddy (iced coffee). Enjoy the smoothies, sandwiches, salads and pita pizzas too.

Tasty Crust
DINER $

(☑808-244-0845; 1770 Mill St; breakfast $6-17, lunch & dinner $7-17; ⊙6am-9pm Mon, to 10pm Sun & Tue-Thu, to 11pm Fri & Sat) The old-school American diner gets a Hawaiian twist at this low-frills locals' joint. Breakfast standbys like Denver omelets and banana pancakes jostle for attention with *loco moco*, Spam, and fried rice with egg. Settle in among the families, crying babies and breakfast-steak-eating businesspeople for a solid budget meal on your way to 'Iao Valley.

808 on Main
BURGERS $

(☑808-242-1111; www.808onmain.com; 2051 Main St; mains $9.50-18; ⊙10am-8pm Mon-Fri) Serving hearty salads, sandwiches and burgers, this new restaurant has simple airy decor and fairy lights inside. The *pupu* (snacks) menu includes dishes like Buffalo Brussels sprouts with hot sauce and blue cheese, and kimchi pork balls with goat cheese and sambal aioli. *Pupu*, beer and wine are discounted during the daily happy hour deal from 3pm to 6pm.

A Saigon Café
VIETNAMESE $$

(☑808-243-9560; cnr Main & Kaniela Sts; mains $10-29; ⊙10am-9.30pm Mon-Fri, to 8.30pm Sun) The oldest and best Vietnamese restaurant on Maui is out of the way, but it rewards the search. Menu stars include Buddha rolls in spicy peanut sauce and aromatic lemongrass curries.

Giannotto's Pizza
ITALIAN $$

(☑808-244-8282; www.giannottospizza.com; 2050 Main St; pizza slice $2-4, mains $7-27; ⊙11am-9pm Mon-Sat, to 8pm Sun) Brando, Sinatra and the Sopranos look down in approval from the cluttered walls of Giannotto's, a family-run pizza joint known for its home recipes.

☆ Entertainment

'Iao Theater
THEATER

(☑808-242-6969; www.mauionstage.com; 68 N Market St; ⊙box office 11am-3pm Mon, Wed & Fri) Nicely restored after years of neglect, this 1928 art-deco theater, which once hosted big names such as Frank Sinatra, is now the venue for community theater productions.

🛍 Shopping

Bird-of-Paradise Unique Antiques
ANTIQUES

(56 N Market St; ⊙9am-3pm Mon-Fri, 10am-2pm Sat) This place is stuffed to the gills with vintage Hawaiiana.

WAILUKU TO 'IAO VALLEY STATE MONUMENT

It's hard to believe today, but the route from Wailuku to 'Iao Valley was the site of Maui's bloodiest battle. In 1790 Kamehameha the Great invaded Kahului by sea and drove the defending Maui warriors up 'Iao Stream. As the valley walls closed in, those unable to escape over the mountains were slaughtered. The waters of 'Iao Stream were so choked with bodies that the area was named Kepaniwai (Dammed Waters).

Native Intelligence
GIFTS & SOUVENIRS

(☑808-249-2421; www.native-intel.com; 1980 Main St; ⊙10am-5pm Mon-Fri, to 4pm Sat) Hula instruments, koa bowls and finely handcrafted items.

Brown-Kobayashi
ANTIQUES

(38 N Market St; ⊙11am-4pm Mon-Fri, to 3pm Sat) Museum-quality Asian antiques.

ⓘ Information

First Hawaiian Bank (www.fhb.com; 27 N Market St) ATM available here.

Maui Visitors Bureau (☑800-525-6284, 808-244-3530; www.gohawaii.com/maui; 1727 Wili Pa Loop; ⊙8am-4:30pm Mon-Fri) For local info pop into the Maui Visitors Bureau or visit its website to download or order a Maui visitor's guide. Also represents Lana'i and Moloka'i.

Post Office (☑808-244-1653; www.usps.com; 250 Imi Kala St; ⊙9am-4pm Mon-Fri, to noon Sat)

'Iao Valley State Monument

As you drive out of Wailuku, 'Iao Valley's emerald lushness envelops you, concluding with an explosion of riparian and mountain greenery at **'Iao Valley State Monument** (Map p130; ☑808-587-0400; per car $5; ⊙7am-7pm), deep inside the bosom of the West Maui Mountains. The scenery is dramatic, with sheer peaks soaring in all directions, most notably 'Iao Needle. Rising above the lush rainforest, and caressed by passing mist, this rock pinnacle stands as a monument to your journey, while marking the entrance to the mysterious, uninhabited valley beyond. Most will never go beyond

'IAO VALLEY & CENTRAL MAUI 'IAO VALLEY STATE MONUMENT

the viewpoint, but the park extends clear up to Pu'u Kukui (5788ft), Maui's highest and wettest place.

Unfortunately, in late 2016 the area suffered severe flood damage. At the time of writing it was closed for repairs; trails through the park were also closed. Check the Department of Land & Natural Resources (http://dlnr.hawaii.gov) website before your visit.

◉ Sights & Activities

After entering the 'Iao Valley State Monument, just after the parking lot, you'll reach a bridge. If the water is high you may see local kids taking bravado jumps from the bridge to the rocky stream below. Don't even think about doing this. Take your dip further on, remembering that flash floods do occur here.

After crossing this bridge you will come to two **short trails** that start opposite each other. Both take just 10 minutes to walk and shouldn't be missed. The upper path leads skyward up a series of steps, ending at a sheltered lookout with a close-up view of 'Iao Needle. The lower path leads down along 'Iao Stream, skirting the rock-strewn stream bed past native hau trees with their fragrant hibiscus-like flowers. Look around and you'll be able to spot fruiting guava trees as well. The lower path returns to the bridge by way of a garden of native Hawaiian plants, including patches of taro.

'Iao Needle   LANDMARK

(Map p130) Rising straight up to 2250ft, this velvety green pinnacle is Maui's iconic landmark. Most people shoot their mandatory photos from the bridge near the parking lot. A better idea, though, is to take the walkway just before the bridge that loops downhill by 'Iao Stream. This leads to the nicest angle, one that captures the stream, bridge and 'Iao Needle together.

The pinnacle takes its name from 'Iao, the daughter of Maui. According to legend, Maui and the goddess Hina raised their beautiful daughter deep in this hidden valley to shelter her from worldly temptations. But a merman (half-man, half-fish) swam into the valley one night and took 'Iao as a lover. When Maui discovered the affair he snatched the merman and threatened to cast him out to sea. 'Iao pleaded that she could not live without the sight of her beloved, so instead Maui turned him into a needle of stone.

'Iao Valley Trail   HIKING

This little-known dirt trail heads deep into 'Iao Valley. It begins on the lower trail after the bridge, over the fence near the end of the cement path, and is marked by a 'Stay on Marked Trails' sign. Beautiful and pristine, it leads through the jungle, paralleling 'Iao Stream, and ends at a steep cliff.

Great views lead back past Wailuku to the sea. This is your only chance to walk into the valley. Allow for a two-hour round-trip.

Waikapu

Located in the foothills of the West Maui Mountains, Waikapu was once a taro farming area but is now a large tract of land with thousands of residents. For visitors, highlights include vast open spaces, a top-notch golf course and a thrilling zipline.

◉ Sights & Activities

Maui Tropical Plantation   FARM

(Map p130; ☑ 808-244-7643; www.mauitropicalplantation.com; 1670 Honoapi'ilani Hwy; admission free, tram tour adult/child 3-12yr $20/10; ⊙ 9am-5pm, tram tours 10am-4pm, departing every 45min; ℗) This longstanding tourist attraction is a cross between a farm, a shopping mall and a theme park. The large gift shop stocks art, aloha wear and gift food. Various plantation huts offer everything from chocolate to jewelry to ziplining (hours vary). Kumu Farms adds organic produce and gourmet products, while a historic house contains photographs of old Waikapu Valley.

★ Flyin Hawaiian Zipline   ADVENTURE SPORTS

(Map p130; ☑ 808-463-5786; www.flyinhawaiianzipline.com; 1670 Honoapi'ilani Hwy, Maui Tropical Plantation; per person $185) Wheeeee! Adrenaline junkies will revel in this new ziplining addition. Located high in the crumpled folds of the West Maui Mountains, this course spans nine valleys with eight lines, including one 3600ft monster, achieving speeds of more than 50mph. Allow four to five hours. Minimum age: 10 years old; weight 75lb to 250lb.

★ King Kamehameha Golf Club   GOLF

(Map p130; ☑ 808-249-0033; www.kamehamehagolf.com; 2500 Honoapi'ilani Hwy; morning round $205; ⊙ 6:30am-6:30pm) The only 18-hole private club on Maui, and the island's most challenging course, is surprisingly

A FRANK LLOYD WRIGHT MASTERPIECE

The clubhouse at the King Kamehameha Golf Club is Maui's great anomaly: a building that should be known worldwide is hardly mentioned on the island, or visited by anyone save its members.

The spectacular rose building looks like a set from *Star Wars*, and is beautifully sited in the Waikapu Valley, at the foot of the West Maui Mountains. A whopping 75,000 sq feet in area, it can be seen from the slopes of Haleakalā. Originally designed as a much smaller home by famed American architect Frank Lloyd Wright, it contains many artistic flourishes, including art glass, etched designs and an elegant Hawaiian art collection.

Wright adapted the design for three successive clients, including Marilyn Monroe, but never broke ground. In 1988, three decades after his death, Japanese investors purchased the plans, intent on building a clubhouse in Maui. They poured $35 million into the project, including further adaptation by one of Wright's apprentices. Then the Japanese economy collapsed in 1999, the club closed, and the greens turned brown. In 2004 another Japanese investor bought the property, and spent $40 million more. Today the club is working to fill its roster, but this is no reflection on the course, or the magnificent building that crowns it.

The public is welcome to tour the building free of charge, and to visit the restaurant. A brochure about the building and the art collection is available at the entrance. Note that the clubhouse is a short drive up the hill beyond the pro shop.

friendly to the public. One-day guests can enjoy a round of golf for less than most resort courses. The extraordinary bi-coastal vistas are matched only by the spectacular Frank Lloyd Wright clubhouse, considered by *Golf Digest* as possibly the best in the country.

Kahili Course GOLF
(Map p130; ☑ 808-242-4653; www.kahiligolf.com; 2500 Honoapiʻilani Hwy; greens fees incl cart $75-95; ☺ 6am-6:30pm) Nestled at the base of the West Maui Mountains, just down the street from its private sister, King Kamehameha Golf Club, this beautiful public course is in outstanding condition and offers great value. The topography is very hilly, but otherwise the course is only moderately difficult. There are no adjacent properties in sight, so no, you won't break any windows.

Maui Zipline ADVENTURE SPORTS
(Map p130; ☑ 808-633-2464; www.mauizipline. com; 1670 Honoapiʻilani Hwy, Maui Tropical Plantation; per person $110; ☺ 9am-3:30pm) Located on the grounds of Maui Tropical Plantation, this is an extremely tame, five-line course designed for families, with a low five-year-old, 50lb limit and dual lines. The zip over a pond adds some spice. However, without any discount for kids, families pay a lot for this two-hour experience.

🍴 Eating

Mill House Dining FUSION $$$
(Map p130; ☑ 808-270-0333; www.millhouse-maui.com; 1670 Honoapiilani Hwy, Maui Tropical Plantation; dinner $18-55; ☺ 11.00am-9pm) With an emphasis on local farm-fresh food, the recently opened Mill House Dining is impress-your-friends-dining without being stuffy. Inventive dishes take the form of pork belly with fennel jam, carrot and brassica, or Hawaiian kampachi fish with soubise (onion sauce), Vietnamese dipping sauce, cucumber, cashew, basil and mint. Some ingredients are actually hand-picked from the beautiful setting – the surrounding plantation's fields.

Maʻalaea

Maʻalaea is the jumping-off point for exploring Maui's coastline by boat. Many tour companies work out of this cute little harbor. The biggest draw is the whale-waching and snorkeling trips that run from here to Molokini – a submerged volcanic crater offshore with excellent visibility. Maʻalaea Bay is home to a surf-spot pipeline, which, when the winds and swells align, can produce fast barrels. It's no coincidence that Maui's first windmill farm marches up the slopes here in windy Maʻalaea. By midday the winds pick up and you might need to hold on to your hat.

WORTH A TRIP

MOLOKINI

Molokini is a volcanic crater sitting midway between the islands of Maui and Kaho'olawe. Half of the crater has eroded, leaving a pretty 18-acre crescent moon that rises 160ft above the sea. But what lies beneath is the main attraction. Steep walls, ledges and an extraordinary fringing reef attract white-tipped reef sharks, manta rays, turtles, abundant fish – and some 1000 visitors per day, most armed with a snorkel and mask. Basic snorkeling trips from Ma'alaea Harbor start from about $90 per person. For more info call or visit the **Ma'alaea Harbor Activities** (Map p130; ☑808-280-8073; www.maalaeaharboractivities.com; Ma'alaea Harbor; ⏰9am-8pm) hut. Trips also leave from Kihei. Avoid discounted afternoon tours: the water is calmest and clearest in the morning, but it can get rough and murky later.

Beaches

Ma'alaea Bay   BEACH
Ma'alaea Bay is fronted by a 3-mile stretch of sand, running from Ma'alaea Harbor south to Kihei. Access is from Haycraft Park at the end of Hauoli St in Ma'alaea and from several places along N Kihei Rd including **Kealia Beach**, which parallels the Kealia Coastal Boardwalk. Parking is limited, but the beach is mostly deserted.

Sights

Maui Ocean Center   AQUARIUM
(Map p130; ☑808-270-7000; www.mauiocean center.com; 192 Ma'alaea Rd; adult/child 3-12yr $28/20; ⏰9am-5pm Sep-Jun, to 6pm Jul & Aug; 🚼) This midsize aquarium showcases Hawaii's dazzling marine life, including many species found nowhere else. The floor plan takes you on an ocean journey, beginning with nearshore reefs teeming with colorful tropical fish and ending with deep-ocean sealife. The grand finale is a 54ft clear acrylic tunnel that leads through a large tank as sharks and rays glide by. Local ordinance prevents exhibition of live cetaceans, so there's no dolphin show.

Activities

Wicked winds from the north shoot straight out toward Kaho'olawe, creating excellent windsurfing conditions that, unlike elsewhere, persist throughout the winter. The bay also has a couple of hot surfing spots. The **Ma'alaea Pipeline** (Map p130), south of the harbor, freight-trains right and is the fastest surf break in all Hawaii. Summer's southerly swells produce huge tubes here.

Shark Dive Maui   DIVING
(Map p130; ☑808-270-7000; www.maui oceancenter.com/sharkdive; Maui Ocean Center, 192 Ma'alaea Rd; 2hr experience incl admission to aquarium for diver & viewing guest $200; ⏰8:15am Mon, Wed & Fri) Shark Dive Maui takes intrepid divers on a daredevil's plunge into the 750,000-gallon deep-ocean tank at Maui Ocean Center to swim with around 20 sharks, including a black-tip reef shark, a hammerhead and, gasp, a tiger shark.

Da Beach House   ADVENTURE SPORTS
(Map p130; ☑808-986-8279; ww.dabeachhouse maui.com; Harbor Shops at Ma'alaea, 300 Ma'alaea Rd; surfboard rental per day from $30; ⏰10am-6pm) Rents water-sports equipment and beach chairs. Sells hats, sunblock, towels, swimwear and other beach goods.

Tours

The tour operators at Ma'alaea Harbor have consolidated reservations at the Ma'alaea Harbor Activities hut, facing Slip 47. Here you can book fishing trips, snorkeling excursions, dinner, cocktail and sunset cruises, and seasonal whale-watching trips. They're great at comparison shopping.

Pacific Whale Foundation   BOATING
(Map p130; ☑808-249-8811; www.pacific whale.org; 300 Ma'alaea Rd, Ma'alaea Harbor Shops; cruises adult/child 7-12yr from $35/20; ⏰schedules vary; 🚼) Led by naturalists, these boat tours do it right, offering snorkeling lessons and wildlife talks. Snacks are provided and kids under 12 go free on certain cruises. Half-day tours concentrate on Molokini; full-day tours add Lana'i. There's a great variety of tours, including whale-watching, dinner and cocktail cruises and, for the explorer, raft tours to Lana'i. Prices vary.

Quicksilver   BOATING
(Map p130; ☑808-662-0075, 808-442-3267; www. quicksilvermaui.com; Slip 44, Ma'alaea Harbor; adult/child 7-12yr $90/60) If you want more of a party scene for your day on the water, hop aboard this sleek double-decker catamaran.

Once you're done snorkeling off Molokini, your crew cranks up Jimmy Buffett and serves a barbecue lunch.

✗ Eating

★ **Ma'alaea General Store & Cafe**   CAFE $
(Map p130; ☎808-242-8900; www.maalaea store.com; 132 Ma'alaea Rd; mains $2-13; ⊗6am-6pm Mon-Sat, to 5pm Sun; ☎⏚) Located in the only original building left from the days when Ma'alaea was a small Japanese fishing village, this friendly general store and cafe offers deli eats, fresh-baked bread, and a rare focus on veggie and gluten-free solutions. Plus giant fudge brownies! The porch is a great place to dive into its signature Reuben while watching the world go by.

Hula Cookies & Ice Cream   DESSERTS $
(Map p130; ☎808-243-2271; www.hulacookies. com; 300 Ma'alaea Rd, Ma'alaea Harbor Shops; cookie $1.50, ice cream $3-6; ⊗10am-6pm) The freshly baked cookies and Maui-made ice cream here are chock-full of macadamia nuts, pineapple and coconut. A good place to take the kids after visiting the nearby aquarium.

Beach Bums Bar & Grill   BARBECUE $$
(Map p130; ☎808-243-2286; www.beachbums hawaii.com; 300 Ma'alaea Rd, Ma'alaea Harbor Shops; breakfast $8-13, lunch & dinner $10-26; ⊗8am-9pm) For harbor views and barbecue, settle in at this lively eatery. Beach Bums uses a wood-burning rotisserie

smoker to grill up everything from burgers and ribs to turkey and Spam. Come from 3pm to 6pm for drafts from $2.50, or from 5pm to 8pm Monday to Friday to enjoy live local music.

❶ Getting There & Away

Ma'alaea has good connections to the rest of Maui's public bus system. The Maui Bus ($2) connects the Harbor Shops at Ma'alaea with Lahaina, Kahului and Kihei. Service depends on the route, but buses operate hourly from around 6am to 8pm.

Kealia Pond National Wildlife Refuge

For a quick escape from Central Maui's traffic and urban hustle and bustle, pull over for a stroll at this tranquil refuge.

◉ Sights & Activities

Kealia Pond National Wildlife Refuge   WILDLIFE RESERVE
(Map p130; ☎808-875-1582; www.fws.gov/refuge/kealia_pond; Mokulele Hwy, 6-mile marker; ⊗7:30am-4pm Mon-Fri) 🅵 **FREE** A birdwatcher's oasis, the Kealia Pond National Wildlife Refuge harbors native waterbirds year-round and hosts migratory ducks and shorebirds from October to April. In the rainy winter months Kealia Pond swells to more than 400 acres, making it one of the largest natural ponds in Hawaii. In summer it shrinks

'IAO VALLEY & CENTRAL MAUI KEALIA POND NATIONAL WILDLIFE REFUGE

THE STORY OF KAHO'OLAWE

The sacred but uninhabited island of Kaho'olawe lies 7 miles southwest of Maui. It has long been central to the Hawaiian rights movement, and many consider the island a living spiritual entity, a *pu'uhonua* (refuge) and *wahi pana* (sacred place).

Yet for nearly 50 years, from WWII to 1990, the US military used Kaho'olawe as a bombing range. Beginning in the 1970s, liberating the island from the military became a rallying point for a larger resurgence of Native Hawaiian pride. Today, the bombing has stopped, the navy is gone and healing the island is considered both a symbolic act and a concrete expression of Native Hawaiian sovereignty. For a more detailed historic timeline for the island, visit www.kahoolawe.hawaii.gov.

The island (11 miles long and 6 miles wide) and its surrounding waters are now a reserve that is off-limits to the general public because of the unexploded ordnance. However, **Protect Kaho'olawe 'Ohana** (PKO; www.protectkahoolaweohana.org; volunteer fee 4/5 days $150/180) conducts monthly visits to pull weeds, plant native foliage, clean up historic sites and honor the land. It welcomes respectful volunteers who are ready to work (not just sightsee). Visits are scheduled during or near the full moon; the volunteer fee covers food and transportation. You'll need your own sleeping bag, tent and personal supplies. For more details see the 'Huaka'i' section on the PKO website. Note: these trips book up at least two years ahead.

GREEN POWER
....

Windy central Maui is a major league player in the field of alternative energy, with a percentage of Maui's electricity needs coming from the 50ft high windmills located approximately 2000ft above Ma'alaea on the mountain area known as Kaheawa Pastures. It's the windmills that hold the greenest future, with 34 of them lining the ridge above Ma'alaea. In addition, Maui has roughly 700 registered electric cars and 117 charging ports. Solar power has also gained momentum on the island, with more than 60,000 homes and businesses installing it since 2001. Looking forward, the plan is to harness geothermal power on Maui by 2040.

to half the size, giving it a skirt of crystalline salt (Kealia means 'salt-encrusted place').

You can view the pond from the coastal boardwalk on N Kihei Rd, as well as from the refuge's **visitor center** (Map p130) off Mokulele Hwy at the 6-mile marker. In both places, you're almost certain to spot wading Hawaiian black-necked stilts, Hawaiian coots and black-crowned night herons – all native water birds that thrive in this sanctuary. The visitor center occupies an abandoned catfish farm with footpaths atop the levees that separate the old fishponds, a layout that allows you to get very close to the birds, and this is also the best place to see wintering osprey, a majestic fish hawk that dive-bombs for its prey in the fishponds.

★**Kealia Coastal Boardwalk**   WALKING
(Map p130; www.fws.gov/refuge/kealia_pond; Kealia Pond National Wildlife Refuge) This wonderful elevated boardwalk by Ma'alaea Bay seems to go on forever. It traverses over 2000ft of wetlands, making it a magnet for birders but also a great nature walk for anyone. Interpretive plaques and benches help along the way. In winter you may spot humpback whales. It's located 350yd north of the 2-mile marker on N Kihei Rd.

Pu'unene

Sugar was the lifeblood of Pu'unene until the end of 2016. Fields of cane expanded out from the Hawaiian Commercial & Sugar (C&S) Company's rusty old mill, the last of its kind in Hawaii. This industrial hulk still looms high, and not so long ago it belched smoke when boiling down sugarcane, making the whole area smell of molasses. Hidden nearby are the remains of the plantation village, including an old schoolhouse and a long-abandoned church. This is a great place to grasp what old island life would have been like – it's truly untouched by tourism.

◉ Sights

Alexander & Baldwin Sugar
Museum   MUSEUM
(Map p130; ☑808-871-8058; www.sugarmuseum. com; 3957 Hansen Rd; adult/child 6-12yr $7/2; ☉9:30am-4.30pm, last entry 4pm) This homespun museum occupies the former residence of the sugar mill's superintendent. There's the usual display of industrial machinery, including a working model of a cane-crushing plant, but what lingers afterward is the human story. One exhibit traces how the sons of missionaries took control of Maui's fertile valleys and dug the amazing irrigation system that made large-scale plantations viable.

Compelling B&W photographs illuminate the labor and recreational aspects of plantation life. An early-20th-century labor contract on display, from the Japanese Emigration Company, committed laborers to work the cane fields 10 hours a day, 26 days a month, for $15.

🛍 Shopping

Old Pu'unene Bookstore   BOOKS
(Map p130; ☑808-871-6563; www.mfol.org; near E Camp 5 Rd; ☉9am-4pm Tue-Sat) This shack has served as a used books store since 1913. It's a bit musty, but the selection is wide and it still sells most of them for a quarter! Pick up secondhand DVDs and CDs here too. All proceeds go to Maui Public Libraries.

RON DAHLQUIST/GETTY IMAGES ©

PHOTO IMAGE/GETTY IMAGES ©

Top: Looking out to
Kaho'olawe (p145),
with Molokini in the
distance

Bottom: Wind turbines
(p67)

Kihei & South Maui

Best Places to Eat

➡ Monkeypod Kitchen (p164)

➡ Fork & Salad (p158)

➡ Café O'Lei (p159)

➡ Matteo's Osteria (p164)

➡ Coconut's Fish Cafe (p158)

➡ Da Kitchen Express (p159)

Best Places to Drink

➡ Monkeypod Kitchen (p164)

➡ 5 Palms (p160)

➡ Dog & Duck (p161)

➡ South Shore Tiki Lounge (p161)

➡ Red Bar at Gannon's (p165)

➡ Maui Brewing Co (p160)

Why Go?

Sunsets are a communal affair in South Maui – just look at the throngs crowding the beach wall at Kama'ole Beach Park II in the late afternoon. It's a scene repeated up and down the coast here every day.

With miles of strip malls, condo complexes and upscale resorts, Kihei and Wailea look too commercial and over-built at first glance. But dig deeper. You'll find a mixed plate of scenery and adventure, stretching from Kihei to Makena and beyond, that's truly unique. You can snorkel reefs teeming with turtles, kayak to remote bays or sail in an outrigger canoe. The coral gardens are so rich you can dive from the shore. And the beaches? Undeniably glorious, whether you're looking to relax beneath a resort cabana or to discover your own pocket of sand. Add reliably sunny weather, quiet coastal trails and a diverse dining scene and South Maui's a pretty irresistible place to land.

When to Go

High season stretches from mid-December through mid-April, when crowds flock to Kihei and South Maui for the Christmas holidays and whale-watching. To avoid the heaviest crowds, visit in April and May or September through mid-December.

The best month for viewing humpback whales off the coast is February. The World Whale Day celebration is held in Kihei in the middle of February.

Movie stars arrive from the mainland in mid-June for the Maui Film Festival in Wailea. Visitors can watch a movie under the stars – and right on the beach – during this five-day extravaganza.

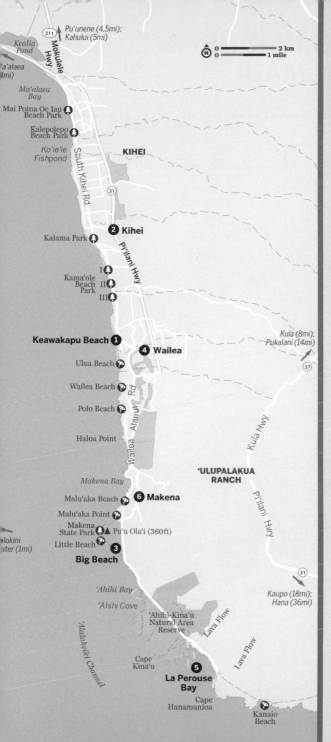

Kihei & South Maui Highlights

1 **Keawakapu Beach** (p154) Watching the sun drop below the horizon from a golden crescent of sand.

2 **Kihei** (p154) Digging into a heaping plate of *loco moco* on the patio of Hawaiian-style Kihei Caffe, or sampling four flagship beers at the Maui Brewing Co.

3 **Big Beach** (p167) Sunbathing on a remote stretch of gleaming sand tucked between wild forests and deep-blue waters in Makena State Park.

4 **Monkeypod Kitchen** (p164) Savoring a mai tai and wood-fired pizza during the convivial happy hour.

5 **La Perouse Bay** (p150) Hiking the Hoapili Trail through an eerie yet beautiful field of black lava.

6 **Makena** (p166) Snorkeling beside graceful green turtles at Turtle Beach, or paddling across Makena Bay in search of whales and marine life.

HIKING IN KIHEI & SOUTH MAUI

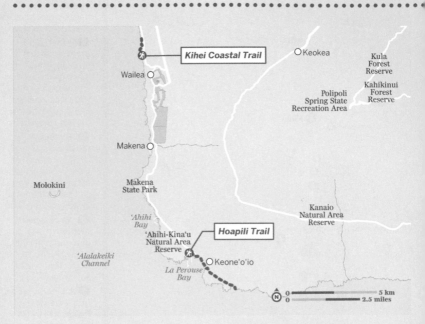

HOAPILI TRAIL

START LA PEROUSE BAY
END KANAIO BEACH
LENGTH 2 MILES ONE WAY; HALF-DAY
DIFFICULTY MODERATE

This section of the ancient King's Trail follows the coastline across jagged lava flows. Be prepared: wear hiking boots, bring plenty to drink, use sunscreen, start early and tell someone where you're going. It's a dry area with no water and little vegetation for shade, so it can get very hot.

From the **La Perouse Bay parking lot**, walk south beside the coast to pick up the **trail**, which begins at the edge of an inky black field of jagged *a'a* lava. The trail tracks the coast here, but a few short side trails lead to the ruins of the ancient Hawaiian community of **Keone'o'io**. Do not disturb the structures.

The trail then curves alongside the coast, passing through a cove then entering a kiawe forest hugging the sandy beach. You might encounter a few foraging goats. After the trail leaves the beach, at about 0.7 miles, you'll see an opening in a metal fence to your left, where the trail heads into an expansive lava field. It's also possible to continue straight along the coast, following a spur trail for 0.75 miles down to the light beacon at the tip of Cape Hanamanioa.

Turn left through the **fence opening**, walking inland to the **Na Ala Hele sign**. From here, follow the King's Hwy as it climbs through rough lava. King Pi'ilani instigated the construction of the the King's Trail more than 300 years ago to encourage commerce. The 200-mile highway once circled the entire island of Maui. As the sun rises and you trudge across the rocky trail through the black lava, you might feel as if you're slowly roasting. But views of the lava and ocean are superb. The trail continues through an older lava flow, returning to the coast at **Kanaio Beach**. Although the trail continues, it becomes harder to follow and Kanaio Beach is the recommended turn-around point.

Trails never stray far from the coast in sunny South Maui, whether they're meandering over rocky bluffs or powering through old lava fields. All are gorgeous, but start early to beat the midday heat.

If you don't include the lighthouse spur, the round-trip distance to Kanaio Beach is about 4 miles. For more details visit www.hawaii-trails.org, the state's trail and access website.

KIHEI COASTAL TRAIL

START KEAWAKAPU BEACH
END KAMA'OLE BEACH PARK III
LENGTH 0.6 MILES ONE WAY; ONE HOUR
DIFFICULTY EASY

This short trail meanders along coastal bluffs ideal for whale-watching and quiet meditation. You might even see an outrigger canoe glide past.

Begin a few steps south of the trailhead on the golden sands of **Keawakapu Beach** (p154), a beautiful place to stretch before your walk. Head north, walking between the rocky coast and the **Mana Kai Maui** (2960 S Kihei Rd). A morning yoga class is held on the beach here daily. Cross the parking lot to the trail, which tracks the lava-rock coast just west of the tidy lawn behind the **Kihei Surfside Resort** (2936 S Kihei Rd). Follow the small trail signs north along the coast.

At the end of the lawn, continue heading north on the seaside path. The island of Kahoolawe breaks the western horizon.

Weathered signage beside the trail discusses the island's role as a navigational training spot for ancient Hawaiians, who were extremely skilled long-distance paddlers.

Walk north past the **Kihei boat ramp**, picking up the trail as it unfurls across a coastal bluff offering expansive views of the sea. The path here is made of packed gray gravel outlined in white coral. Curiously, when the trail was being built, a storm washed hundreds of yards of bleached coral onto the shore here. The coral was not originally planned for the trail construction, but the volunteers building the trail consulted with a Hawaiian kahuna (priest) and were told ancient trails were often outlined in white coral so they could be followed at night. The Hawaiian gods were thanked for the gift of coral, which was then incorporated into the trail.

Along the bluff, look for the burrows of 'ua'u kani (wedge-tailed shearwaters), ground-nesting seabirds that return to the same sites each spring. The birds lay a single egg and remain until November, when the fledglings are large enough to head out to sea. The trail ends beyond the grassy lawn at the southern end of **Kama'ole Beach Park III** (p154).

LAZY DAYS

Dreaming of lounging in a tropical country club? Then make your way to south Kihei and Wailea, where relaxing is done in style – and usually framed by palm trees.

MORNING STROLLS

Early risers will be treated to watercolor hues and sweet tranquility on a sunrise stroll on the Wailea boardwalk or the Kihei Coastal Trail. Empty kayaks sit on the beach, outrigger-canoe clubs skim past shore and wildlife frolics in its last moments of peace.

A DAY ON THE BEACH

Oh, the golden strands of south Maui. World-class snorkeling is just offshore and an army of paddle boards are ready to rent. Stylish groups of honeymooners, hipsters and rich retirees amp up the people-watching. And reading on the beach never looked so pretty.

ENJOYING THE AMENITIES

World-class spas, golf courses and tennis courts are only a shuttle ride away in Wailea. Chef-driven restaurants beckon from the resorts, as do infinity pools and splashy wonderlands. In south Kihei, sunsets at Keawakapu Beach are free, unless you add in a 5 Palms cocktail. And you should.

1. Wailea Beach Walk (p163)
2. Andaz Maui resort, Wailea (p162)
3. Keawakapu Beach (p154)

Kihei

Two reasons to visit Kihei? The beaches and your budget. Yes, it's overrun with strip malls and traffic, but with 6 miles of easy-to-access beaches, loads of affordable accommodations and a variety of dining options, it offers everything you need for an enjoyable beach vacation. An energetic seaside town, Kihei also works well for short-trip vacationers seeking reliable sunshine – on average Kihei is sunny 276 days per year. It's also home to the island's busiest bar scene.

To zip from one end of Kihei to the other, take the Pi'ilani Hwy (Hwy 31). It runs parallel to and bypasses the stop-start traffic of S Kihei Rd. Well-marked crossroads connect these two routes.

🏖 Beaches

Water conditions vary with the weather, but swimming is usually good. For the most part, these beaches have sandy bottoms with a fairly steep drop, which tends to create good conditions for bodysurfing, especially in winter.

The beaches below are listed from north to south. The further south you travel, the better the beaches. At the northern end of Kihei, swimming is not advised, but kayaking is good in the morning. Windsurfers set off in the afternoon. Rocky points divide Kama'ole Beach into three very popular sections, called Kam I, Kam II and Kam III.

For a list of facilities at each county beach, visit www.mauicounty.gov. or call ☎ 808-879-4364.

Kalepolepo Beach Park   BEACH
(Map p157; S Kihei Rd at Ka'ono'ulu St; P 🚻) This compact park beside the headquarters for the Humpback Whale National Marine Sanctuary is a nice spot for families with younger kids. A grassy lawn is fronted by the ancient Ko'ie'ie Fishpond (p156), whose stone walls create a shallow swimming pool with calm waters perfect for wading. There are also picnic tables, a grill and an outdoor shower.

Charley Young Beach   BEACH
(Map p155; 2200 S Kihei Rd; P) On a side-street, out of view of busy S Kihei Rd, this neighborhood beach is the least-touristed strand in Kihei. It's a real jewel in the rough: broad and sandy, and backed by swaying coconut palms. You're apt to find fishers casting their lines, families playing volleyball and someone strumming a guitar. It also has some of the better bodysurfing waves in Kihei.

Beach parking is on the corner of S Kihei Rd and Kaia'u Pl. To get to the beach, walk to the end of Kaia'u Pl.

Kama'ole Beach Park I   BEACH
(Map p155; 2400 S Kihei Rd; P) A pretty, golden-sand beach with full facilities and lifeguards, plus a volleyball court and a parking lot. Travelers with disabilities can access the ocean at Kam I using accessibility ramps and the sand beach chair. For details about the status of the sand beach chair (available 8:30am to 3:30pm), check the Kamaole I listing at www.mauicounty.gov or call ☎ 808-270-6136.

Kama'ole Beach Park II   BEACH
(Map p155; 2550 S Kihei Rd) This lovely beach has beautiful golden sand as well as full facilities and lifeguards.

Kama'ole Beach Park III   BEACH
(Map p155; 2800 S Kihei Rd; P 🚻) Another beach covered in a blanket of golden sand, Kama'ole Beach Park III has full facilities and lifeguards, plus a playground and parking lot. Great spot for a beach day. The shaded picnic tables starting filling up early on weekends. Also has ADA parking, pathways and beach access.

The southern end of Kama'ole Beach Park III has some nearshore rocks harboring a bit of coral and a few colorful fish, though it pales in comparison to the snorkeling at beaches further south.

★ Keawakapu Beach   BEACH
(Map p155; ☎ 808-879-4364; www.mauicounty.gov/Facilities; P) From break of day to twilight, this sparkling stretch of sand is a showstopper. Extending from south Kihei to Wailea's Mokapu Beach, Keawakapu is set back from the main road and is less visible than Kihei's main roadside beaches just north. It's also less crowded, and is a great place to settle in and watch the sunset.

With its cushiony soft sand, Keawakapu is also a favorite for sunrise yoga and wake-up strolls. The ocean is a perfect spot for an end-of-day swim. Mornings are best for snorkeling: head to the rocky outcrops that form the northern and southern ends of the beach. During winter look for humpback whales, which come remarkably close to shore here.

There are three beach access points, all with outdoor showers. To get to the southern end, drive south on S Kihei Rd until it dead-ends at a beach parking lot. Near the middle of the beach, there's a parking lot at the corner of Kilohana Dr and S Kihei Rd. Cross S Kihei Rd to the beach access walkway. At the northern end, beach parking can be found in a large access lot north of the Days Inn.

◉ Sights

Hawaiian Islands Humpback Whale National Marine Sanctuary Headquarters
MUSEUM

(Map p157; ☎808-879-2818; http://hawaii humpbackwhale.noaa.gov; 726 S Kihei Rd; ⊙10am-3pm Mon-Fri; 🅿 ♿) FREE The oceanfront deck at the revamped marine sanctuary headquarters, which sits just north of the ancient Koʻieʻie Fishpond, is an ideal spot for viewing the humpback whales that frequent the bay during winter. Free scopes are set up for viewing. Inside, displays and videos provide background, and there are lots of informative brochures about whales and other Hawaiian wildlife. Swing by at 11am on Tuesday or Thursday for the free '45-Ton Talks' about whales.

Congress created the marine sanctuary in 1992 with a mission to protect humpback whales and their habitat. Its efforts have been a success – a majority of humpback whale populations were removed from the endangered species list in September 2016. A moratorium on whaling remains in place, however. The sanctuary extends from the

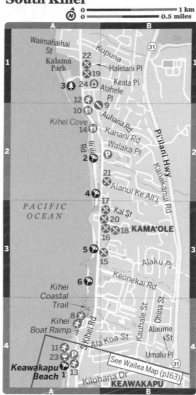

South Kihei

KIHEI & SOUTH MAUI KIHEI

shoreline to ocean depths of 600ft in the waters surrounding the Hawaiian Islands.

Ko'ie'ie Fishpond
HISTORIC SITE

(Map p157; S Kihei Rd at Ka'ono'ulu St; P ♿) In ancient Hawaii, coastal fishponds were built to provide a ready source of fish for royal families. The most intact fishpond remaining on Maui is the 3-acre Ko'ie'ie Fishpond, now on the National Register of Historic Places; it borders both Kalepolepo Beach Park and the Hawaiian Islands Humpback Whale National Marine Sanctuary headquarters.

David Malo's Church
CHURCH

(Trinity Episcopal Church By-the-Sea; Map p157; ☎808-879-0161; www.trinitybts.org; 100 Kulanihako'i St; P) Philosopher David Malo, who built this church in 1852, was the first Hawaiian ordained to the Christian ministry. He was also co-author of Hawaii's first constitution and an early spokesperson for Hawaiian rights. While most of Malo's original church has been dismantled, a 3ft-high section of the wall still stands beside a palm grove. Pews are lined up inside the stone walls. It's really quite beautiful.

Outdoor services are held at 9am on Sunday by Trinity Episcopal Church By-the-Sea. All are welcome.

Kalama Park
PARK

(Map p155; ☎808-879-4364; www.mauicounty. gov/Facilities; 1900 S Kihei Rd; P ♿) Athletes, skate rats and toddlers who need to roam will appreciate this expansive seaside park. Sports facilities include tennis and basketball courts, ball fields and a skateboard park. Also on site are a playground, picnic pavilions, restrooms and showers. Although there is a small beach, behind the whale statue, a runoff ditch carries wastewater here after heavy rains so best swim elsewhere.

🏃 Activities

South Maui's top activities are water-based.

Stand up paddle surfing (SUP) looks easy, and it is a learnable sport, but currents off Maui can carry you down the coast very quickly. Best to start with a lesson before renting a board.

Maui Dreams Dive Co
DIVING, SNORKELING

(Map p155; ☎808-874-5332; www.mauidreamsdiveco.com; 1993 S Kihei Rd; shore dives $69-99, boat dives $139; ⊙7am-6pm) Maui Dreams is a first-rate, five-star PADI operation specializing in shore dives. With this family-run outfit, a dive

trip is like going out with friends. Nondivers, ask about the introductory dive ($89), and, to zoom around underwater, check out the scooter dive ($99 to $129).

Maui Dive Shop
DIVING, SNORKELING

(Map p157; ☎808-879-3388; www.mauidiveshop. com; 1455 S Kihei Rd; 2-tank dives $90-180, snorkel rentals per day $6-9; ⊙7am-8pm) This is a good spot to rent or buy water-sports gear, including boogie boards, snorkels and wet suits. The company provides free transportation from South Maui resorts to tour departure points. Stop by for a free brochure with a map spotlighting good snorkeling spots. This location also rents Jeep Wranglers.

Stand Up Paddle Surf School
SURFING

(☎808-579-9231; www.standuppaddlesurfschool. com; 185 Paka Pl; 90min lesson $199; ⊙8am-2pm) This SUP school is owned by champion paddle-surfer Maria Souza, who was also the first woman surfer to tow into the monster waves at Jaws. Small classes and safety are priorities, and the paddling location is determined by weather and water conditions. Classes fill quickly, so call a few days – or a week – ahead. Multiday and Yoga SUP classes are also available.

Maui Wave Riders - Kihei
SURFING

(Map p155; ☎808-875-4761; www.mauiwaveriders.com; 2021 S Kihei Rd; surfing & SUP lessons adult/child 8-12yr from $65/55; ⊙lessons from 7:30am; ♿) In central Kihei across the street from Kalama Park, Maui Wave Riders offers two-hour surfing and 90-minute SUP lessons. Also rents surf boards and paddleboards.

The Cove
SURFING

(Map p155; S Kihei Rd) At the south end of Kalama Park, these shallow waters off this tiny park are great for beginners, with small waves that break right and left. It can get crowded. You can rent surfboards and sign up for lessons at shops across the street.

Surf Shack
WATER SPORTS

(Map p155; www.surfshackmaui.com; 2960 S Kihei Rd, Mana Kai Maui Resort; ⊙8am-5pm) Spending the day at gorgeous Keawakapu Beach? Stop here to rent snorkel sets ($7 per day), kayaks, (half-day $50), surf boards (half-day $20 to $25) and SUP boards (half-day $50). Beach chairs and coolers also available. Office is on the back side of the resort. Second location at 1993 S Kihei Rd in the Island Building (open 7:30am to 3pm).

North Kihei

bikes. Bike lanes run along both the Pi'ilani Hwy and S Kihei Rd, but cyclists need to be cautious of inattentive drivers making sudden turns across lanes.

👉 Tours

South Pacific
Kayaks & Outfitters   KAYAKING
(☏ 808-875-4848; www.southpacifickayaks.com; kayak rental/tour from $45/74; ⊙ kayak tours 7:15am; 🚸) This top-notch operation leads a variety of kayak-and-snorkel tours from Makena Landing. Tours leave at 7:15am daily, with a few tours also leaving at 10:30am Monday through Friday. Surfing and SUP lessons are also available, as well as hiking trips. Windsurfing and kite-surfing lessons offered at Kanaha Beach Park in Kahului.

It also rents kayaks for those who want to go off on their own, and will deliver them to Makena Landing by reservation.

Blue Water Rafting   RAFTING, SNORKELING
(Map p155; ☏ 808-879-7238; www.bluewater rafting.com; tours $41-140) In a hurry? Try the Molokini Express trip (adult/child $55/45) if you want to zip out to the crater, snorkel and be back within two hours.

Maui Yoga Path   YOGA
(Map p155; ☏ 808-874-5545; www.mauiyogapath.com; 2960 S Kihei Rd, Mana Kai Maui Resort; class $20; ⊙ beach yoga 7-8am, times vary for other classes) Take a morning yoga class on gorgeous Keawakapu Beach. Open to all levels. Iyengar, yoga movement and private classes also available.

South Maui Bicycles   CYCLING
(Map p155; ☏ 808-874-0068; www.southmauibicycles.com; 1993 S Kihei Rd, Island Surf Bldg; per day $22-60, per week $99-250; ⊙ 10am-6pm Mon-Sat) Rents top-of-the-line Trek and Gary Fisher road bicycles, as well as basic around-town

---

SOUTH MAUI FOR KIDS

➡ Ulua Beach (p162)

➡ Hawaiian Sailing Canoe Adventures (p164)

➡ Kama'ole Beach Park III (p154)

➡ Local Boys Shave Ice (p159)

➡ Hawaiian Islands Humpback Whale National Marine Sanctuary Headquarters (p155)

An adventurous half-day trip heads southward on a motorized raft for snorkeling among sea turtles at remote coves along Maui's lava-rock coast, which is beyond La Perouse Bay. Trips depart from the Kihei boat ramp.

🎊 Festivals & Events

Kihei Fourth Fridays FAIR
(www.kiheifridays.com; 1279 S Kihei Rd, Azeka Mauka Shopping Center; ⊘6-9pm 4th Fri of month; 🚼) Part of the Friday Town Parties series, this popular monthly festival draws locals with live music, food trucks and arts and crafts.

World Whale Day CULTURAL
(www.mauiwhalefestival.org; ⊘mid-Feb; 🚼) Organized by the Pacific Whale Foundation, this family-friendly bash celebrates Maui's humpback whales with a parade (9am to 10am), crafts, live music, food booths and environmental displays. It's held at Kalama Park on a Saturday in mid-February.

🍴 Eating

⭐**Fork & Salad** HEALTH FOOD $
(Map p157; ☑808-879-3675; www.forkandsalad maui.com; 1279 S Kihei Rd, Azeka Mauka Shopping Center; mains $9-17; ⊘10:30am-9pm; 🍴) Local farms strut their stuff at this glossy new salad emporium winning raves across Kihei. Step up to the counter, choose a classic or signature salad – or build your own – then add a deliciously seasoned protein, from organic chicken to sustainable shrimp to seared ahi. Ooh and ahh as staff toss it with Hawaiian-inspired dressings. Creamy lilikoi, anyone?

Sandwiches, soups and juices are also on the menu. Takeout menu available.

Coconut's Fish Cafe SEAFOOD $
(Map p157; ☑808-875-9979; www.coconuts fishcafe.com; 1279 S Kihei Rd, Azeka Mauka Shopping Center; mains $12-18; ⊘10am-9pm; 🚼)

For fresh, healthily prepared seafood in a family-friendly setting, try this chill spot in north Kihei. Order at the counter – we recommend the fish tacos – then settle in at one of the communal surfboard tables. All the fish is grilled, all ingredients are homemade (except the ketchup), staff are welcoming and service is quick. Dig in!

Nalu's South Shore Grill BREAKFAST, HAWAIIAN $
(Map p157; ☑808-891-8650; www.nalusgrill.com; 1280 S Kihei Rd, Azeka Makai Shopping Center; breakfast $10-14, lunch & dinner $9-17; ⊘8am-9:30pm; 🍴🚼) A koa canoe hangs overhead, enormous beach photos cover the walls, and two feral chickens strut around like they own the place. Yep, this new open-air eatery may sit in a strip mall, but the decor and dishes embrace all things Hawaiian. Breakfasts are the showstoppers, from acai bowls to three-egg omelets to the vegetarian loco moco. The focus? Healthy, hearty and locally grown.

Tamura's Fine Wine & Liquors SEAFOOD $
(Map p157; ☑808-891-2420; www.tamurasfinewine.com; 91 E Lipoa St; fresh poke per lb $18.99; ⊘9:30am-9pm Mon-Sat, to 8pm Sun) What? Great *poke* from a wine and liquor store? Yep, after browsing the towering aisles, which are stocked high with liquors, wines and beer, head to the tucked-away seafood counter for some of the island's best *poke*. Tamura's sells 10 different varieties, and you can enjoy a free sample or two before making your decision. Aloha, liquor-store *poke*!

808 Deli CAFE $
(Map p155; ☑808-879-1111; www.808deli.com; 2511 S Kihei Rd, Suite 102; breakfast $6-8, lunch $7-9; ⊘9am-5pm) With fresh breads, innovative spreads, gourmet hot dogs and 20 different sandwiches and paninis, this tiny sandwich shop across from Kam II is the place to grab a picnic lunch. For a spicy kick, try the roast beef with pepper jack and wasabi aioli.

Kihei Caffe CAFE $
(Map p155; ☑808-879-2230; www.kiheicaffe.com; 1945 S Kihei Rd, Kihei Kalama Village; mains $7-13; ⊘5am-2pm) Maybe it's the sneaky birds on the patio, or the quick-to-arrive entrees, but dining at this busy Kihei institution is not exactly relaxing. But you know what? That's part of the quirky charm. Order at the inside counter, fill your coffee cup at the thermos, snag a table on the patio then watch

the breakfast burritos, veggie scrambles and loco moco flash by.

Solos, couples, families – everyone's here or on the way. Cash only.

Da Kitchen Express
HAWAIIAN $

(Map p155; ☑808-875-7782; www.dakitchen. com; 2439 S Kihei Rd, Rainbow Mall; breakfast $11-15, lunch & dinner $11-18; ⊙9am-9pm) Da Kitchen is da bomb. Come to this no-frills eatery for Hawaiian plate lunches done right. The local favorite is Da Lau Lau Plate (with steamed pork wrapped in taro leaves), but you won't go wrong with any choice, from charbroiled teriyaki chicken to the gravy-laden loco moco (rice, fried egg and hamburger patty). We particularly liked the spicy kalua pork.

Cafe@LaPlage
CAFE $

(Map p155; ☑808-875-7668; www.cafealaplage. com; 2395 S Kihei Rd, Dolphin Plaza; sandwiches $4-12; ⊙6:30am-5pm Mon-Sat, to 3pm Sun; 🛜) They stack the sandwiches high at this small cafe and coffee shop. At breakfast, choose from five different bagel sandwiches or simply get your bagel slathered in cinnamon-honey butter. Lunchtime paninis include the Maui Melt, with turkey, bacon, pepper jack, avocados and jalapeños. Wi-fi is free, and there are computers up front ($3 for the first 15 minutes, then 15¢ per minute).

Kina'ole Grill
FOOD TRUCK $

(Map p155; ☑808-280-9048; www.facebook.com/kinaolegrillfoodtruck; 77 Alanui Keali'i Dr; plate lunch $14; ⊙11am-7:30pm) Hawaiian-style seafood and meat plate lunches are the tasty specialties at this tropically bright food truck that parks on Alanui Keali'i Rd, not far from Kama'ole Beach Park I. Plates come with rice, mac 'n' cheese, and greens. Cash only.

Eskimo Candy
SEAFOOD $

(Map p157; ☑808-879-5686; www.eskimo candy.com; 2665 Wai Wai Pl; mains $9-18; ⊙10:30am-7pm Mon-Fri; 🚸) Wondering whether to order the seafood chowder? You should. This hearty treat primes the palate for the top-notch fresh seafood served in this busy fishmarket with a take-out counter. Raw-fish fanatics should key in on the *poke* (cubed, marinated raw fish), ahi (yellowfin tuna) wraps and fish tacos. The handful of tables fill quickly at lunchtime. Parents will appreciate the under-$9 kids' menu.

Local Boys Shave Ice
SWEETS $

(Map p155; ☑808-344-9779; www.local boysshaveice.com; 1941 S Kihei Rd, Kihei Kalama Village; shave ice from $4.50; ⊙10am-9pm) Load up on napkins at Local Boys, where they dish up hearty servings of shaved ice drenched in a rainbow of sweet syrups. We like it tropical (banana, mango and 'shark's blood') with ice cream, *kauai* cream and azuki beans. Cash only.

★ Café O'Lei
HAWAIIAN $$

(Map p155; ☑808-891-1368; www.cafeolei restaurants.com; 2439 S Kihei Rd, Rainbow Mall; lunch $8-16, dinner $17-29; ⊙10:30am-3:30pm & 4:30-9:30pm) This strip-mall bistro looks ho-hum at first blush. But step inside. The sophisticated atmosphere, innovative Hawaii Regional Cuisine, honest prices and excellent service knock Café O'Lei into the fine-dining big leagues. For a tangy treat, order the blackened mahimahi with fresh papaya salsa. Look for unbeatable lunch mains, with salads, for under $10, and a sushi chef after 4:30pm (Tuesday to Saturday).

Famous martinis, too.

Fabiani's Bakery & Pizza
ITALIAN, BAKERY $$

(Map p157; ☑808-874-0888; www.fabianis.com; 95 E Lipoa St; pastries under $4, breakfast $8-14, lunch $9-16, dinner $13-21; ⊙7am-9pm) What puts the fab in Fabiani's? Definitely the prosciutto, mozzarella and arugula white pizza with truffle oil. Or wait, maybe it's the linguini with sautéed clams. Or the chef-made pastries preening like celebrities as you walk in the door. Whatever your choice, you'll surely feel fabulous nibbling your meal inside this sparkling Italian eatery and pastry shop. There's also a rather nice bar.

808 Bistro
BISTRO $$

(Map p155; ☑808-879-8008; www.maui808bis tro.com; 2511 S Kihei Rd; breakfast $7-16, dinner $18-29; ⊙7am-2pm & 5-9pm) This open-air eatery showcases hearty comfort food and fresh seafood – think braised short-ribs with garlic mashed potatoes and fresh ahi with a wasabi-panko crust and ponzu sauce. Kiss your diet goodbye at breakfast with the decadent whale pie with ham, hash browns, egg, cheese and gravy. The restaurant sits behind 808 Deli (p158), across the street from Kama'ole Beach Park II.

Nutcharee's Authentic Thai Food
THAI $$

(Map p157; ☑808-633-4840; www.nutcharees. com; 1280 S Kihei Rd, Azeka Makai Shopping Center; mains $11-16; ⊙11am-3pm daily, plus 5-9pm

Sun-Thu, to 9:30pm Fri & Sat) Fans of Nutcharee Case's panang curry with fresh fish no longer have to drive to Hana to get their fix. She closed her beloved East Maui outpost in 2015 and opened this new restaurant soon after. Settle in for her acclaimed noodles and stir-fry dishes and a wide array of curries. Currently BYOB.

Want takeout for dinner? Call early. Dishes are made fresh to order, and if she's got a full house she might stop taking phone orders.

Roasted Chiles   MEXICAN $$
(Map p157; ☑ 808-868-4357; www.hawaiiontv. com/roastedchiles; 1279 S Kihei Rd, Azeka Mauka Shopping Center; lunch $12-16, dinner $15-22; ⊙ 11am-9pm) At most Mexican restaurants on Maui, the food is simply a buffet for the margaritas. But here? The margaritas are excellent, but so is the authentic Mexican cuisine, which is thoughtfully seasoned and pleasantly presented. Start with fresh guacamole or *ono* ceviche then take your pick of savory traditional dishes and an array of sauces, from the complex chocolate *mole* to the creamy green sauce.

Attentive service ties it all together into a great night out.

Pa'ia Fish Market – South Side   SEAFOOD $$
(Map p155; ☑ 808-874-8888; www.paiafishmarket. com; 1913 S Kihei Rd, Kihei Kalama Village; mains $10-21; ⊙ 11am-9:30pm) This new spinoff, from the folks behind the beloved Pa'ia Fish Market in the Upcountry, is a quick and convenient stop for fresh seafood. Across the street from Kalama Park, the open-air eatery serves *ono* and mahi burgers, fish and chips, and seafood pasta. Plate meals arrive with slabs of seasoned local fish and Cajun rice or home fries. It's pricey, but portions are big.

The restaurant is new and lacks the communal buzziness of the Pa'ia mothership – but give it time.

**Sansei Seafood
Restaurant & Sushi Bar**   JAPANESE $$$
(Map p155; ☑ 808-879-0004; www.sanseihawaii. com; 1881 S Kihei Rd, Kihei Town Center; appetizers $4-20, mains $10-57; ⊙ 5:30-10pm, to 1am Thu-Sat) Maui is laid-back, but sometimes you have to plan ahead. Dinner at Sansei is one of those times – make a reservation or queue early for the sushi bar. The creative appetizer menu offers everything from a shrimp cake with ginger-lime chili butter to lobster-and-blue-crab ravioli. Fusion dishes include Japanese

jerk chicken with garlic mashed potatoes and herb *beurre* fondue.

Between 5:30pm and 6pm all food is discounted 25%, and appetizers and sushi are discounted 50% from 10pm to 1am Thursday through Saturday.

✖ Self-catering

**Hawaiian Moons
Natural Foods**   SUPERMARKET $
(Map p155; ☑ 808-875-4356; www.hawaiian moons.com; 2411 S Kihei Rd, Kama'ole Beach Center; sandwiches under $10; ⊙ 8am-9pm; ☑) Newly expanded, this natural foods market draws 'em in for its well-stocked hot and cold salad bars ($8.49 per pound). The soups are so good you might see someone sipping straight from their bowl while checking out! Also sells fresh juices, organic coffee, smoothies, acai bowls and sandwiches.

Foodland   SUPERMARKET $
(Map p155; ☑ 808-879-9350; www.foodland.com; 1881 S Kihei Rd, Kihei Town Center; ⊙ 5am-1am) Handy supermarket known for its delicious *poke* bowls.

☕ Drinking & Nightlife

Most bars in Kihei are across the street from the beach and have nightly entertainment. Kihei Kalama Village, aka the Bar-muda Triangle (or just the Triangle), is a lively place at night, packed with buzzy watering holes.

★ 5 Palms   COCKTAIL BAR
(Map p155; ☑ 808-879-2607; www.5palmsrestau rant.com; 2960 S Kihei Rd, Mana Kai Maui; ⊙ 8am-11pm, happy hour 3-7pm & 9-11pm) For sunset cocktails beside the beach, this is the place. Arrive an hour before the sun goes down because the patio bar, just steps from stunning Keawakapu Beach, fills quickly. During happy hour, sushi and an array of delicious appetizers are half-price, with a one drink minimum, while mai tais and margaritas are $5.75. Popular with tourists and locals.

Maui Brewing Co   BREWERY
(☑ 808-213-3002; www.mauibrewingco.com; 605 Lipoa Pkwy, Maui Research & Technology Park; ⊙ tasting room 11am-10pm, tours noon-3pm) ✦ At Maui Brewing's new Kihei production facility, the lively taproom is open daily for pints and food-truck fare. About two-dozen different beers are on-tap at any given time, flowing straight from holding tanks in the brewery. Tours (per person $15) are offered six times

daily, with a flight of four beers and one full beer from the taproom included in the price.

Reservations recommended for tours.

Dog & Duck
PUB
(Map p155; ☑808-875-9669; 1913 S Kihei Rd, Kihei Kalama Village; ☺8am-2am) This lively Irish pub with a welcoming vibe attracts a younger crowd. And yes, it has sports on TV, but it's not blaring from every corner. Decent pub grub goes along with the heady Guinness draft.

South Shore Tiki Lounge
BAR
(Map p155; ☑808-874-6444; www.southshore tikilounge.com; 1913 S Kihei Rd, Kihei Kalama Village; ☺11am-2am; ☜) The drink maestros at this cozy tropical shack regularly win annual *MauiTime Weekly* awards for best bartenders. Live music daily from 4pm to 6pm. DJs, live music and dancing nightly starting at 10pm.

What Ales You
CRAFT BEER
(Map p155; ☑808-214-6581; www.whatalesyou. com; 1913 S Kihei Rd, Kihei Kalama Village; ☺11am-10pm Tue-Sun, 4-10pm Mon) In the Bar-muda Triangle, What Ales You serves 16 taps of cold craft beer, rotating daily. You'll also find wine and a short menu of appetizers, sandwiches and rice bowls.

Ambrosia Martini Lounge
BAR
(Map p155; ☑808-891-1011; www.ambrosiamaui. com; 1913 S Kihei Rd, Kihei Kalama Village; ☺7pm-1:30am) Nicknamed 'Amnesia' by locals, this compact martini bar brings a hint of nightclub style to Kihei – but without the pretension. Look for live music or a DJ nightly. Two-for-one martinis during happy hour (7pm to 9pm, all night Sunday).

Dina's Sandwitch
PUB
(Map p157; ☑808-879-3262; 145 N Kihei Rd, Sugar Beach Resort; ☺11am-10pm) The mai tais are handcrafted at Dina's, a convivial, come-as-you-are locals' joint in north Kihei. For something decadent, try the Nutty Witches Tit – a scoop of mac-nut ice cream with Myers rum, vodka and banana liqueur. The walls are covered with $1 bills – thousands of dollars' worth according to Dina.

Shopping

Yee's Orchard
FOOD
(Map p157; 1165 S Kihei Rd; ☺11am-5pm Tue-Thu, Sat & Sun) For out-of-this-world mangoes from May through summer, pull over at this 60-year-old fruit stand just north of Longs Drug.

Kihei Kalama Village
MARKET
(Map p155; ☑808-879-6610; 1941 S Kihei Rd; ☺pavilion shops 10am-7:30pm) More than 40 shops and stalls are clustered at this central shopping arcade. For fashionable women's island-wear pop into **Mahina** (www.shop mahina.com). Made-in-Hawaii jams, jellies and sauces are for sale in welcoming **Tutu's Pantry** (www.tutuspantry.com) – free samples are available.

ℹ Information

Bank of Hawaii (☑808-879-5844; www.boh. com; 1279 S Kihei Rd, Azeka Mauka Shopping Center; ☺8:30am-4pm Mon-Thu, to 6pm Fri)

Kihei Police Station (☑808-244-6400; 2201 Pi'ilani Hwy)

Longs Drugs (☑808-879-2033; www.cvs.com; 1215 S Kihei Rd; ☺store 24hr, pharmacy 8am-10pm Mon-Fri, to 7pm Sat & Sun) This convenience store, with a pharmacy, has one aisle loaded up with rubber slippahs (flip flops, yo').

Post Office (Map p157; ☑808-879-1987; www. usps.com; 1254 S Kihei Rd; ☺9am-4:30pm Mon-Fri, 9am-1pm Sat)

Urgent Care Maui Physicians (☑808-879-7781; www.medicalclinicinmaui.com; 1325 S Kihei Rd; ☺8am-6pm) This clinic accepts walk-in patients.

ℹ Getting There & Around

TO/FROM THE AIRPORT

Almost everyone rents a car at the **airport** (p305) in Kahului. Otherwise, expect to pay about $18 to $34 for shuttle service or $30 to $45 for a taxi, depending on your destination in Kihei. The airport is 10 miles from North Kihei and 16 miles from South Kihei.

A few rental car agencies can be found along North and South Kihei Rds. These are good options if you're looking for lower rates or a day-trip rental. **Kihei Rent A Car** (☑808-879-7257; www.kiheirentacar.com; 96 Kio Loop; per day/week from $35/175; ☺7:30am-9pm) rents cars and 4WDs to those aged 21 and over, and includes free mileage. For the lowest rates consider one of the older-model cars (which can be well worn!). Provides Kahului Airport shuttle pick-up and drop-off for rentals over five days.

Uber is available, and rates currently seem to run higher than taxis, ranging from $53 to $101 per ride from the airport, depending on Kihei destination.

BUS

The **Maui Bus** (p33) serves Kihei with two routes. One route, the Kihei Islander, connects Kihei with Wailea and Kahului; stops include

Kamaʻole Beach Park III, Piʻilani Village shopping center, and Uwapo at South Kihei Rd. The other route, the Kihei Villager, primarily serves the northern half of Kihei, with a half-dozen stops along South Kihei Rd and at Piʻilani Village shopping center and Maʻalaea. Both routes operate hourly from around 6am to 8pm and cost $2.

Wailea

The golden-sand beaches in Wailea are the stuff of daydreams, famed for phenomenal swimming, snorkeling, sunbathing and consistently sunny skies.

Beyond the beaches? With its tidy golf courses, protective privacy walls and discreet signage, Wailea looks a bit like a members-only country club. South Maui's most elite haunt, it stands in sharp contrast to Kihei. Don't bother looking for gas stations or fast-food joints; this exclusive community is all about swank beachfront resorts and low-rise condo villas, with all the glitzy accessories.

If you're not staying here, say a loud *mahalo* (thank you) for Hawaii's beach-access laws that allow you to visit anyway, with dedicated public parking lots.

🏖 Beaches

Wailea's fabulous beaches begin at the southern end of Keawakapu Beach in Kihei and continue south toward Makena. All of the beaches that are backed by resorts have public access, with free parking, showers and restrooms. The beaches in this section are listed from north to south.

For a list of facilities at each beach, visit mauicounty.gov or call ☏ 808-879-4364.

Mokapu Beach   BEACH
(Map p163; Halealiʻi Place; Ⓟ) The lovely Mokapu Beach is behind the Andaz Maui resort, on the northern side of a small point between the beaches.

Ulua Beach   BEACH
(Map p163; Halealiʻi Pl; Ⓟ) Snorkelers should head straight for Ulua Beach, to the south of the point. The coral at the rocky outcrop on the right side of Ulua Beach offers Wailea's best easy-access snorkeling.

Not only is it teeming with brilliant tropical fish, but it's also one of the best spots for hearing humpbacks sing as they pass offshore. Snorkeling is best in the morning before the winds pick up and the masses arrive. When the surf's up, forget snorkeling – go bodysurfing instead. Beach access and parking is just south of the Andaz Maui.

★ Wailea Beach   BEACH
(Map p163; access road off Wailea Alanui Dr; Ⓟ 🚻)
To strut your stuff celebrity-style, make a beeline to this sparkling strand, which fronts the Grand Wailea and Four Seasons (p165) resorts and offers a full menu of water activities. The beach slopes gradually, making it a good swimming spot. When it's calm, there's decent snorkeling around the rocky point on the southern end. Most afternoons there's a gentle shorebreak suitable for bodysurfing. Divers entering the water at Wailea Beach can follow an offshore reef that runs down to Polo Beach.

The beach access road is between the Grand Wailea and Four Seasons resorts.

Polo Beach   BEACH
(Map p163; Kaukahi St; Ⓟ) In front of the Fairmont Kea Lani, Polo Beach is seldom crowded. When there's wave action, boogie boarders and bodysurfers usually find good shorebreaks here. When calm, the rocks to the north provide good snorkeling. At low tide, the lava outcropping at the southern end of the beach holds tide pools harboring spiny sea urchins and small fish.

To find it, turn down Kaukahi St after the Fairmont Kea Lani and look for the beach parking lot on the right.

Poʻolenalena Beach   BEACH
(Map p163; Makena Alanui Rd; Ⓟ 🚻) This long and lovely crescent-shaped beach, south of the resorts, is a favorite of local families on weekends. It's rarely crowded though, and the shallow, sandy bottom and calm waters make for excellent swimming. There's good snorkeling off both the southern and northern lava points. The parking lot is on Makena Alanui Rd, a half-mile south of its intersection with Makena Rd.

🏃 Activities

Wailea Golf Club   GOLF
(Map p163; ☏ 808-875-7450; www.waileagolf. com; 100 Wailea Golf Club Dr; greens fee Gold & Emerald $145-240, Old Blue $120-190; ☺ varies, typically 7am-5pm) There are three championship courses in Wailea. The **Emerald course** is a tropical garden that consistently ranks at the top; the rugged **Gold course** takes advantage of volcanic landscapes; and the **Old Blue course** (Map

Wailea

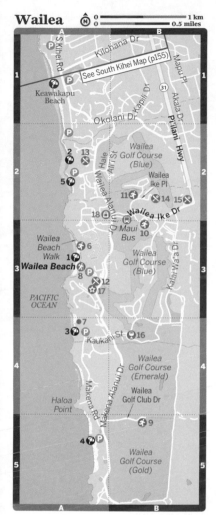

In winter this is a fantastic location for spotting humpback whales. On a good day you may be able to see more than a dozen of them frolicking offshore.

Some of the luxury hotels you'll pass along the walk are worth strolling through as well, most notably the **Grand Wailea Resort** (p000), which is adorned with $35-million-worth of eye-catching international works of art. Stop by for one-hour art collection tours on Tuesdays and Fridays at 10am, which begin at the Na Pua gallery.

In front of the Wailea Point condos you'll find the foundations of three Hawaiian house sites dating to AD 1300; this is also a fine spot to watch the sun drop into the sea.

Wailea Tennis Club   TENNIS
(Map p163; ☑808-879-1958; www.waileatennis.com; 131 Wailea Ike Pl; per person $20, racket rental per day $10; ⊙7am-6pm Mon-Fri, to 5pm Sat

p163; ☑808-879-2530; www.waileagolf.com; 100 Wailea Ike Dr) is marked by an open fairway and challenging greens.

For the cheapest fees, tee off in the afternoon (check times), when 'twilight' rates are in effect. Resort guests also pay less.

Wailea Beach Walk   WALKING
(Map p163) For the perfect sunset stroll, take the 1.3-mile shoreline path that connects Wailea's beaches and the resort hotels that front them. The undulating path winds above jagged lava points and back down to the sandy shore.

SUNSCREEN: ZINC OR TITANIUM ONLY

Heading into the ocean to snorkel? Check your sunscreen bottle. Or better yet, check the label at the store before you buy it. Scientists have determined that many ingredients found in today's sunscreens are, along with other factors, killing coral reefs. What's safe? Zinc and titanium oxide. As posted by the Division of Land & Natural Resources (DLNR) at 'Ahihi-Kina'u Natural Area Reserve, avoid sunscreens with this list of coral-destroying ingredients: oxybenzone, octinozate, avobenzone/ avobenzine, homosalate, octisalate, octocrylene, ethylhexyl methoxycinnamate. For more information, check out the video from the DLNR at https:// vimeo.com/180382413 or visit the Hawaii DLNR website http://dlnr. hawaii.gov.

& Sun) Nicknamed 'Wimbledon West,' this award-winning complex has 11 Plexi-pave courts. Ninety-minute lessons are available (clinic/private $35/140). Courts also open for pickleball – a tennis, badminton and ping-pong combo.

Aqualani Beach & Ocean Recreation　　　WATER SPORTS
(Map p163; ☑808-283-0384; www.aqualani beach.com; 3850 Wailea Alanui Dr, Grand Wailea Resort; snorkel/boogie board/kayak/SUP per hour $10/10/50/50; ⏰7am-5pm) On the beach behind the Grand Wailea, Aqualani rents all the gear you need for ocean fun. Also offers unlimited rentals of all equipment for one day for $99 per person.

☞ Tours

Hawaiian Sailing Canoe Adventures　　　CANOEING
(Map p163; ☑808-281-9301; www.mauisailing canoe.com; adult/child 4-14yr $179/129; ⏰tours 9am; 🚻) Learn about native traditions and snorkel beside sea turtles on a three-hour trip aboard a Hawaiian-style outrigger canoe. Tours depart from Polo Beach.

✫ Festivals & Events

Maui Film Festival　　　FILM
(www.mauifilmfestival.com; Wailea; ⏰mid-Jun) Hollywood celebs swoop in for this five-day extravaganza in mid-June. Join the stars

under the stars at various Wailea locations, including the open-air 'Celestial Theater' on a nearby golf course and the 'Toes-in-the-Sand Cinema' (free) on Wailea Beach.

✕ Eating

Waterfront Deli　　　DELI $
(Map p163; ☑808-891-2039; 3750 Wailea Alanui Dr, Shops at Wailea; sandwiches & salads $3-9; ⏰store 7am-10:30pm, deli 7am-8pm) For a quick, inexpensive meal to go, visit this deli inside the Whalers General Store at the back of the Shops at Wailea.

★Monkeypod Kitchen　　　PUB FOOD $$
(Map p163; ☑808-891-2322; www.monkeypod-kitchen.com; 10 Wailea Gateway Pl, Wailea Gateway Center; lunch $15-27, dinner $15-41; ⏰11:30am-11pm, happy hour 3-5:30pm & 9-11pm; 🚻) 🍴 Happy hours are crowded but convivial at Chef Peter Merriman's latest venture, where the staff, your fellow drinkers and the 36 craft beers on tap keep the alohas real. But microbrews are not the only draw. Gourmet pub grub takes a delicious Hawaiian spin and is typically sourced from organic and local ingredients, with Maui Cattle burgers and plenty of Upcountry veggies.

Woodfired pizzas are $9 during happy hour – mmm, Hamakua wild mushrooms. Kid menu items are under $10.

Matteo's Osteria　　　ITALIAN $$
(Map p163; ☑808-891-8466; www.matteosmaui. com; 161 Wailea Ike Pl; mains lunch $11-16, mains $12-39; ⏰lunch 11:30am-3pm Mon-Fri, happy hour 3-6pm Mon-Fri, dinner 5-9:30pm daily) With 64 wines by the glass, handmade pastas and pizza, and impeccable service, it's no surprise that Matteo's is Wailea's current 'It Girl' despite the strip-mall setting. Savor a white pizza topped with bechamel sauce, beef tenderloin and Maui onions or dig into wide-ribbon pappardelle with braised lamb, tomato ragu and caramelized vegetables. Fresh seafood mains available too.

The $21 lunch special includes salad, a pizza or pasta dish, and a glass of wine.

Pita Paradise　　　MEDITERRANEAN $$
(Map p163; ☑808-879-7177; www.pitaparadise hawaii.com; 34 Wailea Gateway Pl, Wailea Gateway Center; lunch $10-27, dinner $19-32; ⏰11am-9:30pm) Although this Greek taverna sits in a strip mall and lacks ocean views, the inviting patio, the townscape mural and the tiny white lights – not to mention the succulent Mediterranean chicken pita – banish any

locational regrets. Owner John Arabatzis catches his own fish, which are served in everything from pita sandwiches at lunch to grilled kabobs at dinner.

★ Ferraro's   ITALIAN $$$

(Map p163; ☑ 808-874-8000; www.fourseasons. com/maui; 3900 Wailea Alanui Dr, Four Seasons Maui at Wailea; lunch $19-31, dinner $31-49; ⊙ 11:30am-9pm) No other place in Wailea comes close to this breezy restaurant for romantic seaside dining. Lunch strays into fun offerings, such as a lobster melt with avocado and sriracha ailoi, and the black truffle pizza with carmelized Maui onions. Dinner gets more serious, showcasing a rustic Italian menu, plus steak and seafood dishes.

Ka'ana Kitchen   HAWAIIAN $$$

(Map p163; ☑ 808-573-1234; www.maui.andaz. hyatt; 3550 Wailea Alanui Dr, Andaz Maui; breakfast mains $18-29, breakfast buffet $47, dinner $16-57; ⊙ breakfast 6:30am-11am, dinner 5:30-9pm) Ka'ana means 'to share,' and Maui's bounty is shared in high style at this chic spot at the Andaz. At breakfast, the buffet will keep you nibbling fruit, bread, cheese, and cured fish and meats all morning. Locally sourced produce and seafood dishes fill the dinner menu, and they are prepared with global seasonings and cooking methods, keeping the selections creative.

🍷 Drinking & Nightlife

Pint & Cork   BAR

(Map p163; ☑ 808-727-2038; www.thepintandcork. com; 3750 Wailea Alanui Dr, Shops at Wailea; ⊙ noon-2am) This chic gastropub and wine bar, which would look right at home in Manhattan or Los Angeles, opened in 2016. We hear it's already a firm favorite with service-industry crowds looking for late-night noshes and libations. Big TVs overlook the 40ft soapstone bar, keeping sports fans happy. Opens early for games during football season, with a Bloody Mary bar.

Soak up the suds with gourmet pub grub specialties such as kalua pork sliders and garlic parmesan fries.

Mulligan's on the Blue   PUB

(Map p163; ☑ 808-874-1131; www.mulligansonthe-blue.com; 100 Kaukahi St; ⊙ noon-2am) Rising above the golf course, Mulligan's offers entertainment nightly, with anything from a seven-piece dance band to a lively magician to an Elvis-themed dinner show. It's also a good place to quaff an ale while enjoying

the distant ocean view, or catching a game on one of the 14 TVs. Opens early for big games.

Red Bar at Gannon's   COCKTAIL BAR

(Map p163; ☑ 808-875-8080; www.gannons restaurant.com; 100 Wailea Golf Club Dr; ⊙ 8:30am-9pm, happy hour 3-8:30pm) Everyone looks sexier when they're swathed in a sultry red glow. Come to this chic spot at happy hour for impressive food and drink specials, as well as attentive bartenders and stellar sunsets. The bar is located inside Gannon's, Bev Gannon's restaurant at the Gold and Emerald courses' clubhouse.

☆ Entertainment

Four Seasons Maui at Wailea   LIVE MUSIC

(Map p163; ☑ 808-874-8000; www.flyrseasons. com/maui; 3900 Wailea Alanui Dr; ⊙ 5-11:30pm) The lobby lounge has Hawaiian music nightly from 5:30pm to 7:30pm, with hula performances from 5:30pm to 6:30pm.

🛍 Shopping

Shops at Wailea   MALL

(Map p163; ☑ 808-891-6770; www.theshopsat wailea.com; 3750 Wailea Alanui Dr; ⊙ 9:30am-9pm; 🛜) This outdoor mall has dozens of restaurants, galleries and stores, with many shops flashing designer labels such as Louis Vuitton and Gucci, but there are some solid island choices, too. Store hours may vary slightly from mall hours. Parking is free the first hour then $3 per half-hour. Also free for three additional hours with a $25 validated purchase.

ⓘ Information

Shops at Wailea (www.theshopsatwailea.com; 3750 Wailea Alanui Dr; ⊙ 9:30am-9pm) This outdoor mall has an ATM and public restrooms.

Urgent Care Wailea Makena (☑ 808-281-6580; www.urgentcarewaileamakena.com; 100 Wailea Ike Dr; ⊙ 8am-8pm) Urgent care closest to Wailea's resorts. Next to Manoli's Pizza.

ⓘ Getting There & Around

The **Maui Bus** (Map p163; http://www.co.maui. hi.us) operates the Kihei Islander between Wailea and Kahului hourly until 8:27pm. The first bus picks up passengers on Wailea Ike Drive (just east of the Shops at Wailea) at 6:27am and runs north along S Kihei Rd, with a side trip to Pi'ilani Village shopping center, then continues to Queen Ka'ahumanu Center. For Lahaina, pick up the Kihei Villager at Pi'ilani Village, which travels to Ma'alaea.

KIHEI & SOUTH MAUI WAILEA

There, transfer to the Lahaina Islander. Fare is $2 per bus ride.

If you plan to do a lot of sightseeing, consider renting a car at the airport or at one of the Wailea resorts, which may have a rental-car desk and a small fleet on-site.

Makena

Makena still feels wild, like a territorial outpost that hasn't been tamed. It's a perfect setting for aquatic adventurers who want to escape the crowds, offering first-class snorkeling, kayaking and bodysurfing, plus pristine coral, reef sharks, dolphins and loads of sea turtles. And with the closing of the striking Makena Beach & Golf Resort in 2016, the setting has gotten even wilder.

The beaches are magnificent. The king of them all, Big Beach (Oneloa Beach), is an immense sweep of glistening sand and a prime sunset-viewing locale. The secluded cove at neighboring Little Beach is Maui's most popular nude beach – you will see bare buns. Together these beaches form **Makena State Park** (🗓Maui District Office 808-984-8109; http://dlnr.hawaii.gov/dsp/parks/maui; Makena Rd; ⊙6am-6pm; P🚻), but don't be misled by the term 'park,' as they remain in a natural state, with no facilities except for a couple of pit toilets and picnic tables. And those rumors about the nude Sunday evening drum circle? Well…

🏊 Beaches

These golden strands are launchpads for kayaking, snorkeling and diving, but you won't find much commercial support in this remote landscape.

The beaches are listed from north to south.

PANIOLO ROOTS
••••••••••••••••••••••••••••••••••
Sitting beneath the slopes of Upcountry's 'Ulupalakua Ranch, Makena was once a *paniolo* (Hawaiian cowboy) village, home to Hawaiian cowboys who corralled cattle at the landing and loaded them onto barges bound for Honolulu slaughterhouses. To catch a glimpse of Makena's roots, stop at the **Keawala'i Congregational Church** (🗓808-879-5557; www.keawai.org; 5300 Makena Rd; ⊙office 10am-5pm Thu-Sat), just south of Makena Landing.

Makena Bay   BAY
(Makena Landing Rd; P) Want to kayak along the coast? Then drop into this pretty bay. There's no better place on Maui for kayaking – as you might surmise from the collection of kayak-tour vans parked here every morning. When seas are calm, snorkeling is good along the rocks at the southern side of **Makena Landing**, the boat launch that's the center of the action. Makena Bay is also a good place for shore dives; divers should head to the north side of the bay.

Kayakers should paddle south along the lava coastline to Malu'aka Beach, where green sea turtles abound. Kayak-snorkel-tour operators meet just south of the landing for trips. South Pacific Kayaks (p157) will deliver pre-reserved kayaks here for rental at 6:45am (single/double $45/65). There are no kayak shops on-site.

Makena Bay was once a busy port for livestock, pineapples and people, and *paniolo* (Hawaiian cowboys) used to herd cattle onto boats bound for Honolulu from here.

Heading south on Makena Alanui Rd, turn right onto Honoiki St then turn right onto Makena Rd.

Malu'aka Beach   BEACH
(Makena Rd; P🚻) Dubbed 'Turtle Beach,' this golden swath of sand behind the now-closed Makena Beach & Golf Resort is popular with snorkelers and kayakers hoping to glimpse the surprisingly graceful sea turtles that feed along the coral here and often swim within a few feet of snorkelers. Terrific coral is about 100yd out, and the best action is at the southern end of the beach. Come on a calm day – this one kicks up with a little wind, and when it's choppy you won't see anything.

Parking lots, restrooms and showers are at both ends of the beach. On the northern side, park at the lot opposite Keawala'i Congregational Church then follow the road a short distance south. If that lot is full, take the first right after the resort, where there's additional parking.

Little Beach   BEACH
(Pu'u Ola'i Beach; http://dlnr.hawaii.gov/dsp/parks/maui; Makena Rd; ⊙6am-6pm; P) Those folks with the coolers and umbrellas, walking north from the sandy entrance to Big Beach? They're heading to Little Beach, which is part of Makena State Park. Also known as Pu'u Ola'i Beach, this cozy strand is au naturel. Nudity is officially illegal, though

Makena to La Perouse Bay

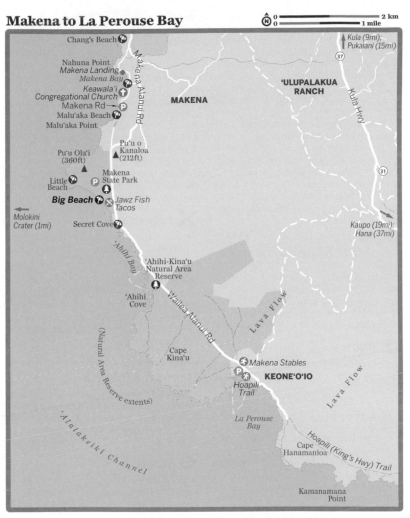

enforcement is at the political whim of the day. The beach is hidden by a rocky outcrop that juts out from Pu'u Ola'i, the cinder hill that marks the northern end of Big Beach. Take the short-but-steep trail over the outcropping.

Little Beach fronts a sandy cove that usually has a gentle shorebreak ideal for bodysurfing and boogie boarding. When the surf's up, you'll find plenty of local surfers here as well. When the water's calm, snorkeling is good along the rocky point. For parking, use the northern lot at Big Beach.

★ **Big Beach** BEACH
(Oneloa Beach; http://dlnr.hawaii.gov/dsp/parks/maui; Makena Rd; ⊙6am-6pm; P) The crowning glory of Makena State Park, this untouched beach is arguably the finest on Maui. In Hawaiian it's called Oneloa, literally 'Long Sand.' And indeed the golden sands stretch for the better part of a mile and are as broad as they come. The waters are a beautiful turquoise. When they're calm you'll find kids boogie boarding here, but at other times the shore-breaks can be dangerous, suitable for experienced bodysurfers

only, who get tossed wildly in the transparent waves.

There are lifeguard stations here. No drinking water is available, so bring your own.

In the late 1960s this was the site of an alternative-lifestyle encampment nicknamed 'Hippie Beach.' The tent city lasted until 1972, when police finally evicted everyone. For a sweeping view of the shore, climb the short trail to the rocky outcrop just north, which divides Big Beach from Little Beach.

The turnoff to the main parking area is a mile beyond the now-closed Makena Beach & Golf Resort. There's a portable toilet here. A second parking area lies 440yd to the south. Thefts and broken windshields are a possibility, so don't leave valuables in your car in either lot.

Secret Cove BEACH
(Makena Rd) This lovely, postcard-size swath of sand, with a straight-on view of Kaho'olawe, is worth a peek – although it's no longer much of a secret. The cove is 440yd after the southernmost Makena State Park parking lot. The entrance is through an opening in a lava-rock wall just south of house No 6900.

Tours

Makena Landing is a popular starting point for kayak tours.

SUNSET DRUM CIRCLE

One of the worst-kept secrets in Makena is the sunset drum circle on Sunday nights at Little Beach. How badly kept? Let's just say there's lots of online footage – and a photo from ABC News – of Aerosmith's Steven Tyler banging a drum on the sand here. He has a house nearby. The scene is pretty chill, but be warned: about 10% to 20% of the crowd is walking around naked and many of these folks are not shy about strutting their stuff. But most everyone is there for the same things: the surf, the sand and the sunset. And maybe some pot brownies. The fire dancing starts after the sun goes down. If you're feeling groovy, check it out. And bring a headlamp. The trail back, which twists over a lava outcrop, is short but it's also steep and rocky. So far, state authorities have kept a distance, but they could shut it all down at anytime. Walk this way...

★ **Aloha Kayaks** KAYAKING
(☎808-270-3318; www.alohakayaksmaui.com; Makena Landing; adult/child 5-9yr $85/60; ☺tours 7:15am) For an eco-minded snorkel-kayak trip with an enthusiastic team of owner-operators, take a paddle with Aloha Kayaks. Owners Griff and Peter have about 10 years of guiding experience apiece. Their mission? To educate guests about the environment and to keep their operations sustainable – and to make sure you see green turtles and other marine life. Whale sightings a possibility in winter.

Trips depart from Makena Landing and Olowalu in West Maui. Wear a swimsuit and sandals.

Eating

Vendors with cold coconuts, pineapples and other fruit are sometimes found along Makena Alanui Dr near Big Beach.

Jawz Fish Tacos FOOD TRUCK $
(www.jawzfishtacos.com; Makena State Park; snacks $4-12; ☺10am-5pm) Get your beach snacks – tacos, burritos, shave ice – at this food truck beside the northernmost Big Beach parking lot.

Beyond Makena

Makena Rd turns adventurous after Makena State Park, continuing for three narrow miles through the lava flows of 'Ahihi-Kina'u Natural Area Reserve before dead-ending at La Perouse Bay.

Sights

'Ahihi-Kina'u
Natural Area Reserve NATURE RESERVE
(☎808-984-8100; http://dlnr.hawaii.gov; Makena Rd; ☺5:30am-7:30pm; P) Although scientists haven't been able to pinpoint the exact date, Maui's last lava flow probably spilled down to the sea here between AD 1480 and 1600, shaping 'Ahihi Bay and Cape Kina'u. Today, the jagged lava coastline and the pristine waters fringing it have been designated a reserve because of its unique marine habitat. Thanks in part to the prohibition on fishing here, the snorkeling is incredible but getting overcrowded. Consider coming for just the scenic drive. Obey all regulations and respect the fragile surroundings.

A few snorkelers head to the little roadside cove 175yd south of the first reserve

OFF THE BEATEN TRACK

LA PEROUSE BAY

Earth and ocean merge at La Perouse Bay with a raw, desolate beauty that's almost eerie. Historians originally thought Maui's last volcano eruption occurred in 1790, but recent analysis indicates the lava flow occurred about 200 to 300 years earlier. Before the blast, the ancient Hawaiian village of Keone'o'io flourished here, and its remains – mainly house and heiau platforms – are scattered among the lava patches.

In 1786 renowned French explorer Jean François de Galaup La Pérouse became the first Westerner to land on Maui. As he sailed into the bay here, scores of Hawaiian canoes came out to greet him. A monument to the explorer is at the end of the road at La Perouse Bay. A lava-rock monument in his honor marks the entrance to the bay area.

From the volcanic shoreline look for pods of spinner dolphins in the bay early in the day. Strong offshore winds and rough waters rule out swimming, but the land is fascinating to explore.

Activities

Located just before the road ends, **Makena Stables** (☎ 808-879-0244; www.makenastables.com; 8299 Makena Rd; 90min trail rides $155-175; ☻ 8am-6pm) offers a morning horseback ride and a sunset tour. Both travel along the rocky lava coast and climb up into the ranchlands. Groups size limited to five people. Must be at least 13 years old to ride.

sign – granted, it offers good snorkeling, but there is a better option. Instead, drive 350yd past the cove and look for a large clearing on the right. Park here and follow the coastal footpath south for five minutes to a black-sand beach with fantastic coral and clear water. Although this area, known informally as The Dumps, used to attract few visitors, the secret is out. Get here well before 9am to nab a decent parking spot – and maybe some solitude. The area now attracts up to 500 people per day.

To snorkel, enter the water from the left side of the beach, where access is easy and recommended by reserve officials. Look for the 'fish' signpost, which marks the entrance point. Snorkel in a northerly direction and you'll immediately be over coral gardens teeming with an amazing variety of fish.

Huge rainbow parrotfish abound here, and it's not unusual to see turtles and the occasional reef shark.

A ranger has been on site at The Dumps parking area recently reminding snorkelers to check their sunscreens before entering the water here. Many suntan lotions contain ingredients that are fatal to reefs (p164). Zinc and titanium oxide are safe.

Large sections of the 1238-acre reserve are closed to visitors until July 31, 2018, which will allow the Department of Land and Resource Management (www.dlnr.hawaii.gov) to protect the fragile environment from tourist wear-and-tear and to develop a long-term protection plan. Visitation in the open areas is still permitted between 5:30am and 7:30pm.

KIHEI & SOUTH MAUI BEYOND MAKENA

North Shore & Upcountry

Best Places to Eat

➡ Mama's Fish House (p183)

➡ Kula Lodge Restaurant (p174)

➡ Hali'imaile General Store (p185)

➡ Mana Foods (p182)

➡ Nuka (p185)

Best Activities for Kids

➡ Farm tour, Surfing Goat Dairy (p190)

➡ Horseback riding, Pi'iholo Ranch Stables (p186)

➡ Spreckelsville Beach (p180)

➡ Makai Glass (p185)

➡ October pumpkin patch, Kula Country Farms (p192)

Why Go?

This wild, lush and sometimes posh region of Maui is home to an extraordinary concentration of variety. In a half-hour drive, you can ascend from the beaches of the North Shore (including the world's windsurfing capital) through the jungle of the lower slopes, and break out into open Upcountry hills, where cowboys still roam the range, and farmers work the island's Garden Belt. Communities change accordingly. The hip surfer town of Pa'ia gives way to Makawao's Old West architecture, which dissolves into a handful of stores in mud-on-boots Keokea, after which the road rolls on to eternity – and maybe, we've heard, to Oprah's house.

The region begs for a lazy country drive, taking in athletic surfers, artsy shops, forest trails, mountain views and organic cafes at your own pace. For the adventurous, there's plenty of ziplining, paragliding and mountain biking.

When to Go

Weather temperatures are pleasant year-round, hovering in the 70s and 80s Farenheit, with a slight dip in winter.

If you love cowboys and parades, plan to visit in early July and catch the Pianolo Parade.

To catch the big-wave action at Jaws near Pa'ia, plan your visit for winter, but note that the biggest surf days vary year to year.

If you're traveling with younger kids, schedule a visit for October so you can stop by the pumpkin patch and corn maze at Kula Country Farm.

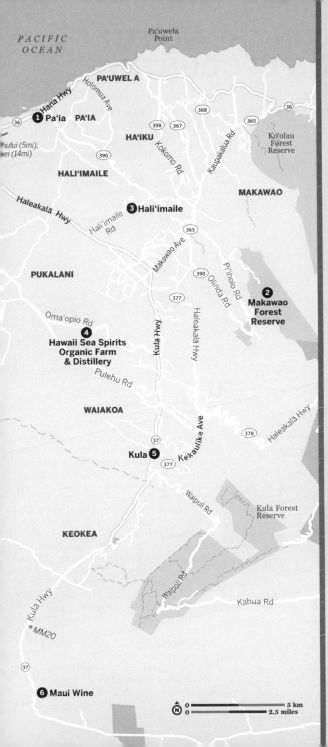

North Shore & Upcountry Highlights

1 Pa'ia (p179)
Sunbathing on the wide sandy strand at HA Baldwin Beach Park, and enjoying a bird's-eye view of expert surfers and windboarders riding the waves at Ho'okipa Beach Park & Overlook.

2 Makawao Forest Reserve (p186)
Exploring moody forest trails that wind through thick stands of pines and eucalyptus trees.

3 Hali'imaile General Store (p185)
Savoring locally sourced cocktails and fusion appetizers during a new happy hour at an old favorite.

4 Hawaii Sea Spirits Organic Farm & Distillery (p189)
Learning how master distillers create fine spirits then sampling the results of their labors.

5 Kula (p190)
Shopping for fresh tropical produce at Kula Country Farms and savoring locavore dishes and the expansive view from Kula Lodge Restaurant.

6 Maui Wine (p193) Sampling pineapple wine and strolling historic grounds once favored by a Hawaiian king.

HIKING IN THE NORTH SHORE & UPCOUNTRY

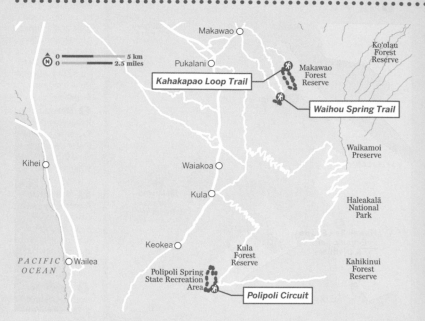

KAHAKAPAO LOOP TRAIL

START/END MAKAWAO FOREST RESERVE PARKING AREA

LENGTH 5.7 MILES; HALF-DAY

Your companions on this walk through the woods? Dog-walkers, mountain bikers and friendly hikers, plus a thick forest. The trees in this reserve are mostly non-native, planted in the early 1900s to protect the watershed after native flora had been destroyed.

To reach Kahakapao Rd and the parking area, follow Pi'iholo Rd for 1.5 miles, turn left on Waiahiwi Rd and turn right after 0.4 miles. Continue to the reserve (open 7am to 7pm). After entering, cross four dips in the road then enter the **parking area** 0.6 miles from the gate.

The trail runs through the Kahakapao Recreation Area within the 2093-acre Makawao Forest Reserve. From the parking area, walk to the **information kiosk** at the back of the lot. A half-mile connector trail, leading to the loop, dives down into the forest just left of the sign. You'll pass a collection of **skill courses and**

pump tracks for both beginner and expert cyclists. Bike-repair tools are attached to a pole by one of the tracks, along with an air pump.

The hard-packed trail is a mix of dirt and clay, often covered in leaves and broken by roots. It can get dangerously slick when wet. And it's often wet. A few single-track bike paths also cross the woods, connecting at various points along the main loop. Beyond the last pump track, the connector trail joins the main loop at another information kiosk.

The right side of the loop is called Kahakapao Loop West. Marked by red arrows, the trail runs 2.2 miles up the side of Haleakalā, twisting through a darkly wooded but lush ravine. One would hardly bat an eye if a hobbit or troll strolled past. The trees occasionally squeak from the wind, adding to the eeriness, especially if you're hiking solo. The trail passes a **picnic table** then twists to the top of the loop. Here, pick up Kahakapao Loop East, which drops through eucalyptus, ash and pine forests on its return to the start of the loop.

Trails twist through thick, sometimes eerie, groves of trees in the Upcountry, a green landscape that sweeps across the steep and often misty slopes of Haleakalā.

POLIPOLI CIRCUIT

START/END POLIPOLI SPRING STATE RECREATION AREA CAMPGROUND
LENGTH 5.3 MILES; HALF-DAY (LONGER IF YOU HIKE FROM THE RESERVE ENTRANCE)

From the Polipoli campground parking area, the Redwood, Plum, Haleakalā Ridge and Polipoli Trails form a worthwhile 5.3-mile loop. The parking area sits at an elevation of 6200ft, so it's cooler here than on the coast. Temperatures can drop below freezing here at night. Wear bright clothing as hunters are active near the park.

To get to the Redwood Trail, follow paved Waipoli Rd to the Kula Forest Reserve. Once the pavement ends, it's another 4 miles to the **campground** (Map p178; Waipoli Rd; campsite $18) and the trailhead. According to the sign, this unpaved stretch requires a 4WD vehicle. You will really see why if the road is wet and muddy.

Proceeding counter-clockwise, the 1.7-mile **Redwood Trail** leads from the right of the parking area. From there you'll descend into a towering redwood forest that feels more like California than Hawaii. You'll pass the **Tie Trail trailhead** and an old ranger's cabin before ending at a former Civilian Conserva-tion Corps camp. The Redwood Trail is open to hikers and mountain bikers. The Plum and Boundary Trails meet here too.

Follow the 1.7-mile **Plum Trail** as it ascends through stands of ash, redwood and sugi trees – all non-native. As the trail name suggests, plum trees also border the trail. From the Plum Trail, pick up the **Haleakalā Ridge Trail**. Stretching 1.6 miles, this scenic path climbs a rift on the southwest slope of the volcano. Look for pine and eucalyptus trees as well as cinders and native scrub.

Complete the loop back to the campground on the short but sweet **Polipoli Trail**, which ribbons beneath cypress trees and cedars, as well as the now-familiar pines.

WAIHOU SPRING TRAIL

START/END TOP OF OLINDA RD
LENGTH 2.4 MILES ROUND-TRIP

For a quiet walk in deep woods, take this cool, tranquil and mostly easy trail, which begins 4.75 miles up Olinda Rd from central Makawao. A half-mile in you'll reach a short loop trail. A steep (and potentially muddy) offshoot from the loop descends to Waihou Spring, but for most the loop will be enough (www.hawaiitrails.org).

CYCLING UPCOUNTRY TO NORTH SHORE

HALEAKALĀ TO PA'IA

START: HALEAKALĀ SUMMIT
END: PA'IA
LENGTH: 34 MILES; HALF-DAY

The 34-mile journey, a 10,000ft drop in elevation, offers tremendous views, a thrilling ride and Upcountry sightseeing, including Makawao. It's also easy – the bikes only have one gear – although you have to be careful to keep your speed down around seriously steep corners (there have been accidents and even deaths).

Guided tours are no longer allowed to begin their trips inside the park. This prohibition does not apply to regular visitors. If riding without a group, you will need to arrange a drop-off or pick-up. Remember that most visitors leave soon after sunrise, so traffic is heaviest early in the morning.

You'll first pass the **Haleakalā Visitor Center** (p205), where you can use the restrooms, grab a park map and replenish your water. Next up is the **Kalahaku Overlook** (p203), which is worth a stop for its lofty view of

the crater. From here, the switchbacks really kick-in. For more water, stop at the **Park Headquarters Visitor Center** (☎ 808-572-4459; www.nps.gov/hale; Hana Hwy, Summit District, Haleakalā National Park; ⏰ 8am-3:45pm) before leaving the park.

Guided bicycle tours begin just downhill from the park entrance, with different companies gathering at separate pull-offs. From the straight stretch of pavement ahead, take your pick of pull-off spots for a photograph. The view of the Maui isthmus, tucked between two coasts and flanked by the West Maui Mountains, is stunning.

Switchbacks tighten as you ride down the green slopes of the volcano. Turn right onto Hwy 377, passing **Kula Lodge** and Marketplace on your left. At the Makawao/Olinda sign turn right onto Kealaloa Rd. Continue to Hanamu Rd until it ends at the **Oskie Rice Arena**. Turn left and twist down Olinda Rd until you reach the cowboy town of Makawao. Cross Makawao Ave. Continue on Baldwin Ave, which passes several galleries and indie shops.

Cycling from the summit of Haleakalā down to seaside Pa'ia has become an island rite of passage.

The scenery opens up as you drop, with sugarcane fields, churches and schools lining the route. As you enter **Pa'ia**, it's time to start thinking about lunch – you have plenty of options.

You can rent bikes at **Maui Cyclery** (p180), or join a tour with **Maui Easy Riders** (p181) or **Haleakalā Bike Co** (p184). The latter also rents bikes.

Top: Haleakalā National Park

Bottom: Cyclists on the downhill route from Haleakalā summit to Pa'ia

GREG ELMES/GETTY IMAGES ©

Pi'iholo Ranch Stables (p186)
Idyap for a Cowboy for a Day experience.

Ho'okipa Beach (p179)
winter afternoons, windsurfers take over at The
'nt, the break furthest west in the bay.

Makawao Forest Reserve (p186)
s magical place is crisscrossed by trails open to
ers and mountain bikers.

Pa'ia (p179)
ia's aging wooden storefronts, splashed
bright colors, house a broad array of indie
sinesses.

North Shore & Upcountry

N
0 ___ 5 km
0 ___ 2.5 miles

PACIFIC OCEAN

Pa'uwela Point

17

Pa'uwela Rd

42
5
PA'UWELA
Holomua Ave
Ha'iku Rd

12
39

See Pa'ia Map (p181)

3

9
Hana Hwy

PA'IA

Baldwin Ave

390

398

32

West Kuiaha Rd
Peahi Rd

East Kuiaha Rd

Kauhikoa Rd

Ulumalu Rd

36

368

45
33
43
37
14

HA'IKU

Kokomo Rd

18

365

MAKAWAO

Ko'olau Forest Reserve

HALI'IMAILE

37

Haleakala Hwy

Kahului (2mi);
Kihei (11mi)

Old Haleakala Hwy

48
6
15
50
38

Kaluanui Rd

See Makawao Map (p187)

13
22
23
Waiahiwi Rd

365

19

Makawao Forest Reserve

PUKALANI

35
34
44
25
47

Makawao Ave

390
377

Olinda Rd

Haleakala Hwy

Oma'opio Rd

16
27

Pulehu Rd

Lower Kimo Dr

29

Pu'u Nianiau (6849ft)

WAIAKOA

Kula Hwy

30

41

26

378

Haleakala Hwy

KULA

4
40

Worcester Glassworks
1

Lower Kula Rd

49

7

21

24

2
Waipoli Rd

Kekaulike Ave

Kula Forest Reserve

Pi'ilani Hwy

KEOKEA
10
36
Keokea Park

11

28

Boundary Trail

Upper Waiakoa Trail

Waipoli Rd

Skyline Trail

Kahua Rd

Kula Hwy

WAILEA

Polipoli Spring State Recreation Area

31

Kahikinui Forest Reserve

Pu'u o Kanaloa (212ft)

37

MM20

46
20

Bully's Burgers (2mi);
Triple L Ranch (2mi)

North Shore & Upcountry

Pa'ia

An eclectic mix of surfers and soul-seekers cluster in Pa'ia, also known as Maui's hippest burg. Once a thriving plantation town of 10,000 residents, it declined during the 1950s when the local sugar mill closed. Then, like some other well-known sugar towns (eg Hanapepe on Kaua'i, and Honoka'a on Hawai'i, the Big Island), Pa'ia successfully reinvented itself. First came an influx of paradise-seeking hippies attracted by low rents. Next came windsurfers attracted by Ho'okipa Beach. Then came the tourists.

Today the town's aging wooden storefronts, splashed in bright colors, house a broad array of indie businesses (for the most part) facing a constant stream of traffic. It still feels like a dusty outpost at times, but that's all part of the vibe.

🏖 Beaches

Ho'okipa Beach Park & Overlook   BEACH
(Map p178; ☑808-572-8122; www.mauicounty.gov/facilities; Hana Hwy, mile marker 9; ⊙5:30am-7pm; ℗) Ho'okipa is to daredevil windsurfers what Everest is to climbers. It reigns supreme as the world's premier windsurfing beach, with strong currents, dangerous shorebreaks and razor-sharp coral offering the ultimate challenge. This is also one of Maui's prime surfing spots. While the action in the water is only suitable for pros, a lookout point on the eastern side of the park offers spectators a great bird's-eye view.

Winter sees the biggest waves for board surfers, while summer has the most consistent winds for windsurfers. To prevent turf battles, surfers typically hit the waves in the morning and windsurfers in the afternoon. In the fall the action includes green sea turtles laying eggs on the beach at dusk. Ho'okipa is just before the 9-mile marker. With a narrow beach and wild surf, this is not the best choice for a long day of sunbathing and swimming.

HA Baldwin Beach Park   BEACH
(Map p178; ☎808-572-8122; www.co.maui.hi.us/facilities; Hana Hwy; ⊗7am-7pm; ⊛) Bodyboarders and bodysurfers take to the waves at this palm-lined county park about a mile west of Pa'ia, at the 6-mile marker. The wide sandy beach drops off quickly, and when the shorebreak is big, swimmers should beware of getting slammed. Calmer waters can be found at the eastern end, where there's a little cove shaded by ironwood trees. Showers, restrooms, picnic tables and well-used sports fields round out the facilities.

The park has a reputation for rowdy behavior after the sun sets, but it's fine in the daytime when there's a lifeguard on duty.

Spreckelsville Beach   BEACH
(Map p178; Kealaki Pl; ⊛) Extending west from HA Baldwin Beach, this 2-mile stretch of sand is a good walking beach. Its near-shore reef makes it less ideal for swimming, but it does provide protection for young kids. If you walk toward the center of the beach, you'll soon come to a section dubbed 'Baby Beach.'

There are no facilities. At the 5-mile marker, turn toward the ocean on Nonohe Pl, then left on Kealakai Pl just before the Maui Country Club.

Tavares Beach   BEACH
(Map p178; Hana Hwy; ℙ ⊛) For a quiet stretch of sand during the week, try this unmarked beach, which is a short drive northeast from downtown, just beyond mile marker 7. The place livens up on weekends when local families arrive with picnics, guitars, dogs and kids. A submerged lava shelf runs parallel to the beach about 25ft from the shore, shallow enough for swimmers to scrape over. Once you know it's there, however, the rocks are easy to avoid, so take a look before jumping in.

⊙ Sights & Activities

Maui Dharma Center   BUDDHIST SHRINE
(Map p181; ☎808-579-8076; www.mauidharmacenter.com; 81 Baldwin Ave; ⊗6:30am-6:30pm; ℙ) Marked by its roadside stupa, this Tibetan Buddhist center offers daily, weekly and monthly prayer and meditation sessions, retreats and Dharma talks. Or just take a quick stroll around the stupa's prayer wheel. The stupa shrine was consecrated by the Dalai Lama in 2007.

Ho'okipa Beach Park   SURFING
(☎808-572-8122; /www.mauicounty.gov/facilities; Hana Hwy; ⊗7am-7pm) You'll find good waves year-round, but the breaks here are best for experienced surfers. In winter, the *really* big waves roll in. There are four surf breaks. Popular and consistent, **Pavilions** is a right-hander. It's closest to the lookout. Just west is **Middles**, which breaks left and right. Furthest west in the bay is **The Point**, which breaks right and is popular with windsurfers, who take over in the afternoon. Just west of the bay is **Lanes**, which breaks left and right, and requires a longer paddle out.

Simmer   WINDSURFING
(Map p181; ☎808-579-8484; www.simmer-hawaii.com; 99 Hana Hwy; sailboards per day $60; ⊗10am-7pm) This windsurfing shop sells gear and stylish men's and women's beachwear.

☞ Tours

Maui Cyclery   CYCLING
(Map p181; ☎808-579-9009; www.gocyclingmaui.com; 99 Hana Hwy; 1-day rental from $30, 1-day ride $150; ⊗8am-5pm Mon-Fri, to 4pm Sat, to noon Sun) What? A no-attitude bike shop? Yep, the folks at Maui Cyclery make you feel welcome the moment you walk in the door. Credit goes to owner Donnie Arnoult, an experienced cyclist who runs one- to multiday cycling 'experiences' across the island. Consider these trips to be supported training rides, with gorgeous scenery and full service backdropping the adventure. Open to all levels. Rentals available too.

Maui Photography Tours   TOURS
(Map p181; www.danielsullivanphotography.com; 149 Hana Hwy; 3hr tour $560) Photography tours with Daniel Sullivan take you to some of the most gorgeous spots on the island, from Hana to the King's Hwy. Sullivan is an acclaimed photographer who has photographed vanishing civilizations around the world. You'll sharpen your skills while capturing some of the island most jaw-dropping scenery. Three- or seven-hour tours available.

You can chat with global-minded Sullivan at his rug, photography and clothing shop, Indigo (p183), in Pa'ia.

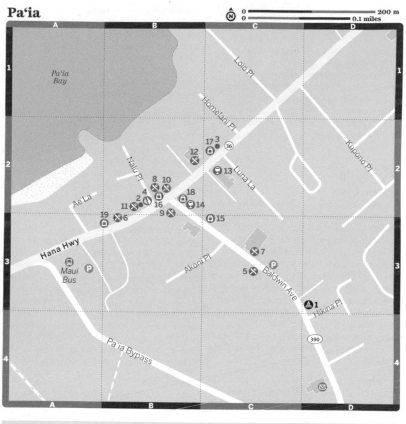

Pa'ia

◎ Sights
1 Maui Dharma Center D3

✪ Activities, Courses & Tours
2 Maui Cyclery B2
3 Maui Photography Tours C2
4 Simmer B2

✪ Eating
5 Café des Amis C3
6 Flatbread Company B3
7 Mana Foods C3
8 Pa'ia Bay Coffee B2
9 Pa'ia Fish Market Restaurant B2

10 Paia Gelato B2
11 Pa'ia Inn Cafe B2
12 Toby's Shave Ice B2

⦿ Drinking & Nightlife
13 Charley's C2
14 Milagros Food Company B2

🛍 Shopping
15 Alice in Hulaland C3
16 Ali'i Kula Lavender - Pa'ia B2
17 Indigo C2
18 Maui Crafts Guild B2
19 Wings Hawaii B3

Maui Easy Riders   CYCLING
(Map p178; ☏ 808-344-9489; www.mauieasyriders.com; Hana Hwy, HA Baldwin Beach Park; per person $119) Offers a four-hour guided tour for groups of up to eight on comfy cruisers. Stops include Makawao and Pa'ia. Departs 9am and 1:30pm. Meet at Baldwin Beach Park. Save $20 by booking online. Staff can arrange a sunrise viewing followed by the bike ride. Also offers a guided tour of the Road to Hana (from $550; not a bike tour).

ISLAND INSIGHTS

The North Shore harbors Maui's most famous big-wave surfing spot: **Jaws** (Pe'ahi; Map p178). When present, the mammoth swell reaches as high as a seven-story building. Surfers are towed in or even dropped by helicopter. Unfortunately for onlookers, there's no legitimate public access to the cliffs above, as the path crosses private land.

🍴 Eating

⭐**Mana Foods** BAKERY, MARKET $
(Map p181; ☎ 808-579-8078; www.manafoodsmaui.com; 49 Baldwin Ave; salad bar $8.99/lb, sandwiches under $9; ⊗8am-8:30pm; 🅿) Dreadlocked, Birkenstocked or just needing to stock up – everyone rubs shoulders at Mana, a friendly health-food store, bakery and deli wrapped into one. Once past the unassuming entrance, you'll find narrow aisles bursting with rare goodies, coffee galore, a fantastic and very busy salad bar, and hot food to go. The mind of Pa'ia made visible.

For a smoothie or healthy breakfast bowl, try the market's new **Maka by Mana Cafe** (www.makabyana.com).

Pa'ia Inn Cafe BREAKFAST $
(Map p181; ☎808-579-6000; http://paiainn.com; 93 Hana Hwy; mains $14-17; ⊗8am-1pm) Watch the chefs whip up your *huevos rancheros* (rancher's eggs) at this pleasant new outdoor cafe tucked behind the Pa'ia Inn. The menu offers a short but appealing mix of breakfast and lunch items, from eggs Benedict to a BLT sandwich with avocado. Pressed juices and smoothies also available. Service can be leisurely, but hey, this is Maui. Where do you have to be?

Toby's Shave Ice DESSERTS, SEAFOOD $
(Map p181; ☎808-579-9745; 137 Hana Hwy; small shave ice $5, poke $11-13; ⊗10am-6pm) Come for the shave ice, stay for the...*poke*? Oh yeah, the *poke* (seasoned raw fish) at this low-frills joint is the bomb. And if you like it spicy, try the suicide *poke*. Smiling devil emoji.

Pa'ia Bay Coffee CAFE $
(Map p181; ☎808-579-3111; www.paiabaycoffee.com; 115 Hana Hwy, enter off Nalu Pl; breakfast $7-12, lunch $8-10; ⊗7am-5:30pm; 🛜) The lovely shaded garden is an inviting sanctuary on a hot day at this low-key coffee shop tucked into a busy downtown side street. Grab croissants to go or settle in at a table for Greek yogurt with berries and granola, organic scrambled eggs with goat cheese, or a smoked salmon and avocado sandwich. A local hot spot in the morning.

Note: if you're not a local, you will be checked out. Not a bad thing necessarily, just depends on your mood.

Kuau Store DELI $
(Map p178; ☎ 808-579-8844; www.kuaustore.com; 701 Hana Hwy; sandwiches under $9; ⊗6:30am-7pm) Fuel up with coffee or a healthy juice before a drive on the Hana Hwy. Sandwiches are also available to go at this general store and deli. Look for the photogenic surfboard fence about 1 mile east of downtown Pa'ia.

Café des Amis CAFE $
(Map p181; ☎808-579-6323; www.cdamaui.com; 42 Baldwin Ave; breakfast $6-14, lunch & dinner $4-22; ⊗8:30am-8:30pm Sun-Thu, to 9pm Fri & Sat) Grab a seat in the courtyard at this often-recommended eatery to dine on sweet or savory crepes and a variety of curries. You'll also find vegetarian offerings, creative breakfasts and a tempting array of drinks, from fruit smoothies to fine wines. Note that the wraps may overpower the flavor of the fillings, and that service can be leisurely.

Paia Gelato DESSERTS $
(Map p181; ☎808-579-9201; www.paiagelato.com; 115 Hana Hwy; cones $5; ⊗7am-10pm) Dishes up 24 different flavors of Maui-made gelato. The Sandy Beach is mixed with graham crackers and peanut butter.

Pa'ia Fish Market Restaurant SEAFOOD $$
(Map p181; ☎808-579-8030; www.paiafishmarket.com; 110 Hana Hwy, cnr Baldwin Ave; mains $10-21; ⊗11am-9:30pm; 🚼) The communal picnic tables are perpetually packed inside this long-time favorite, where the fish is always fresh, tasty and affordable. The local favorite is *ono* fish and chips, but the menu includes plenty of other temptations, including charbroiled mahi, Cajun-style snapper, and a Hawaii classic, blackened ahi sashimi. As for those crowded picnic tables, they turn over quickly. Children's menu mains under $6.

Flatbread Company PIZZA $$
(Map p181; ☎808-579-8989; www.flatbreadcompany.com; 89 Hana Hwy; pizzas $13-24; ⊗11am-10pm) 🌿 Wood-fired pizzas made with organic sauces, nitrate-free pepperoni, Maui pineapples – you'll never stop at a

chain pizza house again. Fun combinations abound, from pure vegan to *kalua* pork with goat cheese. Don't want a pizza? Many of those toppings are available in organic salads.

★ Mama's Fish House
SEAFOOD $$$

(Map p178; ☑ 808-579-8488; www.mamasfishhouse.com; 799 Poho Pl; mains $32-68; ☉11am-9pm) Mama's is a South Seas dream: superb food, top-notch service and a gorgeous seaside setting. The fish is literally fresh off the boat – staff can even tell you who caught it. The eclectic building successfully integrates everything from driftwood to sugarcane machinery. When the beachside tiki torches are lit at dinnertime, you'll swear you've entered a poster from *South Pacific*.

The only drawback is the eye-popping prices, which match the island's most expensive resorts. Yet no one seems to care. This is a magnet for honeymooners, or for anyone looking for that once-in-a-lifetime Hawaii experience. Located on Hana Hwy, 1.5 miles east of Pa'ia town. Reservations essential; holidays book out three months ahead.

🍷 Drinking & Nightlife

Charley's
BAR

(Map p181; ☑ 808-579-8085; www.charleysmaui.com; 142 Hana Hwy; ☉7am-10pm Sun-Thu, to 2am Fri & Sat) Pa'ia's legendary saloon has been slingin' suds and pub grub since 1969. In its heyday it was a magnet for visiting rock stars, who were known to take to the stage. While that scene has moved on (OK, there's a slim chance part-time resident Willie Nelson will pop in), this is still the town's main music venue.

It has dinner music Tuesday to Thursday, DJs and bands Friday and Saturday, and open mic night Monday. Check the website for the schedule. Willie's son Lukas and his band Promise of the Real played here in 2016.

Milagros Food Company
BAR

(Map p181; ☑ 808-579-8755; www.milagrosfoodcompany.com; 3 Baldwin Ave; ☉11am-10pm) With sidewalk tables perched on Pa'ia's busiest corner, an island-style Tex-Mex menu (mains $10 to $16) and a variety of margaritas, this bar-restaurant is the perfect spot for a late-afternoon pit stop. Happy hour is from 3pm to 6pm, with $4 house margaritas.

🛍 Shopping

★ Indigo
ARTS & CRAFTS

(Map p181; ☑ 808-579-9199; www.indigopaia.com; 149 Hana Hwy; ☉10am-6pm) Step into this inviting boutique for a shopping trip through Central and Southwest Asia. The gorgeous handcrafted rugs, one-of-a-kind furnishings and traditional crafts were collected by the owners, Daniel Sullivan and Caramiya Davies-Reid. Sullivan also sells vibrant photographs taken during his travels, while Davies-Reid designs breezy dresses and custom bathing suits.

You can check out Sullivan's brilliant photographs from a hike around the island on the King's Hwy in his book *The Maui Coast: The Legacy of the King's Highway*.

★ Maui Crafts Guild
ARTS & CRAFTS

(Map p181; ☑ 808-579-9697; www.mauicraftsguild.com; 120 Hana Hwy; ☉10am-6pm) Perched on the corner of the Hana Hwy and Baldwin Ave, this longstanding artists' co-op store sells everything from pottery and jewelry to hand-painted silks and natural-fiber baskets at reasonable prices. All artists must be full-time Maui residents.

Ali'i Kula Lavender – Pa'ia
GIFTS & SOUVENIRS

(Map p181; ☑ 808-579-8060; www.aliikulalavender.com; 115 Hana Hwy; ☉8am-6pm) Pop into this tiny shop for lotions and other lavender-infused products from the farm up the road in Kula.

Wings Hawaii
CLOTHING, JEWELRY

(Map p181; ☑ 808-579-3110; www.wingshawaii.com; 69 Hana Hwy; ☉10am-8pm) For truly unique clothing and jewelry – they call it beach boho chic – stop by this small shop that sells locally designed womenswear.

Alice in Hulaland
GIFTS & SOUVENIRS

(Map p181; ☑ 808-579-9922; www.aliceinhulaland.com; 19 Baldwin Ave; ☉10am-6pm) Kitschy but fun souvenirs and Hawaiiana, plus trendy fashions.

ℹ Information

Bank of Hawaii (☑ 808-579-9511; www.boh.com; 35 Baldwin Ave; ☉8:30am-4pm Mon-Thu, to 6pm Fri)

Post Office (Map p181; ☑ 808-579-8866; www.usps.com; 120 Baldwin Ave; ☉9am-4pm Mon-Fri, 10:30am-12:30pm Sat)

CROSSTOWN TRAFFIC

For a surfer town bursting with healthy bodies, Pa'ia sure has some clogged arteries. Roads, that is. If you're heading Upcountry from Kahului, avoid the main intersection at Baldwin Ave by taking the bypass. If you're staying awhile, head for the town lot first, as parking is a problem. And if you're heading on to Hana, check your gas gauge: Pa'ia has the last filling station on the highway, and Hana's has been known to run dry.

Getting There & Around

Pa'ia is 6.5 miles from the Kahului Airport. The **Maui Bus** (Map p181; Hana Hwy, east of Bypass Rd) operates the Ha'iku Islander between the airport and Pa'ia ($2) every 90 minutes from 5:40am to 8:40pm. The bus stop is located on the Hana Hwy beside the city parking lot on the right as you enter town, just beyond the Pa'ia Bypass Rd.

Ha'iku

Ha'iku is a lot like old Pa'ia, before tourism took hold. Both have their roots in sugarcane – Maui's first 12 acres of the sweet stuff were planted in Ha'iku in 1869, and the village once had both a sugar mill and pineapple canneries. Thanks to its affordability and proximity to Ho'okipa Beach, it's also a haunt of pro surfers, who've helped rejuvenate the town.

Nestled in greenery, this is a low-key place to stay, with many excellent accommodations and restaurants for its size. To get an early start on the Road To Hana, consider spending the night here.

Activities

Kalakupua Playground PARK
(Fourth Marine Division Memorial Park; Map p178; 808-572-8122; www.mauicounty.gov; Kokomo Rd, mile marker 2; 8am-7pm;) Known as 'Giggle Hill,' the jungle gym and playground – complete with turrets, boardwalks and slides – is great for kids. The 40-acre park here also has playing fields and covered picnic pavilions. The park was the site of a marine training ground and camp during World War II.

Haleakalā Bike Co CYCLING
(Bike Maui; Map p178; 808-575-9575; www.bikemaui.com; 810 Ha'iku Rd, Ha'iku Marketplace;

sunrise bike tour $135) Want to watch the sunrise then bike down the volcano at your own pace? Then book the Sunrise Special. After an early-morning van ride to the summit, followed by the sunrise, you'll be dropped off just outside the park with a bike, helmet, backpack, rain gear and a map. From there it's 23 twisty miles down to Ha'iku. Be back by 4pm. Check-in is 3am.

Not an early riser? Try the Summit Deluxe Trip. After a 9am check-in, this trip climbs to the summit of the volcano for a guided tour, which is followed by a self-guided downhill ride ($105 per person).

Also rents bikes ($40 to $55 per day) if you want to tackle roads and trails in and around the park on your own. Rental includes a bike rack and its installation.

Eating

Baked on Maui BAKERY, CAFE $
(Map p178; 375 W Kuiaha, Pa'uwela Cannery; breakfast $9-10, lunch $8-10; 6:30am-5pm) Delicious homemade food, including fresh baked bread, a full breakfast menu and great sandwiches, makes this *the* local stop prior to tackling the Road to Hana. From Pa'ia turn right on West Kuiaha and continue on until you reach the huge Pa'uwela Cannery building, now business space.

Veg Out VEGETARIAN $
(Map p178; 808-575-5320; www.veg-out.com; 810 Kokomo Rd, Ha'iku Town Center; mains $7-10, 12in pizza $10-18; 10:30am-7:30pm Mon-Fri, 11:30am-7:30pm Sat & Sun;) Tucked inside a former warehouse, this rasta-casual vegetarian eatery serves up a dynamite burrito loaded with beans, hot tofu and jalapeños. Also right on the mark are the taro cheeseburgers and pesto-chèvre pizzas.

Sala Dang THAI $
(Map p178; 808-463-4166; 824 Kokomo Rd; mains $13-24; 11am-9pm Mon-Sat) Tuk Tuk Thai closed up its popular food truck and moved across the street to a cottage. And it looks like the crowds have followed. Now known as Sala Dang, and serving noodle, curry and stir fry dishes, this cozy joint is hoppin'.

Ha'iku Grocery Store SUPERMARKET $
(Map p178; 808-575-9291; 810 Ha'iku Rd, Ha'iku Marketplace; 6am-9pm) Now owned by Foodland, this market sells bento boxes and hot food in addition to the usual groceries.

★ Nuka   JAPANESE $$
(Map p178; ☑ 808-575-2939; www.nukamaui.com; 780 Ha'iku Rd; lunch $5-12, dinner small plates $4-22, mains $12-20, rolls $9-19; ⊙ 10am-1:30pm & 4:30-10pm Mon-Fri) One of Maui's best dining options marries a traditional Japanese restaurant with a jazzy cafe, offering the classics, such as sushi and tempura, alongside exotic rolls and *otsumami* (tapas). From the menus to the decor to the website, everything is presented with sophistication, and without inflated prices. And oh, that Nuka Roll. Now open for lunch serving noodles, burgers and an acai bowl.

No reservations. There may be a line by 6:15pm.

Colleen's   AMERICAN $$
(Map p178; ☑ 808-575-9211; www.colleensinhaiku. com; 810 Ha'iku Rd, Ha'iku Marketplace; breakfast $7-13, lunch $6-16, dinner $11-30; ⊙ 6am-10pm) From morning to evening, this boisterous bistro is the Ha'iku hangout, for locals and visitors alike. Menu choices are straightforward – burgers, salads and build-your-own pizzas among them – but cooked to perfection, and supported by a wide range of craft beers. Excellent coffee and big breakfasts drag 'em in early.

Looking for greens and protein? Try the roasted beet salad with goat cheese and grilled chicken. Delicious!

🍸 Drinking & Nightlife

Maui Kombucha   TEAHOUSE
(Map p178; ☑ 808-575-5233; www.mauikombucha. com; 810 Ha'iku Rd, Ha'iku Marketplace; 12oz tea $5, mains $7-13; ⊙ 8am-8pm Mon-Fri, to 5pm Sat & Sun) Welcome to 'The Booch,' home of Ha'iku's alternative drink, kombucha. This hip hole-in-the-wall overflows with fermented tea (with bubbles!) and a lively crowd. Also serves chai tea and cold-pressed coffee. The veggie fare changes daily, but expect wraps, salads and lots of fun. Faces Kokomo Rd in the Ha'iku Marketplace.

Hali'imaile

The tiny pineapple town of Hali'imaile is jumping these days. Named for the sweet-scented maile plants – used in lei-making – that covered the area before pineapples took over, it recently welcomed a new micro-distillery and a new glass-blowing studio. Both are housed in Quonset huts across the road from the old general store (c 1918), which has been transformed into one of Maui's top restaurants. This bustling collection of businesses is the heart of the community.

👉 Tours

Hali'imaile Distilling Company   FOOD & DRINK
(Map p178; ☑ 808-633-3609; www.haliimaile distilling.com; 883 Hali'imaile Rd; $10; ⊙ 10am-4pm Mon-Fri) The whiskey casks are emblazoned with *paniolo* (Hawaiian Cowboy) mustaches at this new micro-distillery, where tours end with samples of three 'luxury' spirits, all infused with local ingredients. Production is overseen by master distiller Mark Nigbur, who built the glass stills you'll see on the tour.

Be sure to sample the flagship Pau Vodka. Distilled from Maui pineapples, it's clean and pure with just a hint of sweetness.

The company also produces Sammy's Beach Bar Rum, a joint venture with Van Halen frontman Sammy Hagar. Hagar is a part-time Maui resident – and a Mark Nigbur doppelganger. There are tours every 30 minutes. Best to reserve ahead.

🍴 Eating

★ Hali'imaile General Store   HAWAIIAN $$$
(Map p178; ☑ 808-572-2666; www.bevgannon restaurants.com; 900 Hali'imaile Rd; lunch $14-26, dinner $32-44; ⊙ 11am-2:30pm & 3-5:30pm Mon-Fri, plus 5:30-9pm daily; 🐾) The culinary sorceress behind this destination dining spot is chef Bev Gannon, who was one of the original forces behind the Hawaii Regional Cuisine movement. A steady flow of in-the-know diners beats a track to this inviting outpost – the building was a general store during the plantation era – to feast on her fusion creations, such as crab-topped pizza and Asian pear duck tostadas.

With appetizers under $11 and cocktail specials, the recently introduced happy hour is drawing crowds. The happy-hour tacos are *muy bueno* (very good).

🛍 Shopping

Makai Glass   ARTS & CRAFTS
(Map p178; ☑ 808-269-8255; www.makaiglass. com; 903 Hali'imaile Rd; ⊙ 11am-6pm Mon-Sat) Walk up to the 2nd-floor viewing area of this spacious gallery, inside a large Quonset hut, to watch glassblowers at work in the studio below. How they craft the glass into fantastic sculptures seems just short of magic. The *honu* (green sea turtles) are especially cool. It's a nice place to browse and hangout before the distillery tour next door.

Makawao

Dubbed Maka Wow on local T-shirts, this attractive town is a mélange of art haven and *paniolo* culture, with a twist of New Age sensibility. A ranching town since the 1800s, its false-front buildings and hitching posts look transported from the Old West. Today the surrounding hills still contain cattle pastures and ranches, but also expensive homes, as these cool and quiet uplands have become a choice residential area. Meanwhile, the town below has filled with attractive galleries and cafes. The main action is at the intersection of Baldwin Ave and Makawao Ave, where you can enjoy browsing, a fine meal and a bit of nightlife.

◉ Sights

Sacred Garden of Maliko GARDENS
(Map p178; 🖉 808-573-7700; www.sacredgarden-maui.com; 460 Kaluanui Rd; ⊙10am-5pm; ℗) **FREE** Need a meditative moment? The nonprofit Sacred Garden of Maliko, a self-described healing sanctuary, has a pair of rock-garden labyrinth walks guaranteed to reset the harmony gauge. One's in an orchid greenhouse; the other's in a *kukui* (candlenut tree) grove beside Maliko Stream. It's a peaceful place, with sitting areas, to relax. Also sells plants and gifts, with complimentary tea and hot chocolate.

Hui No'eau Visual Arts Center ARTS CENTER
(Map p178; 🖉 808-572-6560; www.huinoeau.com; 2841 Baldwin Ave; ⊙9am-4pm; ℗) **FREE** Occupying the former estate of sugar magnates Harry and Ethel Baldwin, Hui No'eau is a regal setting for a community arts center. In 1917 famed architect CW Dickey designed the main plantation house, which showcases the Hawaiian Regional architectural style he pioneered. You can visit the galleries, which exhibit island artists, and stroll the grounds, where you'll find stables converted into art studios.

The gift shop sells quality ceramics, glassware and prints created on site. At the front desk, pick up a brochure with a map and list of things to do. A fantastic coffee truck parks here in the morning. The center is just north of the 5-mile marker.

Makawao History Museum MUSEUM
(🖉 808-572-2482; 3643 Baldwin Ave; ⊙10am-5pm Mon-Sat, 11am-5pm Sun) **FREE** Step into this tiny museum for an overview of the town's cowboy past, with lots of ranching tools on display plus black-and-white photos of the town and its former inhabitants. There's also a display exploring the town's multicultural roots. You can pick up a historic Makawao walking tour map here too ($1).

🏃 Activities

**Makawao Forest
Reserve Trails** HIKING, MOUNTAIN BIKING
(Map p178; www.mauimountainbike.org; Kahakapau Rd, Makawao Forest Reserve; ⊙7am-7pm) Walking into the thick and towering trees at this 2093-acre reserve feels like an journey into a fantasy novel. This magical place, which still feels undiscovered, is crisscrossed by trails open to hikers and mountain bikers. The 5.75-mile multiuse Kahakapao Loop Trail (p172) is the primary trail. It parallels a ravine before arcing back through cool upland forest. Trails are very slick when wet.

If dry, these volcanic clay trails are also great for running. You will pass two small pump tracks a short distance from the trailhead. The trails are a joint effort between state agencies and the Maui Mountain Bike Coalition. At press time, trail maps and visitor information had not been added to state-run recreational websites. For a helpful map showing the various trails and their uses, visit www.mauimountainbike.org/kahakapao-recreation-area. Rent bikes in Pa'ia.

To reach Kahakapao Rd, head up Pi'iholo Rd for 1.5 miles, turn left on Waiahiwi Rd and turn right after 0.4 miles. Continue to the reserve.

Pi'iholo Ranch Stables HORSEBACK RIDING
(Map p178; 🖉 808-270-8750; www.piiholo.com; 325 Waiahiwi Rd; per person Cowboy for a Day $349, 2/3hr rides $229/349; ⊙Mon-Sat; ⊕) Want to round-up cattle like a *paniolo*? Then giddyap for the Cowboy for a Day experience. In a secluded glen, high up on the edge of a rainforest, this family-run cattle ranch, now six generations old, also offers two- and three-hour group horseback rides for up to six people with mountain, valley and pasture views galore. All rides are private.

Pi'iholo Ranch Zipline ADVENTURE SPORTS
(Map p178; 🖉 808-572-1717; www.piiholozipline.com; 799 Pi'iholo Rd; zip tours $99-180, canopy tours $99; ⊙tours 8am-3pm, reservations 7am-7pm; ⊕) This operation offers two options: a standard dual-line course of four/five lines, the latter with a 2800ft finale that hits 600ft in altitude, and a six/seven-line

Makawao

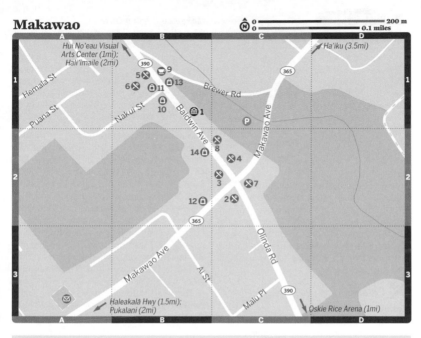

Makawao

◎ Sights
1 Makawao History Museum...................B1

✖ Eating
Casanova Deli.............................(see 2)
2 Casanova Italian Restaurant................C2
3 Komoda Store & Bakery.......................C2
4 Makawao Garden Café.........................C2
5 Makawao Steak House.........................B1
6 Market Fresh Bistro............................B1
7 Polli's..C2
8 Rodeo General Store............................C2

◎ Drinking & Nightlife
9 Sip Me!..B1

⑪ Shopping
10 Designing Wahine Emporium................B1
11 Hot Island Glass...............................B1
12 Maui Hands......................................B2
   Viewpoints Gallery.........................(see 11)
13 Volcano Spice...................................B1
14 Wertheim Contemporary.....................B2

canopy course. You can bring your own Go-Pro cam to mount on your helmet, but bring your own head straps. The Hike & Zip combo ($219) includes a waterfall hike on the Hana Hwy.

☞ Tours

808 Off the Grid OUTDOORS
(Map p178; ☎ 808-495-7560; www.808offthegrid. com; 325 Waiahiwi Rd; 2/3hr tour $250/330; ⊘ tours 8am and 11am Mon-Sat) Hop into a rugged all-terrain vehicle for a tour of the vast ranch lands surrounding Pi'iholo Ranch. The trip bounces over green pastures with expansive views of the coast and the West

Maui mountains, and stops by private pools and waterfalls on the property.

✸ Festivals & Events

Makawao Third Friday FAIR
(www.mauifridays.com; Baldwin Ave; ⊘ 6-9pm 3rd Fri monthly; 🚶) On the third Friday of every month the center of Makawao turns into a pedestrian zone and laid-back street party from 6pm to 9pm, with food, arts and crafts and live music.

Maui Polo Club SPORTS
(www.mauipoloclub.com; Olinda Rd/Haleakalā Hwy; adult/child under 12yr $10/free; ⊘ 1:30pm, gates open 12:30pm; 🚶) A friendly tailgating party

VIEWS AND VERTIGO

For a steep scenic drive with plenty of twists and turns, head into the hills above Makawao along Olinda Rd, which picks up in town where Baldwin Ave leaves off. Turn left onto Pi'iholo Rd near the top, and wind back down into town. The whole crazy loop takes about half an hour. Combine with **Waihou Spring Trail** (p173) for a cool midway break.

surrounds these Sunday matches held behind Oskie Rice Arena, 1 mile above town on Olinda Rd, early September through mid-November; and at the Manduke Baldwin Polo Arena, 1.7 miles up Haleakalā Highway from Makawao Ave, from early April to late June. Dress is casual to island dressy (ie your best aloha shirt).

✖ Eating

Market Fresh Bistro INTERNATIONAL $
(Map p187; ☑808-572-4877; marketfreshbistro. com; 3620 Baldwin Ave; breakfast $12-20, lunch $9-16; ⊙9-11am & 11:30am-3pm Tue-Sat, 9am-2pm Sun, 6-8:30pm Thu) Foodies love the sophisticated tastes at this relaxing farm-to-table cafe, whose philosophy of 'global influence, local ingredients' has rapidly made it one of Makawao's best dining options. Insiders descend here Thursday evenings at 6pm for a special prix-fixe dinner ($75), but call ahead to make sure it's on and make a reservation. Located inside the Shops at the Courtyard.

Komoda Store & Bakery BAKERY $
(Map p187; 3674 Baldwin Ave; ⊙7am-4pm Mon, Tue, Thu & Fri, to 2pm Sat) Celebrating its 100th birthday in 2016, this homespun bakery, legendary for its mouthwatering cream puffs, stick doughnuts and guava-filled *malasadas* (Portuguese fried doughnuts), is a Makawao landmark. Arrive early, as it often sells out by noon.

Rodeo General Store DELI $
(Map p187; ☑808-572-1868; 3661 Baldwin Ave; mains $7-9; ⊙6:30am-8pm Sun-Thu, to 9pm Fri & Sat) The deli counter at this busy general store sells a variety of to-go meals, from salads and sandwiches to Hawaiian *poke* and plate lunches. The *kalua* pork is tender and oh-so tasty. Everything is made from scratch. Also sells beer and liquor.

Makawao Garden Café CAFE $
(Map p187; ☑808-573-9065; 3669 Baldwin Ave; mains under $9; ⊙11am-3pm Mon-Sat) On a sunny day there's no better place in town for lunch than this outdoor cafe tucked into a courtyard at the northern end of Baldwin Ave. It's strictly sandwiches and salads, but everything's fresh, generous and made to order by the owner herself.

Casanova Italian Restaurant ITALIAN $$
(Map p187; ☑808-572-0220; www.casanovamaui. com; 1188 Baldwin Ave; lunch $9-20, dinner $14-44; ⊙11:30am-2pm Mon-Sat, plus 5:30-9:30pm daily) Classic Italian dishes. Juicy Maui-raised steaks. Innovative pizzas cooked in a kiawe-fired oven. It's hard to go wrong at this long-time Upcountry favorite. Casanova doubles as an entertainment venue, with a happening dance floor and DJs or live music on Wednesdays and weekends (10pm to 1am). Wednesday night is Ladies Night, when women get in free.

For a casual lunch, try one of the hearty sandwiches at the attached **deli** (☑808-572-0220; www.casanovamaui.com; 1188 Makawao Ave; mains $7-9; ⊙7:30am-5:30pm Mon-Sat).

Polli's MEXICAN $$
(Map p187; ☑808-572-7808; www.pollismexican restaurant.com; 1202 Makawao Ave; most mains $13-24, tacos $5; ⊙11am-10pm) Parked on the corner of Baldwin Ave and Makawao Ave, this friendly and reliable Tex-Mex restaurant is a longtime favorite. Have a cerveza at the small bar, or tackle sizzling fajitas in the nearby booths. Four children's plates available for $5 each. Margaritas are $4 during happy hour (4pm to 5:30pm Monday to Friday).

Makawao Steak House STEAK $$$
(Map p187; ☑808-572-8711; www.cafeolei restaurants.com; 3612 Baldwin Ave; mains $14-34; ⊙restaurant 5-9pm Tue-Sun, bar from 4:30pm Tue-Sun; ♿) What's a cowboy town without a steak house? Or a saloon? You get both here, along with a warm Upcountry atmosphere. Dining solo? Grab a seat at the welcoming bar. Owned by the Cafe O'Lei franchise, the varied menu offers something for everyone, including the kids. Five mains for $6 each on the children's menu.

🍷 Drinking

Gypsy Maui Coffee Truck COFFEE
(Map p178; ☑808-298-3320; www.facebook. com/gypsymaui; 2841 Baldwin Ave, Hui No'eau Visual Arts Center; ⊙8am-noon Mon-Fri) Fans of

Bulletproof coffee will find a new favorite after sipping the Gypsy ($5), a creamy blend of espresso, coconut oil and buffalo butter. Served from a food truck on the front lawn of Hui No'eau Visual Arts Center, the other specialty coffees here are also superb. Tasty snacks ($4 to $7) such as avocado toast, plus the gorgeous backdrop, make this a perfect pit stop.

Sip Me! COFFEE
(Map p187; ☑ 808-573-2340; www.sipmemaui.com; 3617 Baldwin Ave; ⊙ 6am-5pm Mon-Sat, 7am-4pm Sun; 🛜) Who's settling in to this chic-but-inviting new spot for cold-brew toddies, cold-pressed juices and smoothies sourced with local produce? Yoga lads and ladies, hipsters in cowboy hats and the occasional mom-and-daughter team. All here for caffeine, conversation and the wi-fi. The pastry counter is loaded with croissants, cinnamon rolls and quiches, plus gluten-free treats. Sit inside or on the patio.

It's a bit of a scene, but we like it. And the 12oz coffee is $1.50. Nice!

🛍 Shopping

⭐ **Wertheim Contemporary** ART
(Map p187; ☑ 808-573-5972; www.wertheim contemporary.com; 3660 Baldwin Ave; ⊙ 11am-5pm) Showcases the extraordinary art of Andreas Nottebohm, who etches flat sheets of aluminum to create an illusion of depth. You won't believe your eyes. Also shows works by local, national and globally known artists.

Maui Hands ART
(Map p187; ☑ 808-572-2008; www.mauihands.com; 1169 Makawao Ave; ⊙ 10am-6pm Mon-Sat, to 5pm Sun) A fascinating collection of high-quality Hawaii art, primarily from Maui, including photography, koa, ceramics, photographs and a mix of traditional and contemporary paintings. Worth a stop.

Volcano Spice FOOD
(Map p187; ☑ 808-572-7729; www.volcanospice company.com; 3621 Baldwin Ave; ⊙ 11am-5pm Mon-Sat, to 3pm Sun) An enticing array of spicy rubs and hot sauces are sold in this tiny shop on Baldwin Ave. If you're a hot-sauce fiend, there are plenty to sample – just bring some water!

Viewpoints Gallery ART
(Map p187; ☑ 808-572-5979; www.viewpoints gallerymaui.com; 3620 Baldwin Ave; ⊙ 10:30am-5pm) This classy gallery hosts more than three dozen of the island's finest artists, and feels like a welcoming museum.

Designing Wahine Emporium GIFTS & SOUVENIRS
(Map p187; ☑ 808-573-0990; www.designing wahine.com; 3640 Baldwin Ave; ⊙ 10am-6pm Mon-Sat, 11am-5pm Sun) Decorative pillows, jewelry, children's clothing, Maka Wow tanks, quality gifts and much else fill this classic plantation cottage.

ℹ️ Information

Post Office (☑ 808-572-0019; www.usps.com; 1075 Makawao Ave; ⊙ 9am-4:30pm Mon-Fri, to 11am Sat)

ℹ️ Getting Around

Minit Stop (☑ 808-573-9295; www.minitstop. com; 1100 Makawao Ave; ⊙ 5am-11pm) There's no bank in town, but this convenience store has gas and an ATM. It also serves legendary fried chicken: your budget lunch.

Pukalani & Around

True to its name, which means Heavenly Gate, Pukalani is the gateway to the lush Upcountry. Most visitors just drive past Pukalani on the way to Kula and Haleakalā, unless they need food or gas (the last before the park). The big draw? The Saturday-morning Upcountry farmers market – the selection is amazing.

To reach the business part of town, get off Haleakalā Hwy (Hwy 37) at the Old Haleakalā Hwy exit, which becomes Pukalani's main street.

🏃 Activities

Pukalani Country Club GOLF
(Map p178; ☑ 808-572-1314; www.pukalanigolf. com; 360 Pukalani St; greens fees with cart $63, with clubs $81; ⊙ 7am-dusk) With its clubhouse in a mobile home, the Pukalani Golf Club doesn't present a pretty face, but the course is in excellent condition and one of the best deals on the island. Come after 2:30pm and golf the rest of the day for just $35 – cart included. Small clubhouse cafe on site.

🧭 Tours

⭐ **Hawaii Sea Spirits Organic Farm & Distillery** DISTILLERY
(Map p178; ☑ 808-877-0009; www.hawaii seaspirits.com; 4051 Oma'opio Rd; adult/child & youth under 21yr $10/free; ⊙ tours 9:30am-4pm) From the sugarcane stalks to the bottling room to the end-of-tour tasting,

the 45-minute guided tour at this family-run vodka and rum distillery tells an interesting story about the organic ethos of the company. Ocean Vodka, the flagship vodka, is made with deep-ocean mineral water sourced off the coast of Hawai'i (Big Island). Tastings are outdoors beside the sugarcane.

Surfing Goat Dairy   FOOD & DRINK
(Map p178; ☑ 808-878-2870; www.surfinggoat-dairy.com; 3651 Oma'opio Rd; ⊙ store 9am-5pm Mon-Sat, to 2pm Sun; ⊕) 'Da' fetta mo betta' is the motto at at this 42-acre farm, the source of all that luscious chèvre adorning the menus of Maui's top restaurants. There's a well-stocked store and various child-friendly 'ag tours' are offered. Free samples of cheese are provided to all visitors. Feel free to bring wine, order some cheese and enjoy the view at the outdoor seating area.

🍴 Eating

⭐ Upcountry Farmers Market   MARKET $
(Map p178; www.upcountryfarmersmarket.com; 55 Kiopaa St; ⊙ 7-11am Sat) It's a rainbow of color at this happening farmers market: yellow apple-bananas; orange carrots; green broccoli; red strawberries. Plus starfruit, avocados, honey – if it's edible and it grows on Maui, it's here. Several dozen local farmers – and a food truck or two – share fruit, vegetables and locally prepared fare in the parking lot just beyond Longs Drugs at the Kulamalu Shopping Center.

This place is rockin' by 8:30am – get here early for the best selection. Lots of free samples too.

Farmacy Health Bar & Grill – Pukalani   HEALTH FOOD $
(Map p178; ☑ 808-868-0443; www.facebook.com/Farmacyhealthbarpukalani; 55 Pukalani St; salads & sandiwiches $10-11, acai bowls $6-15; ⊙ 8am-5:30pm) 🌱 Craving a healthy lunch? Pop into Farmacy for a juice, smoothie or acai bowl – all fruit-loaded and fresh. A spin-off of the Farmacy in Wailuku, this place blends health and great taste with a bit of artistic flair. Plenty of good veggie-filled sandwiches too. Order at the counter and then grab a seat on the sidewalk patio.

Pukalani Superette   SUPERMARKET $
(Map p178; ☑ 808-572-7616; www.pukalanisuperette.com; 15 Makawao Ave; prepared meals $3-10; ⊙ 5:30am-9pm Mon-Fri, 6:30am-9pm Sat, 7am-8pm Sun) A popular choice for prepared hot meals – *kalua* pork, chili chicken, Spam musubi etc.

Foodland   SUPERMARKET $
(Map p178; www.foodland.com; 55 Pukalani St, cnr Old Haleakalā Hwy & Pukalani St; ⊙ 24hr) Located in the Pukalani Terrace Center, just off the highway, this always-open supermarket is a convenient pit stop for people heading up and down the mountain.

ℹ️ Information

Bank of Hawaii (☑ 808-572-7242; www.boh.com; 55 Pukalani St, cnr Old Haleakalā Hwy, Pukalani Terrace Center; ⊙ 8:30am-4pm Mon-Thu, to 6pm Fri) The last bank and ATM before reaching Kula and Haleakalā National Park.

Kula

It's cooler in Kula – refreshingly so. Think of this Upcountry heartland as one big garden, and you won't be far off. So bountiful is Kula's volcanic soil, it produces most of the onions, lettuce and strawberries grown in Hawaii and almost all of the commercially grown protea. The latest addition, sweet-scented lavender, is finding its niche, too. The magic is in the elevation. At 3000ft, Kula's cool nights and sunny days are ideal for growing all sorts of crops – making Kula synonymous with fresh veggies on any Maui menu.

⊙ Sights

⭐ Worcester Glassworks   GALLERY
(Map p178; ☑ 808-878-4000; www.worcesterglassworks.com; 4626 Lower Kula Rd; ⊙ 10am-5pm Mon-Sat) This family-run working studio and gallery produces some amazing pieces, particularly the sand-blasted glass in natural forms (eg seashells). Visitors are welcome to watch the artists and their solar-powered furnaces at work. The adjacent store offers gorgeous pieces for sale. Call ahead to confirm it's open. Look for the small sign at the house just south of Kula Bistro. It's very welcoming.

Ali'i Kula Lavender   GARDENS
(Map p178; ☑ 808-878-3004; www.aklmaui.com; 1100 Waipoli Rd; $3; ⊙ 9am-4pm) Perched on a broad hillside with panoramic views of the West Maui Mountains and the central Maui coast, this charming lavender farm is a scenic place to relax. Distractions include fragrant pathways, a gift shop with lavender

products, and a lanai with sweeping views where you can enjoy a scone and a cup of lavender tea.

Kula Botanical Garden GARDENS
(Map p178; ☑808-878-1715; www.kulabotanicalgarden.com; 638 Kekaulike Ave; adult/child 6-10yr $10/3; ☺9am-4pm) 🍃 Walking paths wind through themed plantings, including native Hawaiian specimens and a 'taboo garden' of poisonous plants. Because a stream runs through it, the garden supports water-thirsty plants that you won't find in other Kula gardens. After a rain the whole place is an explosion of color.

Holy Ghost Church CHURCH
(Map p178; ☑808-878-1261; www.kulacatholiccommunity.org; 4300 Lower Kula Rd; ☺8am-6pm) Waiakoa's hillside landmark, the octagonal Holy Ghost Church, was built in 1895 by Portuguese immigrants. The church features a beautifully ornate interior that looks like it came right out of the Old World, as indeed much of it did. The gilded altar was carved by renowned Austrian woodcarver Ferdinand Stuflesser and shipped in pieces around the Cape of Good Hope.

🏃 Activities

Proflyght Paragliding PARAGLIDING
(Map p178; ☑808-874-5433; www.paraglidemaui.com; Waipoli Rd; paraglide 1000ft $115, 3000ft $225; ☺office 7am-7pm, flights 2hr after sunrise) Strap into a tandem paraglider with a certified instructor and take a running leap off the cliffs beneath Polipoli Spring State Recreation Area. The term 'bird's-eye view' will never be the same. Must be at least eight years old and under 230lb.

Want to watch the gliders and their colorful chutes float on the breeze? Drive up Waipoli Rd just beyond Ali'i Kula Lavender in the morning, pull over and look up. Gorgeous!

Skyline Eco-Adventures ADVENTURE SPORTS
(Map p178; ☑808-878-8400; www.zipline.com; 18303 Haleakalā Hwy; zipline tour adult/child under 18yr $120/60; ☺8:30am-2pm) Maui's first zipline has a prime location on the slopes of Haleakalā. The five lines are relatively short (100ft to 850ft) compared with the competition, although a unique 'pendulum zip' adds some spice. Good for newbies. Feeling *really* adventurous? Try its new Haleakalā Hike & Bike tour ($250). It includes a summit sunrise, biking down the volcano then ziplining. Up at 2am!

👉 Tours

O'o Farm FOOD & DRINK
(Map p178; ☑808-667-4341; www.oofarm.com; 651 Waipoli Rd; tours $58; ☺farm tour 10:30am-2pm Mon-Fri, coffee tour 8:30-10:30am Wed & Thu) Whether a gardener or a gourmet, you're going to love a tour of this Upcountry farm, which supplies Pacifico restaurant and the Feast at Lele. Where else can you help harvest your meal, give the goodies to a gourmet chef and feast on the bounty? On the new 'Seed to Cup' Coffee Tours you'll learn about coffee cultivation.

✨ Festivals & Events

Holy Ghost Feast CULTURAL
(www.kulacatholiccommunity.org; ☺May; 👪) This festival celebrates Kula's Portuguese heritage. Held at the Holy Ghost Church in the spring on Pentecost weekend (50 days after Easter). It's a family event with games, craft vendors, a farmers market and a free Hawaiian-Portuguese lunch on Sunday.

🍴 Eating

La Provence CAFE $
(Map p178; ☑808-878-1313; www.laprovencekula.com; 3158 Lower Kula Rd, Waiakoa; pastries $3-6, lunch $11-14, crepes $4-13; ☺7am-2pm Wed-Sun) One of Kula's best-kept secrets, this little courtyard restaurant in the middle of nowhere is the domain of Maui's finest pastry chef. Popular offerings include ham-and-cheese croissants, chocolate-filled pastries, and filled crepes. Weekends offer a brunch menu that draws patrons from far and wide. Try the warm goat cheese and Kula greens salad. Hours may fluctuate so call before driving here. Cash and check only.

★ Kula Lodge Restaurant HAWAIIAN $$$
(Map p178; ☑808-878-1535; www.kulalodge.com; 15200 Haleakalā Hwy; breakfast $12-27, lunch $18-42, dinner $26-42; ☺7am-9pm) Assisted by its staggering view, perhaps the best of any Maui restaurant, Kula Lodge has reinvented itself to great effect. Inside, veteran Chef Marc McDowell has the kitchen humming to a farm-to-table variety menu. Locally sourced salads are delicious. Outside, brick ovens provide build-your-own pizzas served under cabanas (11am to 8pm). A spectacular sunset here is the perfect ending to a day on the summit.

★ Kula Bistro
ITALIAN $$$

(Map p178; ☎ 808-871-2960; www.kulabistro.com; 4566 Lower Kula Rd; breakfast $9-17, lunch & dinner $12-39; ⊙ 7:30am-10:30am Tue-Sun, plus 11am-8pm daily) Is everyone in town here or what? Yup, sure looks like it. And we think we know why. This superb family-owned bistro offers a friendly dining room, sparkling service and delicious home cooking, including fabulous pizza and huge servings of coconut cream pie (enough for two). BYOB wine from Morihara Store across the street. No corkage fee.

🛍 Shopping

Kula Country Farms
FOOD

(Map p178; www.kulacountryfarms.com; Kula Hwy; ⊙ 10am-5pm Tue-Fri, to 4pm Sat & Sun; ⊞) If you're driving past this large produce stand in October with the kids, you will have to pull over for the happenin' Pumpkin Patch. Resistance is futile – and the place does look fun. Otherwise, stop by for fresh fruit, vegetables and flowers from local farms, as well as a good selection of Maui-sourced jams, sauces and honeys, plus farm-themed gifts.

Keokea

Blink-and-you'll-miss it Keokea is the last real town before Hana if you're swinging around the southern part of the island. The sum total of the town center consists of a coffee shop, an art gallery, a gas station and two small stores, the Ching Store and the Fong Store. The last two announce one of Hawaii's many immigrant populations. Drawn by rich soil, Hakka Chinese farmers migrated to this remote corner of Kula at the turn of the 20th century. Their influence is still found throughout the village.

But the village isn't entirely off the world's radar – media powerhouse Oprah Winfrey has a home and property in the area. With small-town friendliness, a low-key vibe and a gorgeous backdrop of green fields and a deep blue sea, this is a pleasant place to hide out for a few hours. Or days.

⊙ Sights & Activities

Sun Yat-sen Park
PARK

(Map p178; ☎ 808-572-8122; www.mauicounty. gov//Facilities; Kula Hwy & Kamaole Rd; ℗) For a time Sun Yat-sen, father of the Chinese nationalist movement, lived in Keokea. He's honored at Sun Yat-sen Park, found along the Kula Hwy (Hwy 37), 1.7 miles beyond

Grandma's Coffee House. The park has picnic tables and is a great place to soak up the broad vistas that stretch clear across to West Maui.

St John's Episcopal Church
CHURCH

(Map p178; ☎ 808-878-1485; www.stjohnsmaui.org; 8992 Kula Hwy; ⊙ services 7:30am & 9:30am Sun) Overlooking a gorgeous view of the coast, this local landmark (c 1907) still bears its name in Chinese characters. Hosts the annual Kula Fest in early fall.

Thompson Road
SCENIC DRIVE

(Map p178; Thompson Rd) Just up from Grandma's Coffee House, this narrow country road swoops briefly through emerald green pastures, flanked by a lava rock wall. Beyond the wall? More green and the deep blue coast. You'll be pulling over for photos, especially if clouds are adding a bit of sparkle to the light. It's magical – so drive slowly and please respect the neighbors.

🍴 Eating

★ Grandma's Coffee House
CAFE $

(Map p178; ☎ 808-878-2140; www.grandmascoffee. com; 9232 Kula Hwy; pastries $4, sandwiches $8-10; ⊙ 7am-5pm, to 8pm Wed-Sat) 🍃 Worthy of a Norman Rockwell painting, this charming island landmark with its creaking screen door and carved wooden tables grows its own coffee and dishes up deli lunches. Take your goodies out on the lanai and eat right under the coffee trees. Coffee is $1.50 – nice!

ℹ Information

Kula Hospital (☎ 808-878-1221; www.maui-memorialmedical.org; 100 Keokea Pl; ⊙ emergency room 24hr, clinic 8am-4:30pm Mon-Fri)

'Ulupalakua

The sprawling 18,000-acre 'Ulupalakua Ranch, which anchors this green landscape, is home to 2300 brood cattle, as well as a small herd of Rocky Mountain elk, which dot the hillside pastures. The ranch is still worked by *paniolo*, Hawaiian cowboys who have been here for generations. Today most people stop by to visit the bustling winery, which sits on 'Ulupalakua Ranch land, about 6 miles beyond Keokea.

Hwy 37 winds south through ranch country, offering good views of Kaho'olawe and the little island of Molokini. With a stop at the winery, the drive to 'Ulupalakua is a nice half-day excursion from Central Maui and Pa'ia. After the vineyard, it's another 25 dusty, bumpy miles to Kipahulu along the remote Pi'ilani Hwy.

Activities

Triple L Ranch HORSEBACK RIDING

(☑ 808-280-7070; www.triplelranchmaui.com; 15900 Pi'ilani Hwy; 90min/2hr $135/160, half-/full day $285/375; ⊙ 9am-6:30pm) Unique on Maui, these personalized trail rides offer the opportunity to explore the volcanic Ka'naio region, from a 90-minute outing around the cattle ranch to half- and full-day excursions to the sea and back. You won't be running into anyone else. Beach rides include a Bully's Burger – straight from the ranch. For ages 12 and over. Reserve 24 hours ahead.

Tours

Maui Wine WINE

(Map p178; ☑ 808-878-6058; www.mauiwine.com; 14815 Pi'ilani Hwy; ⊙ 10am-5:30pm, tours 10:30am & 1:30pm) ⚑ Formerly Tedeschi Vineyards, Maui's sole winery offers free tastings in its historic stone cottage and twice-daily 30-minute tours, also complimentary. It produces a noteworthy variety, from grape wines to novelty wines, using local fruit to great effect. Try the sweet Maui Splash, a light blend of pineapple and passion fruit, then stroll the historic grounds.

The new 75-minute King's Tour ($50 per person, 3:30pm Thursday and 2:30pm Saturday) takes guests across the property, where the last reigning king of Hawaii would visit. This tour includes tastings of estate wine from the vineyard, sampled in the historic Old Jail.

To learn more about the history of the ranch – which was established in the mid-1800s – step into the small exhibit room beside the tasting area.

POLIPOLI SPRING STATE RECREATION AREA

On the upper slopes of Haleakalā, the remote and heavily forested **Polipoli Spring State Recreation Area** (Map p178; ☑ 808-984-8109; http://dlnr.hawaii.gov/dsp/parks/maui; Waipoli Rd; ⊙ 6am-6pm; 🅿) is the place for solitary hiking. Check the park website or call before you make the drive. Trails and facilities are often closed due to weather damage, with downed trees and flash-flood damage often affecting the trails. The park sits at 6200ft so it can get chilly at night.

Festivals & Events

'Ulupalakua Holiday Tree Lighting CULTURAL

(☑ 808-878-6058; www.mauiwine.com; 14815 Pi'ilani Hwy; ⊙ Dec; 🎪) On a Saturday in early December, 'Ulupalakua Ranch sponsors a fun holiday bash on the lawn of Maui Wine. Come by for children's games, live music, an outdoor movie and the lighting of a 25ft-tall decorated Monterey pine. There's wine tasting too. Admission is free, but the winery requests that guests bring a canned good for Maui Food Bank.

Eating

'Ulupalakua Ranch Store DELI $

(Map p178; ☑ 808-878-1202; www.ulupalakuaranch.com; Pi'ilani Hwy; burgers $9-12; ⊙ store 9:30am-5:30pm, grill 10am-5pm) ⚑ Sidle up to the life-size wooden cowboys on the front porch and say howdy. Then pop inside and check out the cowboy hats and souvenir T-shirts. If it's lunchtime, mosey over to the grill and treat yourself to an organic ranch-raised elk burger. The meats on the menu are Maui sourced, and Chef Will Munder strives to do the same with the produce.

Haleakalā National Park

Best Places to Hike

→ Keonehe'ehe'e (Sliding Sands) Trail (p196)

→ Pipiwai Trail (p199)

→ Halemau'u Trail (p197)

→ Hosmer Grove Trail (p199)

→ Kaupo Trail (p197)

Best Viewpoints

→ Pu'u'ula'ula (Red Hill) Overlook (p202)

→ Kalahaku Overlook (p203)

→ Pele's Paint Pot Lookout (p206)

→ Haleakalā Visitor Center (p205)

→ Kuloa Point Trail (p199)

Why Go?

To fully experience Maui – or at least peer into its soul – make your way to the summit of Haleakalā. Like a yawning mouth, the huge crater opens beneath you, in all its raw volcanic glory, caressed by mist and, in the experience of a lifetime, bathed in the early light of sunrise. Lookouts on the crater's rim provide breathtaking views of the moonscape below, and the many cinder cones marching across it.

The rest of this amazing park, which is divided into two distinct sections, is all about interacting with this mountain of solid lava, and the rare lifeforms that live upon it, some of them found only here. You can hike down into the crater, follow lush trails on the slopes, or put your mountain bike through its paces. For the ultimate adventure, get a permit, bring a tent and camp beneath the stars. However you do it, the experience will stick with you.

When to Go

Temperatures at the summit can be extreme, and they may fluctuate rapidly. Year-round temperatures range from below freezing to 50°F to 60°F. Expect temperatures to drop 3°F for every 1000ft rise in elevation. Crowds clear quickly after sunrise so, if you want to avoid congestion, plan to visit an hour or two after the sun comes up.

The Kipahulu area is warmer and wetter. Expect daytime temperatures averaging 70°F to 80°F year-round. At night, the temperature average is 65°F to 75°F.

Park visitation numbers remains fairly consistent year-round, but winter and summer are considered the busiest seasons.

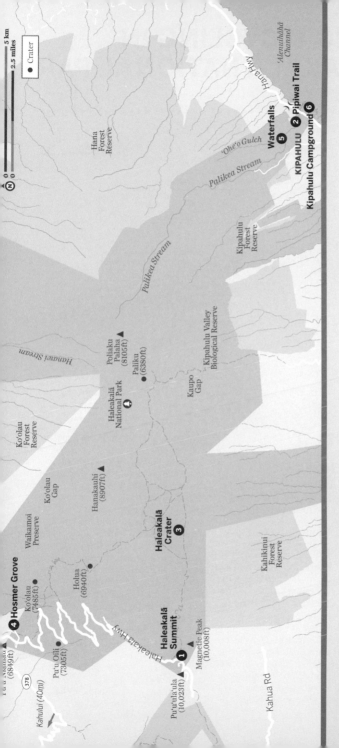

Haleakalā National Park Highlights

❶ Haleakalā Summit (p202) Watching the day break above the clouds, or peering at the cosmos after sunset.

❷ Pipiwai Trail (p199)

Checking out gorgeous waterfalls and a magical bamboo forest.

❸ Haleakalā Crater (p196) Hiking past cinder cones and other natural wonders on

the Keonehe'ehe'e (Sliding Sands) Trail.

❹ Hosmer Grove (p203) Scanning for native birds while ogling the towering – but non-native – trees.

❺ Waterfalls (p199) Taking a photo of the cascading 'Ohe'o Gulch pools from the Kuloa Point Trail.

❻ Cabins & Campgrounds (p207) Spending the night in the depths of the crater or steps from the pounding sea.

HIKING & CYCLING IN HALEAKALĀ NATIONAL PARK

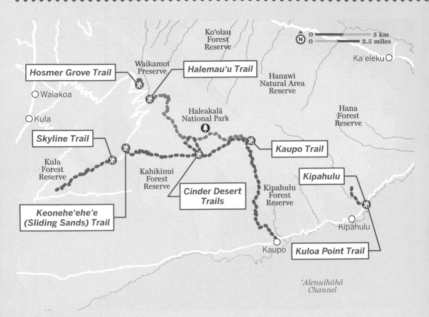

SUMMIT AREA

KEONEHEʻEHEʻE (SLIDING SANDS) TRAIL

START/END HALEAKALĀ VISITOR CENTER
LENGTH 18.4 MILES ROUND-TRIP; TWO DAYS
DIFFICULTY STRENUOUS

The **path** (www.nps.gov/hale) descends into an unearthly world of stark lava sights and ever-changing clouds. The trailhead is at the entrance to the **visitor center** (p205) parking lot, beside Pa Kaʻoao (White Hill). This hike is best done in two days, so secure a Paliku camping or cabin permit in advance.

The first thing you'll notice? The silence. The only sound is the crunching of volcanic cinders beneath your feet. If you're pressed for time, just descending 20 minutes will reward you with an into-the-crater experience and fabulous photo opportunities. The

climb out, unfortunately, takes nearly twice as long.

The first 6 miles follow the southern wall, with great views. Vegetation is minimal, but you may see green kūpaoa plants and shimmering silverswords. At the first major **overlook**, after the long straightaway, you can see cinder cones dotting the bottom of the crater. The views only improve from here. Switchbacks drop from the overlook. A spur trail to Ka Luʻu o ka Ōʻō cinder cone, which arises to your left about 2 miles down, has been closed. Enjoy the **view** from where you are. Next up? A field of silverswords. After that a narrow path squeezes through a tall lava formation, framing the peaks ahead.

Four miles down, after an elevation drop of 2500ft, Keoneheʻeheʻe Trail intersects with a **spur** that leads north into the cinder desert, where it connects with the Halemauʻu Trail after 1.5 miles.

Continuing on Keoneheʻeheʻe, head across the crater for 2 miles to Kapalaoa. Verdant ridges rise on your right, giving

From cinder cones to silverswords, the sights are otherworldly when hiking inside Haleakalā crater. Waterfalls and a bamboo forest keep views wild on the coast. And biking? Hold on tight!

way to ropy *pahoehoe* (smooth-flowing lava). Kapalaoa is reached after roughly four hours. From here to **Paliku** (☎808-572-4459, cabin reservation 877-444-6777; www.nps.gove/hale; camp-site free; cabin for 1-12 people $75), the descent is gentle and the vegetation gradually increases. Paliku (6380ft) is beneath a sheer cliff at the eastern end of the crater. In contrast to the crater's barren western end, this area receives heavy rainfall, with ohia forests climbing the slopes.

After an overnight in Paliku cabin or the adjacent campground, retrace your steps to the visitor center.

HALEMAU'U TRAIL
START/END 3.5 MILES ABOVE PARK HEADQUARTERS VISITOR CENTER
DISTANCE 7.4 MILE ROUND-TRIP
DIFFICULTY MODERATE

With views of crater walls, lava tubes and cinder cones, the Halemau'u Trail down to the Holua campground and back – 7.4 miles round-trip – can be a memorable day hike. Just be sure to start early before the afternoon clouds roll in and visibility vanishes. The first mile is fairly level and offers a fine view of the crater with Ko'olau Gap to the east.

The trail then descends 1400ft along 2 miles of switchbacks to the crater floor and on to **Holua campground** (6940ft). You'll see impressive views of the crater walls rising a few thousand feet to the west. Several lava tubes are visible from the trail, but since endangered species use them for shelter, the Park Service has made them off-limits.

If you have the energy, push on another mile to reach some colorful cinder cones, being sure to make a short detour onto the **Silversword Loop**, where you'll see these unique plants in various stages of growth. In summer, their tall stalks should be ablaze with hundreds of maroon and yellow blossoms. But be careful – half of all *'ahinahina* (silversword plant) today are trampled to death as seedlings, mostly by careless hikers who wander off trails and inadvertently

crush the plants' shallow, laterally growing roots. The trail continues another 6.3 miles to the **Paliku cabin**.

The trailhead to Halemau'u is 3.5 miles above the Park Headquarters Visitor Center and about 6 miles below the Haleakalā Visitor Center. There's a fair chance you'll see nene (native geese) in the parking lot.

CINDER DESERT TRAILS
START/END HALEAKALĀ CRATER
DISTANCE VARIES
DIFFICULTY MODERATE

Two spur trails connect Keonehe'ehe'e (Sliding Sands) Trail, near Kapalaoa cabin, with the Halemau'u Trail between Paliku and Holua cabins. If you're camping you may have time to do them both, as the trails are not very long. The spur trail furthest west takes in many of the crater's most kaleidoscopic cones, and the viewing angle changes with every step.

If you prefer stark, black and barren, the other spur trail takes you through *'a'a* (rough, jagged lava) and pahoehoe (smooth-flowing lava) fields.

Both trails end up on the northern side of the cinder desert near Kawilinau, also known as the **Bottomless Pit**. There's not much to see, as you can't really get a good look down the narrow shaft. The real prize is the nearby short loop trail, where you can sit for a while in the saddle of Pele's Paint Pot Lookout (p206), the crater's most brilliant vantage point.

KAUPO TRAIL
START HALEAKALĀ CRATER
END KAUPO
DISTANCE 8.6 MILES
DIFFICULTY VERY STRENUOUS

The most extreme of Haleakalā's hikes is the Kaupo Trail, which starts at the Paliku campground and descends to Kaupo on the southern coast. Be prepared for ankle-twisting conditions, blistered feet, intense tropical sun, torrential showers and a possibly hard-to-follow path. Your knees will take a pounding as you descend more than 6100ft over 8.6 miles.

The first 3.7 miles of the trail drop 2500ft in elevation before reaching the park boundary. It's a steep rocky path through rough lava and brushland, with short switchbacks alternating with level stretches. From here you'll be rewarded with spectacular **ocean views**.

The last 4.9 miles pass through Kaupo Ranch property on a rough 4WD trail as it descends to the bottom of **Kaupo Gap**, exiting into a forest where feral pigs snuffle about. Here trail markings become vague, but once you reach the dirt road, it's another 1.5 miles to the end at the eastern side of the Kaupo Store.

The 'village' of **Kaupo** is a long way from anywhere, with light traffic. Still, you'll probably manage a lift. If you have to walk the final stretch, it's 8 miles to the **'Ohe'o Gulch campground**.

Because this is such a strenuous and remote trail, it's not advisable to hike it alone. No camping is allowed on Kaupo Ranch property, so most hikers spend the night at the Paliku campground and then get an early start.

SKYLINE TRAIL
START SCIENCE CITY
END POLIPOLI SPRING STATE RECREATION AREA
DISTANCE 8.5 MILES, FOUR HOURS
DIFFICULTY MODERATE

This cinematic trail, which rides the precipitous spine of Haleakalā, begins just beyond the summit at a lofty elevation (9750ft) and leads down to the campground at Polipoli Spring State Recreation Area (6200ft). Get an early start to enjoy the views before clouds take over.

To get to the trailhead, go past Pu'u'ula'ula (Red Hill) Overlook and take the road to the left just before Science City. The road, which passes over a cattle grate, is signposted not for public use, but continue and you'll soon find a Na Ala Hele sign marking the trailhead.

The Skyline Trail starts in barren open terrain of volcanic cinder, a moon walk that passes more than a dozen cinder cones and craters. The first mile is rough lava rock. After three crunchy miles, it reaches the tree line (8500ft) and enters native mamane forest. In winter mamane is heavy with flowers that look like yellow sweet-pea blossoms. There's solitude on this walk.

JEREMY WOODHOUSE/HOLLY WILMETH/GETTY IMAGES ©

Kipahulu Bamboo Forest

If the clouds treat you kindly, you'll have broad views all the way between the barren summit and the dense cloud forest. Eventually the trail meets the Polipoli access road, where you can either walk to the paved road in about 4 miles, or continue via the Haleakalā Ridge Trail and Polipoli Trail to the campground.

If you prefer treads to hiking boots, the Skyline Trail is also an exhilarating adventure on a mountain bike. Just look out for hikers!

HOSMER GROVE TRAIL
START/END: HOSMER GROVE CAMPGROUND
DISTANCE: 0.5 MILES
DIFFICULTY: EASY

Anyone who is looking for a little greenery after hiking the crater will enjoy this shaded woodland walk, as will birders. The half-mile loop trail starts at Hosmer Grove campground, 0.75 miles south of the Park Headquarters Visitor Center, in a forest of lofty trees.

The exotics here were introduced in 1910 in an effort to develop a lumber industry in Hawaii. Species include fragrant incense cedar, Norway spruce, Douglas fir, eucalyptus and various pines. Although the trees adapted well enough to grow, they didn't grow fast enough at these elevations to make tree harvesting practical.

After the forest, the trail moves into native shrubland, with *'akala* (Hawaiian raspberry), mamane, *pilo, kilau* ferns and sandalwood. The *'ohelo*, a berry sacred to the volcano goddess Pele, and the *pukiawe*, which has red and white berries and evergreen leaves, are favored by nene.

Listen for the calls of the native *'i'iwi* and *'apapane*; both are fairly common here. The *'i'iwi* has a very loud squeaking call, orange legs and a curved salmon-colored bill. The *'apapane*, a fast-moving bird with a black bill, black legs and a white undertail, feeds on the nectar of bright red ohia flowers, and its wings make a distinctive whirring sound.

KIPAHULU AREA

PIPIWAI TRAIL
START/END NEAR VISITOR CENTER
DISTANCE 4 MILES ROUND-TRIP; TWO HOURS
DIFFICULTY MODERATE

Ready for an adventure? This fun **trail** (www.nps.gov/hale; Kipahulu Area, Haleakalā National Park) ascends alongside the 'Ohe'o streambed, rewarding hikers with picture-perfect views of waterfalls and an otherworldly trip through a bamboo grove. The trail starts on the *mauka* (inland) side of the visitor center and leads up to Makahiku Falls (0.5 miles) and Waimoku Falls (2 miles). To see both falls, allow about two hours return. Can be muddy!

Along the path, you'll pass large mango trees and patches of guava before coming to an overlook after about 10 minutes. **Makahiku Falls**, a long bridal-veil waterfall that drops into a deep gorge, is just off to the right. Thick green ferns cover the sides of 200ft basalt cliffs where the water cascades – a very rewarding scene for such a short walk.

Continuing along the main trail, you'll walk beneath old banyan trees, cross Palikea Stream (killer mosquitoes thrive here) and enter the wonderland of the **Bamboo Forest**, where thick groves of bamboo bang together musically in the wind. The upper section is muddy, but boardwalks cover some of the worst bits. Beyond the bamboo forest is **Waimoku Falls**, a thin, lacy 400ft waterfall dropping down a sheer rock face. When you come out of the first grove, you'll see the waterfall in the distance. Forget swimming under Waimoku Falls – its pool is shallow and there's a danger of falling rocks.

Wear your grippy water shoes for this one.

KULOA POINT TRAIL
START/END: NEAR VISITOR CENTER
DISTANCE/DURATION: 0.5 MILES; 20 MINUTES
DIFFICULTY: EASY

Even if you're tight on time, take this 20-minute stroll! The **Kuloa Point Trail** (www.nps.gov/hale; Kipahulu Area, Haleakalā National Park), a half-mile loop, runs from the visitor center down to the lower pools and back. A few minutes down, you'll reach a broad grassy knoll with a gorgeous **view** of the Hana coast. On a clear day you can see Hawai'i, the Big Island, 30 miles away across 'Alenuihaha Channel.

The large freshwater **pools** along the trail are terraced one atop the other and connected by gentle cascades. They may look calm, but flash floods have taken several lives here, so the Park Service does not recommend swimming in them.

MICHELE FALZONE/GETTY IMAGES ©

MONICA AND MICHAEL SWEET/GETTY IMAGES ©

FLEETHAM DAVE/GETTY IMAGES ©

3

1. Pipiwai Trail (p199)
This moderate trail rewards hikers with picture-perfect waterfalls and an otherworldly bamboo grove.

2. Haleakalā National Park Summit Area (p202)
Seeing Haleakalā's crater open beneath you in all its raw glory is an experience of a lifetime.

3. 'Ahinahina (Silversword; p202)
The silversword has been brought back from the brink of extinction, but still faces environmental threats.

4. Pele's Paint Pot (p206)
The lookout at Pele's Paint Pot is the crater's most brilliant vantage point.

❶ Information

Haleakalā National Park (☎ 808-572-4400; www.nps.gov/hale; Summit District: Haleakalā Hwy, Kipahulu District: Hana Hwy; 3-day pass car $20, motorcycle $15, individual on foot or bicycle $10; [P] [🚻]) has two very different sections, the ethereal Summit Area and the coastal Kipahulu Area. There is no direct road connection between them. Thus travelers typically visit the summit on one day, and the Kipahulu Area on another (usually heading to or from Hana). One entrance ticket is good for both areas.

If you plan to watch the sunrise, remember to make a reservation at www.recreation.gov within 60 days of your visit, which covers your vehicle, or sign up for a commercial tour. You cannot enter the park between 3am and 7am without the reservation receipt and photo ID of the reservation-holder.

Summit Area

History

Ancient Hawaiians did not inhabit the summit, but they came up the mountain and built heiau (temples) at some of the cinder cones. The primary goddess of Haleakalā, Lilinoe (also known as the mist goddess), was worshipped here. Today, Native Hawaiians still connect spiritually on the summit, and also come to study star navigation.

In 1916 Haleakalā became part of Hawai'i National Park, along with its Big Island siblings, Mauna Loa and Kilauea. In 1961 Haleakalā National Park became an independent entity; in 1969 its boundaries were expanded down into the Kipahulu Valley. And in 1980 the park was designated an International Biosphere Reserve by Unesco.

There are currently 51 federally listed (endangered and threatened) species in the park, the largest number in any US national park. This includes 40 plant species, six birds, one bat, one monk seal, one sea turtle and two damselfly species.

◉ Sights

The summit is an unabashed showstopper. Often referred to as the world's largest dormant volcano, the floor of Haleakalā is a colossal 7.5 miles wide, 2.5 miles long and 3000ft deep – nearly as large as Manhattan. In its prime, Haleakalā reached a height of 12,000ft before water erosion carved out two large river valleys that eventually merged to form Haleakalā crater. Technically, as geologists like to point out, it's not a true 'crater,' but to sightseers that's all nitpicking. Valley or crater, it's a phenomenal sight like no other in the US national park system.

★ **Pu'u'ula'ula (Red Hill) Overlook**   VIEWPOINT
(www.nps.gov/hale; Haleakalā Hwy; [P]) You may find yourself standing above the clouds while exploring Pu'u'ula'ula (10,023ft), Maui's highest point. The **summit building** provides a top-of-the-world panorama from its wraparound windows. On a clear day you can see Hawai'i (Big Island), Lana'i, Moloka'i and even O'ahu. When the light's right, the

---

SILVERSWORD COMEBACK

Goats ate them by the thousands. Souvenir collectors pulled them up by their roots. They were even used to decorate parade floats. It's a miracle any of Haleakalā's famed *'ahinahina* (silverswords) are left at all.

It took a concerted effort to bring them back from the brink of extinction, but Haleakalā visitors can once again see this luminous relative of the sunflower in numerous places around the park, including Kalahaku and Pu'u'ula'ula (Red Hill) Overlooks and Silversword Loop (p197).

The *'ahinahina* takes its name from its elegant silver spiked leaves, which glow with dew collected from the clouds. The plant lives for up to 50 years before blooming for its first and last time. In its final year it shoots up a flowering stalk that can reach as high as 9ft. During summer the stalk flowers gloriously with hundreds of maroon and yellow blossoms. When the flowers go to seed in late fall, the plant makes its last gasp and dies.

Today the *'ahinahina* faces new threats, including climate change and loss of its pollinators, ants. But at least its fragile natural environment has been protected. After years of effort, the National Park Service has finished fencing the entire park with a 32-mile-long fence to keep out feral goats and pigs. You can do your part by not walking on cinders close to the plant; this damages the shallow roots that radiate out several feet just inches below the surface.

RESPONSIBLE HIKING

To protect Haleakalā's fragile environment, keep to established trails and don't be tempted off them, even for well-trodden shortcuts through switchbacks. And for your own sake, come prepared. Remember the climate changes radically as you cross the crater floor. In the 4 miles between Kapalaoa and Paliku cabins, rainfall varies from an annual average of 12in to 300in! Take warm clothing in layers, sunscreen, rain gear, a first-aid kit and lots of water. Hikers without proper clothing risk hypothermia.

Here are recommended day hikes, depending on how much time you have available:

Ten hours If you're planning a full-day outing, and you're in good physical shape, the 11.2-mile hike that starts down Keonehe'ehe'e (Sliding Sands) Trail (p196) and returns via Halemau'u Trail (p197) is the prize. It crosses the crater floor, taking in both a cinder desert and a cloud forest, showcasing the park's amazing diversity. Get an early start. As for getting back to your starting point, hitchhiking is allowed in the park and there's a designated place to hitch on Haleakalā Hwy opposite the Halemau'u trailhead.

Three hours For a half-day experience that offers a hearty serving of crater sights, follow Keonehe'ehe'e (Sliding Sands) Trail down to where it goes between two towering rock formations, before dropping steeply again. It takes one hour to get down. However, the way back is a 1500ft elevation rise, making the return a strenuous two-hour climb.

One hour Take to the forest on the Hosmer Grove Trail (p199) and see the green side of Haleakalā National Park.

---

colors of the crater are nothing short of spectacular, with grays, greens, reds and browns.

An 'ahinahina garden has been planted at the overlook, making this the best place to see these luminous silver-leafed plants in various stages of growth.

Hosmer Grove   FOREST
(www.nps.gove/hale; off Haleakalā Hwy; P) A pleasant half-mile loop trail winds through Hosmer Grove, which is home to non-native tree species – including pine, fir and eucalyptus – as well as native scrubland. The site is also popular with campers and picnickers. The whole area is sweetened with the scent of eucalyptus and alive with the red flashes and calls of native birds. Hosmer Grove sits on a side road just after the park's entrance booth.

Drive slowly on the road in, as this is one of the top places to spot nene, a rare goose that is also the state bird.

Leleiwi Overlook   VIEWPOINT
(www.nps.gov/hale; Haleakalā Hwy) For your first look into the crater, stop at Leleiwi Overlook (8840ft), midway between the Park Headquarters Visitor Center and the summit. The overlook also provides a unique angle on the ever-changing clouds floating in and out. You can literally watch the weather form at your feet. From the parking lot, it's a five-minute walk across a gravel trail to the overlook.

En route you'll get a fine view of the West Maui Mountains and the flat isthmus connecting the two sides of Maui.

Kalahaku Overlook   VIEWPOINT
(www.nps.gov/hale; Haleakalā Hwy; P) Don't miss this one. Kalahaku Overlook (9324ft), 0.8 miles beyond Leleiwi Overlook, offers a bird's-eye view of the crater floor and the ant-size hikers on the trails snaking around the cinder cones below. At the observation deck, plaques provide information on each of the volcanic formations that punctuate the crater floor. From the deck you'll also get a perfect angle for viewing both the Ko'olau Gap and the Kaupo Gap on the rim of Haleakalā.

Between May and October the 'ua'u (Hawaiian dark-rumped petrel) nests in burrows in the cliff face at the left side of the observation deck. Even if you don't spot the birds, you can often hear the parents and chicks making their unique clucking sounds. Of about 20,000 'ua'u remaining today, most nest right here at Haleakalā, where they lay just one egg a year. These seabirds were thought to be extinct until sighted in the crater during the 1970s.

A short trail below the parking lot leads to a field of native 'ahinahina (silversword), ranging from seedlings to mature plants.

This overlook is only accessible on the way down the mountain.

Haleakalā Summit Area

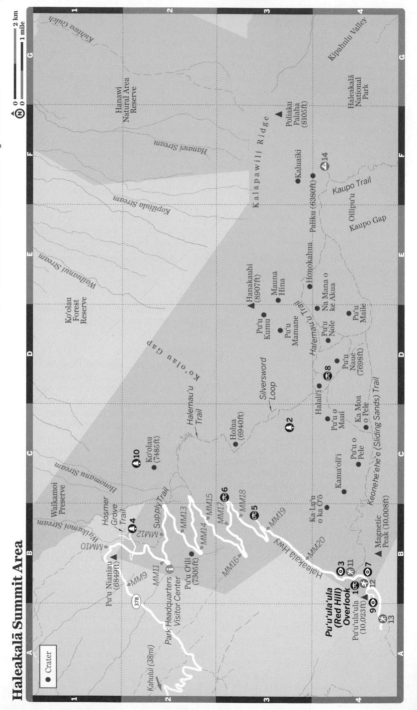

Haleakalā Summit Area

Haleakalā Visitor Center
CULTURAL CENTER, VIEWPOINT

(www.nps.gov/hale; Haleakalā Hwy; ☉ sunrise-3pm; P) Perched on the rim of the crater at 9745ft, this visitor center is the park's main viewing spot. And what a magical sight awaits. The ever-changing interplay of sun, shadow and clouds reflecting on the crater floor creates a mesmerizing dance of light and color. The center has displays on Haleakalā's volcanic origins and details on what you're seeing on the crater floor 3000ft below.

Nature talks are given, books on Hawaiian culture and the environment are for sale, and there are drinking fountains and restrooms here. Hikers, note that it may be easier to fill a thermos at the water filling station at the Park Headquarters Visitor Center.

By dawn the parking lot fills with people coming to see the sunrise show, and it pretty much stays packed all day. Leave the crowds behind by taking the 10-minute hike up **Pa Ka'oao (White Hill)**, which begins at the eastern side of the visitor center and provides stunning crater views.

Waikamoi Preserve
NATURE RESERVE

(☏ 808-572-7849; www.nature.org; ☉ hiking tour 2nd Sat of the month) This windswept native cloud forest supports one of the rarest ecosystems on earth. Managed by the Nature Conservancy, the 8951-acre preserve provides the last stronghold for hundreds of species of native plants and forest birds. Open only by guided tour, the preserve is a place to look for the *'i'iwi* and the *'apapane* (both honeycreepers with bright red feathers).

The yellow-green *'amakihi* flies among the preserve's koa and ohia trees.

A four- to five-hour hiking tour currently runs the second Saturday of the month starting at 8am. To make reservations and confirm the meet-up location (currently in Pukalani), phone the number above, or email (hike_waikamoi@tnc.org), the Nature Conservancy. The hike is moderately strenuous. Bring rain gear. Due to concerns about the spread of Rapid Ohia Death, no one who has visited the Big Island within six months of the tour date may access the preserve.

Science City
LANDMARK

(Haleakalā Observatories; www.ifa.hawaii.edu) As the sun rises, this collection of domed observatories shimmers just beyond the summit. Nicknamed Science City and managed by the University of Hawai'i, this area is unfortunately off-limits to visitors, as it houses some very interesting equipment – much of it studying the sun and outer space.

Pan-STARRS surveys the heavens for earth-approaching objects, both asteroids and comets, that might pose a danger to our planet. It is the most powerful survey system in the world in terms of combined field of view, resolution and sensitivity. The Air Force's Ground-Based Electro-Optical Deep Space Surveillance system performs a similar function. It is capable of identifying a basketball-size object 22,000 miles away. After years of delay, the Daniel K Inouye Solar Telescope is now under construction. When complete it will be the world's most powerful solar telescope. Operations are expected to begin in 2019.

The Institute for Astronomy at the University of Hawai'i holds free monthly public talks at its office in Pukalani. For more information see www.ifa.hawaii. edu/haleakalanew. The website contains fascinating videos of past lectures.

Magnetic Peak
MOUNTAIN

(www.nps.gov/hale) The iron-rich cinders in this flat-top hill, which lies immediately southeast of the summit building (the direction of Hawai'i, the Big Island), pack enough magnetism to play havoc with your compass. Modest as it looks, it's also – at 10,008ft – the second-highest point on Maui.

Pele's Paint Pot Lookout   VIEWPOINT
(www.nps.gov/hale) Along the loop trail south of Kawlinau, this is the crater's most brilliant vantage point.

Activities

Cycling

Cycling downhill from the summit to the sea, via Makawao and Pa'ia, is a popular pursuit. Several companies lead tours to the summit but, due to past problems, they cannot begin the cycling part of the tour within the park. Cycling must begin outside park boundaries. If you want to explore the summit, tour vans will typically shuttle you to the top for a short visit then drive you down to a permissible starting point. From here, you will either pedal at your own pace or ride with a guide-led group, depending on the tour company. Many people combine a sunrise trip with a downhill ride, requiring a very early start.

Individual cyclists who are not part of a commercial tour are allowed to pedal from the summit without restriction. If you choose this option, you would need to arrange a bike rental and transportation on your own. This is a cheaper option. Bike racks are typically provided with the rental for free or for a small fee. For rental equipment see Crater Cycles (p133) in Kahului, or Maui Cyclery (p180) in Pa'ia.

Mountain Biking

The Skyline Trail (p198) is a wild ride from Science City Access Rd down to Polipoli Spring State Recreation Area. The trail may occasionally close due to weather damage. Check its status at www.hawaiitrails.org or one of the local bike shops.

Ranger Talks

Stop at the Park Headquarters Visitor Center to see what's happening. Free **ranger talks** on Haleakalā's unique natural history and Hawaiian culture are given at the Haleakalā Visitor Center and the Pu'u'u-

la'ula (Red Hill) Overlook; the schedule varies, but there are usually one or two each day.

Stargazing

On clear nights, stargazing is phenomenal on the mountain. You can see celestial objects up to the seventh magnitude, free of light interference, making Haleakalā one of the best places on the planet for a sky view.

The park no longer offers star talks. These are now run by concessionaires. You can also pick up a free star map at the Park Headquarters Visitor Center and have your own cosmic experience.

Maui Stargazing   OUTDOORS
(✆808-298-8254; www.mauistargazing.com; 60-90min tour adult/child under 16yr $104/89; ☉office 8am-4pm) Watch the sun drop below the horizon from the summit then scan the skies to study the cosmos. Look for deep-sky objects through a 12in Dobsian telescope – the largest portable telescope out there. Tours meet at Kula Lodge (p174).

Volunteering

Volunteers on Vacation   VOLUNTEERING
(✆808-249-8811; www.volunteersonvacation.org; Haleakalā National Park) The Pacific Whale Foundation runs drop-in volunteer projects in the park, which occur on the first and third Sundays of the month. Volunteers work on projects that help protect the park's fragile ecosystem, such as removing invasive plants. There is no charge to participate, transportation is free, and admission to the park is included.

Friends of Haleakalā National Park   VOLUNTEERING
(✆808-876-1673; www.fhnp.org; Haleakalā National Park) This multiday volunteer opportunity is sponsored by Friends of Haleakalā National Park. This totally volunteer-led operation involves up to a dozen visitors, who hike into the wild and stay for two nights in cabins owned by the National Park Service. Volunteers perform one of a number of tasks ranging from cabin maintenance to plant removal to nene habitat improvement.

See the website for trip leader email addresses and phone numbers.

Camping & Cabins in the Crater

For one of the most unique overnight experiences in Hawaii, if not the entire US, consider camping in the crater or spending the night in one of its three rustic cabins. To spend the night at Haleakalā is to commune with nature.

🛏 Camping

All of the backcountry camping options are primitive. None have electricity or showers. You will find pit toilets and limited nonpotable water supplies that are shared with the crater cabins. Water needs to be filtered or chemically treated before drinking; conserve it, as water tanks occasionally run dry. Fires are allowed only in grills and are prohibited entirely in times of drought. You must carry in all your food and supplies, and carry out all your trash. Also be aware that during periods of drought you'll be required to carry in your own water.

THE SUNRISE EXPERIENCE

Haleakalā' means 'House of the Sun.' So it's no surprise that, since the time of the first Hawaiians, people have been making pilgrimages up to Haleakalā to watch the sun rise. It is an experience that borders on the mystical. Mark Twain called it the 'sublimest spectacle' that he had ever seen.

In recent years the number of cars arriving at the summit has often exceeded the number of available parking spaces, leading to severe overcrowding. To escape the crowds, visitors have strayed into fragile endangered species habitats or dangerous areas. Cars parking outside designated areas also threaten the fragile landscape and could block emergency vehicles. The stats? In January of 2016, park officials said that the number of cars exceeding parking spaces occurred 98% of the time, with an average of 600 people on the summit. In 2017, to manage crowds and protect the park, the park service began requiring reservations for those arriving between 3am and 7am.

Reservations can be made up to 60 days in advance and cost $1.50 per car. They can only be made at www.recreation.gov, and the reservation fee is separate from the entrance fee. You can also catch the sunrise with a commercial tour group.

Plan to arrive at the summit an hour before the actual sunrise; that will guarantee you time to see the world awaken. Around that point the night sky begins to lighten and turn purple-blue, and the stars fade away. Ethereal silhouettes of the mountain ridges appear. The gentlest colors show up in the fragile moments just before dawn. The undersides of the clouds lighten first, accenting the night sky with pale silvery slivers and streaks of pink.

About 20 minutes before sunrise, the light intensifies on the horizon in bright oranges and reds. Turn around for a look at Science City, whose domes turn a blazing pink. For the grand finale, the moment when the disk of the sun appears, all of Haleakalā takes on a fiery glow. It feels like you're watching the earth awaken.

Come prepared – it's going to be c-o-l-d! Temperatures hovering around freezing and a biting wind are the norm at dawn and there's often a frosty ice on the top layer of cinders. If you don't have a winter jacket or sleeping bag to wrap yourself in, bring a warm blanket from your hotel. However many layers of clothes you can muster, it won't be too many.

The best photo opportunities occur before the sun rises. Every morning is different, but once the sun is up, the silvery lines and the subtleties disappear.

One caveat: a rained-out sunrise is an anticlimactic event, but stick around. Skies may clear and you can enjoy a fantastic hike into the crater.

If you just can't get up that early, sunsets at Haleakalā have inspired poets as well.

NENE WATCH

The native nene, Hawaii's state bird, is a long-lost cousin of the Canada goose. By the 1950s hunting, habitat loss and predators had reduced its population to just 30. Thanks to captive breeding and release programs, it has been brought back from the verge of extinction and the Haleakalā National Park's nene population is now about 200.

Nene nest in shrubs and grassy areas from altitudes of 6000ft to 8000ft, surrounded by rugged lava flows with sparse vegetation. Their feet have gradually adapted by losing most of their webbing. The birds are extremely friendly and love to hang out where people do, anywhere from cabins on the crater floor to the Park Headquarters Visitor Center.

Their curiosity and fearlessness have contributed to their undoing. Nene don't fare well in an asphalt habitat and many have been run over by cars. Others have been tamed by too much human contact; so, no matter how much they beg for your peanut butter sandwich, don't feed the nene. It only interferes with their successful return to the wild.

The nonprofit Friends of Haleakalā National Park runs an Adopt-a-Nene program. For $30 you get adoption papers, information about your nene, a certificate and postcard. The money funds the protection of nene habitat.

Permits are required for backcountry camping in the crater. They are free and issued at the Park Headquarters Visitor Center on a first-come, first-served basis between 8am and 3pm up to one day in advance. Photo identification and a 10-minute orientation video are required. Camping is limited to three nights in the crater each month, with no more than two consecutive nights at either campground. Because only 25 campers are allowed at each site, permits can go quickly when larger parties show up, a situation more likely to occur in summer.

Keep in mind that sleeping at an elevation of 7000ft is not like camping on the beach. You need to be well equipped – without a waterproof tent and a winter-rated sleeping bag, forget it.

🛏 Wilderness Cabins

Three rustic cabins dating from the 1930s lie along trails on the crater floor at Holua, Kapalaoa and Paliku. Each has a wood-burning stove, a propane burner, 12 bunks with sleeping pads (but no bedding), pit toilets and a limited supply of water and firewood. There is no electricity. Hiking distances to the cabins from the crater rim range from 4 miles to just over 9 miles. There's a three-day limit per month, with no more than two consecutive nights in any cabin. Each cabin is rented to only one group at a time.

The cabins can be reserved online up to six months in advance. A photo ID is required for the permittee, and all of those staying in the cabin must watch a 10-minute wilderness orientation video.

ℹ Information

Pack plenty of snacks, especially if you're going up for the sunrise. No food or bottled water is sold anywhere in the park. You don't want a growling stomach to send you back down the mountain before you've had a chance to see the sights.

Bring extra layers of clothing. The temperature can drop dramatically at any point in the day.

Kipahulu Visitor Center (☎808-248-7375; www.nps.gov/hale; Hana Hwy, Kipahulu District, Haleakalā National Park; ⊙9am-4:30pm)

Park Headquarters Visitor Center (☎808-572-4459; www.nps.gov/hale; ⊙8am-3:45pm) Less than a mile beyond the entrance, this visitor center is the place to pick up brochures, a trail map and a map of the stars for stargazing. You can also buy a nature book, get camping permits and find information about ranger talks and other activities offered during your visit. If you're going hiking, you'll want to make sure your water bottles are filled before leaving here. Keep an eye out for nene wandering around the grounds; most nene deaths are the result of being hit by cars.

The water filling station is beside the restrooms.

DANGERS & ANNOYANCES

This park can be a seriously dangerous place to drive, due to a combination of sheer drops with no guardrails, daily doses of thick mist, and strong wind. Exercise extra caution on winter afternoons, when a sudden rainstorm can add ice to the list.

Obey warning signs. They often mark a spot where a visitor has been hurt or killed by a fall, a flash flood or falling rocks.

The weather can change suddenly from dry, hot conditions to cold, windswept rain. Although the general rule is sunny in the morning and cloudy in the afternoon, fog and clouds can blow in at any time, and the windchill can quickly drop below freezing. Dress in layers and bring extra clothing.

At 10,000ft the air is relatively thin, so expect to tire more quickly, particularly if you're hiking. The higher elevation also means that sunburn is more likely.

Visitors rarely experience **altitude sickness** at the summit. An exception is those who have been scuba diving in the past 24 hours, so plan your trip accordingly. Children, pregnant women and those in generally poor health are also susceptible. If you experience difficulty breathing, sudden headaches and dizziness, or more serious symptoms such as confusion and lack of motor coordination, descend immediately. Sometimes driving down the crater road just a few hundred feet will alleviate the problem. Panicking or hyperventilating only makes things worse.

ENTRANCE FEES & PASSES

Haleakalā National Park (p202) never closes, and the pay booth at the park entrance opens before dawn to welcome the sunrise crowd. The pay booth accepts credit cards, not cash. The fee covers both sections of the park. If you're planning several trips, or are going on to Hawai'i (Big Island), consider buying an annual pass ($25), which covers all of Hawaii's national parks. The Interagency Annual Pass ($80) covers the entrance fee for all national parks and federally run recreation sites for one year; it includes the pass holder and three adults.

MAPS

A current hiking trail map can be downloaded from the park's official website (www.nps.gov/hale). Other planning materials and books can be purchased online from the park's partner: www.hawaiipacificparks.org.

🛈 Getting There & Around

Getting to Haleakalā is half the fun. Snaking up the mountain it's sometimes hard to tell if you're in an airplane or a car – all of Maui opens up below you, with sugarcane and pineapple fields creating a patchwork of green on the valley floor. The highway ribbons back and forth, and in some places as many as four or five switchbacks are in view all at once.

Haleakalā Hwy (Hwy 378) twists and turns for 11 miles from Hwy 377 near Kula up to the park entrance, then another 10 miles to Haleakalā summit. It's a good paved road, but it's steep and winding. You don't want to rush, especially when it's dark or foggy. Watch out for cattle wandering freely across the road.

The drive to the summit takes about 1½ hours from Pa'ia or Kahului, two hours from Kihei and a bit longer from Lahaina. If you need gas, fill up the night before, as there are no services on Haleakalā Hwy.

On your way back downhill, be sure to put your car in low gear to avoid burning out your brakes.

There is no public bus service to the park.

Kipahulu Area

☉ Sights

Kipahulu Visitor Center   CULTURAL CENTER
(☏ 808-248-7375; www.nps.gov/hale; Hana Hwy, Kipahulu Area, Haleakalā National Park; 3-day pass car $20, motorcycle $15, person on foot or bicycle $10; ☉ park 24hr, visitor center 9am-4:30pm) Rangers offer cultural history talks and demonstrations on the lives and activities of the early Hawaiians who lived in the area now within park boundaries. Guided hikes along the Pipiwai Trail are currently offered on Sundays at 10am by reservation. Hikes last two hours. To reserve a spot, call the visitor center after 9am the prior Sunday. Meet at the visitor center.

🏃 Activities & Tours

Kipahulu 'Ohana   CULTURAL
(☏ 808-248-8558; www.kipahulu.org; per person $49; ☉ tours 10am & 2pm) Kipahulu was once a breadbasket, or more accurately a poi bowl, for the entire region. For fascinating insights into the area's past, join the ethnobotanical tour led by Kipahulu 'Ohana, a collective of Native Hawaiian farmers who have restored ancient taro patches within the national park. Includes a sampling of Hawaiian foods and intriguing details about the native plants and ancient ruins along the way.

The two-hour outing includes about 3 miles of hiking and concentrates on the farm activities. The tour meets outside the Kipahulu Visitor Center; advance reservations required.

🛈 Getting There & Around

To explore the park in depth and on your own schedule, you will need to rent a car. There is no public bus service to either district of the park. The summit is 40 miles from Kahului, just over an hour's drive. Kipahulu is 55 miles from Kahului via the Road to Hana. Expect the drive to take at least two hours. Guided tours also stop at both sections of the park.

The Road to Hana

Best Places to Eat

➡ Huelo Lookout (p216)

➡ Ke'anae Landing Fruit Stand (p221)

➡ Coconut Glen's (p223)

➡ Up In Smoke (p223)

➡ My Thai Food (p223)

➡ Halfway to Hana (p221)

Best Views

➡ Ke'anae Peninsula Lookout (p221)

➡ Wailua Valley State Wayside (p221)

➡ Wai'anapanapa State Park (p225)

➡ Honomanu Bay (p220)

Why Go?

There's a sense of suspense you just can't shake while driving the Road to Hana, a serpentine road lined with tumbling waterfalls, lush slopes, and rugged coasts – and serious hairpin turns. Spanning the northeast shore of Maui, the legendary Hana Hwy ribbons tightly between jungle valleys and towering cliffs. Along the way, 54 one-lane bridges mark nearly as many waterfalls, some tranquil and inviting, others so sheer they kiss you with spray as you drive past. The drive is ravishingly gorgeous, but certainly not easy.

Roadside distractions? Eden-like swimming holes, sleepy seaside villages and hiking trails through cool forests. If you've never tried smoked breadfruit, explored a spring-fed cave or gazed upon an ancient Hawaiian temple, set the alarm early. As for rental cars, Jeeps and Mustangs are the ride of choice.

Once you've left Ha'iku behind, houses give way to thick jungle, and the scenery gets more dramatic. One quirk? After the 16-mile marker on Hwy 36, the Hana Hwy becomes Hwy 360 and the mile markers begin again at zero.

When to Go

Driving the Road to Hana is an extremely popular activity. The highway is busy year-round. For slightly lighter crowds, visit in the Maui off-season (April, May and September through mid-December).

If you're limited to a day trip, start your drive at dawn or as soon after sunrise as you can. Parking next to the top waterfalls gets harder as traffic increases.

If you have two days, spend the night in Hana. On the drive back, pull over at the sites and waterfalls that you missed.

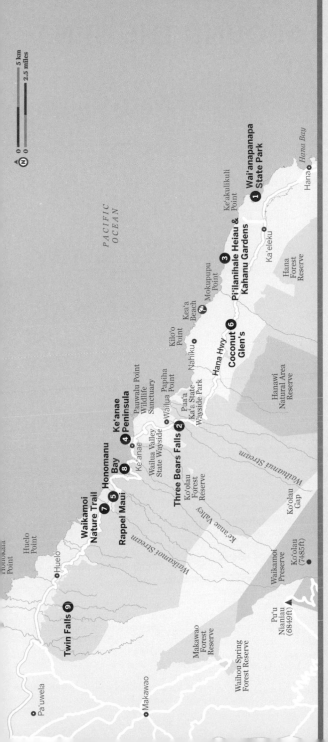

The Road to Hana Highlights

❶ Wai'anapanapa State Park (p225) Exploring stunning natural attractions along a rugged lava coast.

❷ Three Bears Falls (p221) Photographing three lovely cascades from one roadside spot.

❸ Pi'ilanihale Heiau & Kahanu Gardens (p224) Admiring Polynesia's greatest temple, and tropical plants.

❹ Ke'anae Peninsula (p220) Strolling a seaside village evoking the best of Old Hawaii.

❺ Rappel Maui (p219) Adventuring beside waterfalls.

❻ Coconut Glen's (p223) Slurping chili chocolate ice cream at a roadside stand.

❼ Waikamoi Nature Trail (p212) Leaving the safety of your car for a jungle hike.

❽ Honomanu Bay (p220) Watching a tropical river spill from a valley into the sea.

❾ Twin Falls (p216) Hiking followed by a splash.

HIKING AROUND THE HANA HIGHWAY

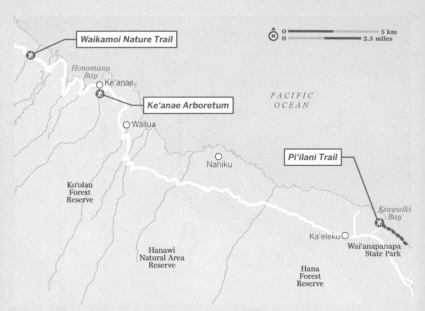

Waikamoi Nature Trail

Honomanu Bay
Keʻanae

Ke'anae Arboretum

Wailua

PACIFIC OCEAN

Nahiku

Pi'ilani Trail

Keawaiki Bay

Koʻolau Forest Reserve

Ka'eleku
Wai'anapanapa State Park

Hanawi Natural Area Reserve

Hana Forest Reserve

WAIKAMOI NATURE TRAIL

START/END WAIKAMOI NATURE TRAIL PARKING AREA
LENGTH 1 MILE
DIFFICULTY EASY

Tree-huggers, lace up your walking shoes. The majestic sights and spicy scents along this 1-mile loop through a leafy forest will introduce you to a global array of tropical trees and ferns. On windy days, you might hear trees 'squeaking' as they sway and stretch high above you.

The signposted trailhead is 0.5 miles past the 9-mile marker. There's a dirt pull-off **parking area** wide enough for several cars. Wear shoes you don't mind getting dirty – this trail can get very muddy after it rains. There are two picnic tables on the hike: one beside the trailhead and one at the summit of the hike. It's 0.5 miles from the trailhead to the summit picnic area.

After a short climb from the parking area, walk past the trailhead picnic table and take the path to your right. You're soon welcomed by a **sign** that reads 'QUIET Trees at Work' and a stand of grand reddish *Eucalyptus robusta*, one of several types of towering eucalyptus trees that grow along the path. Trees native to Australia and Pacific islands are labeled along the way.

In about five minutes you'll reach a ridge at the top of the loop. You'll be treated to fine views of the winding Hana Hwy. After a few steps up the spur trail to your right, you'll enjoy great **views** of a huge green pincushion: a bamboo forest, facing you across the ravine.

As you climb the spur, watch your footing. Roots here are thick and slippery. You'll pass through a small bamboo grove before reaching a **clearing** and a **covered picnic table** at the top of the ridge. There's not much to see from the summit due to the thick foliage. Return to the main trail and follow the remainder of loop back down. Look right for a short path to an **overlook with a bench** as you descend. From here it's an easy walk

It's trails gone wild along the Road to Hana, where the daily dance of rain and sunshine makes trail maintenance a very tough job. HIghlights? Jungle flora, lava coasts and island history.

through the trees – which include a labeled Hawaiian koa – back to the parking area.

PI'ILANI TRAIL

START PA'ILOA BEACH
END KAINALIMU BAY
LENGTH 3 MILES
DIFFICULTY MODERATE

This gem of a coastal trail offers a private, reflective walk on top of a raw lava field several feet above the sea, with refreshing views. The route follows an ancient footpath known as the King's Trail that once circled the island. Some of the worn stepping-stones along the path date from the time of Pi'ilani, a king who ruled Maui in the 14th century.

The trail packs a lot up front, so even if you just have time for the first mile, you won't regret it. In spots the loose gravel path skirts sheer, potentially fatal drops into the sea – exercise caution and leave the kids behind. Bring water as there is no shade the entire way, and good hiking shoes, as it gets rougher as you go along. The trail parallels the coast the entire way.

This hike begins at the black-sand shores of **Pa'iloa Beach** then runs beside the ocean along lava sea cliffs. You'll soon pass a **burial ground**, a natural sea arch and a blowhole that roars to life whenever there's pounding surf. Watch for endangered Hawaiian monk seals basking onshore. Note that walkway improvements begun in 2016 may alter the trail route here slightly.

Look for the ruins of the **Ohala Heiau** as you continue, but don't disturb this ancient lava-rock platform. After 0.75 miles you'll view **basalt cliffs** lined up all the way to Hana, and ironwood encroaching the shoreline. Round stones mark the way across lava and a grassy clearing, fading briefly over a rugged sea cliff. A dirt road comes in from the right as the trail arrives at Luahaloa, a ledge with a small **fishing shack**. Inland stands of ironwood heighten the beauty of the last mile of clifftop walking. Stepping stones hasten the approach to **Kainalimu Bay** ahead, as the trail dips down a shrubby ravine to a quiet, black-cobble beach.

Dirt roads lead another mile south to Hana. Alternatively, you can walk inland to the asphalt road, and either walk or hitch back to Wai'anapanapa State Park.

KE'ANAE ARBORETUM

START/END 0.6 MILES AFTER MILE MARK 16, ROAD TO HANA
DISTANCE 1.2 MILES ROUND-TRIP; 30 MINUTES
DIFFICULTY EASY

For a pleasant stroll through amazing tropical flora, pull over 0.6 miles after the 16-mile marker for the Ke'anae Arboretum. The trail here follows the Pi'ina'au Stream past magnificent shade trees and other plants, much of it labeled by name and country of origin. It's a lovely side trip. Park opposite the entrance gate and follow the paved trail. It turns to dirt and finally grows in after you hit a fence.

1. Wai'anapanapa State Park (p224)

Swim in a cave, sun on a black-sand beach, explore ancient Hawaiian sites.

2. Road to Hana

The serpentine Road to Hana is lined with tumbling waterfalls, lush slopes, and rugged coasts.

3. Huelo Lookout (p216)

Grab a drinking coconut and French crepe, or a smoothie and slice of banana bread.

4. Hana Lava Tube (p224)

Also known as the Ka'eleku Caverns, this cave was formed by ancient lava flows and once served as a slaughterhouse.

❶ HANA TRIPS TIPS

➜ Hundreds of cars are making the journey each day. To beat the crowd, get a sunrise start.

➜ Fill up the tank in Pa'ia or Ha'iku; the next gas station isn't until Hana, and the station there sometimes runs dry.

➜ Bring snacks and plenty to drink.

➜ Wear a bathing suit under your clothes so you're ready for impromptu swims.

➜ Bring shoes that are good for hiking as well as scrambling over slick rocks.

➜ Pull over to let local drivers pass – they're moving at a different pace.

➜ The drive can feel a bit rushed at times: If you want to slow down, consider spending one or two nights in Hana – you can visit the attractions you missed on the way back the next day.

➜ Leave valuables at your hotel or take them with you. Smash-and-grab thefts do occur.

❶ Getting There & Away

To drive the Road to Hana at your own place, rent a car. The drive kicks off on the eastern fringe of Haiku, near Huelo, 20 miles east of Kahului International Airport (p305).

Several tour companies run Road to Hana trips, with buses and shuttles pulling over for key waterfalls and other roadside attractions. **Valley Isle Excursions** (p304), which includes breakfast and lunch on its Road to Hana tours, leaves Hana via the Pi'ilani Hwy, with a final stop at **Maui Wine** (p193).

There is no public bus service to Hana or anywhere along the Road to Hana.

Twin Falls

Just after the 2-mile marker a wide parking area with a fruit stand marks the start of the trail to **Twin Falls** (Map p218; P 🚻). Local kids and tourists flock to the pool beneath the lower falls, about a 10-minute walk in. Twin Falls garners attention as the 'first waterfall on the road to Hana.' It can get a bit crowded, but if you're traveling with kids or you're up for a short, pleasant hike, this is a good one. Two photogenic falls and a swimming hole are your reward.

To get to the falls, follow the main trail across a stream. Turn left at the trail junction just ahead. Continue a short distance then climb over the aqueduct. The falls are straight ahead. You will have to do a bit of wading to get there. Turn around if the water is too high. If there's been a recent flash flood, the trail to upper falls may close.

We have seen smashed glass in the overflow parking area, so if you have valuables, take them with you as a precaution.

Huelo

With its abundant rain and fertile soil, Huelo once supported more than 50,000 Hawaiians, but today it's a sleepy, scattered community of farms and enviable cliffside homes.

The double row of mailboxes and a green bus shelter after a blind curve, 0.5 miles past the 3-mile marker, mark the start of the narrow road that leads into the village. The only sight, Kaulanapueo Church, is a half-mile down.

It's tempting to continue driving past the church, but not rewarding, as the road shortly turns to dirt and dead-ends at gated homes. There's no public beach access.

◉ Sights

Kaulanapueo Church CHURCH
(Map p218; Door of Faith Rd; P) Constructed in 1853 of coral blocks and surrounded by a manicured green lawn, this tidy church remains the heart of the village. It has been built in early Hawaiian missionary style, with a spare interior and a tin roof topped by a green steeple. Swaying palm trees add a tropical backdrop. There are no formal opening hours, but the church may be unlocked during the day.

✕ Eating

Huelo Lookout HEALTH FOOD $
(Map p218; ☎ 808-280-4791; www.huelolookout. coconutprotectors.com; 7600 Hana Hwy; snacks $6-10; ⊗ 8am-5:30pm) 🌱 The fruit stand itself is tempting enough: drinking coconuts, pineapples, smoothies, acai bowls, banana bread and French crepes. But it doesn't stop there: take your goodies down the steps, where there's a shack selling waffles and sugarcane juice, and a table with a coastal panorama.

Ko'olau Forest Reserve & Around

This is where the Road to Hana starts to get wild! As the highway snakes along the edge of the Ko'olau Forest Reserve, the jungle takes over and one-lane bridges appear around every other bend. Ko'olau means 'windward,' and the upper slopes of these mountains experience a mighty 200in to 300in of rain annually, making for awesome waterfalls.

Kailua

After the 5-mile marker you'll pass through the village of Kailua. This little community of tin-roofed houses is largely home to employees of the East Maui Irrigation (EMI) Company. EMI operates the extensive irrigation system carrying water from the rainforest to the thirsty sugarcane fields in central Maui.

After leaving the village, just past the 6-mile marker, you'll be treated to a splash of color as you pass groves of **painted eucalyptus** with brilliant rainbow-colored bark. Roll down the windows and inhale the sweet scent of these majestic trees introduced from Australia.

Ko'olau Ditch

For more than a century the Ko'olau Ditch has been carrying up to 450 million gallons of water a day through 75 miles of flumes and tunnels from Maui's rainy interior to the dry central plains. You can get a close-up look by stopping at the small pull-off just before the bridge after the 8-mile marker. Just 30ft above the road you'll see water flowing through a hand-hewn, stone-block section of the ditch before tunneling into the mountain.

Waikamoi Stream Area & Waterfalls

⊙ Sights

Waikamoi Falls   WATERFALL
(Map p218; Hana Hwy; P) There's only space for a few cars before the bridge at the

---

OFF THE BEATEN TRACK

THE KING'S TRAIL

Attention adventurers: this one is hard to beat. Over 300 years ago, King Pi'ilani (of heiau fame, p224) led the construction of a path around the entire island of Maui in an effort to improve commerce between its far-flung regions. Today the King's Trail, or what's left of it, offers the opportunity to see the island in a unique and unforgettable way: by walking around it. The 200-mile trail skirts the coastline the entire way, providing access to remote areas where traditional Hawaiian life is still practiced. It can be covered in eight to nine days, if you push it. But be careful – this is not for the faint of heart. The trail has not been maintained in its entirety. There are places where it disappears, or where the highway has been built upon it. There are cars, steep cliffs and crazy dogs to contend with. And you'll need to bring lots of water.

If you only have time for a taste, try a section such as the Lahaina Pali Trail (p126) from Ma'alaea to Papalaua Beach, the Hoapili Trail (p150) from La Perouse Bay to Kanaio, or the **Pi'ilani Trail** (☑808-984-8109; http://dlnr.hawaii.gov/dsp/parks/maui; Wai'anapanapa State Park, off Hana Hwy) between Wai'anapanapa State Park and Hana Beach Park, where the ancient trail once began. A complete itinerary looks like this:

Day 1 Ha'iku–Waihe'e

Day 2 Waihe'e–Kahakuloa

Day 3 Kahakuloa–Napili

Day 4 Napili–Oluwalu

Day 5 Oluwalu–Kihei

Day 6 Kihei–Kanaio

Day 7 Kanaio–Kaupo

Day 8 Kaupo–Hana

Day 9 Hana–Ha'iku

For more information, contact Daniel Sullivan at Indigo (p183) in Pa'ia. He's not only walked the entire trail, but created an extraordinary photographic record, which he includes in his book *The Maui Coast: Legacy of the King's Highway* (www.danielsullivan. photoshelter.com).

Road to Hana: Twin Falls to Keʻanae

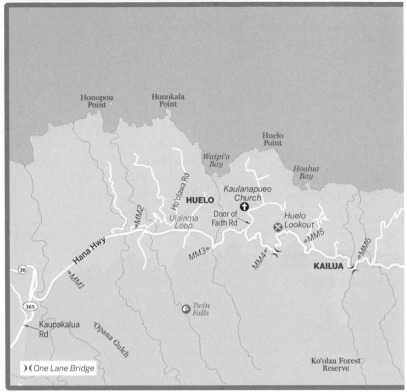

10-mile marker, but unless it's been raining recently don't worry about missing this one. The East Maui Irrigation Company diverts water from the stream, so the falls are usually a trickle. After the bridge, a green canopy of bamboo hangs over the road.

Garden of Eden Arboretum GARDENS
(Map p218; ☑808-572-9899; www.mauigarde-nofeden.com; 10600 Hana Hwy; adult/child $15/5; ⊗8am-4pm; Ⓟ) Why pay a steep $15 per person – not per carload, mind you – to visit an arboretum when the entire Road to Hana is a garden? Well, it does offer a tamer version of paradise. The winding paths are neatly maintained, the flowers are identified, and the hilltop picnic tables sport gorgeous views, including ones of Puohokamoa Falls and Keopuka Rock, which was featured in the opening shot of *Jurassic Park*. A good choice for those not up for slippery jungle trails.

There's also a nifty art gallery, the **Fractal Gallery**, located within, its entrance guard-ed by peacocks. The arboretum is 0.5 miles past the 10-mile marker.

Puohokamoa Falls WATERFALL
(Map p218; Hana Hwy) Immediately after the 11-mile marker you'll pass Puohokamoa Falls. This waterfall no longer has public access, but you can get a glimpse of it from the bridge, or a photogenic bird's-eye view from the Garden of Eden Arboretum.

Haipuaʻena Falls WATERFALL
(Map p218) For a secluded dip, Haipuaʻena Falls, 0.5 miles past the 11-mile marker, provides a deep and serene pool. Since you can't see the pool from the road, few people know it's there. So it's not a bad choice if you *forgot* your bathing suit.

There's space for just a couple of cars on the Hana side of the bridge. To reach the falls, walk 50yd up the left side of the stream. Wild ginger grows along the path, and ferns hang from the rock wall beside

the waterfall, creating an idyllic setting. Be aware of slippery rocks and flash floods.

Tours

★ **Rappel Maui**   ADVENTURE SPORTS
(Map p218; ☎808-270-1500; www.rappelmaui.com; Hana Hwy, 10600 Hana Hwy; $200; ☺tours 7am, 8am, 10am & 11:30am) 'Are you insane?' That's the general reaction to telling people you are rappelling (abseiling) down the face of a waterfall. The magic of this outfit is that it makes this way-out sport seem easy by the end, even if you have no previous experience. Van pick-up at Central Maui Park-n-Ride available. Lunch provided.

After a 60ft instructional rappel down a dry cliff, you'll go straight down a 50ft waterfall, then a more difficult 30-footer, after which you'll swim to the finish line. This is real adventure, yet in the hands of the highly experienced and low-key Dave Black, it's

also safe – and a compelling alternative to all those ziplines.

Eating

Garden Gourmet Cafe   CAFE $
(Map p218; 10600 Hana Hwy, near Garden of Eden ticket booth; lunch mains $8-9; ☺10am-5pm; P) Starving on the Hana Hwy? Pop into this local secret just before the ticket booth at the Garden of Eden. Here you'll find pizza, wraps, tacos and daily smoothies. May close on Tuesdays.

Kaumahina State Wayside Park

Clean restrooms and a grassy lawn with picnic tables make this roadside park a family-friendly stop. The park comes up 350yd after the 12-mile marker. Take the short walk up the hill past the restrooms for an eye-popping view of coastal scenery. No drinking water.

For the next several miles, the scenery is absolutely stunning, opening up to a new vista as you turn round each bend. If it's been raining recently, you can expect to see waterfalls galore crashing down the mountains.

Honomanu Bay

◉ Sights

Honomanu Park PARK
(Map p218; ☑ 808-248-7022; www.mauicounty.gov/Facilities; Hana Hwy; P) Honomanu Bay's rocky black-sand beach is used mostly by local surfers and fishers. Surfable waves form during big swells, but the rocky bottom and strong rips make it dangerous if you're not familiar with the spot; there's no lifeguard here.

Honomanu Stream, which empties into the bay, forms a little pool just inland from the beach that's good for splashing around, and on weekends local families take the young 'uns here to wade in its shallow water. Walk to the end of the beach, look back up the stream, and take in the valley – ooh!

Kalaloa Point VIEWPOINT
(Map p218; Hana Hwy; P) For a fascinating view of the coast, stop at the pull-off on the ocean side of the highway, 0.6 miles past the 14-mile marker. From the point you can look clear across Honomanu Bay and watch ant-size cars snaking down the mountain cliffs on the other side.

Ke'anae

What awaits you at the halfway point on the drive to Hana? Dramatic landscapes and the friendliest seaside village on the route. And we haven't even mentioned the delicious banana bread.

Starting way up at the Ko'olau Gap in the rim of Haleakalā Crater and stretching clear down to the coast, Ke'anae Valley radiates green, thanks to the 150in of rainfall each year. At the foot of the valley lies Ke'anae Peninsula, created by a late eruption of Haleakalā that sent lava gushing all the way down Ke'anae Valley and into the ocean. Unlike its rugged surroundings, the volcanic peninsula is perfectly flat, like a leaf floating on the water.

Sights come up in quick succession. After you pass the YMCA Camp 0.5 miles past the 16-mile marker, the arboretum pops up on

the right and the road to Ke'anae Peninsula heads off to the left around the next bend.

◉ Sights

Ke'anae Arboretum HIKING
(Map p218; https://hawaiitrails.org) 🏃 For a pleasant stroll through amazing tropical flora, pull over 0.6 miles after the 16-mile marker for the Ke'anae Arboretum. The trail here follows the Pi'ina'au Stream past magnificent shade trees and other plants, much of it labeled by name and country of origin. It's a lovely side trip that takes about 30 minutes total.

Park opposite the entrance gate and follow the paved trail. It turns to dirt and finally grows in after you hit a fence. The trail is 0.6 miles one way.

★ Ke'anae Peninsula VILLAGE
(Map p218; Ke'anae Rd; P ♿) This rare slice of 'Old Hawaii,' home to an 1860s church and a wild lava coast, is reached by taking Ke'anae Rd on the *makai* (seaward) side of the highway just beyond Ke'anae Arboretum. Families have tended stream-fed taro patches here for generations.

The rock islets you see off the coast from Ke'anae Park – Mokuhala and Mokumana – are seabird sanctuaries. Turn around here, as there's a private residential area beyond, with nothing else to see. There are public restrooms (open 8am to 7pm) across from the small parking area.

➡ **Ke'anae Congregational Church** CHURCH
(Lanakila 'Ihi'ihi o Iehova Ona Kaua; Map p218; off Keanae Rd) Marking the heart of the village is this church, built in 1860. Enter over the steps of the adjacent cottage. The church is made of lava rocks and coral mortar, uncovered by whitewash. It's a welcoming place with open doors and a guest book. Note the cameo portraits in the adjacent cemetery.

➡ **Ke'anae Park** PARK
(Map p218; ☑ 808-248-7022; www.mauicounty.gov/Facilities; Keanae Rd; ⊙ 8am-7pm; P ♿) Ke'anae Park has a scenic coastline of jagged black lava and hypnotic white-capped waves. Forget swimming, as the water is rough and there's no beach.

Ching's Pond NATURAL FEATURE
(Map p218) The stream that feeds Ke'anae Peninsula pauses to create a couple of swimming holes just below the bridge, 0.9 miles after the 16-mile marker. You won't see anything by driving by, but if you pull off

immediately before the bridge you'll find a deep crystal-clear pool beneath. It's best to observe the pool but not to take a dip. Locals often swim here, but there are 'No Trespassing' signs. The waters are also susceptible to dangerous flash floods.

According to one local source, a flood could be close if the water here is murky.

Ke'anae Peninsula Lookout VIEWPOINT
(Map p218; Hana Hwy; P) For a superb bird's-eye view of the lowland peninsula and village, including the patchwork taro fed by Ke'anae Stream, stop at the paved pull-off just past the 17-mile marker on the *makai* side of the road. There's no signpost, but it's easy to find if you look for the yellow tsunami speaker. If it's been raining lately, look to the far left to spot a series of cascading waterfalls.

Eating

★Ke'anae Landing
Fruit Stand HEALTH FOOD $
(Aunty Sandy's Banana Bread; Map p218; 📱808-248-7448; 210 Ke'anae Rd; banana bread $6, snacks $4-6; ⊙8:30am-2:30pm) 'Da best' banana bread on the entire road to Hana is baked fresh every morning by Aunty Sandy and her crew, and is so good you'll find as many locals as tourists pulling up here. You can also get fresh fruit, hotdogs, sandwiches and drinks at this stand, located in the village center just before Ke'anae Park.

Halfway to Hana FAST FOOD $
(Map p218; www.halfwaytohanamaui.com; 13710 Hana Hwy; lunch mains $7-9; ⊙8:30am-4pm) This aptly named old-timer has been slinging burgers, dogs and ice cream to midway travelers for 30 years. The only ATM on the highway is here, as well as portable restrooms. Also sells shave ice, and the homemade beef jerky will see you through to the other side.

Ke'anae to Nahiku

Waterfalls are a highlight on the twisting stretch of the highway between Ke'anae and Nahiku. Feeling hungry? Nahiku is a good place to pull over for a late lunch or afternoon snack.

Sights

Wailua Valley State Wayside VIEWPOINT
(Map p222; http://dlnr.hawaii.gov/dsp/parks/maui; Hana Hwy; P) Just before the 19-mile marker, Wailua Valley State Wayside lookout comes up on the right. The overlook provides a broad view into verdant Ke'anae Valley, which appears to be 100 shades of green. You can see a couple of waterfalls (when they're running), and Ko'olau Gap, the break in the rim of Haleakalā crater, on a clear day. Turn toward the sea for an outstanding view of Wailua Peninsula as well – don't miss this.

A word of caution: the sign for the wayside appears at the last moment, so be on the lookout.

Wailua Peninsula Lookout VIEWPOINT
(Map p222; Hana Hwy; P) For the most spectacular view of Wailua Peninsula, stop at the large paved pull-off on the ocean side of the road 0.25 miles past the 19-mile marker. There's no signpost but it's not hard to find as two concrete picnic tables mark the spot. Grab a seat, break out your snack pack and ogle the taro fields and jungle vistas unfolding below.

★Three Bears Falls WATERFALL
(Map p222; Hana Hwy) Got your camera? This beauty takes its name from the triple cascade that flows down a steep rockface on the inland side of the road, 0.5 miles past the 19-mile marker. Catch it after a rainstorm and the cascades come together and roar as one mighty waterfall. There's limited parking up the hill to the left after the falls.

You can scramble down to the falls via a steep ill-defined path that begins on the Hana side of the bridge. The stones are moss-covered and slippery, so either proceed with caution or simply enjoy the view from the road.

Pua'a Ka'a State Wayside Park PARK
(Map p222; http://dlnr.hawaii.gov/dsp/parks/maui; Hana Hwy; ⊙6am-6pm; P) 🌿 The highway cuts right through this delightful park whose name, Pua'a Ka'a, means Rolling Pig. Some unlucky passersby will see just the restrooms on the ocean side of the road and miss the rest. But you brought your beach towel, didn't you? Cross the highway from the parking area and head inland to find a pair of delicious waterfalls cascading into pools. The park is 0.5 miles after the 22-mile marker.

The best for swimming is the upper pool, which is visible just beyond the picnic tables. To reach it, you'll need to cross the stream, skipping across a few rocks. Beware of falling rocks beneath the waterfall, and flash floods. To get to the lower falls, which

Road to Hana: Wailua to Wai'anapanapa State Park

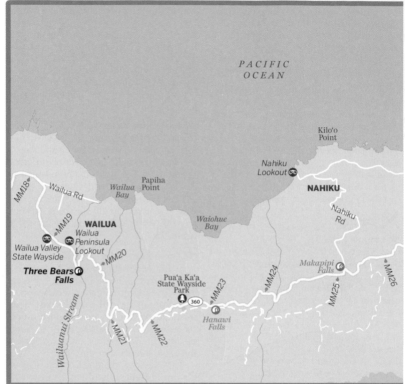

drop into a shallow pool, walk back over the bridge and walk upstream. Be sure to catch the view from the bridge.

Hanawi Falls   WATERFALL
(Map p222; Hana Hwy) A waterfall with a split personality, Hanawi Falls sometimes flows gently into a quiet pool and sometimes gushes wildly across a broad rockface. No matter the mood, it always invites popping out the camera and snapping a pic. The falls are 175yd after the 24-mile marker. There are small pull-offs before and after the bridge.

Makapipi Falls   WATERFALL
(Map p222; Hana Hwy) This powerful cascade makes its sheer plunge right beneath your feet as you stand on the ocean side of the Makapipi Bridge, 175yd after the 25-mile marker. Most waterfall views look up at the cascades, but this one offers a rare chance to experience a waterfall from the top. You don't see anything from your car so if you

didn't know about it, you'd never imagine this waterfall was here. And sometimes it isn't, as it flows intermittently.

You'll find pull-offs before and after the bridge.

Nahiku

The rural village of Nahiku is down near the coast, and cut by Nahiku Rd. Apart from an attractive lookout point, there's not much to tempt visitors. However, just before the 29-mile marker you'll find the Nahiku Marketplace. The jungle's best attempt at a strip mall, it ranges from a tent to a tin roof. Inside you'll find a fruit stand, and several small eateries and shops with very flexible opening hours. If you're hungry, you'll want to stop. The food's tempting and this is the last place for a meal until you reach Hana.

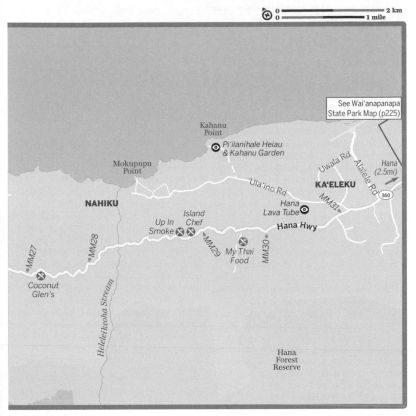

◉ Sights

Nahiku Lookout VIEWPOINT

(Map p222; Nahiku Rd) If you're looking for a visual feast, turn left just past the 25-mile marker. After winding down to the sea over 2.5 miles, you'll find a great coastline view with waves crashing against the shore. This is a fine picnic spot and a good place to stretch your legs.

✘ Eating

Coconut Glen's ICE CREAM $

(Map p222; ☎808-979-1168; www.coconutglens. com; Hana Hwy, Mile 27.5; scoop of ice cream $7; ☺10:30am-5:30pm; ✐) ✿ From his inviting roadside shack Coconut Glen (aka Glen Simkins, who could double for Willy Wonka) is trying to 'change the world one scoop at at time.' Pull over for his 100% vegan ice cream, which comes in six flavors – check the chalkboard – and is so tasty you won't notice it's

made from coconut milk, not cream. The chili chocolate is delish. Cash only.

Up In Smoke HAWAII REGIONAL $

(Map p222; Hana Hwy, Nahiku Marketplace; mains $4-9; ☺10am-5pm Sun-Wed) This bustling barbecue stand at the Nahiku Marketplace is *the* place to try kiawe-smoked breadfruit and *kalua* pig tacos.

Island Chef SEAFOOD $

(Map p222; Hana Hwy, Nahiku Marketplace; mains $12-20; ☺11am-5pm) The coconut shrimp here is so good that it brings people out from Hana.

My Thai Food THAI $

(Map p222; Hana Hwy, Nahiku Marketplace; mains $12-13; ☺11am-5pm Tue-Sat) ✿ Proof positive that you can now get Thai food absolutely anywhere. Owner Jen uses only fresh-caught Hana fish in her savory curries. The green papaya salad and pad Thai get rave reviews.

'Ula'ino Road

'Ula'ino Rd begins at the Hana Hwy, just south of the 31-mile marker. Cottage rentals, restaurants and food stands become more prevalent along the Hana Hwy between 'Ula'ino Rd and the town of Hana.

★ **Pi'ilanihale Heiau &**
Kahanu Garden HISTORIC SITE
(Map p222; ☎ 808-248-8912; www.ntbg.org; 650 'Ula'ino Rd; adult/child under 13yr $10/free, guided tour $25/free; ⊙ 9am-4pm Mon-Fri, 9am-2pm Sat, tours Mon-Fri; P ⊞) The most significant stop on the entire Road to Hana, this site combines a 294-acre ethnobotanical garden with the magnificent Pi'ilanihale Heiau, the largest temple in all of Polynesia. A must-do tour provides fascinating details of the extraordinary relationship between the ancient Hawaiians and their environment. This is perhaps the best opportunity in Hawaii to really understand what traditional Hawaiian culture was like prior to contact with the West. Amazingly, very few people visit.

Pi'ilanihale Heiau is an immense lava stone platform with a length of 450ft. The history of this astounding temple is shrouded in mystery, but there's no doubt that it was an important religious site. Archaeologists believe construction began as early as AD 1200 and continued in phases. The grand finale was the work of Pi'ilani (Pi'ilanihale means House of Pi'ilani), the 14th-century Maui chief who is also credited

with the construction of many of the coastal fishponds in the Hana area.

The temple occupies one corner of Kahanu Garden, near the sea. An outpost of the National Tropical Botanical Garden (which also runs the Allerton and McBryde gardens on Kaua'i), Kahanu Garden contains the largest collection of breadfruit species in the world, with over 120 varieties. Breadfruit is significant because, as its name suggests, its nutritional value makes it a dietary pillar, and hence a weapon to combat global hunger. The garden also contains a living catalog of so-called canoe plants, those essentials of traditional life brought to Hawaii in the canoes of Polynesian voyagers, along with a hand-crafted canoe house.

The very best way to unlock the relationship between the heiau (ancient temple), the plants, and their beautiful parklike surroundings, where palms sway in the breeze, is to take a guided tour, something the entire family will enjoy. These are given Monday through Friday at noon or 1pm and last two hours. Reserve by phone or by emailing kahanu@ntbg.org beforehand. The only other option is a self-guided tour by brochure. The site is located 1.5 miles down 'Ula'ino Rd from the Hana Hwy.

Hana Lava Tube CAVE
(Ka'eleku Caverns; Map p222; ☎ 808-248-7308; www.mauicave.com; 305 'Ula'ino Rd; self-guided tour $12.50; h10:30am-4pm; pc) Who's afraid of the dark? Test yourself at the end of this underground walk by flipping off your flashlight. Eerie! One of the odder sights on the Road to Hana, this mammoth cave was formed by ancient lava flows. It once served as a slaughterhouse – 17,000lb of cow bones had to be removed before it was opened to visitors!

Winding your way through the extensive cave, which reaches heights of up to 40ft, you'll find a unique ecosystem of dripping stalactites and stalagmites. The journey is well signed, takes about 45 minutes, and is a perfect rainy-day activity. Admission includes flashlights and hard hats. If you want to lose the kids, an adjoining **botanical maze** made from red ti plants is no extra charge beyond the ticket price. Hana Lava Tube is half a mile from the Hana Hwy.

Wai'anapanapa State Park

Swim in a cave, sun on a black-sand beach, explore ancient Hawaiian sites, use the

Wai'anapanapa State Park

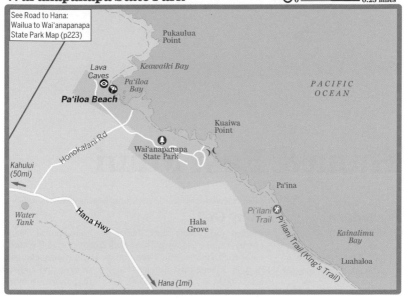

See Road to Hana:
Wailua to Wai'anapanapa
State Park Map (p223)

Pukaulua
Point

Lava
Caves

Keawaiki Bay

Pa'iloa
Bay

Pa'iloa Beach

PACIFIC
OCEAN

Kuaiwa
Point

Honokalani Rd

Wai'anapanapa
State Park

Kahului
(50mi)

Pa'ina

Water
Tank

Hana Hwy

Pi'ilani
Trail

Hala
Grove

Pi'ilani Trail (King's Trail)

Kainalimu
Bay

Luahaloa

Hana (1mi)

public restrooms – this is one cool park. A sunny coastal trail and a seaside campground make it a tempting place to dig in for awhile. Honokalani Rd, which leads into **Wai'anapanapa State Park** (☑808-248-4843; http://dlnr.hawaii.gov/dsp/parks/maui; off Hana Hwy; P⚿), is just after the 32-mile marker. The road ends overlooking the park's centerpiece, the jet-black sands at Pa'iloa Bay. Go early and you'll have it all to yourself. Most sights are within a short walk of the parking areas.

A large-scale construction project to improve the park's coastal walkway began in September 2016.

There are no restaurants, markets or vendors in the park.

🌂 Beaches

★ Pa'iloa Beach   BEACH
(☑808-984-8109; P) The small beach here is a stunner – hands down the prettiest black-sand beach on Maui. Walk on down, sunbathe, enjoy. But if you jump in, be very cautious. It's open ocean with a bottom that drops quickly and water conditions that are challenging, even for strong swimmers. Powerful rips are the norm (Pa'iloa means 'always splashing') and there have been several drownings here.

◉ Sights

Lava Caves   CAVE
(☑808-984-8109; P) A 10-minute loop path north from the beach parking lot leads to a pair of lava-tube caves. Their gardenlike exteriors are draped with ferns and colorful impatiens, while their interiors harbor deep spring-fed pools with resident fish. Wai'anapanapa means 'glistening waters' and the pools' crystal-clear mineral waters reputedly rejuvenate the skin. They will invigorate – these sunless pools are refreshingly brisk!

On certain nights of the year, the waters in the caves take on a red hue. Legend says it's the blood of a princess and her lover who were killed in a fit of rage by the princess's jealous husband after he found them hiding together here. Less romantic types attribute the phenomenon to swarms of tiny bright-red shrimp called 'opaeula, which occasionally emerge from subterranean cracks in the lava.

❶ Information

Division of State Parks (☑808-984-8109; http://dlnr.hawaii.gov/dsp/hiking/maui; 54 S High St, Room 101, Wailuku; ⊘8am–noon Mon-Fri)

Hana & East Maui

Best Places to Eat

➡ Hana Farms Clay Oven Pizza (p238)

➡ Hana Burger Food Truck (p238)

➡ Thai Food by Pranee (p236)

➡ Surfin' Burro (p238)

➡ Shaka Pops (p238)

Best Scenic Views

➡ Hamoa Beach (p235)

➡ Pu'u o Kahaula Hill (p235)

➡ St Joseph Church (p241)

➡ Hana Ranch Restaurant (p238)

➡ Skyview Soaring (p235)

Why Go?

Rugged and remote, East Maui is the go-to spot for Maui-ans looking to get away from it all. Instead of golf courses and beach resorts, you'll see a place that's hardly changed in ages. Overgrown jungles, lonely churches and narrow roads to the coast – it's wild yet welcoming. In slow-moving Hana you'll learn to talk story – l-o-n-g story – with people who take a personal approach to everything. You'll want more than a few hours here. If you keep going – and you should – you'll reach Haleakala National Park, followed by sleepy Kipahulu, which makes Hana look urban. Then it's a wild drive on the Pi'ilani Hwy to Kaupo, where the main street has one building. Finally you'll disappear into miles of open country on the back side of Haleakalā: one spectacular drive. From beginning to end you'll find off-the-grid farms, under-the-radar restaurants, secluded beaches and voices from the past.

When to Go

Hana never feels crowded, but the Road to Hana does get busy. Popular food trucks will have lines at lunch and top attractions get busier as the day goes on. Leave early for your day trip or spend the night in Hana to get a jump on the crowds.

In April Hana hosts the East Maui Taro Festival (p236), the region's biggest party.

Hana is on the rainy side of the island, and you will en-counter rain year-round – but it usually passes quickly.

For slightly lighter crowds, visit in Maui's off-season (April, May, September through mid-December).

PACIFIC
OCEAN

Pukaulua
Point

360 Hana Hwy

Ka'eleku

Wai'anapanapa
State Park

2 **Hana
Farms**

Nanu'alele
Point

Waikoloa
Beach **7M**

Hana

Pu'u o Kahaula **5**
Hill

Hanawi
Natural Area
Reserve

Haleakalā
National Park **1**

Hana Forest
Reserve

Hana Burger **6**
Food Truck

Koki
Beach **7M**

Palikea Stream

Kapi'a Stream

Hamoa **Hamoa** **1**
Beach

Waiho'i Valley

'Opau
Bay

Kipahulu Valley

Waiohonu Stream

Kipahulu Valley
Biological
Reserve

Keawa
Bay

Wailua **3**
Falls

Kipahulu
Forest
Reserve

Kipahulu
Forest
Reserve

Ono Organic **4**
Farms

Hana Hwy Kipahulu

Kaupo **7** **7M** Mokulau
Beach

31

'Alenuihāhā
Channel

N 0 _____ 5 km
0 _____ 2.5 miles

Hana & East Maui Highlights

1 **Hamoa Beach** (p235)
Sunning and surfing on
picture-perfect tropical
shores.

2 **Hana Farms** (p238)
Joining locals for delicious
clay-oven pizza topped with
produce fresh from the field.

3 **Wailua Falls** (p240)
Ogling the most dramatic

cascade on a drive full of
drama.

4 **Ono Organic Farms**
(p240) Tasting exotic fruit on
a tour of an oh-so-local farm.

5 **Pu'u o Kahaula Hill**
(p235) Hiking to a hilltop with
sweeping views of Hana.

6 **Hana Burger Food Truck**

(p238) Biting into a juicy
grass-fed burger beside the
Hana Hwy.

7 **Kaupo** (p241) Pulling
off the Pi'ilani Hwy to savor
a photogenic view of green
pastures, black lava and blue
sea.

ROAD TRIP: PI'ILANI HIGHWAY

Spectacular road trip taking you from lush jungle to crashing sea

This spectacular coastal drive starts out in lush jungle, with snaking bends through numerous gulches. Once it enters the dry side of the island, the road breaks out into magnificent wide-open scenery, from the crashing sea to the volcano above. And hardly anyone is on it. There are no gas stations or other services, so stock up and fuel up beforehand.

The untamed Pi'ilani Hwy (Hwy 31) is also known as the Back Road to Hana. It travels 25 ruggedly scenic miles between Kipahulu and 'Ulupalakua.

Leaving **❶ Kipahulu** you'll drive beneath intimidating – and very crumbly – sheer cliffs,

fortunately covered in protective chain. The Pi'ilani Hwy officially starts at the **❷ Kalepa Bridge**, near mile marker 38.5. The most hair-raising bend comes a short distance later, after the stand selling 'spring-chilled coconutz.' Drive slowly and honk. It's a tight one-way turn between a cliff and the sea with no railings. You may have to back up if you meet another car. And yes, it's as scary as it sounds.

The road remains tight and twisty and the pavement soon gives way to short dirt stretches. The open side of Haleakalā Crater becomes visible and a mile later you'll enter Kaupo. This scattered community is the stomping

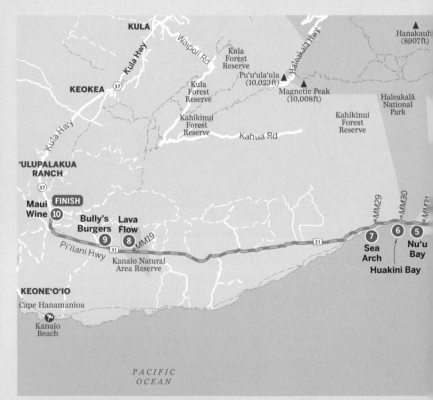

Start Kipahulu

End Maui Wine, 'Ulupalakua

Length 25 miles; two hours

ground of *paniolo* (Hawaiian cowboys), many of them fourth-generation ranch hands working at Kaupo Ranch.

As the only lowlands on this section of coast, Kaupo was once heavily settled and is home to several ancient heiau and two 19th-century churches. Today there's one commercial venture here, the ❸ **Kaupo Store** (p241), just beyond mile marker 35.

A mile later ❹ **St Joseph Church** (p241) (1862) is on the left. With its mountain backdrop, this is Kaupo's prettiest site, and prime for photography. You can see enormous waterfalls through Kaupo Gap, the great gash in the side of majestic Haleakalā. Big and photogenic views of green pastures and blue waters open up at mile marker 33.

Past Kaupo village, you enter the dry side of the island. Near the 31-mile marker, a short 4WD road runs down to ❺ **Nu'u Bay** (Map p226) favored by locals for fishing and swimming. If you're tempted to hit the water, stay close to shore to avoid rip tides.

Just east of the 30-mile marker you'll see two gateposts that mark the path to dramatic ❻ **Huakini Bay**. Park at the side of the highway and walk down the rutted dirt drive. It takes just a couple of minutes to reach this rock-strewn beach whipped by violent surf. You may see a few fishermen. After the 29-mile marker, look for for a natural lava ❼ **sea arch** that's visible from the road.

As you approach 'Ulupalakua, eight graceful windmills, which started producing energy in 2012, mark the return of modern times. Pull over just ahead for interpretive signage about the windmills and the Hawaiian people who lived here between AD1500 and 1800.

At the 19-mile marker the road crosses a vast ❽ **lava flow** dating from between AD 1480 and 1600, Haleakalā's last-gasp eruption. This flow, part of the Kanaio Natural Area Reserve, is the same one that covers the La Perouse Bay area.

Just offshore is Kaho'olawe and on a clear day you can even see Hawai'i, the Big Island. It's such a wide-angle view that the ocean horizon is noticeably curved! You'll wonder how anyone could have thought the world was flat!

For lunch, keep an eye out for lonely ❾ **Bully's Burgers** (p241). Don't mind the cow skulls! From there it's 4 miles to ❿ **Maui Wine** (www.mauiwine.com), where you can toast the end of one spectacular drive.

The road is subject to tall tales about its condition. In reality it is rough and narrow in a few spots early on, with a series of unpaved sections later in the drive, but easily driveable. The latter half has brand-new black-top. The highway has also gotten more crowded. Don't follow any vehicle too closely. With so many one-way stretches of road, someone ahead of you may need to stop and back up.

Wash-outs sometimes close the road temporarily, so inquire about conditions at the Kipahulu Visitor Center at the national park.

LAZY DAYS

How laid-back is Hana? We've heard that some honeymooners have left after just one night because it's too quiet and slow-paced. Still interested? Then gear up – or perhaps gear down – for beach days, leisurely lunches, big views and lots of conversation.

ENJOYING THE BEACH

Sunbathing. Shell collecting. Picnics. Maybe a game of croquet. Hana's beach scene tends to be more low-key than others on the island, although you will see surfers and bodyboarders when the surf is up. The ocean can be a bit rough for everyday visitors, but you can snorkel and kayak when seas are calm.

LINGERING OVER LUNCH

Beyond Travaasa Hana, lunch options are communal, with folks queuing at roadside food trucks. Food-truck kitchens aren't big, so residents and tourists alike talk story at picnic tables while they wait. It's a great place to pick up local gossip and tips from fellow travelers.

VIEW FROM PU'U O KAHAULA HILL

The grass covering Pu'u o Kahaula Hill, also known as Lyon's Hill, glows green after a rain – a brilliant welcome mat. A short climb ends at a commanding summit platform with a towering cross and tiki torches. Prepare for thoughts on nature, beauty and maybe even religion as you gaze over Hana town and the coast.

1. Shrimp lunch
2. *Kalua* pork, *lomilomi* salmon and Spam musabi
3. Hamoa Beach (p235)

East Maui

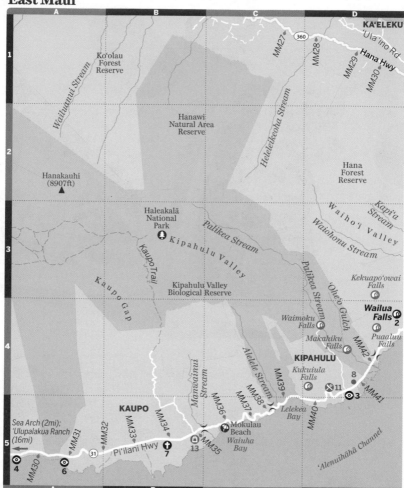

Hana

Heavenly Hana. Is it paradise at the end of the rainbow or something a little bit different? Due to its history and its isolated location at the end of Hawaii's most famous drive, Hana has a legendary aura. But many travelers are disappointed when they arrive to find a sleepy hamlet, population 1235. But that is only because Hana takes more than an hour or two to understand.

Surprisingly, Hana does not try to maximize its benefit from the many day-trippers who arrive each afternoon. This is one of the most Hawaiian communities in the state, with a timeless rural character, and also home to many transplants willing to trade certain privations for a slow, thoughtful and personal way of life in a beautiful natural setting. Though 'Old Hawaii' is an oft-used cliché, it's hard not to think of Hana in such terms. Slow down, spend a night or two and enjoy it.

History

It's hard to imagine little Hana as the epicenter of Maui, but this village produced many of ancient Hawaii's most influential

HANA & EAST MAUI HANA

Enter San Francisco businessman Paul Fagan, who purchased 14,000 acres in Hana in 1943. Starting with 300 Herefords, Fagan converted the cane fields to ranch land. A few years later he opened a six-room hotel as a getaway resort for well-to-do friends and brought his minor-league baseball team, the San Francisco Seals, to Hana for spring training. That's when visiting sports journalists gave the town its moniker, 'Heavenly Hana.'

Hana Ranch and the legendary Hana-Maui hotel (which changed hands many times) were the backbone of the local economy here for decades thereafter. In recent years, the hotel has been sold and transformed into Travaasa Hana. In 2014 the ranch section of Hana Ranch's land holdings, including its cattle operation, was sold to Hana Ranch Stewards LLC. The latter plans to add food production to the mix, with a focus on sustainable agricultural practices.

🏖 Beaches

Hana Bay Beach Park is in downtown Hana. Hamoa Beach and Koki Beach sit alongside photogenic Haneo'o Rd, which loops for 1.5 miles off the Hana Hwy just south of town.

ali'i (chiefs). Hana's great 14th-century chief Pi'ilani marched from here to conquer rivals in Wailuku and Lahaina, and become the first leader of unified Maui.

The landscape changed dramatically in 1849 when ex-whaler George Wilfong bought 60 acres of land to plant sugarcane. Hana went on to become a booming plantation town, complete with a narrow-gauge railroad connecting the fields to the Hana Mill. In the 1940s Hana could no longer compete with larger sugar operations in Central Maui and the mill went bust.

Hana

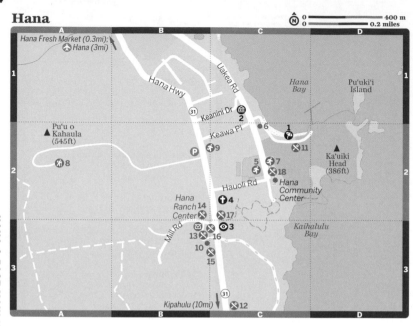

HANA & EAST MAUI HANA

Hana

Hana Bay Beach Park BEACH
(Map p234; ☏ 808-248-7022; www.co.maui.hi.us/ Facilities; 150 Keawe Pl; P ♿) Croquet by the beach? Why not? Welcome to Hana's version of the town plaza, a bayside park where children splash in the surf, picnickers enjoy the view from the rocky black-sand beach and musicians strum their ukuleles. And others play croquet. When water conditions are very calm, snorkeling and diving are good out past the pier. Currents can be strong, and snorkelers shouldn't venture beyond the

headland. Surfers head to **Waikoloa Beach** at the northern end of the bay.

Koki Beach BEACH
(Map p232; Haneo'o Rd; P) This picturesque tan beach sits at the base of red cliffs with views toward tiny 'Alau Island. Bodysurfing is excellent, as it's shallow for quite a distance, but a rip current has been known to sweep people out to sea if they go too far. Shell-picking is good along tide pools by the edge.

★**Hamoa Beach**   BEACH
(Map p232; Haneo'o Rd; P 👫) With its clear water, white sand and hala-tree backdrop, this famous crescent is a little gem; author James Michener once called it the only beach in the North Pacific that actually looked as if it belonged in the South Pacific. When the surf's up, surfers and bodyboarders flock here, though beware of rip currents. When it's calm, swimming is good in the cove.

Public access is down the steps just north of the hotel's bus-stop sign; there's parking for seven or eight cars opposite. Facilities include restrooms.

⊙ **Sights**

Hasegawa General Store   HISTORIC SITE
(Map p234; ☑ 808-248-8231; 5165 Hana Hwy; ⊙ 7am-7pm; P) Need cash? Or maybe some screws? Or how about a bottle of Jim Beam? Or Ben & Jerry's Half-Baked fro yo? The Hasegawa family has operated a general store in Hana since 1910. The narrow aisles inside the tin-roof store are jam-packed with a little bit of everything. And we mean everything, from hardware to produce to tourist brochures. This icon of mom-and-pop shops is always crowded with locals picking up supplies and travelers stopping for snacks and the ATM.

**Wananalua
Congregational Church**   CHURCH
(Map p234; ☑ 808-248-8040; 10 Hauoli St, cnr Hana Hwy & Hauoli St) On the National Register of Historic Places, this church – built in the 1840s – has such hefty walls it resembles an ancient Norman cathedral. The crumbling mausoleums in the cemetery, watched over by the draping arms of a massive banyan tree, are a poignant sight. The church and the courthouse are the only surviving structures from the 1800s in Hana.

Hana Cultural Center   MUSEUM
(Map p234; ☑ 808-248-8622; www.hanacultural center.org; 4974 Uakea Rd; donation $3; ⊙ 10am-4pm Mon-Fri; P) This down-home museum displays some interesting local artifacts. The best is an entire three-bench **courthouse** (c 1871). Although it looks like a museum piece, this tiny court is still used on the first Tuesday of each month when a judge shows up to hear minor cases, sparing Hana residents the need to drive all the way to Wailuku to contest a traffic ticket. Original paintings of Teddy Roosevelt and Admiral Dewey are a blast from the past.

Opening hours seem to be irregular, and the museum is not always open as posted.

Hana Community Center   LANDMARK
(Map p234; ☑ 808-248-7022; www.co.maui.hi.us/ Facilities; 5091 Uakea Rd; P 👫) Anchors the town park, which has a baseball field, tennis courts and a playground, all behind Travaasa Hana.

🏃 **Activities**

★**Skyview Soaring**   GLIDING
(Map p232; ☑ 808-344-9663; www.skyviewsoar ing.com; Hana Airport; 30min/1hr $160/300; ⊙ by reservation) Haleakalā has excellent soaring conditions, and a sailplane is a unique, rewarding and safe way to see the mountain. After he cuts the engine, experienced pilot Hans Pieters will fly over the crater (weather permitting) and let you fly too, before gliding silently back to Hana Airport.

Call in advance for a reservation, or try your luck and visit the airport. Hans has clearly had his own share of luck, as he is one of the few people to have survived being struck by a propeller.

Pu'u o Kahaula Hill   HIKING
(Lyon's Hill; Map p234; Hana Hwy) This paved walkway up Pu'u o Kahaula Hill, behind the Travaasa Hana parking lot (take the small gate in the left corner), makes for a fine 30-minute round-trip walk. It leads to Hana's most dominant landmark, a tasteful memorial to former Hana Ranch owner

---

ⓘ **KAIHALULU (RED SAND) BEACH**
....

You might hear rumors about this cloth-ing-optional red-sand beach, which is tucked in a hidden cove beneath a sheer red cliff, all protected by a volcanic dyke that was created by an ancient fissure.

While unique, the beach and its access trail are located on private property. The steep trail is also narrow, crumbly and dangerous; there have been numerous injuries to hikers who have fallen here, with a few requiring an airlift out for medical care. Also, on the way to and from the beach, the trail runs near an old Japanese cemetery. There is evidence of disrespectful wear and tear to the site caused by careless hikers as they pass the cemetery grounds.

AGRICULTURAL ZONING

One of the keys to understanding Hana is contained in the local zoning regulations. In order to preserve Hana from development, the vast majority of properties are zoned agricultural. As a result, hardly anyone has the right to erect a commercial building. Consequently, almost all restaurants, and some other businesses, inhabit temporary structures, and sometimes hysterically so. You'll find them under thatched huts, tents, and great blue tarps. Ice-cream trucks serve as semi-mobile kitchens. Technically, many of these businesses are still illegal, but as long as they benefit the community, no one cares. The deserted mini-mall down the road from Hasegawa Store bears witness to how effective this informal system can be.

For visitors, the upshot is this: don't be afraid to eat under a blue tarp. Hana's many temporary structures are actually part of its charm.

Paul Fagan: like a mountaintop heiau with a huge cross. All of Hana is laid out below.

Midway up the walkway you'll see a signed trail going off to your left. This leads to Koki Beach (2 miles).

Spa at Travaasa Hana　　SPA
(Map p234; ☑ 888-820-1043; www.travaasa.com; 5031 Hana Hwy, Travaasa Hana; 1hr lomilomi massage $175; ☺ 9am-7pm) If the long drive to Hana has tightened you up, this posh spa can work out the kinks with *lomilomi* (traditional Hawaiian massage). While nicely laid out, and big enough for an army, the rooms are a bit clinical.

Luana Spa　　SPA
(Map p234; ☑ 808-248-8855; www.luanaspa.com; 5050 Uakea Rd; 1hr massage/scrub/facials from $80/100/85) From a papaya pineapple scrub to a nourishing noni wrap, treatments embrace local ingredients and traditions. Offers treatments in a secluded yurt on Ka'uiki Hill, opposite Hana Ballpark. Spa treatments can be combined with an overnight stay in the **yurt** (☑ 808-248-8855; www.luanaspa.com; d $130; ☎).

Hana Ballpark　　TENNIS
(Map p234; ☑ 808-248-7022; www.co.maui.hi.us/Facilities; cnr Uakea Rd & Hauoli St; ☺ sunrise-sunset; ♿) Offers very nice public tennis courts and a playground for kids.

Tours

Hana-Maui Kayak & Snorkel　　CRUISE
(Map p234; ☑ 808-248-7711; www.hanabaykayaks.com; Hana Beach Park; snorkel trip adult/child under 11yr $99/50; ♿) If you're an inexperienced snorkeler, or want to snorkel out beyond Hana Bay, then Kevin Coates is your man. You'll paddle beyond the pier in Hana Bay and sample the reef before rounding the corner into open sea. Kevin's been doing this since 1995, so has an endless number of stories to keep you entertained.

Travaasa Hana Stables　　HORSEBACK RIDING
(Map p234; ☑ 808-270-5276, reservations 808-359-2401; www.travaasa.com; 1hr ride $60; ☺ tours 9am & 10:30am) Enjoy a gentle trail ride through pastures and along Hana's black-lava coastline. Riders must be at least nine years old. Open to nonguests; book at the front desk.

✺ Festivals & Events

★ **East Maui Taro Festival**　　CULTURAL
(www.tarofestival.org; ☺ Apr) Maui's most Hawaiian town throws its most Hawaiian party. If it's native, it's here – a taro pancake breakfast, poi making, hula dancing and a big jamfest of Hawaiian music. Held on the last weekend in April, it's Hana at its finest. Book accommodations well in advance.

Hana Canoe Regatta　　SPORTS
(www.co.maui.hi.us/Facilities; Hana Bay Beach Park; ☺ Apr) Outrigger canoes race out to sea in April, marking the start of canoe season.

Hana Surfing Classic　　SURF MEET
(www.mauisurfohana.org; ☺ Sep) Annual amateur surfing contest held at Koki Beach in mid-September.

✗ Eating

★ **Thai Food by Pranee**　　THAI $
(Map p234; 5050 Uakea Rd; meals $10-15; ☺ 10:30am-4pm) Hana's ever-popular Thai lunch is served from an oversized mobile food truck surrounded by picnic tables. Step up to the counter for a large and tasty meal, including fiery curries with mahimahi and fresh stir-fried dishes. Get there early for the best selection. Located opposite Hana Ballpark.

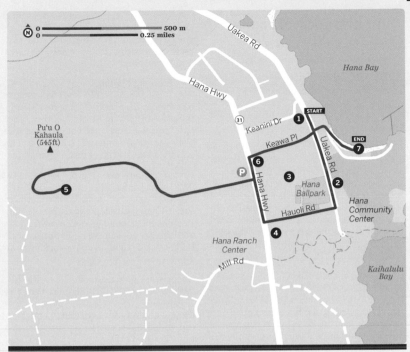

🏃 Walking Tour
Hana Walk

START HANA CULTURAL CENTER
END HANA BAY BEACH PARK
LENGTH 2.5 MILES, ONE HOUR

Artifacts at the **①Hana Cultural Center** (p235) spotlight Old Hawaiian customs, with fishing tools and crafts on display. Step into the tiny 1871 courthouse here to learn about the devastating tsunami that hit northern Maui and Hana in 1946, killing 14 people and destroying 77 homes. The adjacent Kauhale Village replicates the compound of an ancient Hawaiian chieftain.

From here, follow Uakea Rd south, crossing Kiawe Pl. A 'Thai Food' sign on your left marks the driveway to **②Pranee's** beloved Thai food truck. On your right, the back lawn of **③Travaasa Hana** (p236) unfurls in well-manicured glory, merging seamlessly with the town's playing fields. The Hana Community Center is just ahead on your left. At the end of the block turn right onto Hauoli Rd, which divides Travaasa Hana. The resort's seafront cottages are on your left; to your right a row of

suites flanks the broad lawn. Watch for golf carts scooting between the two sections.

The simple but eye-catching **④Wananal-ua Congregational Church** (p235), built in the 1840s, anchors the corner of Hauoli Rd and the Hana Hwy. Cross the highway and walk to the stone wall surrounding the resort's parking lot. Open the gate to follow the half-mile trail to the top of **⑤Pu'u o Kahaula Hill** (p235), also known as Lyon's Hill. It's topped by a large cross. With the right mix of sun and rain clouds, the pastures glow a rich hue of green. Stone benches and tiki torches surround the cross, a simple but powerful memorial to former Hana Ranch owner Paul Fagan. Enjoy the view of Hana.

Return the way you came and cross the Hana Hwy. A sidewalk to the left leads through a small garden before arriving at **⑥Hana Coast Gallery** (p239), home to high-quality Hawaiian-made art. From here, walk carefully along the shoulder of Kiawe Pl down to **⑦Hana Bay Beach Park** (p234). Grab a seat and savor the view of the tranquil sea.

THE BEST LOCAVORE DINING

➡ Ono Organic Farms (p240)

➡ Hana Farms Clay Oven Pizza (p238)

➡ Hana Fresh Market (p238)

➡ Hana Burger Food Truck (p238)

➡ Laulima Farm (p241)

★ **Shaka Pops**   ICE CREAM $

(Map p234; www.shakapopsmaui.com; ice pops $4.75; ⊙11am-4pm Sun-Fri) A friendly *shaka* wave greets travelers passing this happy cart, where frozen treats-on-a-stick come in fresh, tropical flavors. Locally made in small batches, they taste great and are definitely worth a lick. Look for the cart in front of the Hana Ranch Center. Life is a little brighter while slurping a Cocoa Hana Banana popsicle.

Hana Burger Food Truck   BURGERS $

(Map p232; ☑808-268-2820; https://hanaranch.com; 5670 Hana Hwy; mains $12-16) What's that flash of silver on the hill, surrounded by a gorgeous field of green? If you're driving south from Hana and you're hungry, the new burger truck from Hana Ranch might be the gate to heaven. Grass-fed burgers from the ranch, picnic tables scattered across a pasture, and Hamoa Beach down the road. It doesn't get much better.

The *paniolo* burger comes with caramelized onions and a papaya BBQ sauce.

Surfin' Burro   MEXICAN $

(Map p234; Hana Hwy; mains $4-8; ⊙8am-7pm) Tacos? In Hana? Yep, and they're darn good too. Also serves breakfast burritos and fresh-made salsa. Look for the orange food truck parked between the Hotel Travaasa and Hasegawa General Store.

Braddah Hutt's BBQ   BARBECUE $

(Map p234; Hana Hwy; meals $8-15; ⊙10am-2pm Mon-Fri) This place is like a BBQ at your neighbor's house. Here, diners sit on folding chairs under a canvas awning while an extended family cooks away over gas grills. Favorites are the barbecued chicken and the fish tacos. Expect a crowd at noon, and don't take the closing time too seriously: it shuts down when the food runs out.

Barefoot Cafe   AMERICAN, HAWAIIAN $

(Map p234; ☑808-446-5732; Hana Beach Park; breakfast $7-10, lunch $7-14; ⊙breakfast 7am-10am, lunch 11:30am-5pm) Hana Beach Park's fast-food grill serves burgers and hot dogs as well as Hawaiian favorites like an ahi *poke* (seasoned raw fish) bowl and plate lunches. Nearby tables make for great beach-watching.

Ono Farmers Market   MARKET $

(Map p234; ☑808-248-7779; www.onofarms.com; Hana Hwy; ⊙10am-6pm) 🖉 This fruit stand is the place to pick up Kipahulu-grown coffee, jams and the most incredible array of fruit, from papaya to rambutan. Look for it in the parking lot just south of the gas station.

Hana Fresh Market   HEALTH FOOD $

(Map p232; ☑808-248-7515; www.hanahealth. org; 4590 Hana Hwy; mains $10-12; ⊙7am-2pm Mon-Fri) This roadside stand in front of Hana Health sells organic produce grown on site and healthy takeout plates featuring locally caught fish. Smoothies and yogurt bowls are also for sale.

Hasegawa General Store   SUPERMARKET $

(Map p234; ☑808-248-8231; 5165 Hana Hwy; ⊙7am-7pm) This iconic mom-and-pop shop, with groceries and, well, a little bit of everything, has been a local fixture for a century. Has an ATM.

Hana Ranch Store   SUPERMARKET $

(Map p234; ☑808-248-8261; 1 Mill St; ⊙6am-7:30pm) Groceries and liquor.

★ **Hana Farms Clay Oven Pizza**   PIZZA $$

(Map p232; ☑808-248-7553; www.hanafarmsonline.com; 2910 Hana Hwy; pizza $18-20; ⊙4-8pm Fri & Sat) 🖉 Located behind the Hana Farms stand, this little gem is *the* local choice on Friday and Saturday nights. Gourmet pizzas with toppings sourced from the farm emerge from clay ovens piping hot. Gas lamps light picnic tables beneath thatched roofs. And the takeaway pizza box is a folded palm leaf – a Hana classic. We hear plans are afoot to open up on more nights.

Pre-order by phone to avoid waiting.

Hana Ranch
Restaurant   AMERICAN, HAWAIIAN $$

(Map p234; ☑808-270-5280; Mill St, Hana Ranch Center; mains $17-32; ⊙11am-8:30pm) The wall of ukuleles is perfect for an Instagram photo at this revamped restaurant, one of a handful of dinner options in Hana. Enjoy the view of the ocean from inside or from the patio. Serves American and Hawaiian fare.

And to clear up any confusion – the Hotel Travaasa owns this restaurant and its name. The actual Hana Ranch runs the burger truck down the road, which opened in 2016, and Hana Provisions in Pa'ia, which opened in 2015.

🍷 Drinking & Nightlife

Preserve Bar BAR
(Map p234; ☑ 808-248-8211; www.travaasa.com; 5031 Hana Hwy, Travaasa Hana; ☺ restaurant 11:30am-9pm, bar till later) When it comes to Hana nightlife, this is the only game in town. Maui beers, locally inspired cocktails and farm-to-table bar fare are on offer. Local musicians perform Sunday, Tuesday and Wednesday nights, accompanied by hula dancers. Come when there's live music, otherwise the vibe can be eerily quiet and slow-paced.

🛍 Shopping

★Hana Coast Gallery ARTS & CRAFTS
(Map p234; ☑ 808-248-8636; www.hanacoast. com; 5031 Hana Hwy; ☺ 9am-5pm) Even if you're not shopping, visit this gallery at the northern side of Travaasa to browse the museum-quality wooden bowls, paintings and Hawaiian featherwork from about 40 different Hawaii artists.

Hana Farms FOOD
(Map p232; www.hanafarmsonline.com; 2910 Hana Hwy; ☺ 8am-7pm Sun-Thu, to 8pm Fri & Sat) This small 7-acre farm grows a large variety of tropical fruits, flowers and spices, and transforms them into interesting products. Its well-done roadside stand offers banana breads, exotic fruit preserves, tropical hot sauces, island candies, coffee and spices. A great place to find a unique and tasty gift. The ginger lime soda is refreshing.

May close at 6pm Sunday to Thursday in summer.

ℹ Information

Hana Ranch Center (Mill Rd) is the commercial center of town.
Bank of Hawaii (☑ 808-248-8015; www.boh. com; Mill St, Hana Ranch Center; ☺ 3-4:30pm Mon-Thu, 3-6pm Fri) No ATM.
Hana Health (☑ 808-248-8294; www.hana-health.org; 4590 Hana Hwy; ☺ 7am-6pm Mon-Wed & Fri, 7am-noon & 2-6pm Thu, 8am-noon Sat) At the northern side of town. Physicians on-call for emergency care 24/7.
Post Office (Map p234; ☑ 808-248-8258; www.usps.com; 1 Mill St, Hana Ranch Center; ☺ 11am-4pm Mon-Fri)

ℹ Getting There & Around

Enterprise (☑ 808-871-1511; www.enterprise. com) Travaasa Hana has a very small fleet of cars.
Hana Airport (Map p232; ☑ 808-248-4861; www.hawaii.gov/hnm; Alalele PL) There are twice-daily flights from Kahului to this small airport (and return) with Mokulele Airlines (www.mokuleleairlines.com), cutting a two-hour drive to a 20-minute flight.
Hana Gas (☑ 808-248-7671; cnr Mill Rd & Hana Hwy; ☺ 7am-8pm Mon-Sat, to 6pm Sun)

Haneo'o Road Loop

Author James Michener was so taken by Hamoa Beach along this 1.5-mile scenic loop drive that he compared it to the South Pacific. To see what tickled him, travel south from Hana on the Hana Hwy and turn left onto Haneo'o Rd just before the 50-mile marker.

At the base of a red cinder hill, less than a half-mile from the start of the loop, the chocolate-brown sands of **Koki Beach** attract local surfers. The offshore isle topped by a few coconut palms is **'Alau Island**, a seabird sanctuary. Incidentally, those trees are a green refreshment stand of sorts, planted by Hana residents to provide themselves with drinking coconuts while fishing from the island.

A little further is Hamoa Beach (p235), whose lovely gray sands are maintained by Travaasa Hana but are open to all. The surf here is popular with surfers and boogie boarders. Watch for riptides if you decide to take a dip. Dr Beach named Hamoa one of the top 10 beaches in the US in 2015.

HANA & EAST MAUI HANEO'O ROAD LOOP

VOLUNTEER ON AN ORGANIC FARM

There are so many organic farms wanting volunteer labor in Hawaii that Worldwide Opportunities on Organic Farms (WWOOF), an organization that puts volunteers and organic farms together globally, runs a special Hawaii operation. In East Maui **Hana Farms** and **Ono Organic Farms** (p238) are both sponsors, among others. For a full list of opportunities, see www.wwoof-hawaii.org.

Hana to Kipahulu

The lush drive south from Hana to Kipahulu brims with raw natural beauty. Between its twists and turns, one-lane bridges and drivers trying to take in all the sights, it's a slow-moving 10 miles, so allow yourself a half-hour just to reach Kipahulu.

Along the way you'll pass 'Ohe'o Gulch, your entry point to the Kipahulu section of Haleakalā National Park (p209). This is the undisputed highlight of the drive, offering fantastic falls, cool pools and tropical paths. The area can experience flash floods, so the Park Service does not recommend swimming in the pools. Note: the rest of the park cannot be accessed from here by car.

The tiny community of Kipahulu, which hides estates and organic farms behind its lush facade, hugs the Hana Hwy 1 mile south of the park.

★ **Wailua Falls**   WATERFALL
(Map p232) Before you reach Kipahulu, you'll see orchids growing out of the rocks, and jungles of breadfruit and coconut trees. Around 0.3 miles after the 45-mile marker, you'll come upon the spectacular Wailua Falls, which plunge a mighty 100ft just beyond the road. There are usually plenty of people lined up snapping photos.

Kipahulu

It's hard to imagine, but this sedate community was once a bustling sugar-plantation town. After the mill shut down in 1922, most people left for jobs elsewhere. Today, mixed among modest homes, organic farms and back-to-the-landers living off the grid, are a scattering of exclusive estates, including the former home of famed aviator Charles Lindbergh.

⊙ Sights

Charles Lindbergh's Grave   CEMETERY
(Map p232; Palapala Ho'omau Congregational Church; P) Charles Lindbergh, the first man to fly across the Atlantic Ocean, moved to remote Kipahulu in 1968. After being diagnosed with terminal cancer, he decided to forgo treatment on the mainland and lived out his final days here. Following his death in 1974, Lindbergh was buried in the graveyard of **Palapala Ho'omau Congregational Church**. The church is also noted for its window painting of a Polynesian Christ draped in the red-and-yellow feather capes of Hawaii's highest chiefs.

Lindbergh's grave is a simple granite slab laid upon lava stones in the yard behind the church. The epitaph is a quote from the Bible: 'If I take the wings of the morning, and dwell in the uttermost parts of the sea.' Walk seaward and you'll find a viewpoint aimed at those uttermost parts.

To find the church, turn left 350yd south of the 41-mile marker and follow the road a short distance to the church, which is at the end of a long driveway on the left.

☞ Tours

★ **Ono Organic Farms**   FOOD & DRINK
(Map p232; ☑ 808-248-7779; www.onofarms.com; Hana Hwy; tours adult/child under 10yr $35/free; ⊙ tours 1:30pm Mon-Fri) This fascinating

---

CHARLES LINDBERGH: THE LONE EAGLE

In 1927, at the age of 25, Charles Lindbergh became the first man to fly across the Atlantic Ocean, navigating *Spirit of St Louis* from Long Island to Paris in 33½ hours. Six others had previously died in the attempt. His success brought him instant global fame.

In 1932 tragedy struck, when the Lindberghs' young son was kidnapped and murdered. In the wake of unrelenting press coverage, Lindbergh and his American wife secretly fled to Europe, where they lived until returning to America in 1939. In the meantime Lindbergh helped the US military by providing reports on the growing capabilities of German aircraft.

Lindbergh later traveled frequently to Europe, where he built a secret double life, fathering seven children with three different women in Germany and Switzerland, two of whom were sisters. In total, he had four different families at once. None of the children knew their half-siblings existed until well after his death.

Lindbergh's last years were spent in Kipahulu, where he retreated from the world almost entirely. *Spirit of St Louis* now hangs in the National Air & Space Museum in Washington DC, a fitting monument to a very transatlantic life.

90-minute tour of a wildly exotic business begins with a delicious tasting of tropical fruit. The variety is amazing: ever tried Surinam cherries, rambutan, red bananas, santol or jaboticaba? The tour then heads into the fields of the 300-acre farm, of which 70 acres are planted.

The farm is well hidden on the inland side of the road just south of the national park; look for 'Ono' on the mailbox. If you can't make it here, sample the goods at Ono Farmers Market (p238) in Hana.

 Eating

Laulima Farm MARKET $

(Map p232; www.laulimafarm.com; Hana Hwy; ☺9am-5pm) Pull over for hand-roasted coffee, veggies and fruit, fresh off the adjoining 13-acre farm. Located on Hana Hwy, between the 40- and 41-mile markers.

Kaupo & Around
☉ Sights

Kaupo Store FOOD & DRINKS

(Map p232; ☏808-248-8054; Pi'ilani Hwy; ☺9am-5pm Mon-Sat) Sells snacks and drinks. It's worth popping inside just to see the shelves, which are filled with vintage displays, including a camera collection dating to 1911. Cash only.

St Joseph Church CHURCH

(Map p232; 33622 Pi'ilani Hwy) The church, established by Catholic missionaries in the 19th century, celebrated its 150th anniversary in 2012. The church offers a noon mass the fifth Sunday of the month in months with five Sundays. You can confirm dates at https://friendsofstjoseph-kaupo.org. Visitors are welcome to respectfully stroll the church grounds and historic cemetery.

The church is located between mile markers 33 and 34.

✖ **Eating**

Bully's Burgers BURGERS $

(☏808-268-0123; www.triplelranchmaui.com/Bully_s_Burgers.php; 15900 Pi'ilani Hwy, Triple L Ranch; burgers $10; ☺11am-6.45pm Wed-Sun) You've reached the end of the road. Or the beginning, if you wish. And what do you find but a burger shack – and we mean shack – decorated with cow skulls. No, Bully's has no Michelin stars, just one heck of a burger, thanks to the beef from Triple L Ranch and a few surprising twists, like the spicy chipotle sauce.

Located about 4 miles past Maui Wine (p193) – or the end of the road from Hana. Before making a special trip, call to confirm it's open.

HANA & EAST MAUI KAUPO & AROUND

Lana'i & Moloka'i

Best Places to Eat

➡ Lana'i City Grille (p250)

➡ Pele's Other Garden (p250)

➡ Nobu (p253)

➡ Kualapu'u Cookhouse (p262)

Best Moloka'i Views

➡ Kalawao

➡ Kalaupapa Overlook

➡ Waikolu Lookout

➡ Halawa Valley

➡ Papohaku Beach

Why Go?

Among Hawaii's six main islands, the two with the smallest populations and the least number of visitors could not be more different. Sure, Lana'i and Moloka'i are easily seen from the other across the narrow channel that separates them, but that's where any similarities stop.

Lana'i was never home to many people – its most active time in history was fairly recently when it fully earned its moniker 'the pineapple island' as much of it was given over to cultivation of the spiky fruit. Today, under the ownership of billionaire Larry Ellison, it offers a very low-key island escape from islands that are already an escape.

Moloka'i is a much more varied place. It has a strong cultural past, with many ancient Hawaiian sites and a strong and, at times, almost militant reverence for its heritage. It has great and rugged natural beauty, but remains off the radar for most travelers.

When to Go

From November through to March, jackets are needed at night in lofty, temperate Lana'i City, while east Moloka'i gets very rainy. Beaches stay balmy.

Come April, winter rains have stopped and the islands enjoy breezy tropical comfort until August.

In September and October, Lana'i City and central Moloka'i stay in the sunny 70s (°F), while the coasts are in the lovely low 80s.

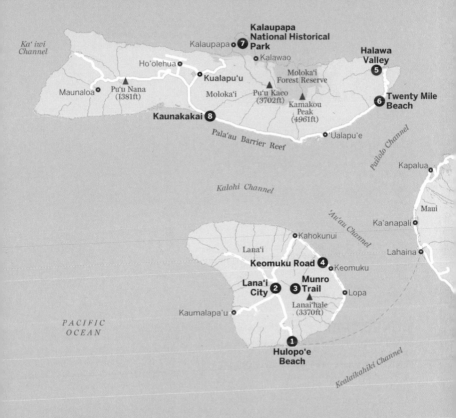

Lana'i & Moloka'i Highlights

1 **Hulopo'e Beach** (p251) Snorkeling the protected reef at the island's best beach.

2 **Lana'i City** (p249) Browsing the shops, then sample the simple cafes, before dozing off in Dole Park.

3 **Munro Trail** (p244) Hiking Lana'i's small, lush heart, stretching above Lana'i City.

4 **Keomuku Road** (p253) Getting lost on this unpaved track to Naha, where you'll find a ghost town and idyllic beaches awaiting discovery.

5 **Halawa Valley** (p261) Hearing echoes of Hawaii's past while hiking in this pristine and deeply spiritual setting of waterfalls.

6 **Twenty Mile Beach** (p260) Discovering underwater delights, or lazing.

7 **Kalaupapa National Historical Park** (p262) Following in the footsteps of America's first saint.

8 **Kaunakakai** (p255) Reliving plantation Hawaii in Moloka'i's main town.

HIKING IN LANA'I & MOLOKA'I

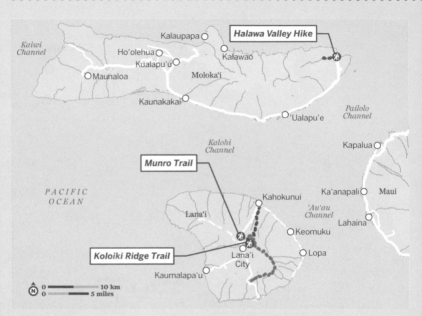

MUNRO TRAIL

START LANA'I CEMETERY
END MANELE RD
LENGTH 12 MILES; FIVE TO SEVEN HOURS
DIFFICULTY MODERATE

This exhilarating 12-mile adventure through verdant forest can be hiked or mountain-biked but not driven. For the best views, and to avoid getting caught at dusk, start early. Hikers should be prepared for steep grades and allow a whole day. Be aware that rains can turn the dirt path into a red swamp. Watch out for sheer drop-offs, especially when mist, fog and clouds limit visibility.

To start, head north on Hwy 44 from Lana'i City. About a mile past the Lodge at Koele, turn right onto the paved road that ends in half a mile at the island's cemetery. The Munro Trail starts left of the cemetery; passing through eucalyptus groves, it climbs the ridge and the path is studded with ohia lehua, ironwood, eucalyptus and Norfolk Island pine trees. The Norfolks, which draw moisture from the afternoon clouds and fog, were planted in the 1920s as a watershed by naturalist George Munro, after whom the trail is named.

The trail overlooks deep ravines cutting across the east flank of the mountain, and passes Lana'ihale (3370ft), Lana'i's highest point. Lookout points dot the trail. On a clear day you can see all of the inhabited Hawaii islands except for distant Kaua'i and Ni'ihau along the route. Stay on the main trail, which descends 6 miles to the central plateau. Keep the hills to your left and make a right turn at the big fork in the road. The trail comes to an end back on Manele Rd (Hwy 440) between Lana'i City and Manele Bay.

You can combine a Munro Trail hike with the Koloiki Ridge Trail. Check the latest conditions with locals beforehand.

On Lana'i, the Munro Trail swoops past non-native trees, ravines and lookouts, while the Koloiki Ridge Trail ends with a panoramic view of the island. It's waterfalls and history in the Halawa Valley on Moloka'i.

KOLOIKI RIDGE TRAIL

START/END LODGE AT KOELE
LENGTH 5 MILES ROUND-TRIP; THREE HOURS
DIFFICULTY MODERATE

This 5-mile hike leads up to one of the most scenic parts of the Munro Trail. It offers sweeping views of remote valleys (where taro was once grown), Maui and Moloka'i.

The trail begins at the rear of the Lodge at Koele on the paved path that leads to the golf clubhouse. From there, follow the sign-posted path uphill past Norfolk Island pines until you reach a hilltop bench with a plaque bearing the poem 'If' by Rudyard Kipling. The heritage center publishes a map that makes following the route easy.

Follow the trail down through a thicket of guava trees to an abandoned dirt service road and you'll intersect with the Munro Trail; after a few minutes you'll pass Kukui Gulch, named for the *kukui* (candlenut trees) that grow there. Continue along the trail until you reach a thicket of tall sisal plants; about 50yd after that bear right to reach Koloiki Ridge, where you'll be rewarded with panoramic views of much of the island.

HALAWA VALLEY

START/END HALAWA VALLEY BEACH PARK
LENGTH 4 MILES ROUND-TRIP; THREE TO FIVE HOURS
DIFFICULTY MODERATE

The hike and spectacle of the 250ft, twin **Moa'ula and Hipuapua Falls**, which cascade down the back of the lush Halawa Valley, are a highlight of many people's Moloka'i visit. They are reached via a straightforward 2-mile trail lined with historical sites. To protect these sites, and because the trail crosses private property, visiting the falls requires a hike with a local guide (p261).

There are numerous cultural sites along the path. You'll also pass through lush tropical foliage. Look for the bright orange blossoms of African tulip trees and the brilliant green of beach heliotrope trees. Among the sights are a burial ground that may date to 650 AD and a seven-tiered stone temple.

Expect muddy conditions and wear stout shoes so you can navigate over river boulders. Some river crossings may be especially perilous. Prepare for voracious mosquitoes, bring water and lunch and have plenty of sunscreen. Most people thrill to a bracing plunge into the pools at the bottom of the falls.

Avoid days when small cruise ships visit Moloka'i as daytripping crowds can lessen the experience. Bring sturdy hiking shoes or sandals, swimsuit, plenty of water, a snack, sunscreen, mosquito repellent and a poncho or protection from the rain.

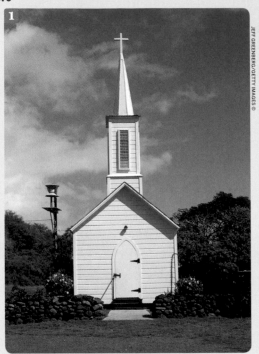

PHIL SCHOFIELD/GETTY IMAGES ©

STEVEN GREAVES/GETTY IMAGES ©

3

OCEAN IMAGE PHOTOGRAPHY/SHUTTERSTOCK ©

1. St Joseph's Church (p260)

Little St Joseph's Church in Kamalo oozes quaint charm.

2. Kalaupapa Trail (p263)

Take a Molokai Mule Ride tour if you're not up to the hike down this *pali* (cliffside).

3. Reef diving

Take a boat ride to the south shores of Lana'i for fantastic diving.

4. Munro Trail (p244)

The Munro Trail is an exhilarating 12-mile adventure through verdant forest.

LANA'I

Although Lana'i is the most central of the Hawaii islands – on a clear day you can see five islands from here – it's also the least 'Hawaiian' one. Now-closed pineapple plantations are its main historic legacy, and the locals are a mix of people descended from immigrant field workers from around the world.

Its signature (imported) Norfolk and Cook Island pines give the island a feel that could just as well come from a remote corner of the South Pacific. And therein lies the charm of Lana'i, a small island (at its widest point only 18 miles across) that's an off-the-beaten-path destination. Hidden beaches, archaeological sites, oddball geology and a sense of isolation let you get away from it all, without going far.

Of course, looming over Lana'i is billionaire owner Larry Ellison, whose efforts to transform the island have proceeded in fits and starts.

🛈 Getting There & Around

AIR

Lana'i Airport (LNY; ☑ 808-565-7942; http://hawaii.gov/lny; off Hwy 440) is about 3.5 miles southwest of Lana'i City. There are no direct flights to Lana'i from the mainland.

Air service is limited to several flights a day on **Ohana** (☑ 800-367-5320; www.hawaiianairlines.com) linking Lana'i to Honolulu. There is also usually one flight to/from Moloka'i.

BOAT

Worth it just for the ride, the **Expeditions Maui–Lana'i Ferry** (☑ 800-695-2624; www.go-lanai.com; adult/child one way $30/20) links Lahaina Harbor (Maui) with Manele Bay Harbor on Lana'i (one hour) several times daily. In winter there's a fair chance of seeing humpback whales; spinner dolphins are a common sight all year, especially on morning sails. Hulopo'e Beach is near the dock; Lana'i tour and activity operators will meet the ferries if you call ahead. Day-trip packages from Maui are popular.

Lana'i

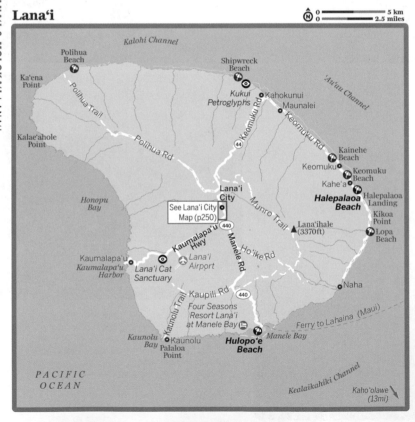

CAR
The island's only gas station, **Lana'i City Service** (p251), sells pricey fuel – a hefty cost for the gas-guzzling rental fleets.

Most vehicle rentals on Lana'i are pricey 4WDs, although these will be necessary for any real explorations.

The main car-rental outfit on the island is an affiliate of **Dollar Rent-a-Car** (☑ 808-565-7227; http://dollarlanai.com; 1036 Lana'i Ave, Lana'i City; 4WD per day $140-200; ☺7am-6pm); however, it's best to make your reservations direct with this office. Having a monopoly on Lana'i translates into steep prices: 4WD Jeeps are available. The firm is owned by Lana'i City Service; note the firm's numerous restrictions on where you can drive your 4WD; confirm these in advance to avoid hefty fines.

Alternatively, other small local firms may offer cheaper rates and allow you to drive to more parts of the island. Most can arrange for pick-up and drop-off at any place on the island. **ABB Executive Rentals** (☑ 808-649-0644; per day $125-180) offers 4WDs and a 2WD car and will arrange pick-up and drop-off. **Lana'i Cheap Jeeps** (☑ 808-649-9517; www.lanaicheapjeeps.com; per day $125-165) rents 4WD Jeeps and Subarus.

TAXI
Rabaca's Limousine (☑ 808-565-6670; rabacalimousine@gmail.com; single ride $10) offers point-to-point rides between the main areas of the island, including the airport. Custom trips to far-flung parts of the island and specialized tours are also available.

Lana'i City

Lana'i City's main square, **Dole Park**, is surrounded by tin-roofed houses and shops, with not a chain in sight. The architecture is little changed since the plantation days of the 1920s, although the gardening is much improved thanks to the efforts of Ellison's island management company, Pulama Lana'i. (Pulama means to care for or cherish.)

Wander between the small but delightfully varied collection of eateries and shops, all with a low-key appeal not found in more touristed places.

⊙ Sights

★Lana'i Culture & Heritage Center   MUSEUM
(Map p250; www.lanaichc.org; 111 Lana'i Ave; ☺8:30am-3:30pm Mon-Fri, 9am-1pm Sat) FREE
This engaging small museum has displays covering Lana'i's often mysterious history; photos and a timeline show its transforma-

A DAY TRIP TO LANA'I
Take the early morning ferry from Lahaina on Maui; keep an eye out for schools of dolphins as the boat approaches Manele Bay. Catch the shuttle into Lana'i City and pour your own coffee for breakfast at **Blue Ginger Café** (p250) before strolling the town's shops and superb **Culture & Heritage Center**. In the afternoon, snorkel at **Hulopo'e Beach** (p251) or dive at Manele Bay before heading back to Maui on the sunset ferry.

tion into the world's pineapple supplier. The lives of the workers are shown in detail and facts such as this jaw-dropper abound: each worker was expected to plant up to 10,000 new pineapple plants per day.

🏃 Activities & Tours

Lana'i Surf School & Surf Safari   SURFING
(☑ 808-649-0739; www.surfinglanai.com; 3hr surf lessons per person $200) Lana'i native Nick Palumbo offers half-day surfing and stand up paddle surfing (SUP) lessons (two-person minimum) at secluded spots. Surfboard and paddleboard rentals from $60 per day including delivery. Also rents boogie boards and kayaks.

★Rabaca's Tours   DRIVING
(☑ 808-565-6670; rabacalimousine@gmail.com; tour for 1-6 people from $95hr) 4WD tours of the island's key sights – many otherwise inaccessible – by an experienced and entertaining guide. Tours are a minimum of three hours. Book in advance.

🎎 Festivals & Events

Pineapple Festival   CULTURAL
(www.lanaipineapplefestival.com) Lana'i's main bash, the Pineapple Festival, is held on or near July 4 and celebrates the island's pineapple past with games and live music at Dole Park (any pineapple you see is imported!).

🍴 Eating

★Lana'i Ohana Poke Market   HAWAIIAN $
(☑ 808-559-6265; 834A Gay St; meals $8-12; ☺10:30am-1pm Mon-Fri) Seating choices at this simple place are limited to picnic tables in the sun or shade. But the *poke* (cubed raw fish mixed with shōyu, sesame oil, salt,

Lana'i City

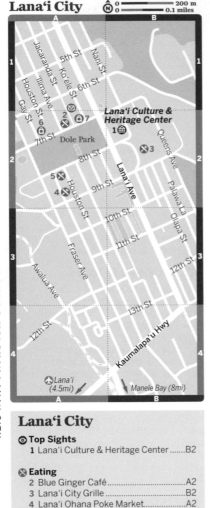

N 0 —— 200 m
0 —— 0.1 miles

Lana'i City

◉ Top Sights

⊗ Eating

⊙ Shopping

chili pepper, 'inamona or other condiments) choices are myriad: spicy tuna, shrimp tempura and more. The raw, cubed fish is superbly fresh and the sauces are spot on. Go early because it closes when they sell out, which is often before 1pm.

Options include divine braised teriyaki beef and perfect mac salad. The coconut shrimp is irresistible.

Blue Ginger Café   CAFE $

(Map p250; ☑ 808-565-6363; www.bluegingercafe lanai.com; 409 7th St; mains $5-15; ⊙ 6am-8pm Thu-Mon, to 2pm Tue & Wed) Don't worry, all the care goes into the food, not the decor at this bare-bones diner, where you can serve yourself a cup of coffee, grab a newspaper, and settle back at a table outside, listening to the wind chimes. Muffins arrive warm from the bakery.

The long menu ranges from breakfasts and salads to burgers, delectable chicken katsu (deep-fried fillets) and more. It's been run by the same family for decades.

★Pele's Other Garden   ITALIAN $$

(Map p250; ☑ 808-565-9628; cnr 8th & Houston Sts; mains $10-25; ⊙ kitchen 11am-2pm Mon-Fri, 5-8pm Mon-Sat, drinks until 9pm) More bistro than deli, this restored plantation house has tables inside and out. Owners Barb and Mark cook creative takes on Italian cuisine and serve up classic spaghetti and meatballs, crispy thin-crust pizza and some first-rate pesto. Salads are made with organic local greens; desserts are large.

There's a fine beer list with 12 brews on tap and a bar menu of snacks such as coconut shrimp. Specials are just that!

★Lana'i City Grille   FUSION $$$

(Map p250; ☑ 808-565-7211; www.hotellanai.com; 828 Lana'i Ave, Hotel Lana'i; mains $28-45; ⊙ 5-9pm Wed-Sun) Famed Maui chef Bev Gannon designed the menu at the charming restaurant within the Hotel Lana'i. Sturdy 1930s schoolhouse furnishings give the wood-floored dining room a vintage air, while the menu combines fresh seafood with various meats in ways both familiar (a perfect rib-eye) and excellent (ahi *poke* tacos).

The bar draws local movers and shakers, pours a fine highball, has a great wine list and is often open until 11pm! On Friday nights there's live Hawaiian music. A recent expansion has added an enticing outdoor terrace.

🛍 Shopping

★Mike Carroll Gallery   ART, BOOKS

(Map p250; ☑ 808-565-7122; www.mikecarroll gallery.com; cnr 7th & Ko'ele Sts; ⊙ 10am-5:30pm Mon-Sat, 9am-2pm Sun) Art-lovers enjoy Mike Carroll Gallery, where you can find the eponymous owner either creating a new work or busy displaying the work of another artist. It's a good source for local books plus Asian antiques.

LIFE WITH LARRY

Decades of sleepy seclusion for Lana'i were interrupted in 2012 when the fabulously wealthy cofounder of Oracle (the huge software developer), Larry Ellison, bought out the island's long-time owner Castle & Cooke (which once ran the ubiquitous pineapple plantations under the Dole name).

It's the biggest change to the island since Castle & Cooke stopped farming and built the Four Seasons resorts in the early 1990s. That the owner is a legendary hard-driving Silicon Valley entrepreneur known for, among other dramatics, winning the America's Cup twice (most recently in 2013), only adds to the interest.

For his estimated $600 million purchase price, Ellison got 98% of Lana'i (the rest is private homes or government land) and a bevy of businesses, such as the resorts. Given that the island has struggled economically since the glory days of pineapples, Ellison's wide-ranging plans for his trophy generated intense interest.

Under the guise of Pulama Lana'i, the Ellison-owned company that manages the island, the changes have been many. Among the notable events are the following:

➡ Construction projects to rebuild parts of the island infrastructure, enact beautification schemes and revitalize core businesses such as the Four Seasons Resort Lana'i put a major strain on the island. During 2016, both of the resorts were closed; the resulting dramatic downturn in visitors caused several long-running businesses to close.

➡ Ellison has discovered that just because you own an island doesn't mean that you're exempt from government regulations. Regulatory hurdles and local political opposition have delayed projects including a new beach resort at Halepalaoa. Issues surrounding approval for a desalination plant caused initiatives like a vast conference center to be put on hold.

➡ During 2016 and into 2017 there was a noticeable slowing in new proposals, leading many locals to fear that the political difficulties had caused Ellison to lose interest in the island and turn his famously high-intensity attentions elsewhere.

For residents, life on Lana'i feels a bit like a soap opera as plans and schemes are floated and then forgotten. Ellison has said he wants the island to be economically self-sufficient, yet achieving this may be the biggest challenge of his life.

Lana'i Art Center ART

(Map p250; ☑ 808-565-7503; www.lanaiart.org; cnr 7th & Houston Sts; ⊙ 10am-4pm Mon-Sat) Staffed by local artist volunteers. You can choose from works in many mediums or learn how to create your own from the artists themselves. A great place to get *very* local recommendations.

ⓘ Information

Bank of Hawaii (www.boh.com; 460 8th St; ⊙ 24hr) One of three ATMs on Lana'i.

Lana'i City Service (☑ 808-565-7227; 1036 Lana'i Ave; ⊙ 6:30am-10pm) The island's one gas station; pricey.

Lana'i Community Hospital (☑ 808-565-8450; 628 7th St; ⊙ 24hr) Offers emergency medical services.

Post Office (Map p250; ☑ 808-565-6517; 620 Jacaranda St; ⊙ 9am-3pm Mon-Fri, 9:30-11:30am Sat)

Hulopo'e & Manele Bays

Lana'i's finest beach (and one of the best in Hawaii) is the golden crescent of sand at Hulopo'e Bay. Enjoy snorkeling, walking to a fabled archaeological site or just relaxing in the shade of palms. Nearby, Manele Harbor provides a protected anchorage for sailboats, other small craft and the Maui ferry, just a 10-minute walk from Hulopo'e Beach. Manele and Hulopo'e Bays are part of a marine-life conservation district that prohibits the removal of coral and restricts many fishing activities.

🏖 Beaches

★**Hulopo'e Beach** BEACH

(off Hwy 440; 🚻) The main beach on the island is kept looking beautiful thanks to the efforts of Panama Lana'i's legions of groundskeepers. Everybody loves this free public beach – locals taking the kids for a swim, tourists on day trips from Maui and

CAT SANCTUARY

Easily Lāna'i's most idiosyncratic sight, the volunteer-run **Lāna'i Cat Sanctuary** (☑ 808-215-9066; http://lanaicat sanctuary.org; off Hwy 440; ◷ 10am-3pm) houses hundreds of feral and abandoned cats. The 3-acre fenced location on a former pineapple field is a feline playground. Visitors are welcomed and will fully discover the range of kitty personalities, from outgoing to standoffish. Donations are vital to buying food and otherwise caring for the cats.

the many visitors who end up losing track of time here.

This gently curving golden-sand beach is long, broad and protected by a rocky point to the south. The **Four Seasons resort** (www.fourseasons.com/lanai; 1 Manele Bay Rd, off Hwy 440) sits on a low seaside terrace on the north side. But the beach is rarely crowded, except on weekends, when picnicking locals descend. Picnic tables shelter under palms and there are public restrooms with solar-heated showers. The ferry dock is an easy 10-minute walk.

For the best snorkeling, head to the left side of the bay, where there's an abundance of coral and reef fish. To the left, just beyond the sandy beach, you'll find a low lava shelf with tide pools worth exploring. Look for the protected shoreline splash pool, ideal for children.

Manele Harbor   HARBOR
(off Hwy 440) During the early 20th century, cattle were herded down to Manele Bay for shipment to Honolulu. These days the herds start in Maui, traveling on day trips to Lāna'i on the ferry. There are a few picnic tables under a shelter and bathrooms here. If you see a huge sailing yacht, it may be Larry's (p251).

◉ Sights & Activities

Pu'u Pehe   NATURAL FEATURE
From Hulopo'e Beach, a path (of around 0.75 miles) leads south to the end of **Manele Point**, which separates Hulopo'e and Manele Bays. The point is actually a volcanic cinder cone that's sharply eroded on its seaward edge. The lava here has rich rust red colors with swirls of gray and black, and its texture is bubbly and brittle – so brittle that

huge chunks of the point have broken off and fallen onto the coastal shelf below.

Cathedrals   DIVING
Diving in and around the bay is excellent. Coral is abundant near the cliffsides, where the bottom quickly slopes off to about 40ft. Beyond the bay's western edge, near Pu'u Pehe rock, is Cathedrals, the island's most spectacular dive site, featuring arches and grottoes amid a large lava tube that is 100ft in length.

Trilogy Lāna'i Ocean Sports runs diving and snorkeling trips in the area.

★**Kapiha'a Village
Interpretive Trail**   HIKING
(www.lanaichc.org/kapihaa.html; Four Seasons Resort Lāna'i) This ancient trail makes for a fine and refreshing walk with superb coastal views. It begins on the coast just beneath the Four Seasons Resort Lāna'i; you'll see a sign as you walk up from the beach. Other signs point out history along the way. Download a guide from the website.

The trail is mostly flat, but dips down into gulches with wisps of beach, and gets very hot at midday. A spur leads to the site of an ancient village, Kapiha'a, and on to the golf clubhouse.

Manele Golf Course   GOLF
(☑ 808-565-2000; www.golfonlanai.com; Four Seasons Resort Lāna'i; greens fees $325; ◷ 7:30am-6pm) This Jack Nicklaus–branded 7039yd course at the Four Seasons resort offers spectacular play along seaside cliffs. The 12th hole challenges golfers to hit across 200yd of ocean surf. It is open only to resort guests.

☞ Tours

Trilogy Lāna'i Ocean Sports   WATER SPORTS
(☑ 808-874-5649; www.sailtrilogy.com; tours from $250) Runs diving and snorkeling trips around Lāna'i, including to the excellent Cathedrals dive site (from $450). On some trips snuba (a system where divers get their air by hose from the surface) is available. Trips use a sailing catamaran; some start on Maui, stopping at Lāna'i for pick-ups. Trips from Lāna'i cost much more than similar trips from Maui.

✗ Eating

Convenience Store   SUPERMARKET $
(Manele Harbor; lunches from $6; ◷ 7am-7pm) This much-needed small store on the harbor has all the basics plus locally prepared

foods for lunch (think rice-based dishes you can heat in the microwave). You can buy your refreshments for the beach or the ferry ride here.

Views at Manele Golf AMERICAN $$

(☑808-565-2000; www.fourseasons.com/manele bay; Four Seasons Resort Lana'i; mains $12-30; ☺kitchen 7am-3pm, bar only 3-6pm) The fantastic coastal panorama from the private cliffside tables here is the best view from any island restaurant, and surprisingly little known. The menu has a broad array of familiar dishes such as salads, sandwiches and burgers; all are prepared with color and flair.

★Nobu JAPANESE $$$

(☑808-565-2832; www.noburestaurants.com/la nai; off Hwy 440, Four Seasons Resort Lana'i; meals $50-200; ☺dinner 6-9:30pm, bar 4:30-10:30pm) The Four Seasons features a branch of the worldwide chain of vaunted high-end Japanese sushi restaurants that just happen to be favorites of Larry Ellison (p251). Newly redesigned, the dining and bar area is on a broad, minimalist-yet-elegant terrace with superb views. The bar serves creative cocktails, including a fabulous sidecar.

One Forty AMERICAN $$$

(☑808-565-2000; www.fourseasons.com/lanai/; Four Seasons Resort Lana'i; dinner mains $45-80; ☺6:30-11am & 6-9pm) Overlooking the ocean, this restaurant offers top-end steaks and fresh local seafood. The setting as the sun goes down is beautiful as you look past the flickering tiki torches and out across the bay. It also offers a bountiful breakfast buffet primarily enjoyed by resort guests.

Keomuku Road

The best drive on Lana'i, Keomuku Rd (Hwy 44) heads north from Lana'i City into cool upland hills, where fog drifts above grassy pastures. Along the way, impromptu overlooks offer straight-on views of the undeveloped southeast shore of Moloka'i and its tiny islet Mokuho'oniki, in marked contrast to Maui's sawtooth high-rises in Ka'anapali off to your right.

The 8-mile road gently slopes down to the coast in a series of switchbacks, through a mostly barren landscape punctuated by eccentrically shaped rocks. The paved road ends near the coast and you are in 4WD country. To the left, a dirt road leads to Shipwreck Beach, while turning right onto Keomuku Rd takes the adventurous to Keomuku Beach or all the way to Naha.

Keep your eyes open – sightings of wild mouflon sheep on the inland hills are not uncommon. Males have curled-back horns, and dominant ones travel with a harem. You may also see white-spotted axis deer.

Shipwreck Beach

Unlike many places worldwide named Shipwreck Beach, where the name seems fanciful at best, you can't miss the namesake wreck here. A large WWII tanker sits perched atop rocks just offshore. Unlike a metal ship (which would have dissolved decades ago), this one was part of a series made from concrete. It was dumped here by the Navy after the war.

Start your beach exploration by taking the sandy road that runs 1.4 miles north from the end of Hwy 44, past some beach shacks. Park in the large clearing overlooking a rocky cove which is known locally as Po'aiwa and has good snorkeling among the rocks and reef, as well as protected swimming over the sandy bottom. The main beach runs north of here.

Kukui Petroglyphs HISTORIC SITE

From the lighthouse foundation, trail markings lead directly inland about 100yd to the Kukui petroglyphs, a cluster of fragile carvings marked by a sign reading 'Do Not Deface.' The simple figures are etched onto large boulders on the right side of the path.

Kahokunui to Naha

Keomuku Rd from Kahokunui to Naha is just the journey for those looking for real adventure on Lana'i. Overhanging kiawe trees shade long stretches of the 12-mile dirt road, which varies from smooth to deeply cratered (and impossibly soupy after storms). This is where your 4WD will justify its daily fee, as you explore the ruins of failed dreams and discover magical beaches. If the road is passable, driving the entire length should take about an hour. The reef-protected shore is close to the road but usually not quite visible.

⊙ Sights

★Halepalaoa Beach BEACH

Running southeast from the pier at Halepalaoa Landing is the reef-protected and shaded Halepalaoa Beach, which seems to have come

THE GARDEN OF THE GODS

The only fertilizer that might work in this garden is cement. Often weirdly shaped volcanic rocks are strewn about this seemingly martian landscape. Multihued rocks and earth, with a palette from amber to rust to sienna, are stunning.

It's utterly silent up here and you can see up to four other islands across the white-capped waters. The colors change with the light – pastel in the early morning, rich hues in the late afternoon.

Reached via the unpaved Polihua Rd, the stretch leading to the Garden of the Gods is fairly good, although often dusty. It generally takes about 30 minutes from town. Polihua Road starts near the stables at the Lodge at Koele.

Kaunolu

Perched on a majestic bluff at the southwestern tip of the island, the ancient fishing village of Kaunolu thrived until its abandonment in the mid-19th century after missionary-transmitted disease had ravaged the island's population. Now a registered National Historic Landmark, Kaunolu boasts the largest concentration of stone ruins on Lana'i, including **Halulu Heiau**. The temple once served as a *pu'uhonua* (place of refuge), where taboo-breakers fled to elude their death sentences. There are over 100 building sites here.

Northwest of the heiau (ancient stone temple), a natural stone wall runs along the perimeter of the sea cliff. Look for a break in the wall at the cliff's edge, where there's a sheer 63ft drop known as **Kahekili's Jump**. The ledge below makes diving into the ocean a death-defying thrill, but is recommended for professionals only. It's said that Kamehameha the Great would test the courage of upstart warriors by having them leap from this spot.

To reach little-visited Kaunolu, follow Kaumalapa'u Hwy (Hwy 440) 0.6 miles past the airport, and turn left onto a partial gravel and dirt road that runs south through abandoned pineapple fields for 2.2 miles. A carved stone marks the turn onto a much rougher but still 4WD-capable road down to the sea. After a further 2.5 miles you'll see a sign for a short **interpretive trail**, which has well-weathered signs explaining the history of Kaunolu. Another 0.3 miles brings you to a parking area amid the ruins.

from desert-island central casting. In winter, the number of whales breaching offshore may outnumber the humans basking on the sand.

Halepalaoa Landing   HISTORIC SITE
Just under 2 miles southeast along the road from Keomuku, you reach Halepalaoa Landing, from which the sugar company planned to ship out its product. But little was accomplished during its short life (1899–1901), other than to shorten the lives of scores of Japanese workers, who are buried in a small **cemetery** that has a sign reading 'Japanese Memorial Shrine'.

Keomuku   HISTORIC SITE
The center of the short-lived sugarcane plantation, Keomuku is 6 miles southeast of Maunalei. The highlight is the beautifully reconstructed **Ka Lanakila o Ka Malamalama Church**, which was originally built in 1903.

Maunalei   HISTORIC SITE
Less than a mile from the end of paved Hwy 44 is Maunalei. An ancient heiau (stone temple) sat there until 1890, when the Maunalei Sugar Company dismantled it and used the stones to build a fence and railroad. Shortly after the temple desecration, the company was beset by misfortune, as saltwater filled the wells and disease decimated the workforce.

Naha   HISTORIC SITE
Four miles south of Halepalaoa you come to Naha, which is both the end of the road and the site of ancient fishponds just offshore. With the wind whistling in your ears, this is a dramatic and desolate setting where the modern world seems very far away.

MOLOKA'I

The popular local T-shirt proclaiming 'Moloka'i time is when I want to show up' sums up this idiosyncratic island perfectly: feisty and independent, while not taking life too seriously. The moniker 'Friendly Isle' means slowing waaay down and taking your sense of rhythm from the locals.

Moloka'i is often cited as the 'most Hawaiian' of the islands, and in terms of bloodlines this is true – more than 50% of the residents are at least part Native Hawaiian. But whether the island fits your idea of 'most Hawaiian' depends on your definition. If your idea of Hawaii includes great tourist facilities, forget it.

But if you're after a place that best celebrates the islands' geography and indigenous culture, then Moloka'i is for you. Ancient Hawaiian sites in the island's beautiful tropical east are jealously protected and restored, and island-wide consensus eschews development of the often sacred west.

❶ Getting There & Around

The Maui ferry no longer runs.

Renting a car is essential if you intend to explore the island or if you are renting a house or condo and will need to shop. All of Moloka'i's highways and primary routes are good, paved roads. The free tourist map, widely available on the island, is useful.

AIR

A taxi from the airport costs around $30 to Kaunakakai. **Hele Mai Taxi** (☑808-336-0967; www.molokaitaxi.com) services the island. Many accommodations can arrange transfers.

Moloka'i Airport (MKK, Ho'olehua; Map p256; ☑808-567-9660; http://hawaii.gov/mkk; Ho'olehua) Small: you claim your baggage on a long bench. Single-engine planes are the norm; sit right behind the cockpit area for spectacular views forward. Because of weight limits for individual bags (40lb), pack a small duffel bag in case you have to redistribute your belongings.

Makani Kai Air (☑808-834-1111; http://makanikaiair.com) Offers scheduled and charter flights to Kalaupapa plus Honolulu (its fares on this route are often the cheapest).

Mokulele Airlines (☑866-260-7070; www.mokuleleairlines.com) Has frequent services to Honolulu and Maui, flights from Moloka'i don't require security checks.

Ohana (☑800-367-5320; www.hawaiianairlines.com) The commuter carrier of Hawaiian Airlines serves Honolulu, Lana'i and Maui from Moloka'i.

BUS

MEO Bus (☑808-553-3216; www.meoinc.org; bus trips free; ☑Mon-Fri), a government economic development service, runs a free shuttle bus around Moloka'i, roughly from 6am to 4pm. From a stop by Misaki's market in Kaunakakai routes go east past the Hotel Moloka'i to Puko'o at mile marker 16, west to Maunaloa via the airport and to Kualapu'u. The buses run roughly every two hours but it is essential that you confirm all details in advance and with the driver if you are hoping to make a round-trip. Stops are not marked.

CAR

Most rental cars are technically not allowed on unpaved roads. If you intend to explore remote areas, such as the Kamakou Preserve, you'll need a vehicle with high clearance, probably a 4WD. Book well in advance, especially if planning a weekend visit. But if you're feeling lucky in low season, walk-in rates at the airport can be half those found online.

There are two gas stations in Kaunakakai. Expect sticker shock.

Alamo Rental Car (www.alamo.com; Moloka'i Airport, Ho'olehua) has a desk at the airport; reserve well in advance. The main office is just across the small parking area.

Local outfits often have the lowest rates. **Mobettah Car Rentals** (☑808-308-9566; www.mobettahcarrentals.com; car & SUV rental per week $340) offers cheap weekly rates on cars; it arranges pick-ups and drop-offs at the airport. **Molokai Car Rental** (☑808-336-0670; www.molokaicars.com; 109 Ala Malama Ave, Kaunakakai; car rental per day from $45; ☑9am-3pm Mon-Fri, to noon Sat) is a small local firm with a limited selection of cars and vans.

Kaunakakai

View a photo of Moloka'i's main town from 50 years ago and the main drag won't look much different today. Worn wood-fronted buildings with tin roofs that roar in the rain seem like refugees from a Clint Eastwood western. But there's no artifice to Kaunakakai – it's the real deal. All of the island's commercial activities are here and you'll visit it often – if nothing else, for its shops and services.

⊙ Sights

Kaunakakai Wharf PORT
(Map p256; Kaunakakai Pl) The busy commercial lifeline for Moloka'i. OK, it's not that busy... A freight barge chugs in, skippers unload catches of mahimahi (white-fleshed fish also called 'dolphin') and a buff gal practices for a canoe race. A roped-off area with a floating dock provides a kids' swim area.

Kapua'iwa Coconut Grove HISTORIC SITE
(Map p256; Maunaloa Hwy) As Moloka'i was the favorite island playground of King Kamehameha V, he had the royal 10-acre Kapua'iwa Coconut Grove planted near his

Moloka'i

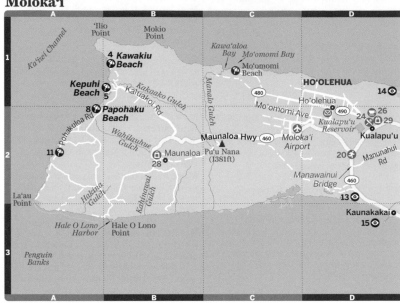

Moloka'i

sacred bathing pools in the 1860s. Standing tall, about a mile west of downtown, its name means 'mysterious taboo.' Be careful where you walk (or park) when you visit, because coconuts frequently plunge silently to the ground, landing with a deadly thump.

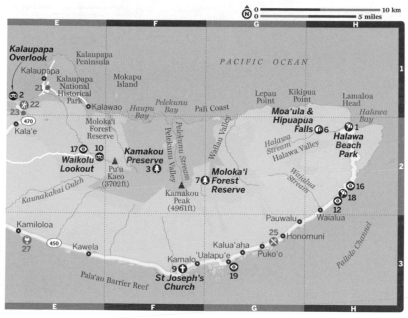

Activities

★ Moloka'i Bicycle
CYCLING

(Map p258; ☎ 808-553-5740; www.mauimolokai bicycle.com; 80 Mohala St, Kaunakakai; bike rental per day/week from $25/75; ⊙ 3-6pm Wed, 9am-2pm Sat & by appointment) This shop's owner, Phillip Kikukawa, has a great depth of knowledge about cycling across the breadth of the island. He'll do pick-ups and drop-offs outside his opening hours. As well as offering repairs, parts and sales, there is a wide selection of bikes to rent, including mountain bikes. Prices include helmet, lock, pump, maps and much more.

Beach Break Moloka'i
OUTDOORS

(Map p256; ☎ 808-567-6091; Holomua Jct, cnr Hwys 460 & 470; ⊙ 10am-4pm Mon-Sat) Offers a wide range of surf gear for sale. Surfboard rentals start at $20 per day and there are many kinds available, including stand up paddleboards (SUPs). Snorkeling sets are $10 per day, and you can also rent beach gear including chairs, coolers and umbrellas. Sale items include yoga mats.

☞ Tours

★ Moloka'i Outdoors
OUTDOORS

(☎ 808-553-4477, 877-553-4477; www.molokai-out doors.com; SUP/kayak tour adult/child from $68/35,

7-8hr island tour $166/87; ⊙ hours vary) Moloka'i Outdoors can custom-design adventures and arrange activities. Paddling and SUPs are its specialty and it can also arrange tours across the island. Kayak and SUP rentals (from $42 per day) can also include transport and pick-ups across the island (from $35).

★ Walter Naki
CULTURAL TOUR, BOAT TOUR

(Molokai Action Adventures; ☎ 808-558-8184) Walter Naki, who is also known for his cultural tours and treks, offers deep-sea fishing, whale-watching and highly recommended North Shore boat tours that include the Pali Coast. Prices negotiable.

Moloka'i Fish & Dive
OUTDOORS

(Map p258; ☎ 808-553-5926; www.molokai fishanddive.com; Ala Malama Ave, Kaunakakai; 2-tank boat dives incl equipment $165; ⊙ 6am-7pm) This is really the Big Kahuna of activities on the island. It operates fishing trips and rents gear. If you have a vague notion of something you'd like to do, come here and see what staff advise. It has a range of beach accessories such as chairs ($5) and umbrellas ($4).

✨ Festivals & Events

Ka Moloka'i Makahiki
CULTURAL

(Kaunakakai; ⊙ late Jan) The ancient makahiki festival, held after the year's main harvest

Kaunakakai

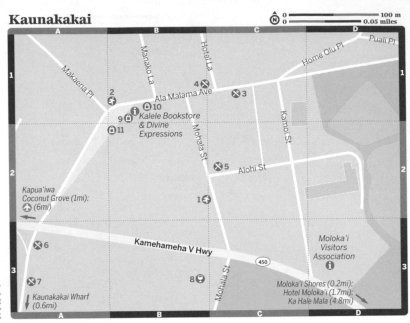

was complete, is still celebrated on Moloka'i. It features traditional ceremonies, an Olympics-esque competition of ancient Hawaiian sports, crafts and activities.

Moloka'i Ka Hula Piko   CULTURAL
(www.kahulapiko.com; ⊙May or Jun) **FREE** As Moloka'i is known as the birthplace of hula, its three-day hula festival has some profound roots. It opens with a solemn ceremony at 3am at Pu'u Nana (the site of Hawaii's first

hula school), followed by a festival including performance, food and crafts. Confirm the dates in advance.

✗ Eating

★ **Maka's Korner**   CAFE $
(Map p258; ☑808-553-8058; cnr Mohala & Alohi Sts; meals $5-10; ⊙7am-9pm Mon-Fri, 8am-1pm Sat & Sun) A dead-simple corner location belies the fine yet basic fare here. Moloka'i's best burgers come with excellent fries, although many patrons are simply addicted to the mahimahi (white-fleshed fish also called 'dolphin') sandwich (go nuts and order it dressed with two-shrimp tempura). Pancakes are served throughout the day. Sit at the tiny counter or at a picnic table outside.

Moloka'i Burger   BURGERS $
(Map p258; ☑808-553-3533; www.molokai burger.com; 20 Kamehameha V Hwy; mains $5-10; ⊙7am-9pm; 🛜) Moloka'i's only drive-through restaurant is a slick operation. The burgers come in many forms but are all thick and juicy. (Try a ramen burger, which is sandwiched between squares of fried noodles.) The dining room is inoffensive; the front terrace peacefully shady. Soft-serve ice cream is a treat.

Kanemitsu Bakery BAKERY $

(☑ 808-553-5855; 79 Ala Malama Ave; loaf of bread $5; ⊙ 5:30am-5pm Wed-Mon, hot bread 7:30am-11pm Tue-Sun) Known for its Moloka'i sweet bread and crackers (the macadamia-nut ones are extraordinary). Otherwise, you'll be surprised such good fresh-baked stuff can come from such a low place. Note: the best stuff is usually gone by 1pm.

Friendly Market SUPERMARKET $

(Map p258; ☑ 808-553-5595; 90 Ala Malama Ave; ⊙ 8:30am-8:30pm Mon-Fri, to 6:30pm Sat) The best selection of any supermarket on the island. In the afternoon fresh seafood from the wharf often appears.

Moloka'i Pizza Cafe PIZZA $

(Map p258; ☑ 808-553-3288; Kaunakakai Pl; meals $9-18; ⊙ 10am-10pm Mon-Thu, to 11pm Fri & Sat, 11am-10pm Sun) Order at the counter or have a seat in the starkly lit dining area at this pizza joint offering everything from salad and sub sandwiches to burgers and pasta. Lazy cooks can get their pizza half-baked (it's neither thick nor thin) and finish cooking it in their rental unit.

🍷 Drinking & Nightlife

★**Hale Kealoha** LOUNGE

(Map p256; ☑ 808-553-5347; Kamehameha V Hwy, Hotel Moloka'i; mains $15-25; ⊙ 7am-9pm) The Hotel Moloka'i's simple waterfront bar and restaurant has waterfront views and skippable food. However the don't-miss highlight are the local *kapuna* (elders) who gather at a long table to play Hawaiian music on 'Aloha Fridays' from 4pm to 6pm. The music always draws a crowd; the performers range from those with some languid and traditional hula moves to jam sessions with a ukulele.

It's a true community gathering with some of the people who are the heart and soul of local culture and who delight in showing off their traditional talents. Don't miss.

Paddler's Inn PUB

(Map p258; ☑ 808-553-3300; www.molokaipad dlersinn.com; 10 Mohala St; mains $8-20; ⊙ 8am-1am; 🛜) The island's only real pub has a large outside terrace that makes up in cheer what it lacks in charm. The long menu is served until about 9pm. Regular items include deep-fried pub grub, burgers, steaks and simple pastas; however, there are many specials on various theme nights. Watch for live performances by local musicians many nights.

🛍 Shopping

★**Kalele Bookstore & Divine Expressions** BOOKS

(☑ 808-553-5112; http://molokaispirit.com; 64 Ala Malama Ave; ⊙ 10am-5pm Mon-Fri, 9am-2pm Sat; 🛜) New and used books, local artworks and loads of local culture and travel advice. Few locals walk past without dropping in to say hi.

Moloka'i Art from the Heart ART

(Map p258; ☑ 808-553-8018; http://molokaigal lery.com; 64 Ala Malama Ave; ⊙ 9:30am-5pm Mon-Fri, 9am-2:30pm Sat) Run by local artists, this small shop is packed with arts and crafts. Works in all mediums can be found here; quality ranges from the earnest to the superb. The T-shirts with local sayings are the real sleepers in the souvenir department.

Saturday Morning Market MARKET

(Map p258; Ala Malama Ave; ⊙ 8am-2pm Sat) This weekly market at the west end of Ala Malama Ave is the place to browse local crafts, try new fruits, stock up on organic produce and pick up some flowers. You'll find most of Moloka'i here before noon.

ℹ Information

Bank of Hawaii (www.boh.com; Ala Malama Ave; ⊙ 8:30am-1pm & 2-4pm Mon-Thu, to 6pm Fri) Has one of several 24-hour ATMs in town.

Moloka'i General Hospital (☑ 808-553-5331; www.molokaigeneralhospital.org; 280 Homeolu Pl; ⊙ 24hr) Emergency services.

Moloka'i Visitors Association (MVA; Map p258; ☑ 808-553-3876; www.gohawaii.com/molokai; 2 Kamoi St; ⊙ 9am-3pm Mon-Fri) This simple office can help with info about member businesses. Look for events updates at www.facebook.com/MolokaiVisitorsAssociation.

ℹ Getting There & Away

Kaunakakai is a walking town. **Rawlin's Chevron** (cnr Maunaloa Hwy/Hwy 460 & Ala Malama Ave; ⊙ office 6:30am-8:30pm Mon-Sat, 7am-6pm Sun) has credit-card-operated pumps, making it the only round-the-clock gas station on the island.

East Moloka'i

The oft-quoted road sign 'Slow down, this is Moloka'i' really applies as you head east on the 27-mile drive on Hwy 450 (aka

FISHPONDS

Starting just east of Kaunakakai and continuing past mile marker 20 along Hwy 450 are dozens of *loko i'a* (fishponds), huge circular walls of rocks that are part of one of the world's most advanced forms of aquaculture. Monumental in size, backbreaking in creation, the fishponds operate on a simple principle: little fish swim in, big fish can't swim out. Some of the ponds are obscured and overgrown by mangroves, but others have been restored by locals anxious to preserve this link to their past. The **Kahinapohaku Fishpond**, about half a mile past mile marker 19, is in excellent shape. Another good one is **'Ualapu'e Fishpond** at mile marker 13.

Kamehameha V Hwy) from Kaunakakai to the Halawa Valley.

Unlike the arid west, this is tropical Moloka'i, with palm trees arching over the road. You'll also catch glimpses of ancient fishponds, stoic old wooden churches, modest family homes, beaches and much more. And watch for dogs sleeping on the yellow line. The final climb up and over into the remote Halawa Valley is breathtaking.

Kawela to Kalua'aha

◉ Sights

★ **St Joseph's Church**　　　　CHURCH
(Map p256; Hwy 450) Only two of the four Moloka'i churches that missionary and prospective saint Father Damien built outside of the Kalaupapa Peninsula are still standing. One of them is quaint little St Joseph's Church (the other is Our Lady of Seven Sorrows). This simple, one-room wooden church, dating from 1876, has a steeple and a bell, five rows of pews and some of the original wavy glass panes. It's just past mile marker 10. The door is usually open.

There is also a lei-draped statue of Father Damien and a little cemetery beside the church.

'Ualapu'e Fishpond　　　　HISTORIC SITE
(Map p256; Hwy 450) A half-mile beyond Wavecrest Resort condo development, at mile marker 13, you'll spot 'Ualapu'e Fishpond on the *makai* (seaward) side of the

road. This fishpond, which is a National Historic Landmark, has been restored and restocked with mullet and milkfish, two species that were raised here in ancient times. It's a good place to ponder the labor involved in moving these thousands of large volcanic rocks.

Puko'o to Rock Point

Puko'o was once the seat of local government (complete with a courthouse, jail, wharf and post office), but the center of island life shifted to Kaunakakai when the plantation folks built that more centrally located town. Nowadays, Puko'o is a sleepy, slow-paced gathering of a few structures.

◉ Sights & Activities

Kahinapohaku Fishpond　　　　HISTORIC SITE
(Map p256; Hwy 450) Ongoing restoration efforts have made this the premier fishpond on the island, tended by *konohiki* (caretakers) who live simply on site. You can see ancient fishing techniques in use today. It is a half-mile east of mile marker 19.

Twenty Mile Beach　　　　BEACH
(Murphy's Beach; Map p256; Hwy 450) Well protected by a reef, the curve of fine sand fronts a large lagoon that is great for snorkeling. Near shore there are rocks and the water can be very shallow, but work your way out and you'll be rewarded with schools of fish, living sponges, octopuses and much more.

Rock Point　　　　NATURAL FEATURE
(Map p256; Hwy 450) The pointy clutch of rocks sticking out, as the road swings left before the 21-mile marker, is called, appropriately enough, Rock Point. This popular **surf spot** is the site of local competitions and it's the place to go if you're looking for east-end swells.

✕ Eating

The market attached to Mana'e Goods & Grindz is small but well-stocked.

★ **Mana'e Goods & Grindz**　　　　HAWAIIAN $
(Map p256; ☑ 808-558-8186; Hwy 450; meals $5-13; ⊙ kitchen 6:30am-4pm daily, store 6:30am-6pm Mon-Fri, to 4pm Sat & Sun; ⊛) Even if it wasn't your only option, you'd still want to stop here. The plate lunches are something of a local legend: tender yet crispy chicken katsu, specials such as pork stew, and standards such as excellent teriyaki burgers and fresh

fish sandwiches served on perfectly grilled buns.

Halawa Valley

With stunningly gorgeous scenery, Halawa Valley enjoys end-of-the-road isolation, which residents guard jealously with gates and 'no trespassing' signs. It was an important settlement in precontact Moloka'i, with a population of more than 1000 and a complex irrigation system.

As late as the mid-19th century, the fertile valley still had a population of about 500 and produced much of the island's taro. Due to past tsunamis, only a few families now remain.

🏖 Beaches

★ Halawa Beach Park BEACH
(Map p256) Halawa Beach was a favored surfing spot for Moloka'i chiefs and is popular today with local kids, although often you won't see a soul. The beach has double coves separated by a rocky outcrop, with the north side a bit more protected than the south.

When the water is calm, there's good swimming and folks launch sea kayaks here, but both coves are subject to dangerous rip currents when the surf is heavy.

Up from the beach, Halawa Beach Park has picnic pavilions, restrooms and non-drinkable running water. Throughout the valley, there's an eerie feel that you can't quite shake, as if the generations that came before aren't sure what to make of it all. Some locals aren't entirely welcoming to visitors.

☞ Tours

See p244 for a hike through the Halawa Valley to Moa'ula and Hipuapua Falls.

★ Pilipo Solatario GUIDE
(Halawa Valley Falls Cultural Hike; ☑808-542-1855, 808-551-1055; www.halawavalleymolokai.com; adult/child $60/35; ☺ hikes most days 9am) Pilipo is a highly recommended guide who has lived most of his life in the Halawa Valley along with his family. He's an amazing storyteller and he regales guests with fascinating details of local culture. The actual hike is usually led by his son. Book well in advance.

Eddie Tanaka HIKING
(☑808-558-8396, 808-658-0191; edward.tanaka@yahoo.com; hikes from $60) Local musician and Moloka'i native Eddie Tanaka will

customize a hike to Moa'ula and Hipuapua Falls. Be sure to spend extra time on culture and lore.

Central Moloka'i

The western section of Central Moloka'i takes in Mo'omomi Beach and the coffee-growing center of Kualapu'u. To the east, the terrain rises sharply to the misty, ancient forests of Kamakou.

Moloka'i's second-most-popular drive (after the Halawa Valley drive in the east) runs from Kualapu'u up Hwy 470 to Pala'au State Park, site of the Kalaupapa Overlook, where you'll find one of the island's most captivating views.

Kamakou Area

The best reason to rent a 4WD vehicle on Moloka'i is for the views from the Waikolu Lookout before discovering the verdant mysteries of the Nature Conservancy's Kamakou Preserve, where you'll find the island's highest peaks. Exploring this secret side of Moloka'i is pure adventure. Besides gazing down into two deep valleys on the island's stunning and impenetrable north coast, you'll explore a near-pristine rainforest that is home to more than 250 native plant species (more than 200 endemic) and some of Hawaii's rarest birds. Although you can't quite reach the island's highest point, Kamakou Peak (4961ft), you'll still get your head in the clouds.

◉ Sights

★ Moloka'i Forest Reserve PARK
(Map p256) The 10-mile drive up to **Waikolu Lookout** takes about 45 minutes, depending on road conditions. You pass through open land with trees and scrubs that is technically the Moloka'i Forest Reserve, although little is developed and signs are few. A mile before the lookout you'll find the 19th-century **Sandalwood Pit**, a grassy depression on the left.

★ Kamakou Preserve PARK
(Map p256) Hiking back through three million years of evolution on the **Pepe'opae Trail** is Kamakou's star attraction. Crossed by a boardwalk, this undisturbed Hawaiian montane bog is a miniature primeval forest of stunted trees, dwarf plants and lichens that make it feel like it's the dawn of time. From

the trail's end at **Pelekunu Valley Overlook**, you'll be rewarded with a fantastic view of majestic cliffs, and, if it's not too cloudy, you'll see the ocean beyond.

To reach the Pepe'opae Trail from Waikolu Lookout, follow Kamakou's main 4WD road 2.5 miles to the marked trailhead; this makes a nice hour-long forest walk in itself.

A great way to see Kamakou is by joining one of the guided hikes led by the **Nature Conservancy** (☑808-553-5236; www.nature.org/hawaii; donation requested; ☉Mar-Oct) on the first or second Saturday of every month. Transportation is provided to and from the preserve.

Kualapu'u

Kualapu'u is the name of both a 1017ft hill and a nearby village. The world's largest rubber-lined reservoir lies at the base of the hill. Its 1.4 billion gallons of water are piped in from the rainforests of eastern Moloka'i and it is the only source of water for the Ho'olehua Plains and the dry West End.

In the 1930s the headquarters of the Del Monte pineapple plantation were located here and a company town grew. Pineapples ruled for nearly 50 years, until Del Monte pulled out of Moloka'i in 1982 and the economy crumbled.

✗ Eating & Drinking

★**Kualapu'u Cookhouse** HAWAIIAN $$
(Kamuela Cookhouse; Map p256; ☑808-567-9655; Hwy 490; mains $6-33; ☉7am-8pm Tue-Sat, 9am-2pm Sun, 7am-2pm Mon) This old roadhouse serves good lunches and is the only place for a meal west of Kaunakakai. Breakfasts feature huge omelets while plate-lunch options include excellent pork *tonkatsu* (breaded and fried cutlets). The dinner menu is more ambitious and includes ribs, steak and spicy crusted ahi (yellowfin tuna). Beer and wine can be purchased at the grocery across the street. Service is endearing. Cash only.

Coffees of Hawaii CAFE
(Map p256; ☑808-567-6830; www.coffeesofhawaii.com; cnr Hwys 470 & 490; ☉7am-4pm Mon-Sat, to 2pm Sun; 🛜) Coffees of Hawaii grows and roasts its own coffee on small plots around its attractive and easily reached setting. You can survey the scene from the verandah and enjoy a cup of the local coffee and a snack.

🛍 Shopping

Blue Monkey GIFTS & SOUVENIRS
(Map p256; ☑808-567-6776; www.bigwindkites.com/bluemonkey; cnr Hwys 470 & 490; ☉10am-5pm Mon-Sat) This large and colorful gift shop in the Coffees of Hawaii buildings offers an excellent selection of local goods and books.

Pala'au State Park

⊙ Sights

★**Kalaupapa Overlook** VIEWPOINT
(Map p256; Pala'au State Park) The Kalaupapa Overlook provides a scenic overview of the Kalaupapa Peninsula from the edge of a 1600ft cliff. It's easy to get the lay of the land from up here and you'll get a good feel for just how far you'll travel if you descend the nearly 1700ft on the trail. Interpretive plaques identify significant landmarks below and explain Kalaupapa's history.

Kauleonanahoa CULTURAL SITE
(Map p256; Pala'au State Park) Kauleonanahoa (the penis of Nanahoa) is Hawaii's premier phallic stone, standing proud in a little clearing inside an ironwood grove, about a five-minute walk from the parking area. The legend goes that Nanahoa hit his wife Kawahuna in a jealous rage and, when they were both turned to stone, he came out looking like a dick, literally. (The stone has been modified through the years to emphasize its appearance.)

Reputedly, women who come here with offerings of lei and stay overnight will soon get pregnant. There's no mention of what happens to men who might try the same thing with some nearby stones that have been carved into a female counterpart to the main rock.

Kalaupapa National Historical Park

The spectacularly beautiful **Kalaupapa Peninsula** is the most remote part of Hawaii's most isolated island. The only way to reach this lush green peninsula edged with long, white-sand beaches is on a twisting trail down the steep *pali*, the world's highest sea cliffs, or by plane. This remoteness is the reason it was, for more than a century, where Hansen's disease (leprosy) patients were forced into isolation.

DON'T MISS

POST-A-NUT

Why settle for a mundane postcard or, worse, an emailed photo of you looking like a tan-lined moron, when it comes to taunting folks in the cold climes you've left behind? Instead, send a coconut. Gary Lam, the world-class postmaster of the **Ho'olehua post office** (☑ 808-567-6144; Pu'u Peelua Ave; ⊙ 8:30am-4pm Mon-Fri), has baskets of them for free. Choose from the oodles of markers and write the address right on the husk. Add a cartoon or two. Imagine the joy when a loved one waits in a long line for a parcel and is handed a coconut! Depending on the size of your nut, postage costs $12 to $22 and takes three to six days to reach any place in the US; other countries cost more and take longer – and you may run into quarantine issues.

If Lam, who takes the time to apply a panoply of colored stamps to each coconut, was in charge of the postal service, its current financial woes would likely vanish. Should you want your nut made especially ornate, Teri Waros of **Kalele Bookstore** (☑ 808-567-9094; http://molokaispirit.com; 64 Ala Malama Ave; ⊙ 10am-5pm Mon-Fri, 9am-2pm Sat; ☎) does custom paint jobs.

From the colony's inception until separation ended in 1969, 8000 patients were forced to come to Kalaupapa. Less than a dozen patients (respectively called 'residents') remain. They have chosen to stay in the only home they have ever known and have resisted efforts to move them away. The peninsula has been designated a national historical park and is managed by the Hawaii Department of Health and the **National Park Service** (☑ 808-567-6802; www.nps.gov/kala).

Since visitor numbers are limited each day, you must have a reservation with Damien Tours.

History

In 1835 doctors in Hawaii diagnosed the state's first case of leprosy, one of many diseases introduced by foreigners. Alarmed by the spread of the disease, King Kamehameha V signed a law that banished people with Hansen's disease to Kalaupapa Peninsula, beginning in 1866.

Hawaiian call leprosy *i mai ho'oka'awale*, which means 'separating sickness,' a reference to how the disease tore families apart. Once the afflicted arrived on Kalaupapa Peninsula, there was no way out, not even in a casket. Early conditions were unspeakably horrible and lifespans short.

Father Damien (Joseph de Veuster), a Belgian priest, arrived at Kalaupapa in 1873. A talented carpenter, he built 300 simple houses, nursed the sick and buried the dead. Damien's work inspired others, including Mother Marianne Cope, who stayed 30 years and came to be known as the mother of the hospice movement. Damien died of leprosy in 1889 at the age of 49.

In 2009 he became Hawaii's (and America's) first Catholic saint.

🏃 Activities

★ Kalaupapa Trail   HIKING

(Map p256) The Kalaupapa trailhead is on the east side of Hwy 470, just north of the mule stables, and is marked by the Pala'au park sign and parked Kalaupapa employee cars. The 3-mile trail has 26 switchbacks, 1400 steps and drops 1664ft in elevation from start to finish.

It's best to begin hiking by 8am, before the mules start to go down, to avoid walking in fresh dung, though you have no choice on the return trip. Allow an hour and a half to descend comfortably. It can be quite an adventure after a lot of rain, though the rocks keep it from getting impossibly muddy. Many find walking sticks a huge help.

🖙 Tours

★ Molokai Mule Ride   TOURS

(Map p256; ☑ 808-567-6088; www.muleride.com; Hwy 470; tour $210; ⊙ tours start 7:45am Mon-Sat) Just an incredible journey, a mule ride is the only way down the *pali* (cliffside) besides hiking, but be prepared – this is not an easy ride. You'll be sore afterwards, even if you're an experienced rider – and it's a safe bet that you've never experienced a ride like this one. Make reservations for the mule ride well in advance.

★ Damien Tours   BUS

(Map p256; ☑ 808-567-6171, 808-221-2153; www.damientoursllc.com; tour $60; ⊙ Mon-Sat) Everyone who comes to the Kalaupapa Peninsula is required to visit the settlement with this tour. If you didn't book through Moloka'i Mule Ride, reservations must be made in advance (call between 4pm and 8pm). Tours last 3½ hours, are done by bus and are accompanied by lots of stories about life in years past. If you're not on the mule ride or other packaged tour, bring your own lunch and a bottle of water. You must be 16 or over.

Pick-ups for the tours are at 10am, whether you arrive on the peninsula on foot, by mule or on a plane.

ℹ️ Getting There & Away

Makani Kai Air (☎877-255-8532, 808-834-1111; www.makanikaiair.com; round-trip tour package from Moloka'i/Honolulu $249/315) Runs regular flights from Ho'olehua on Moloka'i and from Honolulu, which are timed to allow for visits in a day. Packages include your place on **Damien Tours** (p263). A package including walking down, taking the tour and flying back up topside is $149.

West End

Apparently uninhabited, Moloka'i's West End seems just a couple of missed rainfalls from becoming a desert. Much of the land has been controlled by the Moloka'i Ranch. Its fortunes – for better and more recently for much worse – have affected the entire island.

Given the economic woes of Moloka'i Ranch, the atmosphere out west is a bit bleak. With the exception of one superlative store, Maunaloa might as well hold tumbleweed races, while the Kaluakoi resort area is beset by financial troubles. Still, you can ignore all the earthly turmoil on one of the many fine beaches.

Kaluakoi Resort Area

🏖️ Beaches

★ **Kepuhi Beach**   BEACH
(Map p256; off Kenani Kai) You can see why they built the defunct Kaluakoi Hotel here: the beach is a rocky, white-sand dream. However, swimming here can be a nightmare. Not only can there be a tough shorebreak, but strong currents are often present even on calm days.

During winter, the surf breaks close to shore, crashing in sand-filled waves that provide a brutal exfoliation.

A five-minute hike up to the top of **Pu'u o Kaiaka** (Map p256; off Kaiaka Rd), a 110ft-high promontory at the southern end of the beach, is rewarded with a nice view of Papohaku Beach. At the top you'll find the remains of a pulley that was once used to carry cattle down to waiting barges for transport over to O'ahu slaughterhouses. There was also a 40ft heiau on the hilltop until 1967, when the US army bulldozed it (and gave the superstitious another reason to ponder the local run of bad luck). There's plenty of parking in the resort's cracked parking lots.

★ **Kawakiu Beach**   BEACH
(Map p256) Kaluakoi's northernmost beach is also the best. Kawakiu Beach is a broad crescent beach of white sand and bright-turquoise waters. It's partially sheltered from the winds that can bedevil the beaches to the south and when seas are calm, usually in summer, Kawakiu is generally safe for swimming.

When the surf is rough, there are still areas where you can at least get wet. On the southern side of the bay, there's a small, sandy-bottomed wading pool in the rocks; the northern side has an area of flat rocks over which water slides to fill up a shallow shoreline pool. Spindly kiawe trees provide shade. Outside of weekends, you may well have the place to yourself.

To get there, turn off Kaluakoi Rd onto the road to the **Paniolo Hale** condos, but instead of turning left to the condos, continue straight toward the former golf course. Where the paved road ends there's space to pull over and park. You'll come first to a rocky point at the southern end of the bay. Before descending to the beach, scramble around up here for a scenic view of the coast, south to Papohaku Beach and north to 'Ilio Point.

Maunaloa

★ **Big Wind Kite Factory & Plantation Gallery**   ARTS & CRAFTS
(Map p256; ☎808-552-2364; www.bigwindkites.com; 120 Maunaloa Hwy; ⊙10am-4pm Mon-Sat, 1-4pm Sun) Big Wind custom-makes kites for high fliers of all ages. It has hundreds ready to go in stock or you can choose a design and watch production begin. Lessons are available, lest you have a Charlie Brown experience with a kite-eating tree.

There is a range of other goods to browse as well, including an excellent selection of

Hawaii-themed books and artworks, clothing and crafts originating from everywhere, from just down the road to far-off Bali.

West End Beaches

★ Papohaku Beach
BEACH

(Map p256; off Kalua Koi Rd) Straight as a palm tree, the light-hued sands of Papohaku Beach run for an astounding 2.5 miles. The sand is soft and you can often stroll from one end to the other without seeing another soul. Offshore, **Third Hole** is one of the island's most challenging surf breaks.

But just when you think you have found the ultimate strand, consider a few leveling details. That intoxicating surf is also a tangle of undertow and unpredictable currents. And there's no easy shade. You can bring an umbrella, but the often strong winds may send it O'ahu-bound. Those same breezes kick up the fine sand, which can sting on blustery days. So come here for the solitude, but do so with your eyes figuratively, if not literally, wide open.

There are seven turnoffs from Kalua Koi Rd that access the beach and have parking. The first leads to Papohaku Beach Park, a grassy place with picnic facilities under gnarled ironwood and kiawe trees. Bathroom and shower facilities are rugged. You can camp here to the left of the restrooms as you face them from the parking lot, the 'no camping' sign only applies to the area to the right (be sure to read the signs that explain which areas are soaked by the automatic sprinklers on which days). There are seldom any other campers here and the view of the stars at night and the sound of surf is mesmerizing. However, the park can be popular with rowdy folks young and old and occasionally some try to stay the night. Guards are meant to check permits but you may be happier here if you are not alone.

Dixie Maru Beach
BEACH

(Map p256; off Pohakuloa Rd) South of the long stretch of Papohaku Beach, there are small sandy coves surrounded by rocky outcrops. At the southern end of Pohakuloa Rd there's a parking lot with access to a narrow, round inlet, which the ancient Hawaiians knew as Kapukahehu.

It is now called Dixie Maru, after a ship that went down in the area long ago. It's the most protected cove on the west shore, and the most popular swimming and snorkeling area. The waters are generally calmer here than other West End beaches.

Papohaku Beach Park
BEACH

(Map p256; off Kalua Koi Rd) A grassy place with picnic facilities under gnarled ironwood and kiawe trees. The bathroom and shower facilities are rugged.

LANA'I & MOLOKA'I WEST END

Top: Northeast coast of Moloka'i.

Bottom: Kayaking off Lana'i.

Understand Maui

Maui Today

Whether it's commercial development, eco-minded activism or discussions about the modern sovereignty movement, the biggest issues on Maui today are intricately connected with the Hawaiian concept of *aloha 'aina*, which is a term meaning 'love and respect for the land.' Specific issues dominating recent headlines? The closure of the island's last sugar mill, new initiatives geared to protecting the island's parks, and efforts to ban genetically modified crops.

Best on Film

The Devil at 4 O'Clock (1961) Spencer Tracy & Frank Sinatra hang out at Lahaina's Pioneer Inn

Riding Giants (2004) Documentary spotlighting surf culture, with big-wave surfers riding waves off Maui

Just Go With It (2011) Adam Sandler & Jennifer Aniston have misadventures at the Grand Wailea Resort

Hereafter (2011) Clint Eastwood's film shot scenes on Front St in Lahaina

Best in Print

Middle Son (2000) Deborah Iida describes 1950s Maui through the eyes of a sugar-plantation laborer

The Maui Coast: Legacy of the King's Highway (2015) Daniel Sullivan captures the enduring majesty of the historic King's Hwy in this vibrant photo book

A Hawaiian Life (2000) Grammy-winning slack key guitarist and host of the Slack Key Show at Napili Kai Beach Resort, George Kahumoku Jr shares stories about life in Hawaii

Maui: A History (2014) This easy-to-read book by Cummins E Speakman Jr and Jill Engledow tells the story of the Valley Isle

Staying Hawaiian

Hawaiian culture today is about much more than melodic place names and luau shows. Traditional arts and healing arts are experiencing a revival, ancient heiau (temples) and fishponds are being restored, native forests replaced and endangered birds bred and released.

Although few island residents can agree on what shape the fragmented Native Hawaiian sovereignty movement should take, or even if it should exist at all, its grassroots political activism has achieved tangible results. Decades of protest and a federal lawsuit filed by sovereignty activists finally pressured the US military into returning the island of Kaho'olawe (which it had used for bombing practice since WWII) to the state in 1994. In 2011, then-governor Neil Abercrombie signed into law a bill recognizing Native Hawaiians as the state's only indigenous people.

In 2016 Disney released the movie *Moana,* an immediate blockbuster. In the film, Moana, the daughter of an ancient Polynesian chieftain, sets out to sea on a mission to restore her people's seafaring ways. She's helped by the demigod Maui, who is based on an actual figure in Polynesian mythology. Filmmakers worked closely with anthropologists and cultural advisers to stay accurate and culturally sensitive. There were some missteps, however, like the film's depiction of Maui as heroic, but also overweight and slightly buffoonish. Effective storytelling or harmful cultural appropriation? Maybe the key lies in the discussions and awareness sparked since the film's release.

Time Marches On

The sugar mill operated by Hawaiian Commercial & Sugar in central Maui shut down operations in 2016. Owned by Alexander & Baldwin (A&B), a company with roots stretching back to the island's earliest missionaries, the mill had come under intense criticism in recent years for its sugarcane burns. Many residents were concerned that the resulting smoke was linked to lung disease. But the reason for the closure? Past and projected operating losses. The sugarcane plantation, which opened in 1870 and eventually covered 36,000 acres, was the last in Hawaii. Future plans for the land are up in the air, although A&B has discussed using the acreage for a diverse range of agricultural projects.

In Makena, 300 people lost their jobs when the Makena Beach & Golf resort closed for good. The striking, fortresslike hotel and its surrounding property had operated as a resort – last known as the Maui Prince Resort – for 30 years.

In a thoroughly modern move, the State Department of Health granted licenses to eight medical-marijuana dispensaries. Two are for dispensaries in Maui. One of them expects to begin dispensing cannabis products from its office in Kahului in 2017.

Protecting the Parks

In recent years, heavy crowds have flocked to the summit of Haleakalā National Park to watch the sunrise. To control the number of visitors and protect the fragile landscape, the park has decided to require predawn visitors to make an advance trip reservation and pay a small fee. How bad was the crowding? Summit parking lots can accommodate about 150 cars, but the number of vehicles has regularly exceeded 300, with more than 1000 visitors often bumping elbows at sunrise viewpoints.

Officials at the Division of Land and Natural Resources (DLNR) are also considering implementing a parking fee at a popular snorkeling spot – informally known as The Dumps – at remote 'Ahihi-Kina'u Natural Area Reserve. This fragile snorkeling destination can see up to 500 visitors per day. A paved parking lot here is already in the works.

POPULATION: **164,637**

LAND AREA: **1,161.5 SQ MILES**

UNEMPLOYMENT: **2.7%**

if Maui were 100 people

36 would be white
29 would be Asian
11 would be Hispanic or Latino
11 would be Native Hawaiian or Pacific Islander
1 would be African American
12 would be other

belief systems

(% of population)

63 Christian

26 none

8 Buddhist

3 other

population per sq mile

MAUI

BIG ISLAND

O'AHU

 ≈ 50 people

History

Maui's early history mirrors the rest of Hawaii's, with warring chiefs, periods of peace, missionaries, whalers and sugarcane. More recently, tourism has become a driving economic force across Maui and much of the state as a whole.

How does Maui stand apart today? In the 21st century the Valley Isle has been a leader in eco-activism, establishing parks and reserves, banning plastic bags and leading the charge against genetically modified foods.

The Great Canoe Voyages

The earliest Polynesian settlers of Hawaii came ashore around AD 500. Archaeologists disagree on exactly where these explorers came from, but artifacts indicate the first to arrive were from the Marquesas Islands. The next wave of settlers were from Tahiti and arrived around AD 1000. Unlike the Marquesans, who sparsely settled the tiny islands at the northwest end of the Hawaiian Islands, the Tahitians arrived in great numbers and settled each of the major islands in the Hawaiian chain. Though no one knows what set them on course for Hawaii, when they arrived in their great double-hulled canoes they were prepared to colonize a new land, bringing with them pigs, dogs, taro roots and other crop plants.

The Tahitian discovery of Hawaii may have been an accident, but subsequent journeys were not. They were highly skilled seafarers, using only the wind, stars and wave patterns to guide them. Yet, incredibly, they memorized their route over 2400 miles of open Pacific and repeated the journeys between Hawaii and Tahiti for centuries.

And what a story they must have brought back with them, because vast waves of Tahitians followed to pursue a new life in Hawaii. So great were the number of Tahitian migrations that Hawaii's population probably reached a peak of approximately 250,000 by the year 1450. The voyages back and forth continued until around 1500, when all contact between Tahiti and Hawaii appears to have stopped.

The community website www.hawaiihistory.org offers an interactive timeline of Hawaii's history plus essays delving into every aspect of ancient Hawaiian culture, with evocative images and links.

TIMELINE	900,000 years ago	AD 300–600	1000–1300
	The volcanoes that formed Maui rise from the sea; the build-up continues until 400,000 BC.	Polynesian colonists, traveling thousands of miles across open seas in double-hulled canoes, arrive in Hawaii. They most likely came from the Marquesas Islands.	Sailing from Tahiti, a second wave of Polynesians arrives. Their tools are made of stone, shells and bone. They bring taro, sugarcane, coconuts, chickens and pigs.

Royal Power Struggles

From the early days of Polynesian settlement, Maui was divided into separate kingdoms, with rival chiefs occasionally rising up to battle for control of this and other islands in the archipelago.

In the 16th century Pi'ilani, the king of the Hana region, marched north to conquer Lele (now Lahaina) and Wailuku, uniting Maui for the first time under a single royal rule. He continued construction of the King's Hwy, begun by ancient Hawaiians. His son, Kiha-a-Pi'ilani, began building the Pi'ilani Hwy, which would connect with the King's Hwy and form a road that eventually looped 138 miles around Maui.

During the 1780s Maui's King Kahekili became the most powerful chief in all Hawaii, bringing both O'ahu and Moloka'i under Maui's rule.

In 1790, while Kahekili was in O'ahu, Kamehameha the Great of Hawai'i launched a bold naval attack on Maui. Using foreign-acquired cannons and two foreign seamen, Isaac Davis and John Young, Kamehameha defeated Maui's warriors. The battle at 'Iao Valley was so fierce and bloody that the waters of 'Iao Stream ran red for days.

An attack on his own homeland of Hawai'i by a Big Island rival forced Kamehameha to withdraw from Maui, but the battle continued over the years. When the aging Kahekili died in 1794, his kingdom was divided among two quarreling heirs, leaving a rift that Kamehameha quickly exploited.

In 1795 Kamehameha invaded Maui again, now with a force of 6000 canoes. This time he conquered the entire island and brought it under his permanent rule. Later that year Kamehameha went on to conquer O'ahu and unite all of the Hawaiian Islands – except Kaua'i – under his reign.

In 1802, Kamehameha established Lahaina as his royal court, where he built a royal residence made of brick, the first Western-style building in Hawaii. The king of Kaua'i agreed to cede to Kamehameha's rule in 1810, allowing Kamehameha to become the first *mo'i* (king) of the Kingdom of

Native Hawaiian Sites

Pi'ilanihale Heiau (p224)

Haleki'i-Pihana Heiau State Monument (p140)

Brick Palace (p85)

Hauola Stone (p84)

Hoapili Trail (King's Hwy Trail; p150)

Hana Cultural Center (p235)

HISTORY ROYAL POWER STRUGGLES

EARLY LAND DIVISIONS

Before contact with Europeans, rulers on Maui divided the island into 12 districts, each known as a *moku*. Eight of these districts dropped to the sea from Pōhaku Pālaha, a rock on the northeast rim of Haleakalā. The 12 *moku* were further divided into subregions known as *ahupua'a*. These wedge-shaped regions were separated by ridgelines and other natural formations. Each *ahupua'a* contained the resources necessary for the survival of the communities living within the wedge.

Taro is now a Hawaii food staple

1500	1778
The migration voyages between the South Pacific and Hawaii come to an end.	Briton Captain James Cook becomes the first-known Westerner to sight Maui.

Hawaii. Lahaina remained the kingdom's capital until 1845, when King Kamehameha III moved the capital to Honolulu on O'ahu.

European Explorers

On January 18, 1778, an event occurred on the islands that would change the life of Hawaiians in ways inconceivable at the time. On that day British explorer Captain James Cook sighted Hawaii while en route to the Pacific Northwest, in search of a possible 'northwest passage' between the Pacific and Atlantic oceans.

Cook's appearance was not only the first Western contact, it also marked the end of Hawaii's 300 years of complete isolation following the end of the Tahitian voyages. Cook anchored on the Big Island, across the channel from Maui, and stayed long enough to refresh his food supplies before continuing his journey north.

Cook sighted Maui but never set foot on the island. The first Westerner to land on Maui was French explorer Jean-François de Galaup, comte de La Pérouse, who sailed into Keone'o'io Bay (now called La Perouse Bay) on Maui's southern shore in 1786, traded with the Hawaiians and left after two days of peaceful contact.

Here Come the Westerners

After Captain Cook's ships returned to England, news of his discovery quickly spread throughout Europe and America, opening the floodgates to an invasion of foreign explorers, traders, missionaries and fortune hunters.

By the 1820s Hawaii had become a critical link in the strengthening trade route between China and the US, with British, American, French

---

A PLACE OF REFUGE

In ancient Hawai'i, a very strict code – called the kapu (taboo) system – governed daily life. If a commoner dared to eat *moi*, a type of fish reserved for *ali'i* (royalty or chiefs), for example, it was a violation of kapu. Penalties for such transgressions could be harsh, even including death. Furthermore, in a society based on mutual respect, slights to honor – whether of one's chief or extended family – could not be abided.

Although ancient Hawai'i could be a fiercely uncompromising place, it was offered forgiveness for errors. Anyone who had broken kapu or been defeated in battle could avoid the death penalty by fleeing to a *pu'uhonua* (a place of refuge). At the heiau (stone temple), a kahuna (priest) would perform purification rituals, lasting from a few hours up to several days. Absolved of their transgressions, kapu breakers were free to return home in safety.

1786	1790	1810	1819
French explorer La Pérouse becomes the first Westerner to land on Maui.	Kamehameha the Great invades Maui, decimating island warriors in a bloody battle at 'Iao Valley.	Kamehameha the Great moves to Maui, declaring Lahaina the royal seat of the Hawaiian kingdom.	Kamehameha the Great dies and the Hawaiian religious system is cast aside.

and Russian traders all using Hawaii as a mid-Pacific stop for provisioning their ships.

Missionary Activities

By a twist of fate, the first missionaries to Maui arrived at a fortuitous time, when Hawaiian society was in great upheaval after the death of Kamehameha the Great in 1819. The missionaries were able to make inroads with Hawaiian leaders, and it made their efforts to save the souls of the 'heathen' Hawaiians much easier. The *ali'i* (royalty), in particular, were keen on the reading lessons the missionaries offered in the Hawaiian language, which had never before had a written form. Indeed, by the middle of the 1850s, Hawaii had a higher literacy rate than the USA.

Lahaina became a center of activity for missionaries and their various projects. In 1831 Lahainaluna Seminary (now Lahainaluna High School), in the hills above Lahaina, became the first secondary school to be established west of the Rocky Mountains, while Lahaina's newspaper, *Ka Lama Hawaii* (The Hawaiian Luminary), was likewise a first west of the Rockies.

But the New England missionaries also helped to destroy traditional Hawaiian culture. They prohibited hula dancing because of its lewd and suggestive movements and denounced the traditional Hawaiian chants and songs as they paid homage to the Hawaiian gods. In the late 19th century, missionary teachers even managed to prohibit the speaking of the Hawaiian language in schools as another means of turning Hawaiians away from their 'hedonistic' cultural roots – a major turnaround from the early missionary days, when all students were taught in Hawaiian.

In *Blue Latitudes: Boldly Going Where Captain Cook Has Gone Before* (2002), Tony Horwitz examines the controversial legacy of Captain Cook's South Sea Voyage, interweaving amusing real-life adventure tales with bittersweet oral history.

Whalers

The first whaling ship to stop in Maui was the *Balena,* which anchored at Lahaina in 1819. The crew was mostly New England Yankees with a sprinkling of Gay Head Indians and former slaves. As more ships arrived, men of all nationalities roamed Lahaina's streets, most in their teens or twenties and ripe for adventure. Lahaina became a bustling port of call with shopkeepers catering to the whalers; saloons, brothels and hotels boomed.

A convenient way station for whalers of both the Arctic and Japanese whaling grounds, by the 1840s Hawaii was the whaling center of the Pacific. In Lahaina the whalers could transfer their catch to trade ships bound for America, allowing them to stay longer in the Pacific and resulting in higher profits. At the peak of the whaling era, more than 500 whaling ships were pulling into Lahaina each year.

1819

The first whaling ship anchors in Lahaina, Maui.

1820

Christian missionaries arrive, filling the gap left by the abandonment of Hawaii's traditional religion.

JUSTIN DELARA/500PX ©

A breaching humpback whale

Whaling brought big money to Maui and the dollars spread beyond its main port. Many Maui farmers got their start supplying the whaling ships with potatoes. Hawaiians themselves made good whalers, and sea captains gladly paid a $200 bond to the Hawaiian government for each Hawaiian sailor allowed to join their crew. Kamehameha IV even set up his own fleet of whaling ships that sailed under the Hawaiian flag.

Whaling in the Pacific peaked in the mid-19th century and quickly began to burn itself out. In a few short years, all but the most distant whaling grounds were being depleted and whalers were forced to go further afield to make their kills.

The last straw for the Pacific whaling industry came in 1871, when an early storm in the Arctic caught more than 30 ships by surprise, trapping them in ice floes above the Bering Strait. Although more than 1000 seamen were rescued, half of them Hawaiian, the fleet itself was lost.

Missionary Era Sites

Baldwin House (p82)

Hale Pa'i (http://lahainarestoration.org/hale-pai-museum/)

Bailey House Museum (p138)

David Malo's Church (p156)

Sugarcane

Maui's role in sugar production began in 1839, when King Kamehameha III issued small parcels of land to individual growers who were then required to have their crop processed at the king's mill in Wailuku. Half of every crop went to the king. Of the remaining half, one-fifth was taken as a tax to support the government and the remainder went to the grower.

In the heyday of sugar, there were as many as 10 plantations on Maui, cultivating thousands of acres of land throughout the island. One of the most prominent mills, the Pioneer Mill in Lahaina, was founded in 1863 by American entrepreneurs. In 1876 the Hamakua Ditch began transporting water from the rainy mountains to irrigate the dry plains, allowing the plantations to spread. In the 1880s a train began transporting freshly cut sugarcane to Pioneer Mill.

Immigration for Labor

As sugar production increased, sugar barons were worried about the shortage of field laborers, who were mostly Hawaiian. There had been a

---

A BLOODY CONFRONTATION

In January 1790 the American ship *Eleanora* arrived on Maui, eager to trade Western goods for food supplies and sandalwood. Late one night a party of Hawaiian men stole the ship's skiff. In retaliation, Captain Simon Metcalf lured a large group of Hawaiians to his ship under the pretense of trading with them. Instead he ordered his men to fire every shipboard cannon and gun at the Hawaiians, murdering over 100 men, women and children. This tragic event, one of the first contacts between Westerners and Maui islanders, is remembered as the Olowalu Massacre.

1831	1848	1868	1893
Lahainaluna Seminary, the first secondary school west of the Rocky Mountains, is built in Lahaina.	Under the influence of Westerners, the first system of private land ownership is introduced in the islands.	Thousands of Japanese laborers arrive on Maui to work newly planted sugarcane fields.	While attempting to restore Native Hawaiian rights, Queen Lili'uokalani is overthrown by American businessmen.

severe decline in the Native Hawaiian population due to introduced diseases, such as typhoid, influenza and smallpox, for which the Hawaiians had no immunity. To expand their operations, plantation owners began to look overseas for a cheap labor supply. First they recruited laborers from China, then recruiters went to Japan in 1868, and in the 1870s they brought in Portuguese workers from Madeira and the Azores islands.

The labor contracts typically lasted for two to three years, with wages as low as $1 per week. Workers lived in ethnically divided 'camps' set up by the plantations, which included modest housing, a company store, a social hall and other recreational amenities. At the end of their contracts, some workers returned to their homelands, but most remained on the islands, integrating into the multicultural mainstream. Alexander & Baldwin, a company created by the sons of missionaries, opened a sugar plantation on Maui in 1870. The plantation's immigrant past is explored in the on-site museum.

After Hawaii's 1898 annexation, US laws, including racially biased prohibitions against Chinese immigration, were enforced in Hawaii. Because of these new restrictions, plantation owners turned their recruiting efforts to Puerto Rico and Korea. Filipinos were the last group of immigrants brought to Hawaii to work in the fields and mills, between 1906 and 1946.

The Great Land Grab

Throughout the period of the monarchy, the ruling sovereigns of Hawaii fought off continual efforts on the part of European and American settlers to gain control of the kingdom.

In 1848, under pressure from foreigners who wanted to own land, a sweeping land-reform act known as the Great Mahele was instituted. This act allowed, for the first time, the ownership of land, which had previously been held exclusively by monarchs and chiefs. The chiefs had not owned the land in the Western sense but were caretakers of both the land and the commoners who lived and worked on the land, giving their monarchs a portion of the harvest in return for the right to stay.

The reforms of the Great Mahele had far-reaching implications. For foreigners, who had money to buy land, it meant greater economic and political power. For Hawaiians, who had little or no money, it meant a loss of land-based self-sufficiency and enforced entry into the low-wage labor market, primarily run by Westerners.

When King David Kalakaua came to power in 1874, American businessmen had wrested substantial control over the economy and were bent on gaining control over the political scene as well. King Kalakaua was an impassioned Hawaiian revivalist, known as the 'Merrie Monarch.' He brought back the hula, reversing decades of missionary repression

For more than a century beginning in 1866, Moloka'i's Kalaupapa Peninsula was a place of involuntary exile for those afflicted with leprosy (now called Hansen's disease). In *The Colony: The Harrowing True Story of the Exiles of Molokai*, John Tayman tells the survivors' stories with dignity, compassion and unflinching honesty.

1898	1901
Hawaii is annexed by the USA and becomes a US territory.	The Pioneer Inn, Maui's first hotel, is built on the waterfront in Lahaina.

The Pioneer Inn on the Lahaina waterfront

against the 'heathen dance,' and he composed 'Hawaii Ponoi', which is now the state song. The king also tried to ensure a degree of self-rule for Native Hawaiians, who had become a minority in their own land.

Overthrow of the Monarch

When King Kalakaua died in 1891, his sister ascended the throne. Queen Lili'uokalani was a staunch supporter of her brother's efforts to maintain Hawaiian independence.

In January 1893 Queen Lili'uokalani was preparing to proclaim a new constitution to restore royal powers when a group of armed US businessmen occupied the Supreme Court and declared the monarchy to be overthrown. They announced a provisional government, led by Sanford B Dole, son of a pioneer missionary family.

After the monarchy's overthrow, the new government leaders pushed hard for annexation by the US, believing that it would bring greater stability to the islands, and more profits to Caucasian-run businesses. Although US law required that any entity petitioning for annexation must have the backing of the majority of its citizens through a public vote, no such vote was held in Hawaii.

Nonetheless, on July 7, 1898, President William McKinley signed a joint congressional resolution approving annexation. Some historians feel that Hawaii would not have been annexed if it had not been for the outbreak of the Spanish-American War in April 1898, which sent thousands of US troops to the Philippines, making Hawaii a crucial Pacific staging point for the war.

WWII

On December 7, 1941, when Japanese warplanes appeared above the Pearl Harbor area, most residents thought they were mock aircraft being used in US Army and Navy practice maneuvers. Even the loud anti-aircraft gunfire didn't raise much concern. Of course, it *was* the real thing, and by the day's end hundreds of ships and airplanes had been destroyed, more than 1000 Americans had been killed and the war in the Pacific had begun.

The impact on Hawaii was dramatic. The army took control of the islands, martial law was declared and civil rights were suspended. Unlike on the mainland, Japanese Americans in Hawaii were not sent to internment camps because they made up most of the labor force in the cane fields in Hawaii's sugar-dependent economy. Thousands of Japanese Americans, many from Hawaii, eventually fought for the US. Many were decorated for their bravery.

The War Department stationed the 4th Marine Division on Maui, where thousands of marines conducted training exercises for combat

---

Part political statement, part historical treatise, *To Steal a Kingdom: Probing Hawaiian History* (1995) by Michael Dougherty takes a hard look at the legacy of Western colonialism and the lasting impacts of missionary culture on the islands.

1927
Convict road gangs complete the construction of the Hana Hwy.

1941
Japanese warplanes attack Pearl Harbor; Hawaii becomes a war zone under martial law.

VACLAV/SHUTTERSTOCK ©

USS Bowfin Submarine Museum, Pearl Harbor, O'ahu

in the Pacific theater. The marines also had recreation time, with dances, movies, boxing matches and plenty of beer-drinking filling their post-training hours. The marines are memorialized at the 4th Marine Division Memorial Park, the site of their camp and training ground in Ha'iku.

Statehood

Throughout the 20th century numerous Hawaiian statehood bills were introduced in Congress, only to be shot down. One reason for this lack of support was racial prejudice against Hawaii's multi-ethnic population. US congressmen from a still-segregated South were vocal in their belief that making Hawaii a state would open the doors to Asian immigration and the so-called Yellow Peril threat that was so rampant at the time. Others believed Hawaii's labor unions were hotbeds of communism.

However, the fame of the 442nd Regimental Combat Team in WWII went a long way toward reducing anti-Japanese sentiments. In March 1959 Congress voted again, this time admitting Hawaii into the Union. On August 21, President Eisenhower signed the admission bill that officially deemed Hawaii the 50th state.

Hollywood Backdrop

At the time of statehood in 1959, Maui's population was a mere 35,000. In 1961 Maui retained such a backwater appearance that director Mervyn LeRoy filmed his classic *The Devil at 4 O'Clock* in Lahaina, where the dirt roads and untouristed waterfront doubled for the sleepy South Pacific isle depicted in his adventure movie. Spencer Tracy and Frank Sinatra not only shot many of their scenes at Lahaina's Pioneer Inn, but stayed there, too. More recently, Adam Sandler and Jennifer Aniston filmed scenes from *Just Go With It* at the Grand Wailea resort.

Tourism & Development

Statehood had an immediate economic impact on Hawaii, most notably in boosting the tourism industry. Coupled with the advent of jet airplanes, which could transport thousands of people per week to the islands, tourism exploded, creating a hotel-building boom previously unmatched in the US. Tourism became the largest industry on Maui.

In 1962 sugar giant Amfac transformed 600 acres of Ka'anapali canefields on Maui into Hawaii's first resort destination outside Waikiki. Things really took off in 1974 with the first nonstop flight between mainland USA and Kahului, and Maui soon blossomed into the darling of Hawaii's tourism industry.

Its growth spurt hasn't always been pretty. In the mid-1970s developers pounced on the beachside village of Kihei with such intensity that it

American author Mark Twain, who spent time on Maui in the 1860s, began a long tradition of Westerners writing about the state's exoticism in his book *Letters from the Sandwich Isles* (published 1939).

1959	1962	1976	1990
On August 21, Hawaii becomes the 50th state of the USA.	Hawaii's first resort destination outside of Waikiki is built at Ka'anapali Beach in Maui.	Native Hawaiian activists illegally occupy the island of Kaho'olawe.	After much litigation and more than a decade of grassroots Hawaiian activism, the US Navy is forced to stop bombing Kaho'olawe. Control over that island isn't officially returned to the state until 2003.

became a rallying call for antidevelopment forces throughout Hawaii. Recent years have been spent catching up with Kihei's rampant growth, mitigating traffic and creating plans intent on sparing the rest of Maui from willy-nilly building sprees.

Hawaiian Renaissance & Sovereignity Movement

By the 1970s Hawaii's rapid growth meant new residents (mostly mainland transplants) and tourists were crowding island beaches and roads. Runaway construction was rapidly transforming resorts almost beyond recognition, and the relentless peddling of 'aloha' got some islanders wondering what it meant to be Hawaiian. Some Native Hawaiians turned to *kapuna* (elders) and the past to recover their heritage, and by doing so became more politically assertive.

In 1976 a group of activists illegally occupied Kaho'olawe, an island in Maui County dubbed 'Target Island.' The government had taken the island during WWII and used it for bombing practice until 1990. During another protest occupation attempt in 1977, two members of the Protect Kaho'olawe 'Ohana (PKO) – George Helm and Kimo Mitchell – disappeared at sea, instantly becoming martyrs. Saving Kaho'olawe became a rallying cry and it radicalized a nascent Native Hawaiian–rights movement.

When the state held its landmark Constitutional Convention in 1978 it passed a number of important amendments of special importance to Native Hawaiians. For example, it made Hawaiian the official state language (along with English) and mandated that Hawaiian culture be taught in public schools. At the grassroots level, the islands were experiencing a renaissance of Hawaiian culture, with a surge in residents – of all ethnicities – joining hula *halau* (schools), learning to play Hawaiian instruments and rediscovering traditional crafts like feather-lei-making.

In 2011 then-Governor Neil Abercrombie signed into law a bill recognizing Native Hawaiians as the state's only indigenous people and establishing a commission to create and maintain a list of qualifying Native Hawaiians. For those who qualfed, this was the first step toward eventual self-governance.

Climate Change & Eco-Awareness

Mauians know intimately the consequences of global warming. Extended periods of drought have become commonplace. Some years the droughts end with record-setting bursts of torrential rains that wash down the slopes, flooding low-lying communities and muddying the coral reefs. Heavy rains in the fall of 2016 caused severe flooding in parts of central Maui, with heavy damage to 'Iao Valley State Monument and Kepaniwai

History Museums

Whalers Village Museum (p107)

Alexander & Baldwin Sugar Museum (p146)

Lahaina Heritage Museum (p82)

Story of Hawaii Museum (p132)

Wo Hing Museum (p83)

1993

President Clinton signs 'Apology Bill,' acknowledging the US government's role in the kingdom's illegal takeover 100 years before.

2002

Partly as a response to Democratic Party corruption scandals, mainland-born Linda Lingle is elected Hawaii's first Republican governor in 40 years.

Barack Obama at a 2008 campaign rally

Park. At the time of research, both parks were closed and the former is due to reopen in June 2017.

Most Mauians take climate change seriously, and even big-wave surfer Laird Hamilton recognizes climate change as a source of the 100ft surf he rides off Maui's North Shore.

Maui has a long history of protecting the environment. It was the first island in Hawaii to ban single-use plastic bags, and, in a move to decrease their own carbon emissions, Mauians supported the erection of windmills on the island.

Citizens voted in 2014 to temporarily ban the planting of genetically modified organisms until environmental and health impacts could be analyzed. The ban was not implemented due to legal challenges from large-scale GMO producers. In 2016 a federal judge ruled that Maui County could not enact any bans affecting federal agricultural matters, which include genetically modified crops. The ruling may be appealed.

A bit of good environmental news? The National Oceanic and Atmospheric Administration (NOAA) announced that nine out of 14 recognized populations of humpback whales could be removed from the endangered-species list. Humpback whales, as a species, were placed on the list in 1970. Forty years of protective efforts appeared to have paid off. Despite the delisting, a moratorium on whaling will stay in effect.

In her book *The Wave* (2010), Susan Casey chronicles Laird Hamilton's big-wave riding off the coast of Maui.

2008	2011	2016
Born and raised in Oahu, Barack Obama is elected US president with more than 70% of the vote.	Maui was the first Hawaiian island to ban single-use plastic bags. Violaters will be fined $500.	Hawaiian Commercial and Sugar closes its sugar mill in Central Maui, the last still operating in Hawaii.

The People of Maui

The bond that unites all Mauians is a sense of _aloha 'aina_ – a love of the land. Add to this strong family ties and a culture that embraces generosity and hospitality, and you've got a style of community now rarely seen on the hard-charging, rootless US mainland. There's also an appreciation for chitchatting, known as 'talking story' – a refreshingly 'retro' mode of communication still in fashion here.

Island Identity

Above Hula dancer chanting and drumming

Nobody sweats the small stuff on Maui. It's all good. No worries. No problem. And if somebody is noticeably wound up? They're from the mainland, guaranteed. Folks on Maui tend to have sunny dispositions, and they're more laid-back than their mainland cousins, dressing more casually and spending more time outside. On weekends everybody can be found hanging on the beach in T-shirts and bikinis, and wearing those ubiquitous flip-flops known in Hawaii as 'rubbah slippahs.'

Located 2500 miles from the nearest continent, the Hawaiian Islands are practically another country. On Maui, most streets have Hawaiian names, mixed-race people are the norm, and school kids participate in hula contests. You'll find no daylight saving time and no significant change of seasons. The geographical distance puts local, rather than national, news on the front page.

People on Maui never walk by anybody they know without partaking in a little 'talk story,' stopping to ask how someone is doing (and meaning it) and to share a little conversation. Islanders prefer to avoid heated arguments and generally don't jump into a controversial topic just to argue a point. Politically, most residents are middle-of-the-road Democrats and tend to vote along party, racial, ethnic, seniority and local/nonlocal lines.

To locals, it is best to avoid embarrassing confrontations and to 'save face' by keeping quiet. At community meetings or activist rallies, the most vocal, liberal and passionate will probably be mainland transplants. Of course, as more and more mainlanders settle in Hawaii, the traditional stereotypes are fading.

Mauians tend to be self-assured without being cocky. Though Honolulu residents may think other Hawaiian Islands are 'da boonies,' they generally give a different nod to Maui. In the greater scheme of Hawaiian places, Maui is considered the more sophisticated sister, with a more polished scene than the Big Island or Kaua'i.

Lifestyle

Take a Sunday afternoon drive along the West Maui coast and you'll see the same scene repeated at the different beach parks: overflowing picnic tables, smoking grills and multi-generational groups enjoying the sun and surf. On Maui, the *'ohana* (family) is central to island lifestyles. *'Ohana* includes all relatives, as well as close family friends. Growing up, 'auntie' and 'uncle' are used to refer to those who are dear to you, whether by blood or friendship. Weekends are typically set aside for family outings, and it's not uncommon for as many as 50 people to gather for a family picnic.

People are generally early risers, often taking a run along the beach or hitting the waves before heading to the office. Most work a 40-hour week – overtime and the workaholic routine common elsewhere in the US are the exceptions here.

In many ways, contemporary culture in Maui resembles contemporary culture in the rest of the US. Mauians listen to the same pop music and watch the same TV shows. The island has rock bands and classical musicians, junk food and nouvelle cuisine. The wonderful thing about Maui, however, is that the mainland influences largely stand beside, rather than engulf, the culture of the island.

Not only is traditional Hawaiian culture an integral part of the social fabric, but so are the customs of the ethnically diverse immigrants who have settled here. Maui is more than a meeting place of East and West: it's a place where the cultures merge, typically in a manner that brings out the best of both worlds.

Recent decades have seen a refreshing cultural renaissance in all things Hawaiian. Hawaiian-language classes are thriving, local artists and craftspeople are returning to traditional mediums and themes, and hula classes are concentrating more on the nuances behind hand movements and facial expressions than on the stereotypical hip-shaking.

Visitors will still encounter packaged Hawaiiana that seems almost a parody of island culture, from plastic lei to theme-park luau. But the

THE PEOPLE OF MAUI LIFESTYLE

Islanders greet each other with the *shaka* sign, made by folding down the three middle fingers to the palm and extending the thumb and little finger. The hand is then shaken back and forth in greeting. On Maui, it's as common as waving.

Tiki totems

growing interest in traditional Hawaiian culture is having a positive impact on the tourist industry, and authentic performances by hula students and Hawaiian musicians are now the norm. Resorts are adding cultural talks and outrigger-canoe tours.

Folks on Maui are quite accepting of other people, which helps explain the harmonious hodgepodge of races and cultures here. Sexual orientation is generally not an issue and gays and lesbians tend to be accepted without prejudice. In 2013 Hawaii became the 15th state to legalize marriage between same-sex couples.

Most locals strive for the conventional 'American dream': kids, homeownership, stable work and ample free time. Generally, those with less-standard lifestyles (eg B&B owners, artists, singles and world travelers) are mainland transplants.

The median price of a home on Maui dropped during the recession, from $700,000 to about $450,000, but single-family home prices have been rising, with the median sales price of a one-family home increasing to $635,000 by the fall of 2016. This is a steep purchase price when the median annual income for a household in 2015 was $66,476. For working-class people, it generally takes two incomes to make ends meet. According to one recent report, the cost of living in Hawaii is the highest of any state, with the price of groceries and other services, like utilities, much higher than on the mainland. Financially, it can be a tough go in paradise. Yet most agree that nothing compares to living on Maui and would leave only if absolutely necessary.

Multicultural Maui

Maui is one of the most ethnically diverse places in the US. Need proof? Just look at its signature dish: the plate lunch. This platter, with its meat, macaroni salad and two scoops of rice, merges the culinary habits of Native

Ranches across the island offer *paniolo* (Hawaiian cowboy) experiences

Hawaiians with those of a global array of immigrants – Portuguese, Japanese, Korean, Filipino – to create one heaping plate of deliciousness. An obvious metaphor never tasted so good.

But the diversity is both eclectic and narrow at once. That's because Hawaii's unique blend of races, ethnicities and cultures is quite isolated from the rest of the world. On one hand, Hawaii is far removed from any middle-American, white-bread city. On the other, it lacks major exposure to certain races and ethnicities, particularly blacks and Mexican Hispanics, that are prevalent in the US mainland population.

Any discussion regarding multiculturalism must address whether we are talking about locals (insiders) or nonlocals (outsiders). Among locals, social interaction has hinged on old plantation stereotypes and hierarchies since statehood. During plantation days, whites were the wealthy plantation owners and, for years afterward, minorities would joke about their being the 'bosses' or about their privileges due to race. As the Japanese rose to power economically and politically, they tended to capitalize on their 'minority' status, emphasizing their insider status as former plantation laborers. But the traditional distinctions and alliances are fading as the plantation generation dies away.

Of course, any tension among local groups are quite benign compared with racial strife on the US mainland. Locals seem slightly perplexed at the emphasis on 'political correctness.' Just consider the nickname for overdeveloped Kihei in South Maui. It's been dubbed 'Haole-wood' by the locals. Haole? It's the Hawaiian term for Caucasian. Among themselves, locals good-naturedly joke about island stereotypes: talkative Portuguese, stingy Chinese, goody-goody Japanese and know-it-all haole.

When nonlocals enter the picture, the balance shifts. Generally, locals feel a bond with other locals. While tourists and transplants are welcomed,

WHO'S WHO

Haole White person, Caucasian. Often further defined as 'mainland haole' or 'local haole.'

Hapa Person of mixed ancestry, most commonly referring to *hapa haole* who are part white and part Asian.

Hawaiian Person of Native Hawaiian ancestry. It's a faux pas to call a non-native Hawaii resident 'Hawaiian.'

Kama'aina Person who is a resident of Hawaii, literally defined as 'child of the land.'

Local Person who grew up in Hawaii. Locals who move away retain their local 'cred,' at least in part, but longtime transplants never become local. To call a transplant 'almost local' is a compliment.

Neighbor Islander Person who lives on any Hawaiian Island other than O'ahu.

Transplant Person who moves to the islands as an adult.

they must earn the trust and respect of the locals. It is unacceptable for an outsider to assume an air of superiority and to try to 'fix' local ways. Such people will inevitably fall into the category of 'loudmouth haole.'

That said, prejudice against haole is minimal. If you're called a haole, don't worry: it's generally not an insult or threat (if it is, you'll know). Essentially, locals are warm and gracious to those who appreciate island ways.

Island Etiquette

Dial it down a notch when you get to Maui. Big-city aggression and type-A maneuvering won't get you far. As the bumper sticker here says, 'Practice Aloha.'

Remember to take off your shoes when entering a home (most residents wear rubbah slippahs partly for this reason – easy to slip on and off and no socks required).

Don't try to speak pidgin – unless you're really good at it and, when driving, unless you're about to hit someone, don't honk your horn. That's a sure way to attract 'stink eye.'

On narrow roads like the Road to Hana and the Kahekili Hwy, the driver who reaches a one-way bridge first has the right of way, if the bridge is otherwise empty. If facing a steady stream of cars, yield to the entire queue.

Remember the simple protocol when visiting sacred places: don't place rocks at the site as a gesture of thanks; better to use words instead. It is also considered disrespectful to stack rocks or build rock towers. And, don't remove rocks from national parks.

Do ask permission before you pick fruit or flowers from trees on private property.

When surfing, there's a pecking order, and tourists are at the bottom. The person furthest outside has the right of way. When somebody is up and riding, don't take off on the wave in front of them. Wait your turn, be generous and surf with a smile.

Above Polynesian mask

Hawaii's Arts & Crafts

E komo mai (welcome) to these unique Polynesian islands, where storytelling and slack key guitar are among the sounds of everyday life. Contemporary Hawaii is a vibrant mix of multicultural traditions and underneath it all beats a Hawaiian heart, pounding with an ongoing revival of Hawaii's indigenous language, artisanal crafts, music and the hula.

Hula

In ancient Hawai'i, hula sometimes was a solemn ritual, in which *mele* (songs, chants) were an offering to the gods or celebrated the accomplishments of *ali'i* (chiefs). At other times hula was lighthearted entertainment, in which chief and *kama'aina* (commoner) danced together, including at annual festivals such as the makahiki held during harvest season. Most importantly, hula embodied the community – telling stories of and celebrating itself.

Traditionally, dancers trained rigorously in halau (schools) under a kumu (teacher), so their hand gestures, facial expressions and synchronized movements were exact. In a culture without written language, chants were important, giving meaning to the movements and preserving Hawaii's oral history, anything from creation stories about gods to royal genealogies. Songs often contained kaona (hidden meanings), which could be spiritual, but also slyly amorous, even sexual.

Hula still thrives today, with competitions and expositions thriving across the islands.

Island Music

Hawaiian music is rooted in ancient chants. Foreign missionaries and sugar-plantation workers introduced new melodies and instruments, which were incorporated and adapted to create a unique local musical style. *Leo ki'eki'e* (falsetto, or 'high voice') vocals, sometimes just referred to as soprano for women, employs a signature *ha'i* (vocal break, or split-note) style, with a singer moving abruptly from one register to another. Contemporary Hawaiian musical instruments include the steel guitar, slack key guitar and ukulele.

But if you tune your rental-car radio to today's island radio stations, you'll hear everything from US mainland hip-hop beats, country-and-western tunes and Asian pop hits to reggae-inspired 'Jawaiian' grooves. A few Hawaii-born singer-songwriters, most famously Jack Johnson, have achieved international stardom. To discover new hit-makers, check out this year's winners of the Na Hoku Hanohano Awards (www.nahokuhanohano.org), Hawaii's version of the Grammies.

Ukulele

Heard all across the islands is the ukulele, derived from the *braguinha*, a Portuguese stringed instrument introduced to Hawaii in 1879. Ukulele means 'jumping flea' in Hawaiian, referring to the way players' deft fingers swiftly move around the strings. The ukulele is enjoying a revival as a young generation of virtuosos emerges, including Nick Acosta, who plays with just one hand, and genre-bending rockers led by Jake Shimabukuro, whose album *Peace Love Ukulele* (2011) reached number one on Billboard's world music chart.

Both the ukulele and the steel guitar contributed to the lighthearted *hapa haole* (Hawaiian music with predominantly English lyrics) popularized in the islands after the 1930s, of which *My Little Grass Shack* and *Lovely Hula Hands* are classic examples. For better or for worse, *hapa haole* songs became instantly recognizable as 'Hawaiian' thanks to Hollywood movies and the classic *Hawaii Calls* radio show, which broadcast worldwide from the banyan-tree courtyard of Waikiki's Moana hotel from 1935 until 1975.

Can't resist the rhythms of the hula? Look for low-cost (or even free) introductory dance lessons at resort hotels, shopping malls and local community centers and colleges. No grass skirt required!

Cowboy Heritage

Spanish and Mexican cowboys introduced the guitar to Hawaiians in the 1830s. Fifty years later, O'ahu-born high-school student Joseph Kekuku started experimenting with playing a guitar flat on his lap while sliding a pocket knife or comb across the strings. His invention, the Hawaiian steel guitar *(kika kila),* lifts the strings off the fretboard using a movable steel slide, creating a signature smooth sound.

In the early 20th century, Kekuku and others introduced the islands' steel guitar sounds to the world. The steel guitar later inspired the creation of resonator guitars such as the Dobro, now integral to bluegrass, blues and other genres, and country-and-western music's lap and pedal steel guitars. Today Hawaii's most influential steel guitarists include Henry Kaleialoha Allen, Alan Akaka, Bobby Ingano and Greg Sardinha.

Slack Key Guitar

Since the mid-20th century, the Hawaiian steel guitar has usually been played with slack key *(ki ho'alu)* tunings, in which the thumb plays the bass and rhythm chords, while the fingers play the melody and improvisations, in a picked style. Traditionally, slack key tunings were closely guarded secrets among *'ohana* (extended family and friends).

The legendary guitarist Gabby Pahinui launched the modern slack key guitar era with his first recording of 'Hi'ilawe' in 1946. In the 1960s, Gabby and his band the Sons of Hawaii embraced the traditional Hawaiian sound. Along with other influential slack key guitarists such as Sonny Chillingworth, they spurred a renaissance in Hawaiian music that continues to this day. The list of contemporary slack key masters is long and ever growing, including Keola Beamer, Ledward Ka'apana, Martin and Cyril Pahinui, Ozzie Kotani and George Kuo.

Traditional Crafts

In the 1970s, the Hawaiian renaissance sparked interest in artisan crafts. The most beloved traditional craft is lei-making, stringing garlands of flowers, leaves, berries, nuts or shells. More lasting souvenirs include wood carvings, woven baskets and hats, and Hawaiian quilts. All of these have become so popular with tourists that cheap imitation imports from across the Pacific have flooded into Hawaii, so shop carefully and always buy local.

Woodworking

Ancient Hawaiians were expert woodworkers, carving canoes out of logs and hand-turning lustrous bowls from a variety of beautifully grained tropical hardwoods, such as koa and milo. Ipu (gourds) were also dried and used as containers and as drums for hula. Contemporary woodworkers take native woods to craft traditional bowls, exquisite furniture, jewelry and free-form sculptures. Traditionally, Hawaiian wooden bowls are not decorated or ornate, but are shaped to bring out the natural beauty of the wood. The thinner and lighter the bowl, the finer the artistry and greater the value – and the price. Don't be fooled into buying cheaper monkeypod bowls imported from the Philippines.

Fabric Arts

Lauhala weaving and the making of kapa (pounded-bark cloth) for clothing and artworks are two ancient Hawaiian crafts.

Traditionally lauhala served as floor mats, canoe sails, protective capes and more. Weaving the lau (leaves) of the hala (pandanus) tree is the easier part, while preparing the leaves, which have razor-sharp spines, is messy work. Today the most common lauhala items are hats, placemats and baskets. Most are mass-produced, but you can find handmade beauties at specialty stores.

Making kapa (called tapa elsewhere in Polynesia) is no less laborious. First, seashells are used to scrape away the rough outer bark of the wauke (paper mulberry) tree. Strips of softer inner bark are cut (traditionally with shark's teeth), pounded with mallets until thin and pliable, and further softened by being soaked in water to let them ferment between beatings. Softened bark strips are then layered atop one another and pounded together in a process called felting. Large sheets of finished kapa are colorfully dyed with plant materials and stamped or painted by hand with geometric patterns before being scented with flowers or oils.

HAWAII'S ARTS & CRAFTS TRADITIONAL CRAFTS

Hawaii has been the home of many modern painters, and scores of visiting artists have drawn inspiration from the islands' rich cultural heritage and landscapes. *Encounters with Paradise: Views of Hawaii and Its People, 1778–1941*, by David Forbes, is a vivid art-history tour.

Hula dancer

In ancient times, kapa was worn as everyday clothing by both sexes and used as blankets for everything from swaddling newborns to burying the dead. Today authentic handmade Hawaiian kapa cloth is rarely seen outside of museums, fine-art galleries and private collections.

Island Writings

From Outside & Inside

Until the late 1970s, Hawaii's literature was dominated by nonlocal Western writers observing these exotic-seeming islands from the outside. Globetrotters such as Mark Twain and Isabella Bird wrote the earliest travelogues about the islands. Best-selling modern titles include James Michener's historical saga, *Hawaii* (1959), and Paul Theroux's caustically humorous *Hotel Honolulu* (2001). More recently, Hawaii-centered historical fiction written by nonresidents includes *The Last Aloha* (2009), by Gaellen Quinn, and *Bird of Another Heaven* (2007), by James Houston.

Meanwhile, locally born contemporary writers have created an authentic literature of Hawaii that evokes island life from the inside. Leading this movement has been Bamboo Ridge Press (www.bambooridge.com), which for almost four decades has published new local fiction and poetry in an annual journal and has launched the careers of many contemporary writers in Hawaii. The University of Hawai'i Press (www.uhpress.hawaii. edu) and Bishop Museum Press (www.bishopmuseum.org) have also made space for local writers to air their voices, especially with insightful nonfiction writings about Hawaiian culture, history, nature and art.

Pidgin Beyond Plantations

In 1975, *All I Asking for Is My Body*, by Milton Murayama, vividly captured sugar plantation life for Japanese nisei (second-generation immigrants) around WWII. Murayama's use of pidgin opened the door to an explosion of vernacular literature. Lois-Ann Yamanaka has won widespread acclaim for her poetry (*Saturday Night at the Pahala Theatre*, 1993) and stories (*Wild Meat and the Bully Burgers*, 1996), in which pidgin embodies her characters like a second skin.

Indeed, redeeming pidgin – long dismissed by academics and disparaged by the upper class – has been a cultural and political cause for some. The hilarious stories (*Da Word*, 2001) and essays (*Living Pidgin*, 2002) of Lee Tonouchi, a prolific writer and playwright whose nickname is 'Da Pidgin Guerrilla,' argue that pidgin is not only essential to understanding local culture, but is also a legitimate language. Another great introduction to pidgin is *Growing Up Local* (1998), an anthology of poetry and prose published by Bamboo Ridge Press.

Hawaii on Screen

Nothing has cemented the paradisaical fantasy of Hawaii in the popular imagination as firmly as Hollywood. Today, Southern California's 'dream factory' continues to peddle variations on a South Seas genre that first swept movie theaters in the 1930s. Whether the mood is silly or serious, whether Hawaii is used as a setting or a stand-in for someplace else, the story's familiar tropes rarely change, updating the original tropical castaways soap opera and often romantically glossing over the islands' history of colonization.

Hollywood arrived in Hawaii in 1913, more than a decade after Thomas Edison first journeyed here to make movies that you can still watch today at Lahaina's **Wo Hing Museum** (www.lahainarestoration.org/ wo-hing-museum; 858 Front St; adult/child $7/free, incl admission to Baldwin House; ◷10am-4pm) on Maui. By 1939, dozens of Hollywood movies had been shot in Hawaii, including the musical comedy *Waikiki Wedding* (1937), in which Bing Crosby crooned the Oscar-winning song 'Sweet Leilani.' Later favorites include the WWII–themed drama *From Here to Eternity* (1953), the musical *South Pacific* (1958), and Elvis Presley's goofy postwar *Blue Hawaii* (1961). Today, Hawaii actively encourages and supports a lucrative film industry by maintaining state-of-the-art production facilities and providing tax incentives. Hundreds of feature films have been shot in the state, including box-office hits *Raiders of the Lost Ark* (1981), *Jurassic Park* (1993), *Pearl Harbor* (2001), *50 First Dates* (2004), *Pirates of the Caribbean: On Stranger Tides* (2011), *The Hunger Games: Catching Fire* (2013) and *Jurassic World* (2015).

Hawaii has hosted dozens of TV series since 1968, when the original *Hawaii Five-O*, an edgy cop drama unsentimentally depicting Honolulu's gritty side, debuted. In 2010 *Hawaii Five-O* was rebooted as a prime-time drama, filmed on O'ahu. That island also served as the location for the hit series *Lost*, which, like *Gilligan's Island* (the pilot of which was filmed on Kaua'i), is about a group of island castaways trying to get home.

For a complete filmography and a list of hundreds of TV episodes filmed here, including what's currently being shot around the islands, check the Hawaii Film Office website, http://filmoffice.hawaii.gov.

Above Lei floral arrangement

Lei

Greetings. Love. Honor. Respect. Peace. Celebration. Spirituality. Good luck. Farewell. A Hawaiian lei – a handcrafted garland of fresh tropical flowers – can signify all of these meanings and many more. Lei-making may be Hawaii's most sensuous and transitory art form. Fragrant and ephemeral, lei embody the beauty of nature and the embrace of *'ohana* (extended family and friends) and the community, freely given and freely shared.

The Art of the Lei

In choosing their materials, lei makers express emotions and tell a story, since flowers and other plants may embody Hawaiian places and myths. Traditional lei makers may use feathers, nuts, shells, seeds, seaweed, vines, leaves and fruit, in addition to more familiar fragrant flowers. The most common methods of making lei are by knotting, braiding, winding, stringing or sewing the raw natural materials together.

Worn daily, lei were integral to ancient Hawaiian society. In the islands' Polynesian past, they were part of sacred hula dances and given as special gifts to loved ones, as healing medicine to the sick and as offerings to the gods, all practices that continue today. So powerful a symbol were they that on ancient Hawaii's battlefields, a lei could bring peace to warring armies.

Today, locals wear lei for special events, such as weddings, birthdays, anniversaries and graduations. It's no longer common to make one's own lei, unless you belong to a hula *halau* (school). For ceremonial hula, performers are often required to make their own lei, even gathering raw materials by hand.

Modern Celebrations

For visitors to Hawaii, the tradition of giving and receiving lei dates back to 19th-century steamships that brought the first tourists to the islands. Later, disembarking cruise-ship passengers were greeted by vendors who would toss garlands around the necks of *malihini* (newcomers).

In 1927, the poet Don Blanding and Honolulu journalist Grace Tower Warren called for making May 1 a holiday to honor lei. Every year, Lei Day is still celebrated across the islands with Hawaiian music, hula dancing, parades, and lei-making workshops and contests.

The tradition of giving a kiss with a lei began during WWII, allegedly when a hula dancer at a USO club was dared by her friends to give a military serviceman a peck on the cheek when offering him a flower lei.

Lei Etiquette

➡ Do not wear a lei hanging directly down around your neck. Instead, drape a closed (circular) lei over your shoulders, making sure equal lengths are hanging over your front and back.

➡ When presenting a lei, bow your head slightly and raise the lei above your heart. Do not drape it with your own hands over the head of the recipient because this isn't respectful; let them do it themselves.

➡ Don't give a closed lei to a pregnant woman for it may bring bad luck; choose an open (untied) lei or *haku* (head) lei instead.

➡ Resist the temptation to wear a lei intended for someone else. That's bad luck. Never refuse a lei, and do not take one off in the presence of the giver.

➡ When you stop wearing your lei, don't throw it away. Untie the string, remove the bow and return the lei's natural elements to the earth (eg scatter flowers in the ocean, bury seeds or nuts).

You can find lei across the island. Keep a lookout for eye-catching Ni'ihau shell lei.

On the 'Garden Island,' leathery, anise-scented mokihana berries are often woven with strands of glossy, green maile vines. Mokihana trees thrive on the rain-soaked western slopes of Mt Wai'ale'ale.

Landscapes & Wildlife

You don't have to be a geologist, botanist or marine biologist to appreciate the Valley Isle's myriad natural charms, although you might find yourself picking up an interest in a new field of study after a morning snorkel or a hike atop Haleakalā. Trust us, it won't take long to feel the *aloha 'aina* (love for the land), too.

The Land

Above 'Iao Valley State Monument (p141)

Maui is the second-largest Hawaiian island, with a land area of 728 sq miles. Set atop a 'hot spot' on the Pacific Plate, Maui rose from the ocean floor as two separate volcanoes. Lava flows and soil erosion eventually built up a valleylike isthmus between the volcanic masses, linking them in their present form. This flat region provides a fertile setting for sugarcane fields and is home to Maui's largest urban center, the twin towns of Kahului and Wailuku.

The eastern side of Maui, the larger and younger of the two volcanic masses, is dominated by the lofty Haleakalā (10,023ft). This dormant volcano, whose craterlike floor is dotted with cinder cones, last erupted between AD 1480 and 1600. The second, more ancient volcano formed the craggy West Maui Mountains, which top out at the Pu'u Kukui (5788ft). Both mountains are high enough to trap moisture-laden clouds carried by the northeast trade winds, bringing abundant rain to their windward eastern sides. Consequently, the lushest jungles and gushiest waterfalls are found along the Hana Hwy, which runs along Haleakalā's eastern slopes, while the driest, sunniest beaches are on the western coasts.

Flora & Fauna

All living things that reached Maui were carried across the sea on wing, wind or wave – seeds clinging to a bird's feather, or insects in driftwood. Scientists estimate that successful species arrived once every 70,000 years – and they included no amphibians and only two mammals: a bat and a seal.

However, the flora and fauna that made it to Maui occupied an unusually rich and diverse land. In a prime example of 'adaptive radiation,' the 250 flowering plants that arrived evolved into some 1800 native species. Lacking predators, new species dropped defensive protections – thorns, poisons and strong odors disappeared, which explains why they fare so poorly against modern invaders. So many plant and animal species have been lost that the state has been dubbed 'the extinction capital of the world.'

The Polynesians brought pigs, chickens, coconuts and about two dozen other species, not to mention people. The pace of change exploded after Western contact in the late 18th century. Cattle and goats were introduced and set wild, with devastating consequences. Even today, sitting on a Kihei beach looking out at Kaho'olawe in the late afternoon, you'll notice a red tinge from the dust whipping off the island, a consequence of defoliation by wild goats released there a century ago.

But there is progress. On Kaho'olawe the goats are gone and native reforestation has begun; Haleakalā National Park (p202) has made great strides in reintroducing and protecting native species; and the first public garden totally dedicated to endemic Hawaiian species, Maui Nui Botanical Gardens (p132), sits on the site of a former exotic zoo.

LANDSCAPES & WILDLIFE FLORA & FAUNA

Best Places to Honor the Sun

Haleakalā Crater (p202) for sunrise

Wai'anapanapa State Park (p225) for sunrise

Big Beach (Oneloa Beach) (p167) for sunset

Papawai Point for sunset

Fleetwood's on Front St (p94) for sunset

MAUI'S TOP PROTECTED AREAS

'Ahihi-Kina'u Natural Area Reserve (p168) A pristine bay, lava flows and ancient sites; good for hiking and snorkeling.

Haleakalā National Park (p202), Summit Area (Large, dormant volcano; good for hiking, camping and horseback riding).

Haleakalā National Park (p202) Kipahulu Area (With towering waterfalls, cascading pools and ancient sites; good for hiking, swimming and camping).

'Iao Valley State Monument (p141) The park features streams, cliffs and swimming holes; good for hiking and photography.

Kealia Pond National Wildlife Refuge (p145) Bird sanctuary; good for bird-watching.

Molokini Crater (p43) A submerged volcanic crater; ideal for snorkeling and diving.

Pi'ilanihale Heiau & Kahanu Garden (p224) A national botanic garden and ancient site; good for walking.

Polipoli Spring State Recreation Area (p193) With cloud forest and uncrowded trails; good for hiking, camping and mountain biking.

Wai'anapanapa State Park (p225) Lava tubes and a trail over rugged sea cliffs to Hana; good for hiking and camping.

Green sea turtle

If you see a wild animal in distress, report it to the state **Division of Conservation & Resource Enforcement** (DOCARE; 808-643-3567).

Animals

Most of Maui's wildlife attractions are found in the water or on the wing. Hawaii has no native land mammals.

Marine Life

Of the almost 700 fish species in Hawaiian waters, nearly one-third are found nowhere else in the world. Maui's nearshore waters are a true rainbow of color: turquoise parrotfish, bright yellow tangs and polka-dotted puffer fish, to name a few.

Honu (green sea turtles) abound in Maui's waters. To the thrill of snorkelers and divers, *honu* can often be seen feeding in shallow coves and bays. Adults can grow to more than 3ft – an awesome sight when one swims past you in the water. Much less common is the hawksbill sea turtle, which occasionally nests on Maui's western shores.

The sheltered waters between Maui, Lana'i and Moloka'i are the wintering destination for thousands of the North Pacific stock of humpback whales. The majestic creatures are the fifth-largest of the great whales, reaching lengths of 45ft and weighing up to 45 tons. Humpbacks are coast-huggers and are visible from the beach in winter along Maui's west and southwest coasts.

Maui is also home to a number of dolphins. The spinner dolphin (named for its acrobatic leaps) comes into calm bays during the day to rest.

With luck you might see the Hawaiian monk seal, which lives primarily in the remote northwestern Hawaiian Islands, but occasionally hauls out on Maui beaches. It was nearly wiped out by hunting in the 1800s,

Native nene, Hawaii's state bird

but conservation efforts have edged the species back from the brink of extinction – barely, with a total population of about 1153 seals in 2012.

Don't touch, approach or disturb marine mammals; most are protected, making it illegal to do so. Watch dolphins, whales, seals and sea turtles from a respectful distance.

Birds

Many of Hawaii's birds have evolved from a single species, in a spectacular display of adaptive radiation. For example, all 54 species of Hawaiian honeycreepers likely evolved from a single finch ancestor. Left vulnerable to introduced predatory species and infectious avian diseases after humans arrived, half of Hawaii's native bird species are already extinct, and more than 30 of those remaining are still under threat. According to a recent article in *Audubon,* one in three endangered bird species in the US is a Hawaiian bird.

The endangered nene, Hawaii's state bird, is a long-lost cousin of the Canada goose. Nene nest in high cliffs on the slopes of Haleakalā and their feet have adapted to the rugged volcanic environment by losing most of their webbing. Nene have black heads, light-yellow cheeks, a white underbelly and dark gray feathers.

At least three birds native to Maui – the Maui parrotbill, 'akohekohe (crested honeycreeper) and 'alauahio (Maui creeper) – are found nowhere else in the world. The Maui parrotbill and 'akohekohe are federally listed endangered species. The Maui parrotbill exists solely in the Kipahulu section of Haleakalā National Park and in a small section of high-elevation forest on the northeast slope of Haleakalā volcano. The cinnamon-colored *po'ouli* (black-faced honeycreeper) was last seen in 2004 and may already be extinct. Alas, it's unlikely you'll see any of those

RAPID O'HI'A DEATH

A dangerous fungus – it has a 100% mortality rate – is killing native o'hi'a trees on the Big Island. To prevent it from spreading to Haleakalā National Park, officials are asking all visitors who arrive from the Big Island to clean and remove dirt and debris from their shoes, and to spray their shoes, clothing and equipment with a 70% alcohol spray. The o'hi'a tree is found only in the state of Hawaii.

birds. But other native forest birds, including the 'apapane (a vivid red honeycreeper), can be sighted in Hosmer Grove in Haleakalā National Park.

Maui's two waterbird preserves, the Kanaha Pond Bird Sanctuary (p132) and Kealia Pond National Wildlife Refuge (p145), are nesting sites for the ae'o (Hawaiian black-necked stilt), a wading bird with a white underbelly and long orange legs.

For more information about honeycreepers and the Maui parrotbill (there are only 500 left!), visit the **Maui Forest Bird Recovery Project** (www.mauiforestbirds.org) website. This group specializes in recovering endangered honeycreepers. Check the group's website for details about speakers and Maui Brewing Pint Nights, a fundraiser held at the brewery's Kahana location (p113). Through the group, you can also sponsor a tree to be planted on Maui, which will aid in habitat recovery for the birds.

National, State & County Parks

Haleakalā National Park (p202) accounts for nearly 10% of Maui's land area. The park not only offers superb hiking and other recreational activities but also protects Hawaiian cultural sites and the habitat of several endangered species. Maui's numerous state and county parks also play an important role in preserving undeveloped forest areas and much of Maui's coastline. The parks are well used by Maui residents – from surfers to pig hunters – as well as by tourists.

The state's **Department of Land and Natural Resources** (DLNR; ☑808-984-8100; http://dlnr.hawaii.gov) has useful online information about hiking, aquatic safety, forestry and wildlife. The DLNR oversees the **Division of State Parks** (☑808-984-8109; www.hawaiistateparks. org; 54 S High St, Room 101, Wailuku; ☺8am-3:30pm Mon-Fri), which issues camping permits on Maui, and **Nā Ala Hele** (www.hawaiitrails.org), which coordinates public access to hiking trails.

Survival Guide

Directory A–Z

Climate

Lahaina

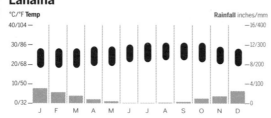

Lana'i City

Kaunakakai

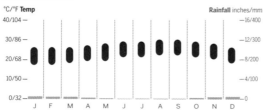

Maui's west coast typically boasts dry, sunny weather, with conditions improving as you continue south from occasionally rainy Kapalua to consistently sunny Kihei and Makena.

Hana and the jungle-covered east Maui offer rainforests and gushing waterfalls. The Upcountry slopes, beneath Haleakalā, commonly have intermittent clouds, making for a cooler, greener respite and ideal conditions for land-based activities such as hiking and horseback riding.

Customs Regulations

➡ Currently each international visitor (21 years of age or older) is allowed to bring 1L of liquor and 200 cigarettes into the USA. You may also bring in up to $100 worth of gift merchandise without incurring any duty. For more complete, up-to-date information, visit the US Customs and Border Protection (www.cbp.gov) website.

➡ Hawaii is a rabies-free state and there are strict regulations regarding the importation of pets, so don't plan on bringing your furry friend on a short vacation.

➡ Many fresh fruits and plants cannot be brought into Hawaii. For complete details, visit the Hawaii Department of Agriculture (http://hawaii.gov/hdoa) website.

Dangers & Annoyances

Agricultural Checks

All luggage and carry-on bags leaving Hawaii for the US mainland are checked by an agricultural inspector using an x-ray machine. You cannot take out fresh flowers of jade vine and Mauna Loa, gardenia, citrus or citrus-related flowers, leaves or plant parts, even in lei, though most other fresh flowers and foliage are permitted. You can take home pineapples and coconuts, but most other fresh fruits and vegetables are banned. Other things not allowed to enter mainland states include plants in soil, berries including fresh coffee berries (roasted beans are OK), cactus and sugarcane.

However, seeds, fruits and plants that have been certified and labeled for export aren't a problem. For more information contact the **Plant Protection & Quarantine Office** (☑808-877-5261; www.aphis.usda.gov).

Hazards & Trespassing

Flash floods, rock falls, tsunami, earthquakes, volcanic eruptions, shark attacks, jellyfish stings and, yes, even possibly getting knocked out by a falling coconut – the potential dangers of traveling in Hawaii might seem alarming at first. But as the old saying goes, statistically you're more likely to get hurt crossing the street at home. The key pieces of advice? Pay attention to your surroundings and watch for changing conditions.

When exploring, remember to mind your manners and watch your step. Hawaii has strict laws about trespassing on both private land and government land not intended for public use. Trespassing is always illegal, no matter how many other people you see doing it. As a visitor to the islands, it's important to respect all 'Kapu' or 'No trespassing' signs. Always seek explicit permission from the land owner or local officials before venturing onto private or public land that is closed to the public, regardless of whether it is fenced or signposted as such. Doing so not only respects the kuleana (rights) of local residents and the sacredness of the land

but also helps to ensure your own safety.

Rental Cars

Rental car break-ins Maui is notorious for smash-and-grabs. Don't leave valuables in the car.

Rental car availability If you see a good rate online before your trip, book the car. Unexpected shortages and rate spikes are not uncommon.

Theft

Maui is notorious for break-ins on parked rental cars. It can happen within seconds, whether in a secluded parking area at a trailhead or in a crowded beach parking lot. Do not leave anything valuable in your car – ever. If you must, pack things well out of sight before you arrive at your destination; thieves wait and watch to see what you put in the trunk.

Tsunamis

Tidal waves, or tsunamis as they're called in the Pacific, are rare, but when they do hit they can be deadly. Maui has a warning system, aired through yellow speakers mounted on telephone poles around the island. Emergency Alert Systems are tested on the first working day of each month at 11:45am for about one minute. If you should hear one at any other time and you're in a low-lying coastal area, immediately head for higher ground.

Emergency & Important Numbers

Emergency	☑911
Country code	☑1
Area code	☑808
International access code	☑011

Electricity

Type A
120V/60Hz

Type B
120V/60Hz

Entry & Exit Formalities

➜ For current information about the USA's entry requirements for travelers, access the Visa section of the **US State Department** (www.travel.state.gov) website and also the Travel section of the US Customs and Border Protection

LEEWARD & WINDWARD

Maui's high central mountains trap the trade winds that blow from the northeast, capturing moisture-laden clouds and bringing abundant rainfall to the windward side of Maui. The jungly road to Hana lies smack in the midst of windward Maui and simply gushes with waterfalls.

The same mountains keep clouds and hence rain from reaching the southwest side of the island. So it's in places such as Kihei and Makena that you'll find the driest, sunniest conditions. It's no coincidence that the great majority of Maui's resorts are found on its dry leeward side.

(www.cbp.gov) website. The Department of Homeland Security's registration program (DHS; www.dhs.gov), called Office of Biometric Identity Management, includes every port of entry and covers nearly every foreign visitor to the USA. Most visitors must register into the US-Visit program and have a digital photo and electronic (inkless) fingerprints taken; the process takes less than a minute. For more information, see the Department of Homeland Security website.

➡ Depending on your home country, you may not need a visa. The **Visa Waiver Program (VWP)** allows citizens of certain countries to enter the USA for stays of 90 days or less without first obtaining a US visa. There are 38 countries currently participating including Australia, France, Germany, Ireland, Italy, Japan, the Netherlands, New Zealand, Norway, Singapore, Sweden, Switzerland and the UK. For a full list of countries and details log onto the State Department's website.

➡ Under the VWP you must have a return ticket (or an onward ticket to any foreign destination) that's non-refundable in the US.

➡ All VWP travelers must register online at least 72 hours before arrival with

the **Electronic System for Travel Authorization** (ESTA; https://esta.cbp.dhs.gov), which currently costs $14. Once approved, registration is valid for two years (or until your passport expires).

➡ With the exception of Canadians and visitors who qualify for the VWP, foreign visitors to the USA need a visa. To apply, you need a passport that's valid for at least six months longer than your intended stay. The process is not free, involves a personal interview and can take several weeks.

➡ Visa applicants may be required to 'demonstrate binding obligations' that will ensure their return home. Because of this requirement, those planning to travel through other countries before arriving in the USA are better off applying for their US visa in their home country rather than on the road.

➡ The validity period for a US visitor visa depends on your home country. The actual length of time you'll be allowed to stay in the USA is determined by US officials at the port of entry.

Passports

➡ A machine-readable passport (MRP) is required for all foreign citizens to enter the USA.

➡ Your passport must be valid for six months beyond

your expected dates of stay in the US.

➡ As of April 1, 2016, you must have an e-passport to enter into the Visa Waiver Program. E-passports contain an electronic chip that is scanned upon arrival to identify the traveler.

Visas

Generally not required for stays of up to 90 days for citizens of Visa Waiver Program countries.

GLBTI Travellers

Maui is a popular destination for gay and lesbian travelers. The state has strong legislation to protect minorities and a constitutional guarantee of privacy that extends to sexual behavior between consenting adults. In 2013 Hawaii became the 15th state to legalize same-sex marriage. That said, people tend to be private so you won't see much public hand-holding or open displays of affection.

There isn't a big, boisterous 'out' scene. Kihei is the most open town on Maui, low-key as it is, and has a hotel, the Maui Sunseeker, catering to gay and lesbian travelers. Websites including www.gogayhawaii.com list LGBTIQ-friendly cafes, bars and events.

Health
Before You Go
HEALTH INSURANCE

International visitors should buy travel insurance for emergencies before they visit Maui. US citizens should check their health insurance policies to see if they are covered for treatments on Maui.

RECOMMENDED VACCINATIONS

No vaccinations are required for a trip to Maui, but it's always worth packing a basic first aid kit and some iodine or peroxide if you're planning on snorkeling near coral.

MEDICAL CHECKLIST

There are plenty of drug stores and pharmacies on Maui, where travelers can pick up household medical items.

➜ Health insurance is a must.

➜ Iodine is a handy extra for your first aid kit if going in the water.

➜ SPF 30+ sun block is advisable for Maui. You can also check the UV rating for your trip at http://uv.willyweather.com

In Maui
AVAILABILITY & COST OF HEALTH CARE

Healthcare is readily available on Maui. Clinics such as Doctors on Call Maui (www.doctorsoncallmaui.com) are open 365 days a year. However, consultations on the island are expensive, ranging from $150 to $200 before tax.

STAPHYLOCOCCUS (MRSA)

It's possible to contract *staphylococcus aureus* (MRSA) in Hawaii and some types of antibiotic-resistant staph infections can be fatal. Staph infections are caused by bacteria that enter the body through an open wound. To prevent infection, practice good hygiene, apply antibiotic ointment to any open cuts or sores and keep them out of recreational water; if they're on your feet don't go barefoot, even on the sand. If a wound becomes painful, looks red, inflamed or swollen, leaks pus or causes a rash or blisters, seek medical help immediately.

TAP WATER

Maui's tap water is safe to drink and meets all standards set out by the federal and state governments. The taste of the water differs in parts of the county, depending on the mineral content in the water. Even though the water is completely safe to drink, travelers who are not used to a particular mineral content may find it unsettles their stomach. Bottled water is supereasy to pick up at supermarkets; a case costs around $4.

Insurance

Getting travel insurance to cover theft, loss and medical problems is highly recommended. Some insurance policies do not cover 'risky' activities such as scuba diving, trekking and motorcycling, so read the fine print. Make sure your policy at least covers hospital stays and an emergency flight home.

Some insurance policies require you to get preauthorization before receiving medical treatment – contact the call center. Keep your medical receipts and documentation for claims reimbursement later.

Paying for your airline ticket or rental car with a credit card may provide limited travel accident insurance. If you already have private US health insurance or a homeowners or renters policy, find out what those policies cover and only get supplemental insurance. If you have prepaid a large portion of your vacation, trip cancellation insurance may be a worthwhile expense.

Worldwide travel insurance is available at www.lonelyplanet.com/bookings. You can buy, extend and claim online any time – even if you're already on the road.

Internet Access

Most towns have cafes offering free internet if you purchase something. Internet is also available at libraries with a $10 non-resident library card, lasting for three months. Most Maui hotels, many condos and B&Bs have wi-fi. Some of the larger hotels offer business centers with computers and internet for guests; fees vary. You can also find free wi-fi at Queen Ka'ahumanu Center in Kahului and at most McDonald's fast food restaurants. When wi-fi is available in an establishment, it's marked in this guide with a symbol 🛜 If you bring a laptop from outside the USA, make sure you bring along a universal AC and plug adapter.

Wi-fi & Internet Service Providers

Common in most hotels; available in some condo units. Free at most McDonald's and with purchases at many cafes.

Legal Matters

Legal rights Anyone arrested in Hawaii has the right to have the representation of a lawyer from the time of their arrest to their trial, and if a person cannot afford a lawyer, the state must provide one for free. You're presumed innocent unless or until you're found guilty in court.

Alcohol laws The legal drinking age is 21. It's illegal to have open containers of alcohol in motor vehicles, and drinking in public parks or on the beaches is also illegal. Drunk driving is a serious crime and can incur stiff fines, jail time and other penalties. In Hawaii, anyone caught driving with a blood alcohol level of 0.08% or greater is guilty of driving 'under the influence' and will have their driver's license taken away on the spot.

Maps

The maps in this guide are sufficient for most exploring. For the most comprehensive road atlas available, pick up a copy of the *Ready Mapbook of Maui County*, which covers virtually every road on Maui, Lana'i and

Moloka'i. It's sold at the Barnes & Noble in Lahaina.

Media

Newspapers Maui's main daily newspaper is the *Maui News* (www.mauinews.com). *Lahaina News* (www.lahainanews.com) is a weekly newspaper focusing on West Maui.

Radio For Hawaiian music and personalities tune into KPOA 93.5FM (www.kpoa.com). Hawaii Public Radio KKUA 90.7FM (www.npr.com) features island programs and music.

TV All major US TV networks and cable channels available.

Money

ATMs are common. Credit cards are widely accepted; often required for car and hotel reservations. The US dollar is the only currency used on Maui.

ATMs

Major banks such as the Bank of Hawaii (www.boh.com) and First Hawaiian Bank (www.fhb.com) have ATM networks throughout Maui that give cash advances on major credit cards and allow cash withdrawals with affiliated ATM cards. In addition to bank locations, you'll find ATMs at most grocery stores, mall-style shopping centers and convenience stores.

Changing Money

If you're carrying foreign currency, it can be exchanged for US dollars at larger banks around Maui.

Credit Cards

Major credit cards are widely accepted on Maui, including at car-rental agencies and at most hotels, restaurants, gas stations, grocery stores and tour operators. Some B&Bs and condos (including some handled through rental agencies) may refuse them.

Tipping

➡ **Taxis Tip** 15% of the metered fare, rounded up to the next dollar.

➡ **Restaurants** Good waiters are tipped 15% to 20%, while very dissatisfied customers make their ire known by leaving 10%. There has to be real cause for not tipping at all.

➡ **Hotels and airports** Give $2 per bag.

➡ **Valets** At least $2 when your car is returned.

Travellers Cheques

Traveler's checks are becoming obsolete. Foreign visitors carrying traveler's checks will find things easier if the checks are in US dollars. Many top-end restaurants, hotels and shops accept US dollar traveler's checks and treat them just like cash.

Out-of-state personal checks are not readily accepted on Maui.

Opening Hours

Opening hours may vary slightly throughout the year. We've provided high-season opening hours; hours will generally decrease in the shoulder and low seasons.

Banks 8:30am–4pm Monday to Friday; some to 6pm Friday and 9am–noon or 1pm Saturday

Bars & clubs noon–midnight daily; some to 2am Thursday to Saturday

Businesses 8:30am–4:30pm Monday to Friday

Post offices 8:30am–4:30pm Monday to Friday; some also 9am–noon Saturday

Shops 9am–5pm Monday to Saturday, some also noon–5pm Sunday; major shopping areas and malls keep extended hours

Post

You can get detailed 24-hour postal information by dialing toll-free ☎800-275-8777 or visiting www.usps.com. First-class mail between Maui and the US mainland usually takes three to four days and costs 47¢ for letters up to 1oz and 34¢ for standard-size postcards. International Global Forever stamps, for postcards and letters, are $1.15.

Public Holidays

When a public holiday falls on the weekend, it's often celebrated on the nearest Friday or Monday instead. These long weekends can be busy, as people from other Hawaiian Islands often take advantage of the break to visit Maui. If your visit coincides with a holiday, be sure to book your hotel and car well in advance.

New Year's Day January 1

Martin Luther King Jr Day Third Monday of January

Presidents Day Third Monday of February

Good Friday March or April

Prince Kuhio Day March 26

Memorial Day Last Monday of May

King Kamehameha Day June 11

Independence Day July 4

Statehood Day Third Friday of August

Labor Day First Monday of September

Discoverer's Day Second Monday of October (celebrated as Columbus Day on the US mainland)

Election Day Second Tuesday of November in even-numbered years

Veterans Day November 11

Thanksgiving Fourth Thursday of November

Christmas Day December 25

Smoking

Tobacco smoking is prohibited in enclosed public places, including restaurants, retail settings and hotel lobbies. Effective January 2016 the prohibition now includes e-cigarettes.

Telephone

Pay phones are a dying breed but you may find them at larger public parks and local community centers. To make long-distance calls consider buying a prepaid phone card at a convenience store or pharmacy.

Always dial ☎1 before toll-free numbers (☎800, ☎888 and ☎877). Some toll-free numbers may only work within the state or from the US mainland, while others work from Canada, too. But you'll only know by making the call.

Cell Phones

International travelers need GSM multiband phones. Buy prepaid SIM cards locally. Coverage can be spotty outside developed areas.

COVERAGE

Cell-phone coverage is good on most of Maui, but spotty in remote areas such as the Road to Hana. Verizon has an extensive cellular network on Maui, and AT&T and Sprint also have decent coverage.

EQUIPMENT

International travelers, take note: most US cell-phone systems are incompatible with the GSM 900/1800 standard used throughout Europe and Asia, and will need a multiband phone. Check with your cellular service provider before departure about using your phone on Maui.

Long Distance & International Calls

Calls to Hawaii If you're calling Maui from abroad, the international country code for the US is ☎1. All calls to Hawaii are then followed by the area code ☎808 and the seven-digit local number.

International calls from Maui To make international calls direct from Maui to any country other than Canada, dial ☎011 + country code + area code + number. To make calls direct to Canada, dial ☎1 + area code + number.

Operator assistance For international operator assistance, dial ☎0. The operator can provide specific rate information and tell you which time periods are the cheapest for calling.

Calls within Hawaii If you're calling from one place on Maui to

SHARK ATTACKS: DO YOU NEED TO WORRY?

Bringing up shark attacks in a guidebook seems rather, well, rude. Our apologies. But shark attacks off the coast of Maui have garnered headlines in recent years. There were seven shark attacks in Maui waters in 2016 and 10 statewide. In 2016 there were no fatal shark attacks, and only two resulted in serious injuries, while five across the state resulted in no injury at all. The norm for Hawaii is roughly four attacks per year.

When and why do they happen? No one is 100% sure. Some scientists think that there may be an increase in incidents in the fall, when female tiger sharks are most likely to be pregnant and perhaps more aggressive. But not all of the recent incidents were at the end of the year. A spike in shark attacks between 2012 and 2013 provoked a Department of Land and Natural Resources study to examine tiger shark behavior off the Maui coast. The study found that islands in the Maui county (Maui, Moloka'i, Lana'i, and Kaho'olawe) have more preferred tiger shark habitats than all the other major Hawaiian Islands combined.

Do you need to be concerned? Not particularly. Although there were two fatal shark attacks in 2013, the last previous shark attack fatality in Hawaii was 2004. According to the International Shark Attack File your odds of being bitten are about 1 in 11.5 million. To be extra cautious, though, try not to swim or snorkel in murky water (which is more likely to appear later in the day) and try to swim where there are lots of people.

any other place on Maui you do not need to dial the ☎808 area code. However, you must dial ☎1 + 808 when making a call from one Hawaiian island to another.

Time

Hawaii does not observe daylight saving time. It has about 11 hours of daylight in midwinter and almost 13½ hours in midsummer. In midwinter the sun rises at about 7am and sets at about 6pm. In midsummer it rises before 6am and sets after 7pm.

Tourist Information

Maui County's tourist organizations have loads of visitor information on their websites and will mail out material to those not online. There's an **information desk** (Map p130; ☎808-872-3893; www. gohawaii.com/maui; Kahului Airport; ⊙5am-10pm) at the Kahului airport.

Local Tourist Offices

Lahaina Visitor Center (☎808-667-9175; www.visitlahaina.com; 648 Wharf St, Old Lahaina Courthouse; ⊙9am-5pm) Located inside the **Old Lahaina Courthouse** (Map p84; ☎visitor center 808-667-9193; http://lahainarestoration. org/old-lahaina-courthouse/; 648 Wharf St, Banyan Tree Park; ⊙9am-5pm) **FREE**, this is an excellent tourist office. You can get gifts, books, info and a walking tour map ($2).

Tours

A number of tour-bus companies operate half-day and full-day sightseeing tours on Maui, covering the most visited island destinations. Popular routes include day-long jaunts to Hana, and Haleakalā trips that take in the major Upcountry sights.

There are also specialized adventure tours such as whale-watching cruises, snorkeling trips to Lana'i and helicopter tours. Details are in the Activities sections for each town.

Polynesian Adventure Tours (☎808-833-3000; www.polyad.com; tours adult from $114, child 3-11yr from $69) Part of Gray Line Hawaii, Polynesian is one of the major Hawaiian tour companies. It offers tours to Haleakalā National Park, Central Maui and 'Iao Valley State Park, and the Road to Hana. It Iso runs short trips from Maui to Pearl Harbor in Oahu (from adult/child $378/357).

Roberts Hawaii (☎800-831-5541; www.robertshawaii. com; tours adult/child 4-11yr $108/79) In operation for more than 70 years, Roberts Hawaii runs three tours: Hana, 'Iao Valley and Lahaina, and Haleakalā National Park.

Valley Isle Excursions (☎808-661-8687; www. tourmaui.com; tours adult/child 2-12yr $148/114) It costs a bit more, but Valley Isle has hands-down the best Road to Hana tour. Vans take just 12 passengers and guides offer more local flavor and less canned commentary. Includes continental breakfast and, in Hana, a BBQ chicken lunch.

Travelers with Disabilities

Maui has decent infrastructure for travelers with disabilities, and most public places comply with Americans with Disabilities Act (ADA) regulations. Many of the major resort hotels have elevators, TTD-capable phones and wheelchair-accessible rooms, while major car-rental companies will install hand controls and provide accessible transportation to the vehicle pick-up site with advance notification. A disability parking placard issued by

other states or countries for parking in designated accessible parking spaces is valid in Hawaii. Most public buses are wheelchair accessible.

Travelers with visual impairments are allowed to bring guide dogs into Hawaii without quarantine, provided they meet the Department of Agriculture's requirements, which include your dog having a current rabies vaccination and a standard health certificate issued fewer than 30 days prior to arrival. Contact the **Animal Quarantine Station** (☎808-483-7151; http://hdoa.hawaii.gov).

Resources

Download Lonely Planet's free Accessible Travel guide from http://lptravel.to/AccessibleTravel.

Volunteering

Opportunities for volunteering abound on Maui. Some require extended time commitments but many ask for just a few hours. The Pacific Whale Foundation and the Hawaii Tourism Authority organize short-term projects on Maui through their joint **Volunteers on Vacation** (☎ext 1 808-249-8811; www. volunteersonvacation.org) program.

Work

Finding serious 'professional' employment is difficult on Maui since the island has a tight labor market. But casual work, such as waiting on tables at restaurants and working on checkout counters in shops, are positions with a lot of turnover, and hence openings, especially in Lahaina. Folks with language, scuba and culinary skills might investigate better-paying employment with resorts.

Transportation

GETTING THERE & AWAY

Air

Maui has a large number of non-stop flights to/from cities on the mainland, including Los Angeles, San Diego, San Francisco, Seattle, Dallas, Chicago and Vancouver, BC. Otherwise it's common to connect through Honolulu. Departure tax is included in the price of a ticket.

Kahului International Airport (OGG; Map p130;☏808-872-3830; http://hawaii.gov/ogg; 1 Kahului Airport Rd) All trans-Pacific flights to Maui arrive in Kahului, the island's main airport. There's a staffed **Visitor Information Desk** in the baggage claim area that's open 7:45am to 10pm daily. There are racks of local travel brochures beside the desk. A huge new rental-car facility and monorail will make the terminal area a construction site through 2019.

Kapalua Airport (JHM;☏808-665-6108; www.hawaii.gov/jhm; 4050 Honoapiilani Hwy) Off Hwy 30, south of Kapalua in West Maui, this regional airport has flights by **Mokulele Airlines** (☏866-260-7070; www.mokuleleairlines.com) to Moloka'i and Honolulu.

To & from the Airport

Roberts Hawaii (☏808-954-8630; www.robertshawaii.com; airport-to-hotel shuttle bus $10 to $44) does not require reservations for its frequent service to most tourist points on the island. There is a booking counter in baggage claim. Book in advance for the shuttle vans of **Hawaii Executive Transportation** (☏800-833-2303, 808-669-2300; www.hawaiiexecutivetransportation.com; 1/2 passengers $26-72/28-80; ☺reservations 7am-11pm) and **Speedi Shuttle** (☏877-242-5777; www.speedishuttle.com; 1/2 passengers $30-80/36-92). The latter carries surfboards.

Sea

The **Expeditions Ferry** (Map p84; ☏808-661-3756; www.go-lanai.com; Lahaina Harbor; adult/child one way $30/20) is worth it just for the ride. It links Lahaina Harbor with Manele Bay Harbor on Lana'i (one hour) several times daily. In winter there's a fair chance of seeing humpback whales; spinner dolphins are a common sight all year, especially on morning sails.

The Moloka'i ferry no longer runs.

GETTING AROUND

For more information on traveling around Maui, see Getting Around (p32).

Air

Mokulele Airlines (☏866-260-7070; www.mokuleleairlines.

CLIMATE CHANGE & TRAVEL

Every form of transportation that relies on carbon-based fuel generates CO_2, the main cause of human-induced climate change. Modern travel is dependent on airplanes, which might use less fuel per kilometer per person than most cars but travel much greater distances. The altitude at which aircraft emit gases (including CO_2) and particles also contributes to their climate change impact. Many websites offer 'carbon calculators' that allow people to estimate the carbon emissions generated by their journey and, for those who wish to do so, to offset the impact of the greenhouse gases emitted, with contributions to portfolios of climate-friendly initiatives throughout the world. Lonely Planet offsets the carbon footprint of all staff and author travel.

com) offers three daily flights from Kahului to tiny **Hana Airport** (Map p232; ☑808-248-4861; www.hawaii.gov/hnm; Alalele PL), cutting a two-hour drive to a 20-minute flight.

Bus

Maui Bus (☑808-871-4838; www.mauicounty.gov/bus; single ride $2, day pass $4) offers an extensive public bus system between the main towns, such as Lahaina, Kihei and Kahului, but not to out-of-the-way places, such as Haleakalā National Park or Hana. Buses come with front-load bike racks.

Car & Motorcycle

The best way to get around is with your own set of wheels, as much of the island is not accessible by bus or bicycle. All the major car rental firms have offices at Kahului Airport. Most of these rental companies also have branches in Ka'anapali and will pick you up at the nearby Kapalua Airport. For a green option, consider

Bio-Beetle in Kahului. Also check out Kihei Rent A Car.

Be sure to check for any road restrictions on your vehicle rental contract. Some car rental agencies, for instance, may prohibit driving on the Kahekili Hwy between Honokohau and Waihe'e and in the Kaupo district of the Pi'ilani Hwy.

Driver's License

➔ US citizens with a driver's license from another state can legally drive in Hawaii if they are at least 18 years old.

➔ International visitors can legally drive in Hawaii with a valid driver's license issued by their home country (minimum age 18).

➔ Car-rental companies will generally accept foreign driver's licenses written in English with an accompanying photo. Otherwise, be prepared to present an International Driving Permit (IDP), obtainable in your home country, along with your foreign driver's license.

Fuel

➔ Gasoline (petrol) is readily available everywhere except

along remote roads (eg Hana Hwy and Kahekili Hwy).

➔ Gas prices in Maui are the highest in the country.

Insurance

➔ Required by law, liability insurance covers any people or property that you might hit. For damage to the rental vehicle, a collision damage waiver (CDW) costs an extra $15 to $20 a day.

➔ If you decline CDW, you will be held liable for any damages up to the full value of the car.

➔ Even with CDW, you may be required to pay the first $100 to $500 for repairs; some agencies will also charge you for the rental cost of the car during the time it takes to be repaired.

➔ If you have vehicle insurance at home, it might cover damages to car rentals; ask your insurance agent before your trip.

➔ Some credit cards offer reimbursement coverage for collision damages if you rent the car with that card; check on this in advance.

➔ Most credit-card coverage isn't valid for rentals over 15 days or for 'exotic' models (eg performance cars, 4WD Jeeps).

Rental

➔ Most rental companies require that you be at least 25 years old, possess a valid driver's license and have a major credit card, not a debit or check card.

➔ Howver, a few major companies will rent to drivers between the ages of 21 and 24, typically for an underage surcharge of around $20 to $30 per day; call ahead to check.

➔ Without a credit card, many agencies simply won't rent you a vehicle, while others require prepayment by cash, traveler's checks or debit card with an additional

DRIVING TIMES

Average driving times and distances from Kahului are as follows. Allow more time during weekday morning and afternoon rush hours, and any time the surf is up on the North Shore.

DESTINATION	MILES	DURATION
Haleakalā Summit	36	1½ hours
Hana	51	2 hours
Ka'anapali	26	1 hour
Kapalua	32	1 hour
Kihei	12	25 minutes
La Perouse Bay	21	50 minutes
Lahaina	23	45 minutes
Makawao	14	30 minutes
'Ohe'o Gulch	61	2¾ hours
Pa'ia	7	15 minutes
Wailuku	3	15 minutes

refundable deposit of $500 per week, proof of return airfare and more.

➜ When you pick up your vehicle, most agencies will request the name and phone number of the place where you're staying. Some agencies are reluctant to rent to visitors who list a campground as their address; a few specifically add 'No Camping Permitted' to car-rental contracts.

Safety Laws

➜ Texting on a handheld device (eg cell phone) while driving is illegal. Talking on a cell phone is only allowed for adult drivers (age 18 and over) who use a hands-free device.

➜ Driving under the influence (DUI) of alcohol or drugs is a serious criminal offense. It's illegal to carry open containers of alcohol (even if they're empty) inside a car. Unless the containers are still sealed and have never been opened, store them in the trunk instead.

➜ The use of seat belts is required for the driver and all passengers, even those riding in the back seat.

➜ Child safety seats are mandatory for children aged three and younger. Those aged four to seven must ride in a booster or child safety seat, unless they weigh over 80lbs, in which case they must be secured by a lap-only belt in the back seat.

Taxi

Taxis operate in the main towns and tourist areas. Uber and Lyft are also available.

Behind the Scenes

SEND US YOUR FEEDBACK

We love to hear from travelers – your comments keep us on our toes and help make our books better. Our well-traveled team reads every word on what you loved or loathed about this book. Although we cannot reply individually to your submissions, we always guarantee that your feedback goes straight to the appropriate authors, in time for the next edition. Each person who sends us information is thanked in the next edition – the most useful submissions are rewarded with a selection of digital PDF chapters.

Visit **lonelyplanet.com/contact** to submit your updates and suggestions or to ask for help. Our award-winning website also features inspirational travel stories, news and discussions.

Note: We may edit, reproduce and incorporate your comments in Lonely Planet products such as guidebooks, websites and digital products, so let us know if you don't want your comments reproduced or your name acknowledged. For a copy of our privacy policy visit lonelyplanet.com/privacy.

OUR READERS

Many thanks to the travelers who used the last edition and wrote to us with helpful hints, useful advice and interesting anecdotes: Ashling Cahill, Jason Hanson, Jennifer Potter, Michael Jones

WRITER THANKS
Amy C Balfour

Thank you Errol Buntuyan and Tim Tattersall for sharing your island insights and recommendations. Monkeypod Kitchen was a blast. JuLee Messerich, thank you for the introductions and the 5 Palms company. A big mahalo to Daniel Sullivan for the Upcountry leads and inspirational island photos. Alex Howard, thank you for trusting me with this awesome assignment. Many thanks to Ryan, Jade, Andrea and the maps and production team for putting it all together.

Jade Bremner

Mahalo to knowledgable coordinating author Amy C Balfour for all her wisdom on both Maui and LP guidebooks, plus Destination Editor Alexander Howard for his quick-fire email responses and support.

Thanks also to local experts Joshua Weisfeld and Travis Morrin for their tips and recommendations. Plus everyone working hard behind the scenes – Cheree Broughton, Dianne Schallmeiner, Jane Grisman and Neill Coen.

Ryan Ver Berkmoes

Teri Waros on Moloka'i was her usual indispensible self. On Lana'i, a shelter cat made me smile and reminded me of an old friend. In Lahaina I'm indebted to the dozens I chatted up who stay genuine despite dealing with tourists all day. On O'ahu I'm indebted to my father, who passed through Pearl Harbor in 1942 to serve in the Pacific yet retained his own love for the islands. And Alexis Ver Berkmoes puts the lime juice in my mai-tai.

ACKNOWLEDGEMENTS

Climate map data adapted from Peel MC, Finlayson BL & McMahon TA (2007) 'Updated World Map of the Köppen-Geiger Climate Classification', Hydrology and Earth System Sciences, 11, 163344.

Cover photograph: Big wave surfing, Maui, Neale Haynes/Alamy ©

THIS BOOK

This fourth edition of Lonely Planet's *Maui* guidebook was researched and written by Amy C Balfour, Jade Bremner and Ryan Ver Berkmoes. The previous edition was written by Glenda Bendure and Ned Friary. This guidebook was produced by the following:

Destination Editor Alexander Howard

Product Editors Ronan Abayawickrema, Amanda Williamson

Senior Cartographer Corey Hutchison

Book Designer Gwen Cotter

Assisting Editors Janice Bird, Andrea Dobbin, Gabrielle Innes, Sandie Kestell, Jodie Lea Martire, Kate Morgan

Assisting Cartographers Hunor Csutoros, Valentina Kremenchutskaya

Assisting Book Designer Fergal Condon

Cover Researcher Naomi Parker

Thanks to Imogen Bannister, Heather Champion, Indra Kilfoyle, Kate Mathews, Clara Monitto, Wayne Murphy, Claire Naylor, Karyn Noble, Genna Patterson, Gary Rafferty, Kirsten Rawlings, Doug Rimington, Jessica Ryan, Victoria Smith, Angela Tinson, Tony Wheeler, Tracy Whitmey

Index

Map Legend

Sights

- Beach
- Bird Sanctuary
- Buddhist
- Castle/Palace
- Christian
- Confucian
- Hindu
- Islamic
- Jain
- Jewish
- Monument
- Museum/Gallery/Historic Building
- Ruin
- Shinto
- Sikh
- Taoist
- Winery/Vineyard
- Zoo/Wildlife Sanctuary
- Other Sight

Activities, Courses & Tours

- Bodysurfing
- Diving
- Canoeing/Kayaking
- Course/Tour
- Sento Hot Baths/Onsen
- Skiing
- Snorkeling
- Surfing
- Swimming/Pool
- Walking
- Windsurfing
- Other Activity

Sleeping

- Sleeping
- Camping

Eating

- Eating

Drinking & Nightlife

- Drinking & Nightlife
- Cafe

Entertainment

- Entertainment

Shopping

- Shopping

Information

- Bank
- Embassy/Consulate
- Hospital/Medical
- Internet
- Police
- Post Office
- Telephone
- Toilet
- Tourist Information
- Other Information

Geographic

- Beach
- Gate
- Hut/Shelter
- Lighthouse
- Lookout
- Mountain/Volcano
- Oasis
- Park
- Pass
- Picnic Area
- Waterfall

Population

- Capital (National)
- Capital (State/Province)
- City/Large Town
- Town/Village

Transport

- Airport
- BART station
- Border crossing
- Boston T station
- Bus
- Cable car/Funicular
- Cycling
- Ferry
- Metro/Muni station
- Monorail
- Parking
- Petrol station
- Subway/SkyTrain station
- Taxi
- Train station/Railway
- Tram
- Underground station
- Other Transport

Note: Not all symbols displayed above appear on the maps in this book

Routes

- Tollway
- Freeway
- Primary
- Secondary
- Tertiary
- Lane
- Unsealed road
- Road under construction
- Plaza/Mall
- Steps
- Tunnel
- Pedestrian overpass
- Walking Tour
- Walking Tour detour
- Path/Walking Trail

Boundaries

- International
- State/Province
- Disputed
- Regional/Suburb
- Marine Park
- Cliff
- Wall

Hydrography

- River, Creek
- Intermittent River
- Canal
- Water
- Dry/Salt/Intermittent Lake
- Reef

Areas

- Airport/Runway
- Beach/Desert
- Cemetery (Christian)
- Cemetery (Other)
- Glacier
- Mudflat
- Park/Forest
- Sight (Building)
- Sportsground
- Swamp/Mangrove

OUR STORY

A beat-up old car, a few dollars in the pocket and a sense of adventure. In 1972 that's all Tony and Maureen Wheeler needed for the trip of a lifetime – across Europe and Asia overland to Australia. It took several months, and at the end – broke but inspired – they sat at their kitchen table writing and stapling together their first travel guide, *Across Asia on the Cheap*. Within a week they'd sold 1500 copies. Lonely Planet was born.

Today, Lonely Planet has offices in Franklin, London, Melbourne, Oakland, Dublin, Beijing and Delhi, with more than 600 staff and writers. We share Tony's belief that 'a great guidebook should do three things: inform, educate and amuse'.

OUR WRITERS

Amy C Balfour

Curator, Kihei & South Maui, North Shore & Upcountry, Road to Hana, Hana & East Maui, Haleakalā National Park Amy first visited Hawaii as a toddler. For this book, she hiked on the King's Trail, explored the Haleakalā crater and sampled vodka on a distillery tour in Hali'imaile. She left Little Beach before things got too wild at the Sunday evening drum circle. Amy has authored or co-authored 30 books for Lonely Planet, including the first two editions of *Discover Maui* and the last three editions of *Hawaii*. Her stories have appeared in *Backpacker*, *Sierra*, *Southern Living* and *Women's Health*.

Read more about Amy at: http://auth.lonelyplanet.com/profiles/amycbalfour

Jade Bremner

'Iao Valley & Central Maui, West Maui Jade has been a journalist for more than a decade. She has lived in and reported on four different regions. Wherever she goes she finds action sports to try, the weirder the better, and it's no coincidence many of her favourite places have some of the best waves in the world. Jade has edited travel magazines and sections for *Time Out* and *Radio Times* and has been a correspondent for the *Times*, *CNN* and the *Independent*. She feels privileged to share tales from this wonderful planet we call home and is always looking for the next adventure.

Ryan Ver Berkmoes

Lana'i, Moloka'i, Lahaina Ryan has written more than 110 guidebooks for Lonely Planet. He grew up in Santa Cruz, California, which he left at age 17 for college in the Midwest, where he first discovered snow. All joy of this novelty soon wore off. Since then he has been travelling the world, both for pleasure and for work – which are often indistinguishable. He has covered everything from wars to bars. He definitely prefers the latter. Ryan calls New York City home.

Read more about Ryan at ryanverberkmoes.com and at @ryanvb

Published by Lonely Planet Global Limited
CRN 554153
4th edition – Sep 2017
ISBN 9781786577047
© Lonely Planet 2017   Photographs © as indicated 2017
10 9 8 7 6 5 4 3 2 1
Printed in China